# Modern Finland

ALSO BY HARALD HAARMANN

*Roots of Ancient Greek Civilization:*
*The Influence of Old Europe* (McFarland, 2014)

# Modern Finland

HARALD HAARMANN

McFarland & Company, Inc., Publishers

*Jefferson, North Carolina*

LIBRARY OF CONGRESS CATALOGUING-IN-PUBLICATION DATA

Names: Haarmann, Harald, author.
Title: Modern Finland / Harald Haarmann.
Description: Jefferson, North Carolina : McFarland & Company, Inc.,
Publishers, 2016. | Includes bibliographical references and index.
Identifiers: LCCN 2016039304 | ISBN 9781476662022
(softcover : alkaline paper) ∞
Subjects: LCSH: Finland—History. | Finland—Intellectual life. |
Ethnology—Finland. | National characteristics, Finnish. | Finland—
Social conditions. | Finland—Economic conditions. | Globalization—Finland. |
Human geography—Finland. | Natural history—Finland. | Social change—Finland.
Classification: LCC DL1012 .H33 2016 | DDC 948.97—dc23
LC record available at https://lccn.loc.gov/2016039304

BRITISH LIBRARY CATALOGUING DATA ARE AVAILABLE

ISBN (print) 978-1-4766-6202-2
ISBN (ebook) 978-1-4766-2565-2

Front cover: (top) Northern lights over Finland (iStockphoto);
(bottom) Sanoma House (left) and the Kiasma Museum of
Contemporary Art in Helsinki (fotoVoyager)

Printed in the United States of America

McFarland & Company, Inc., Publishers
Box 611, Jefferson, North Carolina 28640
www.mcfarlandpub.com

To the Finnish Maiden
on the occasion of her 99th anniversary

# Acknowledgments

I would like to express my thanks to all those who have supported me in this enterprise, with constructive contributions in discussions, fruitful suggestions and information of all kind. My thanks go in particular to my wife, Dr. Pirkko-Liisa Haarmann, former member (now retired) of the Finnish Supreme Court of Justice. Every time we engaged in lively discussions about issues concerning Finland's history and social development, she gave me vital feedback. She read through the manuscript and made suggestions for improvement. I am also grateful to my neighbors and friends who have created a pleasant atmosphere for me.

I had the pleasure to meet with three of Finland's presidents in person, namely Mauno Koivisto (in office from 1982 until 1994), Martti Ahtisaari (1994–2000), and Tarja Halonen (2000–2012). In our conversations I sensed the kind of pragmatism, so typically Finnish, that showed in the ways the presidents assessed Finland's role in the world.

# Table of Contents

# Introduction

## *What Makes a Small Country Like Finland Exceptional?*

To the outsider, the ways of the Finns may seem exotic or somehow mysterious. In Finland, people are more attached to their natural surroundings than in most other post-industrial countries. And this goes with a high degree of technological development and of digitalization that has penetrated almost every nook of Finnish society. In August of 2010, *Newsweek* ranked Finland top as the best country in the world with respect to education, economic competitiveness, civil liberties, quality of life, social security and human development. Since then there has been some fluctuation in the ranking of countries as the best in the world regarding their quality of life, but Finland is still highly ranked. The intention of this book is to dive into Finnishness and to investigate why so much of its fabric may seem exotic (in the eye of outsiders). This book invites the reader to embark on an expedition into Finland's recent past, to discover how Finland became modernized within an unusually short span of time and how Finnish society has constantly and flexibly adjusted to changing conditions.

Finland is known for its advanced technologies, which are displayed, for example, in ship building, electronic industries and communication systems. Some of the world's biggest cruise ships have been built in Finland. During the past decades, Finland has developed high standards in environmental protection; Chinese officials asked Finnish experts and firms for assistance to get the pollution in the big Chinese cities under control. The country stands out with its advanced digitalization of the economic, private and public sectors. Finland is among the countries with high rates of internet users, the penetration rate being 91 percent (as compared to 84 percent in the United States in 2015).

Finnish expertise in a great variety of domains is not accidental but anchored in an efficient educational system which even set standards for other countries. For example, Germany, Italy, and the United Arab Emirates have experimented with the principles of Finnish education. In Finland, professional life and entrepreneurship are open to all citizens. The Finnish labor market can draw on maximum resources since Finnish society is characterized by a far-reaching equality of the sexes. In June 2012, Hillary Clinton, wife of the former U.S. president Bill Clinton (in office from 1993 to 2001), visited Finland to talk about women's roles in society. On the basis of her experiences in this country, she came to the conclusion that, instead of Americans talking to Finnish women about women's lib, it should be women from Finland coming to the United States to talk to American women about this issue. The sense for gender equality has deep roots in Finland, and this showed early in the political arena. Finnish women were given full suffrage (the right to vote and to run for office) as early as 1906.

The successful modernization of Finland was achieved at a price. Until the end of World War II, Finnish society was predominantly agrarian. That changed within a few years when the Finns were forced to boost their industrial capacities in order to rid themselves of the burden of reparations for alleged war damages demanded by the Soviet Union. This concerted huge effort to produce great amounts of industrial goods as payment of reparations to the Soviet Union put a tremendous strain on the whole population. In an atmosphere of uncertainty about what would happen, should Finland not be able to pay its debts in time, many Finns believed the consequences would have been the occupation of Finland by Soviet forces and the annexation of the country to the Soviet empire. Finland experienced a swift modernization and the Finns managed to pay back their war debts in time. The last train loaded with reparation goods for the Soviet Union left Finland on 18 September 1952. That same year, the Olympic Games were held in Helsinki, and this events marked the beginning of a Finnish self-assured society to build its future.

In the years that followed Finland took part in the enterprise of the other Scandinavian countries to build a welfare state, and these efforts materialized in the 1970s and 1980s. Finnish economy balanced trade relations with the West and with the East, and Finland's course of political neutrality gained global recognition. Helsinki became the venue of one of the few global summit meetings during the era of the Cold War when Finland, in 1975, hosted the conference on security and cooperation in Europe. The conference was attended not only by the presidents of European countries but also by those of the superpowers, the USA and the Soviet Union. The agreement that was signed meant recasting the political order in Europe, and the Organization for Security and Cooperation in Europe contributed to reducing ideological tensions in contemporary Europe.

When, in 1995, Finland joined the European Union as a member state, its ties with western Europe were consolidated. Given the country's experience in getting along politically with its neighbor, a former superpower, the input of Finnish politicians and their expertise in contacts between the EU and Russia have come to bear. The attraction of Finland in a worldwide comparison shows in the increase of foreign investments in recent years. Finland's credit rating had been AAA for many years. The rating, though, dropped to AA+ in October 2014 and, for several months, it equaled that of the USA where this rating has been in place since 2011. In early summer 2015, the rating was raised, once again, to AAA. What is positively noted by those international institutions that monitor the development of the world economies are the Finnish government's declared intentions to continue austerity measures and to meet the manifold demands for consolidating national economies after the recent worldwide economic crisis.

Like other EU countries, Finland has accepted refugees. Finland's society has been multicultural and multilingual for many generations, with the traditional national groups of Finns, Finland-Swedes and Saami. With the influx of people from countries outside

Europe new trajectories of language contacts and social integration are being explored. Furthermore, Finland is home to a steadily increasing number of foreign residents.

Finnish products keep going global. This is true in practically all domains of economy (e.g., in forestry: paper), of technology (cruise ships, elevators, networks of telecommunication), of culture (architecture, design, music, computer games). Certain brands play the role of markers of Finnish identity, such as the characters of the Moomins that are as popular in Finland as they are abroad. The Moomins symbolize what the image of Finland stands for in the world: a peace-loving nation that is willing to give humanitarian support to people in areas of crisis and that is prepared to send peacekeepers into the world with a UN mandate.

The Finnish sense of peacekeeping has been activated in numerous operations worldwide to stabilize conditions in formerly war-torn regions. Finnish soldiers have participated in many UN peacekeeping missions. Finnish politicians are sometimes called to function as mediators in challenging international negotiations. Such political efforts have been recognized worldwide, eventually resulting in the awarding of the Nobel Peace Prize to one outstanding mediator, the former president of Finland, Martti Ahtisaari, who knows what he is talking about when he states: "Peace is a question of will."

One must look beneath the surface of things to find out how a small country managed to build a modern society with high living standards and heavyweight economic potential. Finland has a total population of 5.5 million people, which equals the population in the metropolitan areas of some of the world's big cities such as Madrid, Miami or Toronto, or in states of the USA like Colorado or Minnesota. This small nation set in motion after World War II a dynamic drive toward the modernization of their economy which developed at a breathtaking pace. The society did not disintegrate, under the innovational pressure, it has stayed intact and, the collective experience of success certainly strengthened social cohesion among the Finns.

Many people, especially foreigners, have wondered how the Finns can so swiftly adapt to changing situations without losing control of the process of innovation. In recent years, the Finnish economy has been struggling to improve its international competitiveness, and it has to be seen how Finnish adaptive skills can bring about a change. There is good reason to shed light on the various cultural traditions and on Finnish mentality because it is here that one finds the key for an understanding of how the Finns bring their inventiveness to bear. In the Finnish mentality are encapsulated vital features such as being steady, tenacious, straightforward, and pragmatic. Finns do not give in easily and, during times of war, Finns have successfully defended their independence. Once they have set their mind to something they stick to the task until it has been completed. Finns like fair play. Therefore, trust is cherished as a value governing social relations as well as economic transactions. In this book, the cultural, social and intellectual foundations are defined in which modern Finnish society is anchored.

Finland offers a kaleidoscope of recreative environments: wide open landscapes, a rich wildlife (bird watching is popular), fresh air and clean water. The quality of the water in many, if not most of Finland's lakes is that of drinking water. Many tourists visit Finland, in summer for swimming, hiking, fishing, yachting or attending the opera festival in Savonlinna, in winter for skiing and sledge-riding. Lapland is among the preferred destinations. Many visitors come to meet Santa Claus in his home near the Arctic Circle.

One gets the impression that the figure of Santa Claus is as popular among youngsters as it is among adults.

The Finns are known for their love of sauna, ice hockey and rock concerts. They love car racing, and many young Finns practice racing in areas where the terrain is not used for other traffic. Foreigners might not know much about Finland, but those interested in racing sports will remember the champions of the 1990s, Tommi Mäkinen (four-time World Rally Champion) and Mika Häkkinen (Formula One), two of the "flying Finns." During the years 1998 and 1999, the winners of the Formula 1 car racing were divided between two nations. The season's races and the world championship were won either by the Finn Mika Häkkinen or by the German Michael Schumacher.

And there are many other things which the Finns practice and which are less known, such as woman-carrying, mobile phone-throwing or mud soccer for which competitions are organized every year. And Finns like to dance. Perhaps the most popular of the dances is the tango which resembles the tango in Argentina. And yet, the Finnish tango is different, it is … just Finnish.

In order to get an overall picture of what is Finnish and what makes a Finn one has to embark on a travel back in time, to identify the sources of Finnish identity, how these have dynamically interacted to produce the fabric of Finnishness and how the various groups of populations have participated in giving profile to the Finnish nation. The travel in time takes us as far back as the end of the last Ice Age. Why so far back? What has the Ice Age to do with the Finns? If we want to understand why the Saami live in the north, the Finns in central and southern Finland and why the Finland-Swedes settle predominantly in the west and southwest we have to start with the story of those people who populated Finland after the ice shield had melted. In Saami culture and language one finds remainders of the culture of the ancient pioneers who were the first to colonize northern Europe after the ice. The Saami and the Finnish languages play the role of refrigerators which have preserved elements of ancient European cultures, lost elsewhere.

# 1

# How Do People Interact with Nature in Finland?
## *The Natural Environment Vis-à-Vis Human Cultural Space*

Finland is a country in Scandinavia. This statement is true, and yet, perhaps only half true. When one thinks of Scandinavia and of the countries in that region of Europe, certainly Finland comes to mind along with Sweden, Norway and Denmark. In geographical terms, Scandinavia is the peninsula that stretches in the upper north of Europe. Finland is located on the eastern rim of the Scandinavian peninsula and in the more precise term Fenno-Scandia is revealed the special geographical position of this part of Scandinavia. Finland is, by its political history, a part of Scandinavia, but the origins of its population and their languages differ markedly from neighboring Scandinavian countries.

Finland is pictured as "the last wilderness of Europe" (Vuoristo and Vesterinen 2009: 33). It is a land of great extremes, regarding nature, climate and wildlife. The northern part of the country (Lapland), making up about one quarter of the land area, lies above the Arctic Circle. Yet, its climate is less arctic than parts of Canada or of Russian Siberia on the same latitude. This has to do with the North Atlantic Drift Current (i.e., Gulf Stream), the marine current that brings warm and moist air to northern Europe. Without the influence from the Atlantic Drift, Lapland's climate would be overall arctic. Yet, what makes a difference when compared to other Arctic regions, is the short summer season (lasting some 50 days) when temperatures may rise, temporarily, higher than + 25° C (77° F). In the south of Finland, the summer season is much longer, lasting for some 110 days. The country's third largest lake, Lake Inari, is located in the Arctic region. Thanks to the influence of the Gulf Stream the lake is frozen "only" between November to early June and its waters are open about five months a year.

The southern coastline of the country is at 60° northern latitude which is the same as the southern tip of Greenland. This part of Greenland is covered with snow during most of the year but the climatic conditions of Finland's coastline are the reverse. Winterly temperatures with snow and ice, and a frozen sea, may last for three or four months, but for the longest time of the year the sea and the lakes are open and the water warms up so people can swim during the summer season. The fact that Finland knows the difference of the seasons (spring, summer, autumn, winter)—unlike Greenland which only knows a long winter and a very short summerly interval—depends on the dynamics of the Gulf Stream, as in Lapland.

Finland is the land of forests. This has been so since the times when the area was inhabited by early hunters and gatherers. Still today some 70 percent of Finland are covered by forests, most of them exploited as a natural resource for the timber industry. This does not mean that deforestation is random. Instead, those who cut down trees for economic purposes are obliged to take care of the renewal of the vegetation, leaving the options for either saving some mature trees from which seeds may spread or for planting new trees. The Finnish Environmental Administration monitors the exploitation of timber from the countries forests. The norm is that the annual growth rate of trees exceeds the total amount of the timber harvest per year. The state of the environment in Finland has been reviewed for 2013 (Putkuri et al. 2014).

The many water reservoirs, lakes and rivers, in this country make up about 10 percent of the total area. Only 6.5 percent is cultivated land. The area for growing crops was larger in the past. As a consequence of Finland's membership in the European Union, the area of cultivated land had to be reduced. The EU directive demanding a reduction of the area for agricultural cultivation to avoid overproduction is described in a popular Finnish saying as *panna pellot pakettiin* (literally "to put fields in a package"). The new restrictions stand in stark contrast to a long tradition, practiced in Finland, to clear woods for agriculture.

Finland has a population of 5.5 million, with an average of 17 inhabitants per square kilometer. This makes Finland one of the most sparsely populated countries in Europe, the others being Iceland and Norway. About a hundred years ago, the size of the population was only half that of the present-day. There has been a slow growth since 1950 when there were some 4 million people living in Finland. Fertility rates for the Finnish population show a decrease since 1970, with rates below 2.0, which is already a bit below the minimum limit for natural growth.

The spread of the population within the country's boundaries is very uneven. The largest agglomeration is found in the south, in the Helsinki metropolitan area (Greater Helsinki), with the capital Helsinki and also including smaller towns such as Vantaa, Espoo and Kauniainen. In the metropolitan area live some 1.4 million people (in 2014). In the area of Greater Helsinki, population density is 470 inhabitants per square kilometer. In contrast to the densely populated south there are only 2 inhabitants per square kilometer in the Arctic region of Lapland.

Finland's population is highly urbanized, with about 85 percent living in cities and towns. The population in rural areas amounts to some 825,000. In light of such proportions one can easily understand that there is much space for every inhabitant in the wide landscapes of Finland, and there is a commonly held view that every Finn may find a stretch of beach on one of the many lakes or a patch of land on one of the many islands and islets off the shores to build a cottage or a summer house (Finn. *kesämökki*). In Finland, there are more than one million summer cottages. Of these, some 250,000 have been built since 1980 (STV 2014: 242). The trend goes in the direction that summer cottages are ever better equipped, technically, to make them habitable also during the winter season and, as private resorts, for people after their retirement.

As a consequence of this seasonal drift of greater portions of the population into the countryside, demands for higher living-standards have spread to rural areas. During the past decades, a high-level sanitary infrastructure and electricity supply have been established, including even remote parts of the country. There is no village or hamlet in Finland that would lack tap water, a sewage system or electricity. Ever more cottages are equipped with toilets and electricity. A regulation, intended to come into effect in March 2018, stipulates that every household in Finland has to have a functioning drainage system. For most, this is a connection to the communal sewer system. Where there is no such connection available, special technical equipment has to be applied to achieve the goal of ecologically sustainable drainage of used water.

## *The Power of Nature—How the Environment Formed After the Last Ice Age*

When you ask a geologist what is the normal state of Finland's environment, the answer may be: "A big layer of ice, some three kilometers thick." Like other countries in the northern region, Finland's geological history has experienced five Ice Ages, and the last ended only some 12,000 years ago. Fenno-Scandia is experiencing an intermediate period before the coming of yet another Ice Age the beginning of which may be only a few thousand years away. Wherever you are in Finland and whatever natural formation you may view, the environment has been decisively shaped by the movements of the big masses of ice during the periods of permanent ice. In the south, the granite surface of the bedrock has been exposed when the massive ice plate, moving from the north in a southerly direction, scrabbled off everything that was lying on the solid surface. Stones and even boulders that were pushed south by the growing ice-shield have been found in northern Russia and central Europe (e.g., in the surroundings of Berlin). The bedrock in central Europe, unaffected by moving ice, is invisible and covered under thick layers of soft soil.

Finland territory is growing, and this has to be understood literally. During the glacial period the ice sheet was growing continuously, with the effect that ever more weight was put on the ground. As a consequence of the increase in weight the earth below the ice sheet was pressed down, a phenomenon called glacial loading. After deglaciation the ground was relieved of pressure and slowly started to rise. This uplift motion, originally caused by glacial unloading, has continued to the present, and it will keep continuing in the future. The rising of the land (post-glacial rebound) is not a balanced process but rather uneven. So is the speed of the process. While, in the northern part of Great Britain, the land is rising up to 10 cm (4 in) in a hundred years, in northern Finland (northern shore of the Gulf of Bothnia) the uplift motion is rather speedy, with rising land levels of some 9–11 mm (0.35–0.43 in) each year (Vaneeckhout 2008: 61ff.). In the area of Vaasa on the western coast, the motion is about 7.5 mm (0.3 in) per year and, in Pori in the southwest it is some 6 mm (0.23 in)/year. The harbor of Tornio, on the northern shore of the Gulf of Bothnia, had to be relocated several times during its history because the rising land repeatedly interrupted the connection of the harbor with the sea.

The uplift motion has been monitored for long, ever since the discovery of the connection between rising land and Ice Age in the 19th century. in 1890, Gerard De Geer published his theory of this connection and gave evidence from his investigation of old shorelines in Scandinavia. Alluvion, newly surfaced land, is a phenomenon familiar to the inhabitants of southwestern and western Finland. They have witnessed the change of shorelines and the emergence of sandbanks and islets for generations (http://www.fgi.fi/fgi/themes/land-uplift). The "new land" has become an issue of legislation, namely of property rights. Legally, the rising land is the property of the one who owned the water area before the emergence of land. If someone owning land on the shore wants to extend his property into the area of "new land" he has to purchase the land from the one who formerly held the water rights (https://en.wikipedia.org/wiki/Post-glacial_rebound#Legal_status).

One can perhaps say that Finland is blessed by nature since the landmass of its territory will expand in the future, by some 10 square km per year. Geologists have predicted that, a thousand years from now, the Gulf of Bothnia will be separated from the Baltic Sea and the area will be split up into two bigger lakes, with a land bridge connecting Finland with Sweden at the height of Vaasa. The land gain for both countries will amount to thousands of square kilometers by then because the earth crust still has the capacity to rise for another 100 meters (328 feet), causing a constant recession of the waters of the Baltic Sea from the shoreline. Former harbor cities will become inland places unless they are relocated at intervals, such as Tornio.

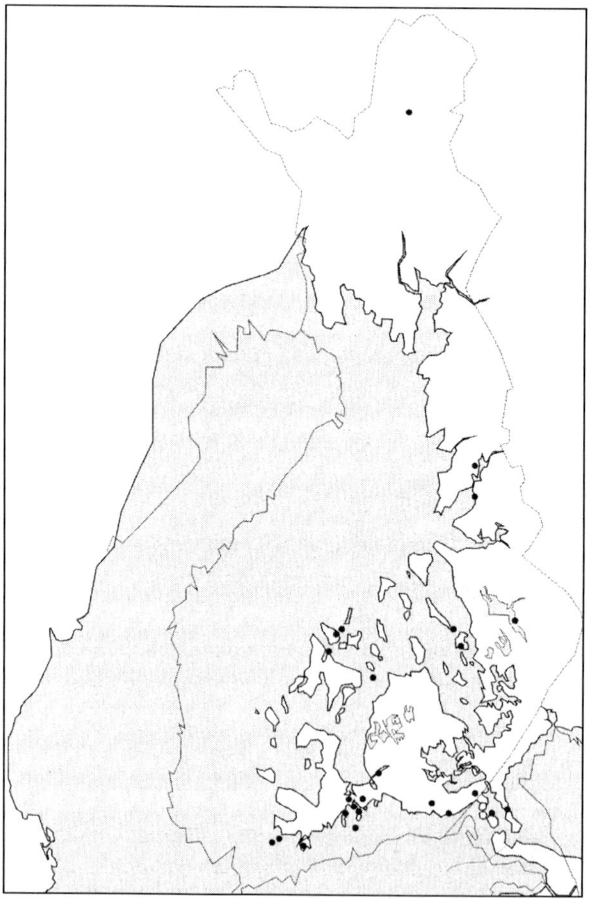

What catches the eye when looking at Finnish landscapes from the air (e.g., google maps) is the multitude of lakes, big and small, that are scattered from the southeast to Lapland. These waters, together with many swamps and wetlands, are the remainders of deglaciation toward the end of the last Ice Age when the melting glaciers and ice sheets produced huge amounts of melting waters, flooding large parts of the country. For long, the southern parts of Fenno-Scandia were covered under the waters of the Yoldia Sea (ca. 11,700–10,700 years BP = before present). From the Yoldia Sea developed the Ancylus Lake (figure 1) from which later emerged the Baltic Sea, after a connection with the North Sea had opened (Raukas 1995). Further east, the big lakes Ladoga and Onega have formed a firm part of the landscape since the post-glacial period. The earliest settlements of people who had arrived from the south are associated with this era (Takala 2004).

**Figure 1: The extension of the Ancylus Lake (ca. 10,000 BP) and the earliest post-glacial settlements in southern Finland (courtesy Hannu Takala).**

Prehistoric global warming caused the end of glaciation, but the melting of the ice sheet did not unfold in a continuous process. The melting started ca. 13,000 years ago and the area of southern Finland had been freed of ice when everything came to a standstill. By 11,500 BP the climate temporarily cooled down again, with the effect that the ice sheet started to grow again, and again scratching rubble and sand from the surface and pushing the material south. This process of a renewed extension of the ice cover lasted several hundred years. By 11,000 BP another sudden warming spike put an end to the motion of the ice and the ice eventually receded, leaving the newly amassed rubble behind. The contours of this terminal moraine of the second movement of the ice are clearly discernible in the landscape. This is a hilly range, called Salpausselkä, that runs, in a west-easterly and further northeasterly direction, through southern Finland.

## How Many Lakes Are There in Finland?

Finland is known as the land of a thousand lakes. Indeed, there are many lakes in this country, but many more than one thousand. According to a geological survey, in Finland, altogether 187,888 lakes are listed that are larger than 5 ares (500 square meters, respectively). The three largest lakes are Saimaa (1,377 square km) in the southeast, Päijänne (1,080 square km) in central Finland and Inari (1,040 square km) in Lapland. Some 300 lakes are larger than 10 square km. "The ecological status of lakes and rivers in Northern Finland, and big lakes throughout the country, is mainly good or high" (Putkuri et al. 2014: 72).

Most of these lakes were formed between 12,000 and 11,000 years ago, toward the end of the last Ice Age. The early history of the melting waters has remained encapsulated in the depth of some lakes. For instance, in some isolated pockets on the bottom of lake Saimaa biologists found melting water from the Ice Age (with a species of microbes that has persisted from that era). There is a species of fish, the Saimaa salmon, that has lived in the lake since the end of the Ice Age (http://www.fishinginfinland.fi/lake_saimaa; 4 March 2015).

"Land of a thousand lakes" is a saying known throughout the world. But when did it originate and why is the number of lakes limited in the English saying? When the Finns speak about lakes in their country then they use the phrase *tuhansien järvien maa* "land of thousands of lakes." The origins of the English saying date back to the end of the 19th century when, in 1899, the first guide book to Finland was published in Great Britain by M. Harland & Son. Its title was *Finland: The Land of a Thousand Lakes*, and it was designed for travellers to get acquainted with the country. In this guide book, the poetic text of a song was presented which was to become Finland's national anthem. The author of this anthem is Johan Ludvig Runeberg (1804–1877), representative of the national movement in Finland. In the tenth verse it says, "*maa tuhatjärvinen*," the meaning of which is ambiguous. It can be translated as "land of thousands of lakes" or "land of a thousand lakes." The second alternative was chosen by the British publisher, and that became the basis for translations into other languages, for example, German (*Land der Tausend Seen*), French (*pays de mille lacs*), and others.

Finland's lake landscape offers some rare species of wildlife, unknown in other parts of Europe. One such species are the grey seals that live in the biggest of the Finnish lakes, Lake Saimaa, in the southeastern part of the country (Hyvärinen et al. 2004). When the last Ice Age ended, the south of Finland was flooded by the melting water. Seals were among the first animal species to inhabit these waters. Once the land mass rose the southern waters were divided, into the western Baltic Sea and the eastern region of Finland's lakes, and the connection with the Baltic Sea was lost. The eastern seals (pusa hispida saimensis, Finnish *saimaannorppa*) became isolated in Lake Saimaa and they adopted to conditions in fresh water while their cousins in the Baltic Sea continued life in salt water. The Saimaa grey seals are on the list of endangered species, they number about 300 and there are zones of protection for this species (Kokko et al. 1999).

## *Finland and Wildlife: Where Are the Polar Bears?*

When people think of wildlife in Finland, what might come to mind is the bear, the "king of the forest" (Pentikäinen 2007). The bear that lives in the Finnish forest is the European brown bear (*ursus arctos*). It is estimated that there are between 1200 and 1500 brown bears in Finland. Many people—Finns themselves and foreigners visiting Finland—go bear watching.

The misunderstanding about the polar bears emerged from the settings of the *Exposition Universelle* (World's Fair) held in Paris between April and November of 1900. At the time, Finland formed part of tsarist Russia but, with its status of an autonomous region (Grand Duchy), Finland was entitled to a pavilion of its own, distinct from that for Russia.

The pavilion, designed by the architects Herman Gesellius, Armas Lindgren and Eliel Saarinen, became famous, and pictures of it were published in several works (e.g., in *Dekorative Kunst* 3, 1900, pp. 457–63; *L'Architecture à l'Exposition Universelle de 1900*, Paris 1900, p. 65, pl. X). There was a recurrent motif that appeared in the architecture of the pavilion and in its surroundings, and that was the bear, the typical animal inhabiting the forests of Finland.

Above the frame of the pavilion's front door, heads of bears in relief formed a picture frieze. On the roof of the pavilion, and in the courtyard, surrounding the pavilion, some sculptures depicting bears were erected. These were sculpted of *staff*, a low-cost material that was a French invention and used for temporary constructions. In fact, all the buildings of the world's fair were demolished after it closed. The *staff* had jute fiber as its core which was then covered with plaster and cement. The sculptures of the bears in their raw state had a whitish color.

Some two weeks before the opening of the fair representatives of the French press visited the site and saw the bear sculptures which had not yet been painted in their final brown color. The journalists wrote their articles and showed themselves impressed by the exquisite Finnish pavilion (*Le Figaro* of 19 September 1900; *Courrier de Saumur* of 27 September 1900). The journalists also talked about the white bears at the Finnish pavilion, and the news about the polar bears spread throughout the world.

The misconception concerning the bear sculptures in their whitish color was somehow reinforced by one of the illustrations that one finds in the guidebook to the exhibition (figure 2). In this illustration, an imaginary scene is added, the shooting of a "white" bear.

The misunderstanding about the white bears turned out to be irrevocable, and the world has persistently retained its cliché about Finland and the polar bears. Nobody could foresee that the journalists would come for a visit of the Finnish pavilion too early, seeing the raw versions of the bear sculptures that caused the misunderstanding. When the Exhibition opened, the sculptures presented themselves in brown color, as was intended. The sculptures in that color represented the species of bear that one could find, in historical times, all over Finland, the brown bear (*Ursus arctos*).

Originally, bears also lived in the southern part of the country although, nowadays, a southern bear is an exception. The presence of the bear in the south lives on in cultural memory and is documented in names of places or landmarks: Pori (Björneborg in Swedish), a town in the southwest (Swedish *björn* means "bear"), Karhumäki ("Bear Hill"), Karhuvuori ("Bear Mountain"), Karhula ("the bear's place") and other names with the element *karhu* ("bear").

---

### The Myth of Finland's Polar Bears

There is a wide-spread belief among foreigners that, in the Arctic region of Scandinavia, one finds polar bears. In March 2010, the zoo in San Diego, California, opened its renewed special section presenting polar bears to the public. On its website, the zoo publicized a map of Europe, indicating the spread of polar bears. According to the map, polar bears live across northern Scandinavia and roam the Arctic tundra in the Finnish province of Lapland as far south as the town of Rovaniemi.

A Finnish tourist who visited the zoo noticed the misleading entry on the map and informed the Finnish consulate. In June 2010, after having been informed through official channels that the map in question contains an important mistake, the management of the zoo withdrew the older map and publicized a corrected version (www.iltasanomat.fi/ulkomaat/art-1288338240297.html; retrieved 23 February 2015). Many Americans, however, still believe that polar bears are found on the European mainland.

In short: there are no polar bears in Finland and there never were, at least not since the end of the last Ice Age. But stereotypes tend to be persistent as one can see from *Vargic's Miscellany of Curious Maps* (2015: 16). On his map of stereotypes Germany is associated with bratwurst, Romania with Dracula, Hungary with gulas, and Finland with polar bears. How came this belief to be so widespread? The association of the polar bear with Finland has its own history, one of misunderstanding.

---

The brown bear is not just any animal. It is the biggest animal not only in Finland but also in Russia. In the folklore and mythology of the Finns, and of those peoples with cultural traditions akin to the Finnish heritage (i.e., the Finno-Ugric minorities in Russia), the bear is not seen as a fearsome animal. Instead, the northern bear is revered and respected.

The bear is a truly holy being for northern people, and this is reflected in a ramified terminology of taboos which developed in a long span of time, among the Ob-Ugrians (Mansi and Khanty) in western Siberia.

> In speaking of the bear, the Ob-Ugrians employ numerous euphemisms of which the following are but a few examples: "animal," "sacred animal," "living animal," "darling old one," "old one of the forest," "swamp animal," "fur-coated old one," "son borne by Koam," "bear man," "bear woman," "uncle old one," "clawed old one," or "shod old one"; a cub is "little one" or "young brother." Generally these names are used in combination with epithets such as "eminent," "divine," "princely" or "majestic" [Honko et al. 1993: 120–21].

Figure 2: Illustration of the Finnish pavilion at the World Exhibition in Paris 1900 (Söderhjelm 1900, supplément illustré).

Since the naming of the bear underlies taboo restrictions, Finnish and related Finno-Ugric languages borrowed expressions from Indo-European languages with which they stood in contact in prehistoric times. The Finnish term for bear (*karhu*, from an Indo-Iranian source) is an example of such kind of borrowing (Itkonen and Kulonen 2001/1: 312). In Finnish oral poetry, the taboo term *otso* is used.

## The Bear and Its Role in Northern People's Cultural Memory

Of all the animals that are depicted in the ancient imagery of the Finno-Ugrians, the bear shows the most vivid persistence. No other animal has been continuously venerated throughout the ages in such a respectful manner as the bear. In the mythical heritage of northern people, totemic conceptualizations of their origins have been preserved, and the bear is perceived as the revered ancestor of the whole clan or ethnic group. "It is a worshipped animal, a cult object, the symbol of tribe and family" (Pentikäinen 1989: 169). As an ancestor spirit the bear is amply celebrated in the oral literature. Ideas about the role of the bear as ancestor spirit may have enhanced the development of the bear cult which was widely practiced in the northern regions.

Since prehistoric times, bear rituals have been practiced throughout northern Eurasia and Eurasian mythology is permeated with tales about the bear. Finland and Lapland are the westernmost extensions of the vast area, called Eurasia, that stretches from northern Europe as far as eastern Siberia. The cultural heritage of the Finns and the Saami shows many resemblances with the cultural traditions and mythical beliefs among the small peoples that inhabit northern Siberia (Haarmann and Marler 2008), memories of the bear cult for one. Although the exact date for the emergence of the bear cult cannot be determined, the rich imagery related to the sacred bear speaks in favor of longevity of the tradition. The most important festival focusing on the sacred bear is the feasting ceremony after the hunt.

Bear-hunting rituals have been practiced among Finno-Ugric peoples throughout the ages. Such performances encompass more than ceremonies that meet the eye; they carry major symbolic meaning relating to aspects of sustainability of the community since the bear-hunting ritual has to be perceived as "an elaborate accumulation of songs, pantomime, drama, feasting, sacrifice and prayer lasting several days.... In their entirety, the ceremonies allowed the community to see the coherence of its central economic, social and religious values and to reaffirm their significance" (Honko et al. 1993: 120).

It is significant that bear festivals among the Ob-Ugrians persisted into the era of the Soviet regime with its atheistic ideals and even survived it.

> During the Soviet era the bear ceremonials did not cease, at least in the north and east. They were so popular that the authorities even thought of declaring them secularised (Balzer 1999, 190), bringing them under a general policy of folklorisation. However, such a decision was never made. Since the fall of the Soviet Union and the renaissance of indigenous customs, some of the bear festivals have become important political manifestations of Khanty (and Ob-Ugrian) unity [Rydving 2010: 35].

Among the Ob-Ugrians, this festival has been continuously celebrated. Westerners had a chance to witness a bear festival in a Khanty village on one of the tributaries of the

Ob river in the late 1980s. To make every single bear feast memorable, the skull of the bear is fixed to a so-called "song stave." "Only the song stave, notched for each song performed during the bear feast, is kept, carefully preserved together with other staves, some of them very old, under the roof of the main village building…. In this way, the past with all its traditions lives on in the family" (Honko et al. 1993: 128–29).

The bonds among members in the community were ritualized as stemming from the union of the bear with an earthly woman (or with a female guardian spirit of nature). "Elements of the bear concept pervade the entire Ob-Ugrian culture, creating one of the world's richest bear cults" (Schmidt 1989: 189). In the cultural memory of the Ob-Ugrians, many stories about the bear have been preserved, in particular about its role in human genesis. The bear is considered to be the son of the sky god. In the myth of origin, the sky god sends his son, the bear, down to earth. There, the bear takes a female spirit of the forest as wife, and their offspring are the first human beings. Thus, the bear becomes the founder of the ancient clans of the Khanty (and Mansi, respectively).

Totemic ancestry relating to the bear is familiar also to the peoples in western Eurasia, for example among the Mordvinians who live on both sides of the central Volga. In their cultural heritage, tales about relationships between the bear and humans have been preserved. Such stories also form part of the oral tradition among Finns, Karelians and Saami (the Skolt Saami, in particular). The totemic motif of the bear mingling with a human being has been chosen as a theme for a Saami feature film, with the Saami title *Guovza* ("The Bear"), that was released in 1994 (Lehtola 2000: 254ff.). The story is of a girl (played by Irene Länsman) who falls in love with a bear that possesses the magic power of transforming into a human being. During the night the transformed bear, a young man, joins the girl in her bed. Their offspring, two boys, inherit the power of transformation from their father. One of the boys kills the bear, his father, and is condemned to exile. The other boy stays with his mother and the bonds that keep them united resemble the relationship of son and mother known from the Greek myth of Oedipus.

The bear has been modeled as sculpture or in relief, engraved as a motif in petroglyphs and painted as a sacred symbol on shamans' drums. In the area of Saami settlement, the bear is depicted in such rock engravings as those in Alta in northern Norway (province of Finnmark), dated between 4200 and 3600 BCE (Helskog 1988: 72f.).

The bear was hunted in the lands of the Saami into the 18th century. In a book published in 1755, Pehr Fjellström, a priest in Swedish Lapland, describes the hunting of the bear and the feast that followed the hunt. The celebrations had ritual character, and these "included the threading of brass rings upon string which was then hung around the necks of hunters. Special food and drink were provided to the men and the women—separately—and for three nights carnal congress was forbidden. As elsewhere in Finno-Ugric cultures, the naming of the bear directly was taboo" (Kent 2014: 225).

The oral literature that has been perpetuated, as a living heritage, among the indigenous peoples of northern Eurasia includes a rich repertory of tales, songs and ceremonial chants relating to the bear and the bear hunt. According to traditional mythology the bear once descended to earth from heaven and, through the bear ritual, the soul of the hunted bear returns to its celestial home.

> A similar background myth of the bear's origins in heaven, his sojourn on earth, and his return, by means of the bear hunt and wake, to his heavenly home appears to have lain behind the Sámi and

Finnish-Karelian bear-hunting rites, though the full details of the myth have been lost, and indeed it is clear that as agriculture increased in importance over the centuries in Finland (not among the Sámi, where instead reindeer-herding became the prevalent means of livelihood) it affected the purpose of the rites, and also probably the underlying myth and attitude towards the bear... [Tolley 2009: 561].

In Finnish folk poetry, the ritual bear feast is celebrated, in manifold local variations over wide areas of the country (Sarmela 1994, map 1).

The bear is called by a taboo-avoiding name: "Good One" or "Great Man" or "handsome one." At the beginning of the ceremony, questions are asked and answers demanded. Then the bear meat is carried inside the house and offered to the participants in the feast. At the end, the skull of the bear is taken out into the forest and fixed to the trunk of a tree.

In connection with the feasting ceremony, there is regular mention of a ritual of the hunter who eats the bear's tongue, its eyes and the ears. Such action which is also described in ceremonial songs may be misinterpreted by outsiders as a sign of domination or manipulation on the side of the hunter. Instead, eating the bear's sense organs and that of speech is an intimate act to transfer the sacred animal's strength and instinct to human beings and it expresses "the idea of profound identification and communication with nature within the ritual—the song was sung to please the forest maidens" (Tarkka 1998: 103).

> Other ritual songs, such as those performed in connection with a successful bear hunt reflect ancient religious traditions shared by other Finno-Ugric peoples. Nineteenth-century songs of greeting a bear as an honored wedding guest show parallels in Saami as well as Khanty and Mansi bear hunting traditions. Because of the bear's tremendous mystical as well as physical power, special care had to be taken to insure that the killed animal's spirit would not be offended. Such remnant songs speak of an age when the fates of men and nature were seen as clearly tied. Returning the bear's bones to the forest was a further way of assuring the continuation of hunting luck [Virtanen and DuBois 2000: 147f.].

In northern Europe, the mythical underpinnings of the bear cult

---

## A Bear Song from Finnish Epic Poetry

The one who brings in the meat:
> Don't beware of the women
> and don't fear the bonnet-heads
> for the women are shining
> and the sons in their half-boots
> the daughters adorned with tin
> for the Good One to come in
> for the Great Man to step in.

The meat on the table:
> I put him upon clean wood
> lay him down on a good board:
> the boards all begin to sing
> and the windows to rejoice
> that the Good One has come in
> that the Great Man has stepped in.

The skull is carried out to be hung on the tree:
> Let us be off, let us go
> up the golden lane
> up the silver road
> where the planks are laid with silk
> planks with silk, swamps with velvet
> and the gates with a black rim.

The skull is fastened to the tree:
> I'll not put him on willow
> nor on sallow set him up:
> I'll put him on a clean tree
> on a good fir tree
> on a fair pine tree
> sit him facing east
> tilting to the north.

When everything has been done, this is said:
> There I left my handsome one
> left the one I keep in mind
> left to watch the moon
> to admire the sun
> sat him facing east
> tilting to the north [excerpts from
> Honko et al. 1993: 187ff.].

still form a vivid part of the people's cultural memory. In the development of folk culture and national culture, the relationship between human beings and the bear has expanded to become manifest in the most exquisite contexts. In some cases, such contexts are revealed in the composition of symbols in the whole of a monument. One such example is the Runeberg monument, celebrating the memory of one of the country's great poets, Johan Ludvig Runeberg (1804–1877).

This monument was created by Johan Ludvig's son, the sculptor Walter Runeberg (1838–1920), erected in the Esplanadi Park in Helsinki, and disclosed to the public in May 1885. At the foot of the pedestal, with the statue of the poet on top, stands the figure of the Finnish Maiden, in the posture of an antique muse and clad in a bear skin, reminiscent of a seer of the ancients and singer of epic songs in the Kalevalaic style (see Chapter 7). Her left arm leans on a tablet, with the Swedish version of the national anthem (*Vårt land*) engraved on it. Under the tablet is a pile of books, underscoring the civilized state of the country and the high level of education of its inhabitants (figure 3).

There is another version of the Finnish Maiden which is also a figure of a young woman clad in a bear skin. This is a statue by the same sculptor, Walter Runeberg, showing her with a sword in her right hand and a shield in her left, on which is inscribed the word LEX (Latin: "law"). This figure symbolizes the Finnish Maiden in her role as protector of the Finnish Constitution (Alho 1997: 63f.). Behind her stands the lion, the heraldic symbol in the Finnish flag. This sculpture of the Finnish Maiden and the lion, imbued with national symbolism, stands at the foot of the monument erected to celebrate Alexander II, the "good Tsar" (see Chapter 8), at the Senate Square in Helsinki. Another version is on display in the state room of the president's palace in Helsinki.

**Figure 3: The Runeberg monument in Helsinki, with the figure of the Finnish Maiden, clad in a bear skin (VårtLandStatue; photograph: Mark A. Wilson; Wilson44691).**

## How Did the Early Inhabitants of Fenno-Scandia Experience Their Environment?

The prehistoric people of northern Europe did not possess writing technology but they made extensive use of a medium that is durable. They told their stories in pictures painted on or engraved into rock surfaces. The rock art of Eurasian peoples is rich and manifold. It provides much information and valuable insights about ancient beliefs and, above all, about how people experienced their natural environment.

There are 127 sites with rock art in Finland, mostly in the southeastern and south-central regions of the country. The inhabitants of Fenno-Scandia started creating such art from about 5000 BCE and this artistic tradition lasted into the second millennium BCE. The style of the pictures, which may be characterized as "sub-naturalistic" (Haarmann 1996), persisted unchanged throughout the period when Finnish rock art was practiced. What we see in the pictures are various animal species: "Although most of the animals would appear to be elk (*Alces laces*), it is possible that some of them portray wild reindeer (*Rangifer tarandus*)" (Lahelma 2008: 25). Pictures of boats show different kind of vessels and these are depicted from various angles. Strokes illustrate the oars that were used. Figures of human beings abound; most of them are male and there are only few pictures of women (see Chapter 3 for the history of women in Finland).

The presence of hunter-gatherers in certain areas, and their activities relating to rock art, can be dated using various methods: studying shoreline changes, artifacts (e.g., arrow points typical of certain local cultures), bones and traces of fire (providing organic material for applying carbon 14 dating methods) near the sites with pictures. The identification of the prehistoric people's anthropological features, based mainly on an investigation of the bone material (DNA analysis) points in the direction of their being the ancestors of the Saami population. Then, the Saami lived further south of the habitats they have occupied since historical times (Seurujärvi-Kari 2000).

The best-known site with prehistoric pictures is Astuvansalmi on the shore of Lake Saimaa in southeastern Finland (Kivikäs 1995: 51ff.). This picture frieze with its numerous motifs is found on the UNESCO list of World Heritage sites. The first rock picture that was documented and studied, at Hvitträsk (on the shore of Juusjärvi), was reported by the famous composer Jean Sibelius in 1911. At many sites, only a few motifs form a visual ensemble. But one finds compositions with dozens or even hundreds of single motifs. The area with the greatest number of motifs of rock art is the Saraakallio, located in central Finland (Kivikäs 1995: 214ff.).

Finnish rock art distinguishes itself from the tradition of rock art in neighboring countries by the special technique that was applied to create pictures. Rock pictures in Finland are painted onto the surface of rocks while those in Norway, Sweden and northern Russia are engraved in the rocky surface. The paint that was used is based on animal fat or blood, mixed with iron oxide which produces brownish-red shades of color. As the result of a natural chemical process the surface with painted pictures was covered by a layer of silicon dioxide, preventing the paint from being washed away by rain. Pictures were painted on the surface of rock walls or waterfront cliffs, and the location of most of the sites in their natural surroundings is awe-inspiring even today (Lahelma 2008: 60f.).

## A Prehistoric Chronicle: Rock Art by the Lakeside

The visual record of northern people's conceptions about their lives and about the world is especially vivid at certain sites, where the ensembles of pictures and their alignment in narrative sequences are so dense as to expose the "annals" of a Stone Age community. Among the rare specimens of a panel densely covered with a multitude of pictures in a naturalistic style, with abstract motifs and with mythological symbolism, is the so-called "roof stone" from Peri Nos (Sawwatejew 1984), a peninsula on the eastern shore of Lake Onega in the Republic of Karelia (Russian Federation; figure 4).

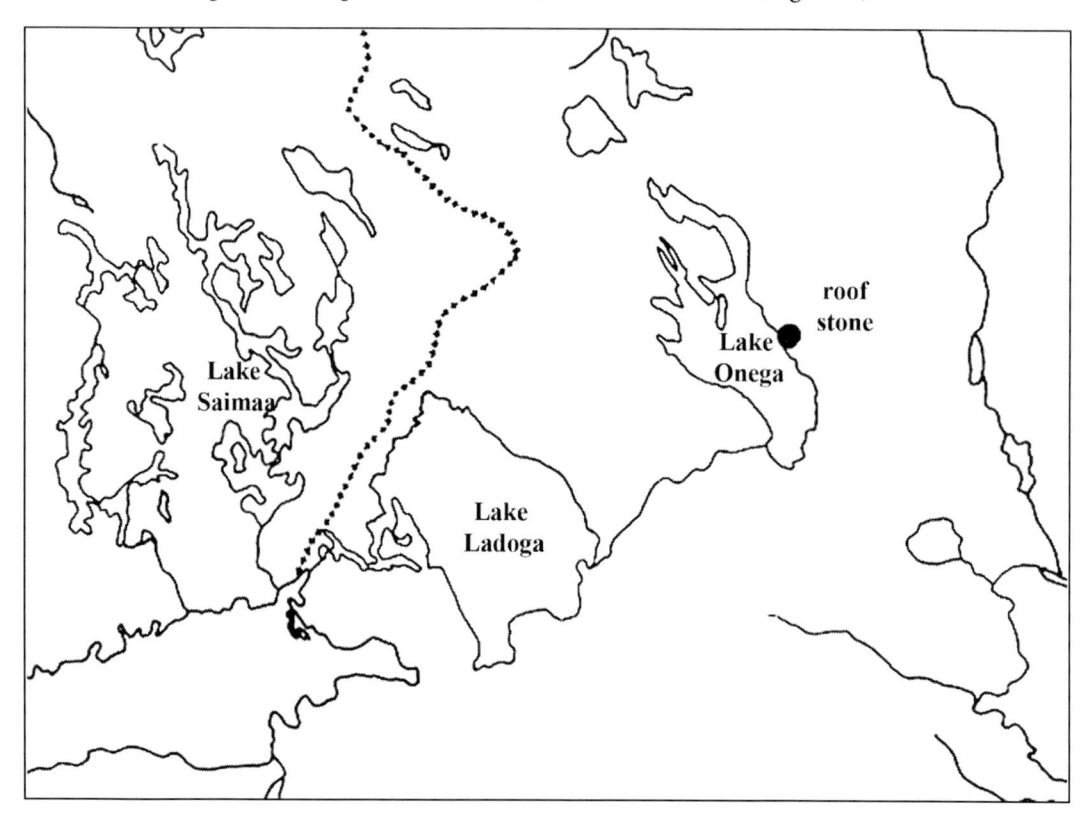

**Figure 4: The great lakes (Lake Ladoga and Lake Onega) on the southeastern periphery of Fenno-Scandia and the location of the "roof stone" (author's material).**

The rock engravings are dated to a period between 2300 and 1700 BCE. The area has been inhabited by local groups of Finno-Ugric populations since prehistoric times. Still today, one finds settlements of the Vepsian people there who speak a Baltic-Finnic language. Peri Nos is one of several sites scattered around Lake Onega (figure 5). This area with rock carvings of mythological significance has been identified as a "prehistoric sanctuary" (Poikalainen 2000).

In the configuration of pictures carved into the smooth surface of the rock, dozens of motifs catch the observer's eye. These motifs are naturalistic as well as abstract. In this dense ensemble of visual components one finds abundant information about hunting and fishing in the prehistoric community, but also about the Onega people's beliefs as

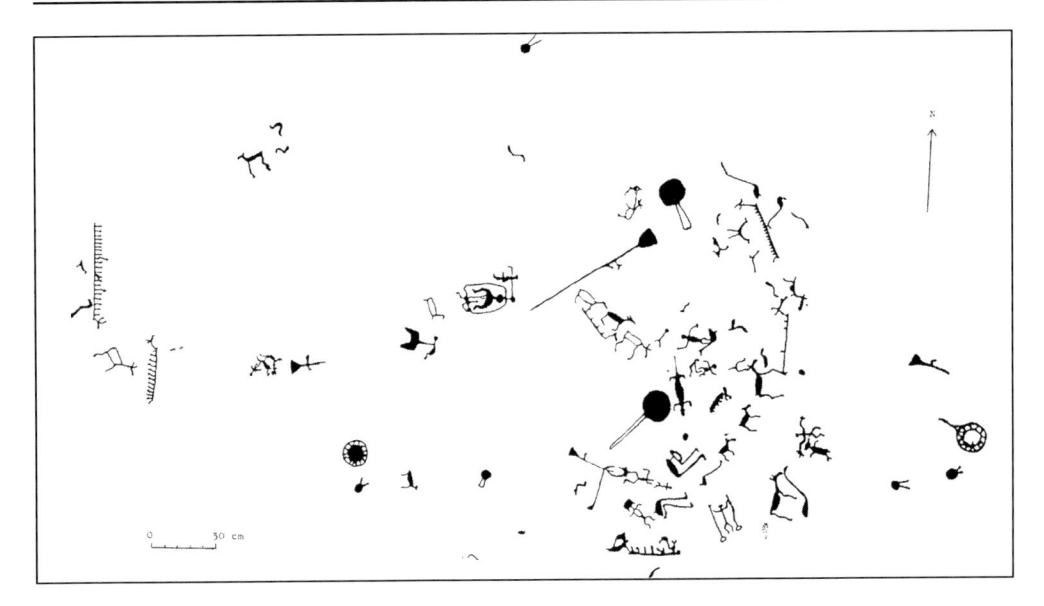

**Figure 5: The ensemble of rock engravings on the "roof stone" from Peri Nos, Lake Onega, Republic of Karelia (from Harald Haarmann, *Language in Its Cultural Embedding* [Berlin: Mouton de Gruyter, 1990], p. 202, fig. 22).**

expressed in central mythological motifs in rituals and ceremonies. How can one arrive at a conclusive interpretation of this visual material which, at first sight, seems to present itself in a rather chaotic disorder?

The key to the understanding of the pictorial composition as a narrative is its relationship to the four directions. The positioning of pictures in the upper part of the ensemble (pointing north) and in the lower part (pointing south) is not coincidental. Similarly, the assemblage of pictures on the right side (pointing east) as opposed to those on the left side (pointing west) is meaningful. Solar disks are positioned on either side of the central composition (see figure 5).

Against the background of this spatio-temporal fixation it is compelling to discern the order of the motifs in the central composition as cyclical (figure 6). The scenery abounds with the depiction of activities of all kinds. Judging simply from the nature of hunting scenes and ceremonial events the annals on the panel cannot represent happenings that occur on one single day. Rather, one has to assert that the scenes depict seasonally bound activities (i.e., east = spring, south = summer, west = autumn, north = winter). This provides a clue to the identification of the pictures as elements of a narrative describing annual activities and events.

When decoding the narrative starting from the northeast direction one arrives at the following tentative reconstruction of a seasonal round (Haarmann 1990: 202ff.):

> **Spring:** (1) After their arrival in early spring wild swans are hunted, from boats or from land, with the help of catapults or boomerang-like devices; (2) With the further melting of lake ice swimming elks that cross bays and rivers, are also hunted;
> **Summer:** (3) During this season, fishing and the hunting of different species of water-fowl are practiced;
> **Autumn:** (4) The hunters set traps and hunt elks, from boats or from land;
> **Winter:** (5) The most important activities seem to be the hunting of elk and deer, and the repairing and construction of traps.

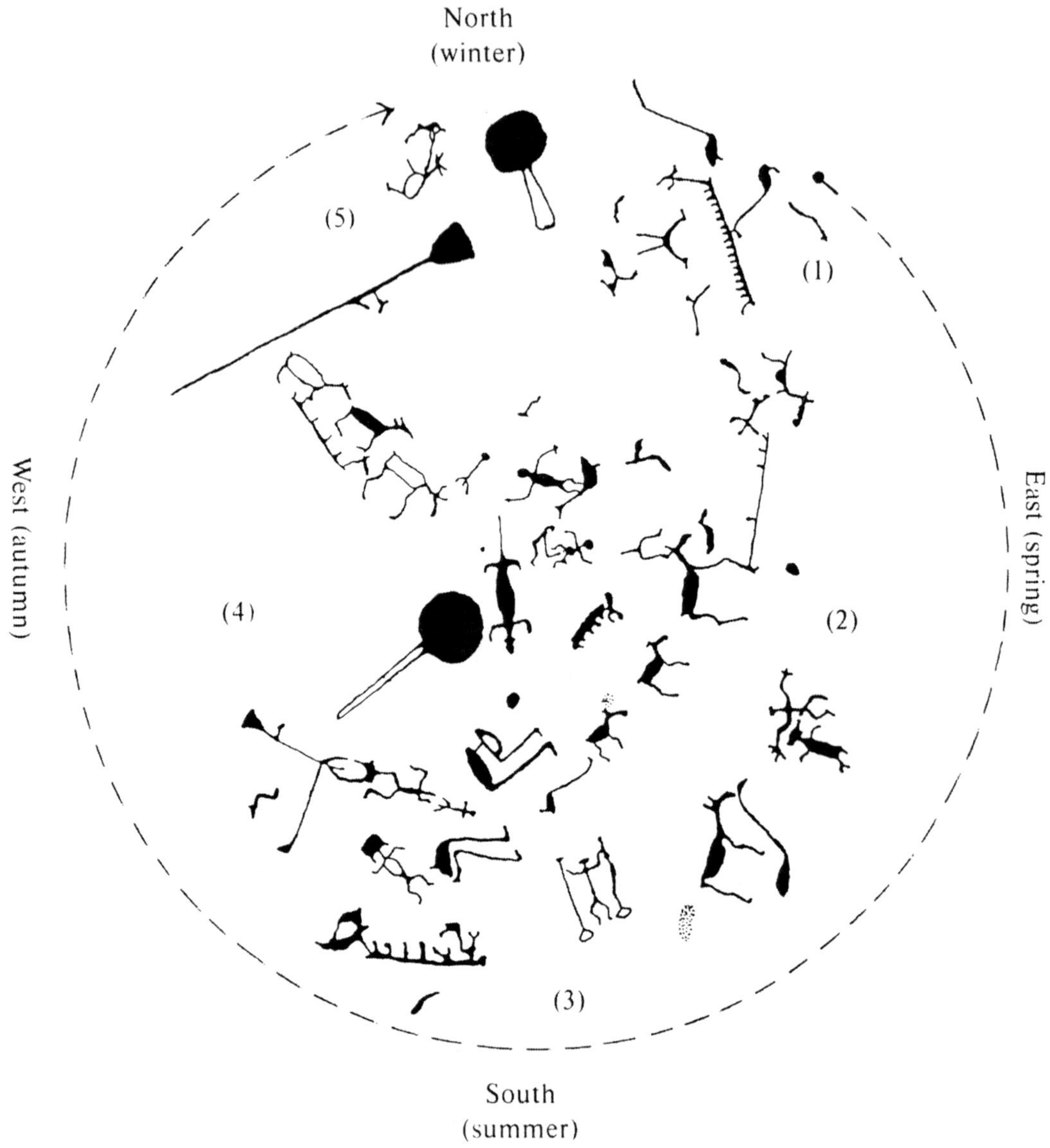

**Figure 6: The central composition of rock engravings on the "roof stone" (from Harald Haarmann, *Language in Its Cultural Embedding* [Berlin: Mouton de Gruyter, 1990], p. 205, fig. 23).**

Certain pictorial configurations can be readily interpreted as describing annual activities, such as hunting elks. Furthermore, there are other motifs in this cyclic narrative which are undoubtedly related to the spiritual life of the Onega people. The decoding of their meaning, however, demands caution.

In view of the Saami linkage with the Onega people's community it does not seem unfounded to highlight the transcendental motifs on the "roof stone" against the background of Saami mythology (Pentikäinen 1995, Helander-Renvall 2006). Certain motifs are of central mythological significance (figure 7).

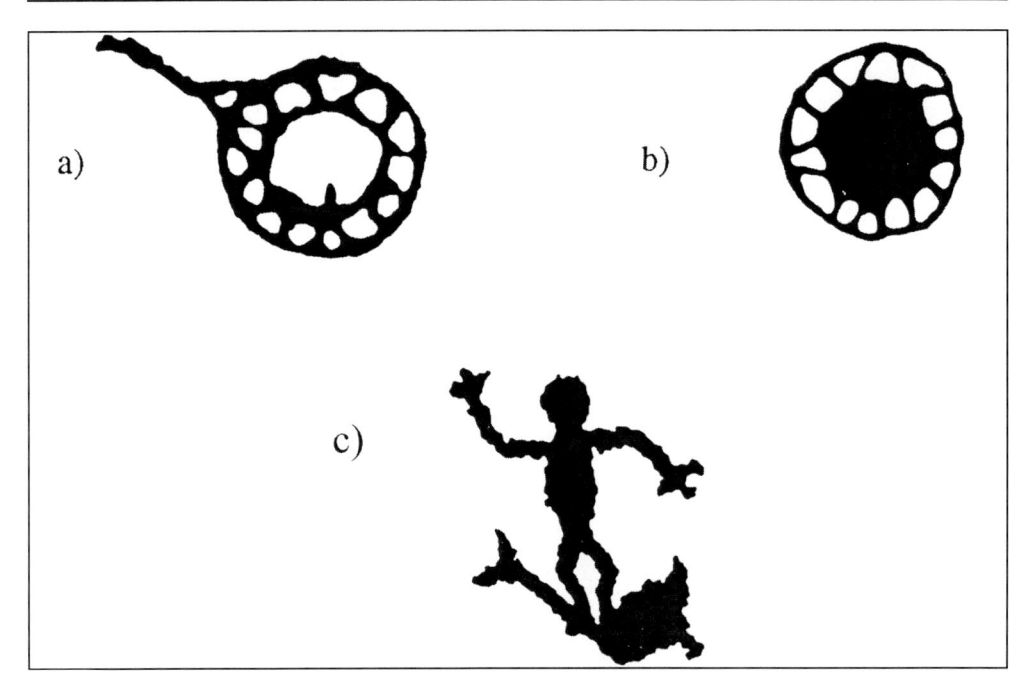

**Figure 7: Symbols with central mythological significance on the "roof stone" (from Harald Haarmann, *Language in Its Cultural Embedding* [Berlin: Mouton de Gruyter, 1990], p. 210, excerpt from fig. 24).**

## The Solar Disk Symbolizing the Giver of Life

The sun is not only an item that everyone can identify as a celestial body, it plays a decisive role for the natural environment and for human ecology. This source of light has impressed people throughout the ages and has attracted their particular attention as documented by the fabric of their mythology. In the mythological tradition, the sun is animated, as a divine figure.

In the beginning, there was the solar deity, Mother Sun. The solar deity is radiant. Light and warmth stream from her. The sun, the source of light and life, is venerated in the mythic tradition of the Saami as a female divinity (Pentikäinen 1995: 120ff.). Her name is Beaivvi nieida ("Sun Maiden").

In the middle of the winter season, the sun does not rise from behind the horizon during the day. This period (called *skabmo* in Saami and *kaamos* in Finnish) lasts for almost two months. The boundary of the Arctic day without sunlight runs near Sodankylä in southern Lapland. At the northernmost tip of Finland (at Utsjoki), *kaamos* extends over 51 days. When the sun finally reappears at the end of January, Saami people would bow to the divinity to honor her and, in former times, a reindeer—preferably a white one—was offered to the Sun Maiden as a sacrifice. The symbol of the sun features on many shaman's drums and is accompanied by various symbols of mythological significance (Autio 2000).

In the panel of rock engravings on the "roof stone," the disk from which a ray of light streams (symbolizing the rising sun) is associated with the eastern direction (figure 7a). The disk with a dark center (symbolizing the setting sun) is associated with the western direction (figure 7b). This arrangement of solar disks illustrates the idea—found in Saami mythology and also among other northern peoples—of the sun's responsibility for human cycles of activity, all part of the contrast between lightness and darkness, between day and night.

The reverence for the sun among the peoples living in the northern region seems well motivated. The amount of light in winter, during the period of the sun's absence, is minimal, compared to the 24-hour presence of the sun during the summer when it does not disappear even at night. This means that the duration of daylight and darkness in the latitude band 60° to 90° N is extremely disproportionate (Przybylak 2003: 6; figure 8).

**Figure 8: A 24-hour rhythm of the never-setting sun in the Arctic summer (author's material).**

There is a special cosmological factor that carries much weight when assessing the significance of the radiating sun for people in the post-glacial period.

> Summers were generally warmer than at present because the tilt of the Earth's axis was greater (thereby enhancing seasonal extremes) and because the Northern Hemisphere summer solstice occurred when the Earth was nearer the Sun on its orbit (at perihelion as opposed to at aphelion as occurs today) ... this caused Northern Hemisphere solar radiation receipt in summer to be about 8 percent greater than it is today [Anderson et al. 2007: 159].

The summer and the winter solstices as well as the spring and autumn equinoxes have been the focus of a sun cult in the North since prehistoric times. The celebration of the summer solstice is a ritual of sun worship which has been very popular among the Baltic-Finnic peoples in northern Europe since ancient times (Honko et al. 1993: 266). "Midsummer, known in Finland as St. John's Day (*Juhannus*, and in Southwest Finland as *mittumaari*, cf. Swedish *midsommar*), has long been the greatest of the summer festivals and it nowadays dominates all others" (Talve 1997: 213f.). In Finland, the custom to burn midsummer bonfires has a long tradition only in the eastern and southern regions. In the 20th century, it has spread to other parts of the country. The bonfire symbolizes the idea of cleansing and that of banishing evil spirits. In north-central Finland (Ostrobothnia), however, the pre–Christian tradition to ward off evil spirits is associated with the burning of bonfires at Easter.

Arguably, the celebration of the summer solstice in the northern part of Scandinavia attracts most attention as an annual event of communal interest, overarching all social groups. The custom of adorning homes with green branches, preferably birch twigs, is practiced by many people, especially in the western and southern parts of Finland (Virtanen and DuBois 2000: 86). Finnish people celebrate midsummer, often in the countryside, amidst family members and friends gathered in the summer houses. In public places, there is dancing and the joyful atmosphere of watching the flaring up and burning down of the bonfire.

Contrasting with this are the habits of experiencing the darkest period of the year. The observation of the winter solstice is marginalized by the celebration of Christmas. This festival is an innovation of the calendar in northern Europe that was introduced during the Middle Ages together with Christianity.

Midsummer as the most typical festival to be celebrated in the home country is not only an event in the annual calendar but also a spiritual focus where people's awareness of the cyclical rhythm of the life cycle ideally crystallizes. In late winter, people's psychology is tuned to moving toward midsummer, and this is like a pull that helps people free themselves from the impression of strenuous days in the late winter period and inspires them to welcome the season of lightness and warmth.

Nothing seems more natural than to assume a similar collective psychology among people of earlier, even prehistoric periods. Then also, a ceremony such as the one to celebrate the event of the summer solstice must have created a similar communal atmosphere as nowadays, binding the members of the communities together in harmony with the deeper significance of the sun and the sacred round of the year in participation within the cycles of Nature.

The experience of the sun rising in the east and setting in the west, common in most parts of the world, is of little use in the Arctic region with its particular light conditions. During the summer season, the sun rises in the northeast, prescribes a wide circle and sets in the northwest. During the fringes of wintertime, the sun rises in the southeast and sets in the southwest. The observation of these fundamental changes in the sun's movements by the prehistoric inhabitants of Finland may have been decisive for the name pattern of the directions. In Finnish, eight main directions are distinguished, each direction with its own name, while, in most languages of Europe, only four main directions are distinguished (well known from the English vocabulary; figure 9).

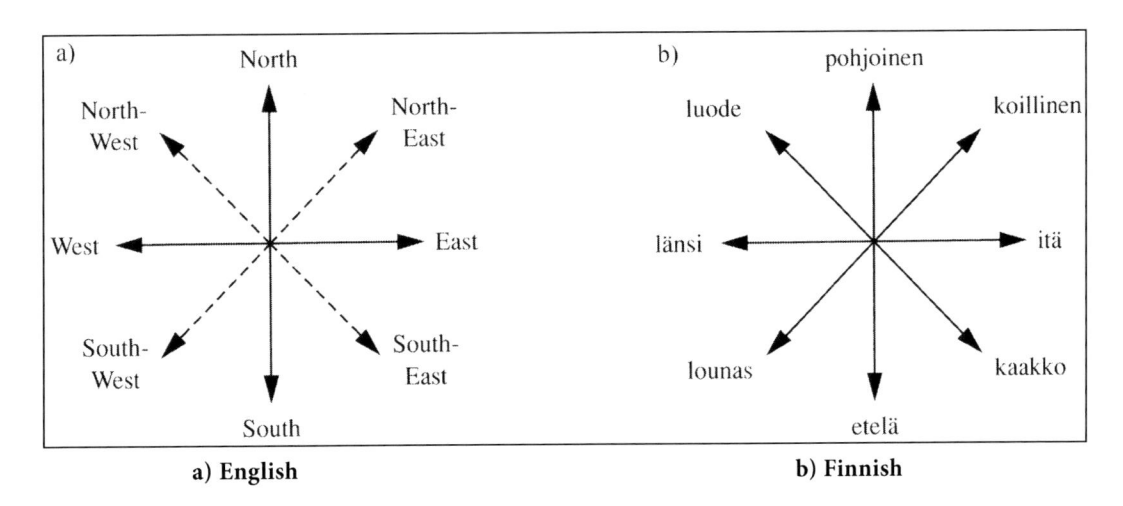

a) English      b) Finnish

**Figure 9: The terminology for geographical directions (author's material).**

The custom to orientate in one's environment by observing the movements of the sun became effective, once a diversified terminology for the directions had been in place. Although no longer needed in the daily life of the urban population, these terminological distinction of the Finnish vocabulary are still in use and are regularly applied by the meteorological service on TV.

## Water Birds as Messengers Between the Worlds

Water birds, ducks and especially wild swans (called *laulujoutsenet* in Finnish), are imbued with mythological significance. The wild swan is very common in the northern regions. Pictures of water birds are found among the rock paintings in southeastern Finland and engraved on the "roof stone" from Lake Onega. In the more than 1100 rock carvings at sites around Lake Onega, 42 percent are images of water birds, the most characteristic contours being those of wild swans (Poikalainen 2000: 259).

The overall significance of water birds in the mythology of the Finno-Ugrians, and especially of the Saami people, is so central that the latter are sometimes called the "people of the wild swan." This notion was coined by the scholar and writer Lennart Meri who was president of Estonia from 1992 to 2001. In 1981, the wild swan became the national bird of Finland and, since 2002, this bird is featured on the one-euro coins minted in Finland. In the traditional Saami calendar, March is called *nuktsamanno* "month of the swan." This is the time when the migratory wild swans return to Lapland.

The ability of water birds to dive and disappear from the surface of the waters has impressed the human mind throughout the ages. It is not surprising that, in the animated world of shamanism, the water bird is seen as the messenger moving from the world of the living to the netherworld, the realm of the ancestors.

In Saami stories about water birds there is one in which the shaman stands on the neck of a wild swan (see figure 7c), almost torturing it, forcing the messenger to reveal things of the netherworld, to give information about the afterlife of the ancestors. There is space, though, for an alternative interpretation of this scene in the rock engravings. The close association of the water bird with the shaman may point at the latter's ability to fly and to the bird's role as a helper to carry its master (or mistress) over mountains and rivers (Hoppál 2001: 85–6).

## *Mythical Realms: Nature and Female Guardian-Spirits of Living Things*

The bear and the wild swan are not the only animals of northern Europe that feature in the tradition of Finno-Ugric myths and popular narrative. Animals such as the elk (moose), the reindeer, the eagle, and others have also left an imprint on people's cultural memory. In light of Finno-Ugric mythology, all living things interact under the protective supervision of Mother Nature. The oral tradition among Finno-Ugrians knows the figure of the Forest Mother and a variety of female guardian-spirits, helpers of the Mistress of Nature. "It is typical of the beliefs of Finno-Ugrians that the earth as well as different elements and natural phenomena of the middle world (water, fire, wind, forest etc.) are incarnated by female deities, 'mother-spirits'" (Ajkhenvald et al. 1989: 158).

## Mother Nature: A Central Mythological Concept

In Eurasian mythology, the various expressions of divine femininity are all manifestations of the Female Principle as the crystallizing focus of the Life Cycle (see Haarmann and Marler 2008: 110ff for a view on major anthropomorphic identities). The figure of the Creatrix, the mythical Ancestral Mother, proliferates into her "daughters," the numerous guardian-spirits of Nature. In Saami mythology, the figure of the Ancestral Mother is called Máttáráhkká.

Artists of our time know how to connect with the old mythical tradition, for example, the performance artist Sanna Karlsson-Sutisna (b. 1965) who dances ballet and creates sculptures with a motor-saw, creating ecological sculptures. Among these are sculpted figures, in half-relief, of female guardian-spirits in tree trunks, sometimes accompanied by mythical creatures such as the wild swan or the bear (Karlsson-Sutisna 2009: 9ff.; figure 10). Karlsson-Sutisna's works have been shown in various international exhibitions, in Sweden (Stockholm), Italy (Genova), Austria (Vienna), France (art park Arques la Bataille in Normandy) and in Indonesia (Bali).

Mother Sun is the Creatrix, the great Ancestral Mother, the force that generates all living things, human beings, animals and plants alike. Representations of the Creatrix are often associated with animals (Martynov 1991: 272), and in the Saami area she is shown giving birth to a reindeer and feeding a reindeer calf (Pentikäinen 1995: 93).

Once the world has been created, the role of the female divinity shifts to that of the Mistress of Nature and of the Protectress of Animals. In the oral tradition of Finno-Ugric peoples, there is a duality, with the figure of a Forest Mother and a variety of female guardian-spirits. The Mistress of Nature is a character with motherly features, giving the fruits of the forest as gifts to people and protecting the animals.

There is a very old tradition of associating living waters (in lakes, rivers and the sea) with a female divinity. In the Finnish epic *Kalevala* (runo I, 111–116), the creation of the world is associated with the goddess Ilmatar, the daughter of the air:

Figure 10: **The female spirit in the trunk of a birch tree (in the Kaivopuisto park in Helsinki, 2004; "Arjen pyhiinvaeltaja," work by Sanna Karlsson-Sutisna; © Kuvasto 2015).**

> Air's young daughter was a virgin,
> Fairest daughter of Creation.
> Long did she abide a virgin,
> All the long days of her girlhood,
> In the Air's own spacious mansions,
> In those far extending regions.

Ilmatar descends to the world ocean, is embraced by winds and waters and becomes pregnant. Ilmatar transforms into the Mother of the Waters, gestates for centuries but cannot give birth. Eventually, a water bird approaches and nests on the goddess' knee. The bird produces an egg that breaks when the goddess moves her leg. The fragments that fall from the egg are the stuff the world is made of (Salo 2013/I: 139f.). In Finnish folklore, there is also the figure of the Maiden of the Lake who sometimes appears to hunters (Sarmela 1994, plate 70). Such beliefs were widespread still in the 19th century when collectors started to record oral folk poetry in writing (Branch 1985).

The concept of a female figure in the imagined world that is responsible for the creation and protection of nature, this key element of nature-oriented Kalevala mythology, shows continuity through time, from the pre–Christian era into Christian society. Among the artists of the Finnish national movement that started out in the 19th century and continued into the 20th century, and also among representatives of Finnish cultural modernism, many draw on Kalevalaic motifs in their works. In 1913, the famous composer Jean Sibelius completed a tone-poem (Op. 70) for soprano and orchestra, *Luonnotar* ("Mistress or Spirit of Nature"), which he dedicated to the Finnish opera diva Aino Ackté (see Chapter 7). The composer had made sketches of the *Luonnotar* already in 1894.

> The Kalevala was a motherlode for Sibelius, and he adapted it in a strikingly individual way. The orchestra may play modern instruments and the soprano may wear an evening gown, but ideally they should convey the power of ancient, shamanistic incantation, as if by recreating by sound they are performing a ritual to release some kind of creative force [Ozorio 2007].

The Kalevalaic tradition kept the composer's mind busy and, one year after the *Luonnotar*, he completed yet another composition (Op. 73): *Aallottaret* ("Mistress of the Sea") which was translated into English as The Oceanides. This composition was commissioned to the United States.

The connection with nature has remained present in the Finnish mindset, and this can be observed in name-giving. Among the preferences for women's names is the tradition to choose name-forms associated with natural phenomena (e.g., Suvi, literally "summer," Lumi "snow," Talvikki "snow," Tuuli, variant Tuulikki, "wind," Aamu "morning," Ilmatar "air maiden," Meri "sea") or with flowers, plants and fruits (e.g., Kanerva "heather," Kirsikka "cherry," Minttu "minth," Orvokki "violet," Pihla "rowan tree," Ruusu "rose," Vuokko "anemone"). This Finnish tradition is reminiscent of similar preferences of name-giving among the Japanese and native Americans.

## Ancient Ties to Living Nature:
## The Shamanistic Tradition

Those who study prehistoric cultures in Eurasia will inevitably encounter an ancient institution, shamanism. Shamanism (or shamanhood, respectively) is perhaps the most widespread pre-scientific worldview in the cultures of the world. With respect to Eurasia and its ancient convergent cultures shamanism is indeed the key to the understanding of how belief systems are overarched by a worldview anchored in beliefs of spirited (or animated) nature.

> The most ancient, the oldest and the most long-lasting institution in the northern hemisphere is shamanism. Shamanism is a family—a clan— institution and it has been present in hunting, gathering and agricultural societies right up to our day, living on in the industrial era [Kare 2000a: 104].

There are regions of the world where the longevity of this nature-oriented worldview is attested to trace its origins to the cultural horizon of the Paleolithic Age. The first scholar to draw attention to the dependency of shamanism on archaic hunting symbolism was Lommel (1965: 18ff.). As for the great age of shamanistic conceptualizations of the natural world these must have been hard-wired in the minds of Paleolithic people: "There is today an understanding that it was in the ancient Paleolithic hunting world that shamanism first took form. There are ever so many indications that account for this conclusion" (Hultkrantz 2001: 6).

The spiritual focus of a shamanistic worldview is on the necessity of a harmonious relationship of human beings with nature. One aspect of a shamanistic worldview is an awareness of the fragile balance of life resources, which enhances the insight that the living conditions and activities of human beings cannot evolve in a kind of antagonistic tension with the life cycle but only in concordance with it. Human beings are supposed to live and breathe in the rhythm of nature in order to minimize conflict when interacting with the world of animals, plants and the spirits.

Since its appearance as a cultural institution among Paleolithic hunter-gatherers shamanism has persisted in many parts of Eurasia and, as a living institution, it can be studied in the Himalayas, in Southeast Asia, in Mongolia, Siberia and in the northeastern corner of Europe (among the Nenets/Yuraks). Among the Saami people of northern Scandinavia, beliefs rooted in shamanism are still vivid as part of cultural memory and in local lore (Rydving 2010: 42f., 52). And this is true for the Finns also. "The remains of shamanism among the Finns demonstrate that shamanism was once practised in a far wider area than when it was recorded in recent centuries" (Tolley 2009: 79).

## Traditional Respect for Nature Meets Modern Environmentalism

From the ways people lived in Finland, in the pre–Christian era, it can be inferred that their attitudes vis-à-vis the natural surroundings were balanced.

> For many hundreds, even thousands, of years, agriculture was largely confined to the coastal strip, where most of the settled population lived; it only made any inroads in the inland areas in the Middle Ages. The interior served two purposes: it was the *erämaa*, "land set aside," regarded as holy in one sense, yet in another a source to be exploited, mainly for hunting, by the settled inhabitants, the lantalaiset, who also practiced agriculture. Its other purpose was as a homeland for the lappalaiset, the semi-nomadic people who made a livelihood from its riches [Tolley 2009: 78f.].

The more humans are attentive to the conditions of living nature surrounding them, the more organic will be the organization of their cultural space. Any form of organization of the cultural space is a manifestation of the intentional interplay of humans with other life-forms and with the inanimate things in nature. Human intentionality demands the steady accumulation of knowledge about the environment in which a person's action is embedded. Knowledge is the foundation of any culture at whatever time in human evolution. The fabric of a culture depends on the quality of knowledge-construction for its creation. Thus, the quality of human knowledge is the arbitrator of the relationship of living things in nature, of their harmony or tension.

The attachment for northern people to nature is easy to understand since the natural environment in Finland has been preserved to a great extent, and such conditions are unknown in most other countries of Europe. Indeed, one finds, in Finland, a dense network of national parks and strict nature reserves (figure 11).

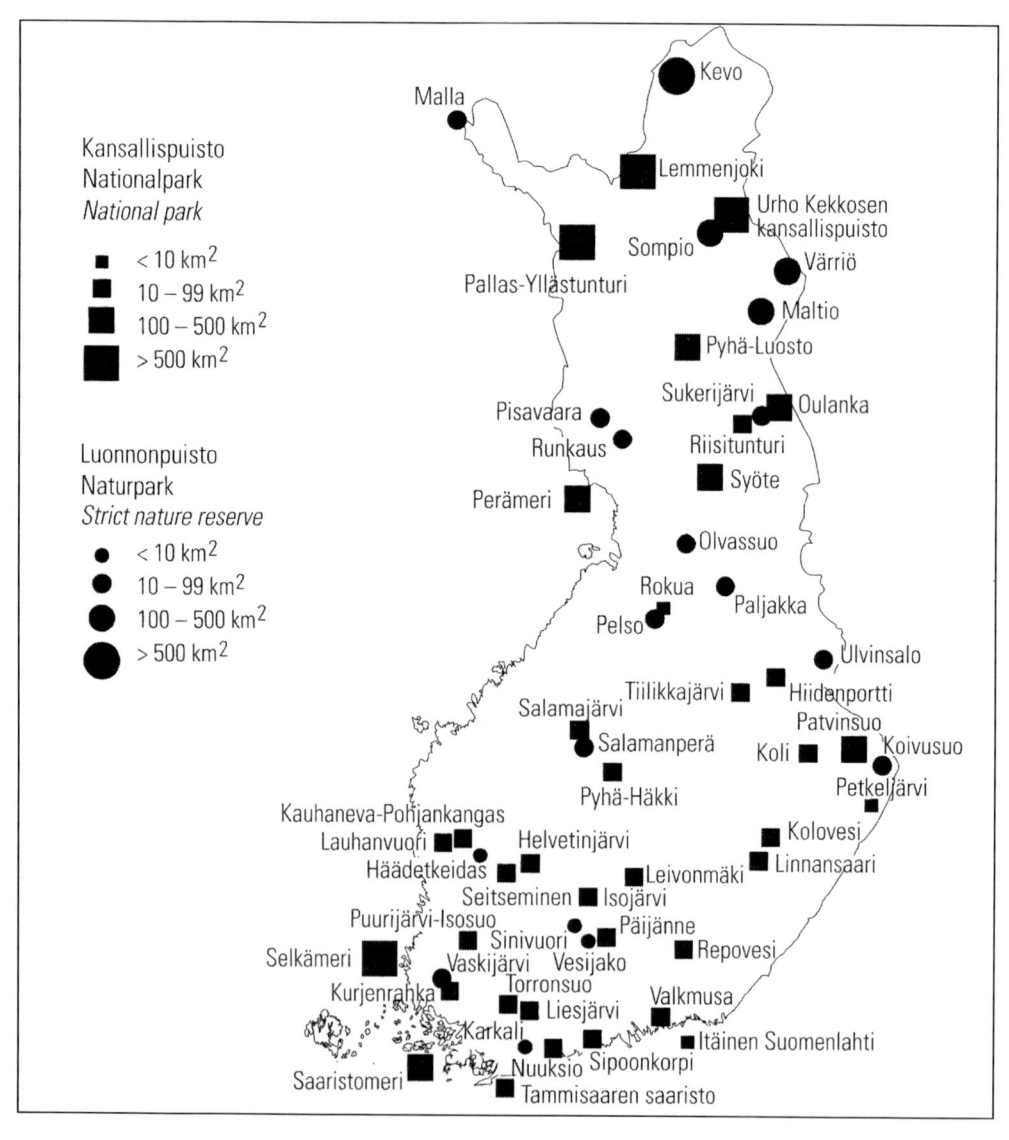

**Figure 11: Natural parks and strict nature reserves in Finland (Finnish Authorities; Forest Administration; STV 2014: 56).**

## Human Interests and the Scope of Nature

When humans construct their cultural space and develop their living conditions, they do it amidst a natural environment. This means that wherever a cultural space is created, it is embedded in natural surroundings. There are two elementary alternatives for how this embedding works: the cultural space unfolds either in harmony or in tension with the natural environment.

Cultural history teaches the valuable lesson that the drifting away from the rhythm of the natural life cycle and the uninhibited exercise of human rule over nature have confronted human beings with seemingly unresolvable contradictions: an ideal of quality of life that contrasts sharply with both the desolate state of an endangered natural environment and the impoverishment resulting from the deconstruction of a former spiritual intactness, a central element of which is respect for nature. The price that future generations will have to pay, socioeconomically, culturally and spiritually, for the uninhibited control of nature of previous generations is rising continually.

Living in a natural environment means interacting with its conditions, profiting from its resources, and responding to the natural life cycle. This experience has challenged human beings from the very beginnings to think seriously about the place of living beings in nature, and this theme is reflected in all religions, although with highly diverse emphases and producing diverse maxims. These maxims, in turn, have different weight in the societies for which they have been formulated, depending on whether religion is perceived as one among other cultural patterns or as a comprehensive mindframe for an embedded worldview.

In some of the world religions, the idea of a balance among all living things in their natural environment is recognizable, as in Buddhism and Hinduism. Some religions have produced a significant philosophy about how humans should interact with other living things in nature (e.g., Eurasian shamanism). The religions in traditional cultures tend to be more nature-oriented than any of the current major world religions.

In other cultures, the role of the natural environment for human society is rather marginalized. This is true, for example, for Islam, a religion with roots in the ancient nomadic cultures of the Arabian peninsula. It is remarkable that Christianity, which originated in a milieu of Hellenistic urban culture of the Near East, has failed to produce any explicit ethical code about human beings and nature. On the contrary, biblical learning is the source of a tradition of thinking where the idea of control over nature is cherished as an expression of the alleged superiority of human beings over all other living things. The Judeo-Christian biblical approach to nature lacks any element of a balance.

The attitudes of people in Fenno-Scandia toward their natural environment, and especially regarding the most common type of landscape, which is forest, have deep roots, with beliefs of the pre–Christian era fusing with certain protective features of Christianity religion.

> The forest has been the mainstay of the life of all the Finnic peoples. The forest was governed by a life-sustaining mother who in Finnish folk incantations ultimately inherited the role of the Virgin Mary. The forest is approached with respect, but timidly: man is a guest, who does not have any self-evident rights over the forest [Pentikäinen 1997: 120].

In the Scandinavian countries and in Finland, issues of environmental protection and engineering have been on the agenda for many years. Jurisdiction requires licensing for the exploitation of natural resources and environmental administration sets standards for water treatment and waste management. Environmental engineering has proliferated into many fields, most of which can be studied at Finnish universities. Among the foreign students who graduate from universities in Finland are many who return to their home country—often a developing nation—and take leading roles in the local environmental management. A special facet in the relationship of people and nature, in the northern tradition, is the persistence of a common sense of respect for nature that is deeply rooted, and nowadays supported by environmental technologies. In the mindset of people living in the northern regions, the principles of environmental ethics are hard-wired, while such principles have to be made explicit for encouraging sensitivity of thought and attitude among other people, in central and western Europe (Taylor 2011).

## The Control of Nature as an Historical Drive in Western Europe

The ideals of a balance of all living things in nature were lost in the societies of western Europe under the impression of the Christian worldview that favored man's control over nature as the maxim of life. The conditioning of the mind to the priority of human control has become typical also in the evaluation of traditional cultures in the eyes of modern scholars who are commonly unaware that the observer's own position—as investigator—may evoke certain pre-evaluations, resulting from the specific tuning of the observer's mind to modern conceptualizations. This means one has to be aware that the approach to analyze cultures may, unconsciously, rest "on the implicit metaphysics of modern mass societies and their valuation of utility over all else" (Hunt 1995: 27).

In fact, many descriptions of culture and their relationship to nature suffer from what might be called the utility syndrome. The idea of utility has become a sort of obsession for people in the information age, and this can be historically explained as a trend in knowledge-construction, giving priority exclusively to technological progress. The utility mentality ultimately roots in the biblical notion of man as the creature chosen by God to govern the earth (Genesis 1, 28–29). In its sublime form, this notion was reinforced by Cartesian philosophical thought, which emphasizes the prominence of human beings as the creatures that are blessed with the capacity of reasoning.

René Descartes (1596–1650) laid the groundwork for what has become known as the Cartesian system in his *Discourse on Method* (1637) and in his masterpiece *Meditations on First Philosophy* (1641). According to Descartes, personal identity was conceptualized as *cogito, ergo sum* (usually translated as "I think, therefore I am"). The individual is perceived as a reasoning entity detached from the natural environment. Nature becomes an object to the active subject, which has dislocated itself from its natural lineage.

> Descartes' explicit aim had been to make men "lords and possessors of nature" ... [and] he portrayed other species as inert and lacking any spiritual dimension. In so doing he created an absolute break between man and the rest of nature, thus clearing the way very satisfactorily for the uninhibited exercise of human rule [Thomas 1983: 34f.].

The utility mentality has persisted and it took a long time until, in the modern age, people have started to learn to critically reflect on the priority of utility, to distance themselves from the utilitarian mentality and to investigate the relationship between people and their environment in a more comprehensive way. The number increases of those who are engaged in culture studies and aware of the existence of a dimension of nonutilitarian relationship of human beings with nature.

> People and animals inhabit a single world in relations of equality, respect, interdependence and co-operation. Animals and people are kin, hence the feelings people retain of closeness, tenderness, indulgence and protectiveness towards animals and why they were seen as so aesthetically captivating and beguiling. Animals and man share a common purpose, a personal and moral relationship. The interconnection between man and nature means that man has no mastery over nature but all his acts can affect it. Man has to allow and assist nature to take its course. The world constitutes a moral order and this order has to be respected [Garlake 1995: 115].

## Respect for Nature in the Northern Region: A Traditional Notion Embraced by Modern Science

The value of insights that may be drawn, as a counterweight to the utility model of culture, from an inspection of nonutilitarian approaches to nature is increasingly appreciated by modern scholarship as a form of scientific analysis, this contrasting sharply with the Cartesian tradition with its notion of an indoctrinated mastery of nature by humans.

This doctrine of mastery of nature by humans spurs egocentrism since the will and aspirations of human beings are attributed higher value than the basic value of recreative nature. If the pursuit of egocentric goals is what defines the meaning of life for an individual then there is no space for a balanced relationship with the natural environment. The nonutilitarian nonsubjective approach to defining the value of nature for community life is understandable in light of a traditional worldview, and yet utterly demanding in a modern consumer society.

> Living a life that is engaged with and so at least partially focused on projects whose value has a nonsubjective source is a way of acknowledging one's non-privileged position. It harmonizes, in a way that a purely egocentric life does not, with the fact that one is not the center of the universe.... In face of this recognition, a life that is directed solely to its subject's own fulfillment, or, to its mere survival or towards the pursuit of goals that are grounded in nothing but the subject's own psychology, appears either solipsistic [standing in isolation from others] or silly [Wolf 2013: 312].

Among the broader public, nonutilitarian values that crystallize in attitudes toward the preservation of the natural environment seemingly enjoy a longer tradition than in scholarly research. And yet, the arguments in favor of the protection of nature that have been repeated in the public debate point at a particular viewpoint that is grounded in rational thinking (Simmons 1993: 168):

(i) *Utilitarian values*
- Scientific: preserving a sample of ecosystems to ensure biotic diversity; conserving gene pools and potentially useful organisms; protecting natural areas for research and monitoring
- economic: providing a particular form of recreation; conserving wildlife; protecting watersheds and water quality; promoting a balanced land use pattern

(ii) *Nonutilitarian values*
- cultural: conserving a cultural heritage; preserving aesthetic values; providing educational opportunities
- ethical: rights of nonhuman entities; social value of exercising restraint over change and transformation.

Ideas such as the conservation of the natural environment as part of the cultural heritage of people who live in close vicinity, the provision of educational opportunities for the younger generation to learn about wildlife, the emphasis given to the rights of nonhuman entities, and other considerations all find their rationale in critical approaches contrasting biblical maxims.

Modern nonutilitarian ideas, regardless of their humane contents, are not rooted, in the Western mind, in a perception of the instructions about living in harmony with nature that have accumulated in the cultural memory of many traditional communities. When Westerners speak about the protection of nature, they follow their own trajectory of argumentation and reasoning, and their understanding of the life cycle of nature may be as artificial as it is among those whose thinking is dominated by utilitarian considerations. Yet, in the cultural memory of the native population in northern Europe, the Saami, who have inhabited their natural environment for thousands of years, the harmonious relationship between nature and human beings is given priority: "there is a strong emphasis on the gift relations between various autonomous powers that include the natural world and on the recognition that *the abundance is given* if those relations in and with the world are nourished" (Kuokkanen 2006: 263).

A special facet in the intellectual orientation of modern environmentalism is naturalism, which combines an appreciation of nature in its own right and its scientific analysis. The extreme manifestation of this kind of approach excludes any religious orientation and considers nature to be all there was, is and will be, without any link to supernatural phenomena. There are also representatives of a soft naturalism who mobilize religious sentiments to highlight the value of nature. "Religious naturalists do not believe that anything exists beyond the world of nature, but they often use religious terminology—words such as mystery and sacred—to express their sense that nature by itself is deserving of a reverential surrender of the mind" (Haught 2013: 175).

In Scandinavia and, particularly in Finland, there has been no break between the world of a traditional respect for the natural environment, a world lost elsewhere, and the intellectual mainstream of the modern era that "recovered" this ideal. Throughout their history, the Finns have been aware of the priority of the natural life cycle, with human beings sharing the benefits of the natural resources, instead of controlling or unilaterally exploiting them.

One finds instances in Finnish folk poetry where the resistance of the pre–Christian respect of nature against the Christian doctrine of its control is addressed in a poetic metaphor. Several men go to the forest to fell a tree, to obtain timber for a church. Their communication with nature is presented in the following poem (Kuusi et al. 1977: 325):

> … they went in search of wood
> … to catch an oak-tree:
> … they found a tree, caught an oak
> … began to hack the oak-tree.
>
> … The oak chattered with its tongue:
> … "What do you men want of me?"
>
> … The men answering said: "I
> … seek wood for a church threshold
> … wood for raising an altar
> … wood where a deacon may sing
> … wood for Mary to lie on."

... The oak answering replied:
... "My wood will not serve for that
... no wood for a church threshold
... wood for raising an altar
... wood where a deacon may sing
... wood for Mary to lie on:
... a wolf has run on my roots
... a bear has lain on my foot
... a squirrel in my branches
... a bird has sung in my top."

The pre–Christian underpinnings of human life, harmonizing with the rhythm of nature, have merged with the intellectual movement of environmental protection to produce a counterweight to utilitarian Cartesianism, and this merger has proven a blessing for the modernization process of Finnish society (see Chapter 3).

The close relationship of the Finnish people with their natural environment was manipulated as a cherished facet of nation-building in the 19th century.

The building blocks of Finnish national romanticism were taken from various sources. Its cornerstone was the symbolism of the 1890s, which had been born in the 1880s as a countermovement to the worship of technology and progress. Symbolism dealt not only with the landscape of the individual soul but also with the soul of the nation. The Finns discovered their province of Karelia and plucked everything suitable for a national style from its vernacular building culture and textile models. At the same time it was realized that there could not be a national soul without nature, so the worship of "national unspoilt nature" became the third pillar of national romanticism [Smeds 1996: 391].

Extreme ecological conditions prevail in the Arctic zone (the circumpolar zone of permanent or extreme cold climate, with average annual temperatures below freezing). Habitation in the Arctic zone expands from the area of Saami settlement in northern Scandinavia over northern Eurasia, Alaska and the Canadian North to the settlements in Greenland (Funk and Sillanpää 1999).

Since the 1970s, environmentalists have listened to representatives of traditional cultures with their background of learned experience from the interaction of their ancestors with natural phenomena. Environmentalists have joined forces with experienced "natives" to jointly articulate their concerns about the damage that is done to the natural and cultural environments of many parts of the world. "The Arctic homeland of the Sámi … can no longer be viewed as part of the periphery of the 'civilised world': the fate of its delicate ecology has worldwide implications" (Kent 2014: 260).

Some of those cultures where people's minds and their knowledge-construction are attuned to a balanced interaction between human activities and natural phenomena reveal extraordinary cases of longevity of this mental matrix. This is true for the local cultures in northern Eurasia, where reindeer herding, hunting and fishing have long been the economic basis for people living under Arctic conditions. Knowledge-construction relating to economic and cultural matters among the Saami in the Arctic region is governed by the priority of avoiding any damaging exploitation of natural resources.

The values of indigenous environmental knowledge as a potential to serve the protection of nature and to safeguard the stability of communities living in a protected environment are not only appreciated in the Arctic zone of Eurasia but in the northernmost region of America as well. The modern trend points in the direction of constructing indigenous environmentalism.

> Incorporating indigenous knowledge into environmental management and sustainable development strategies is crucial and recent international cooperation on Arctic environmental matters has made great headway in acknowledging that indigenous peoples and their communities should be involved at local, regional and national levels in resource management, conservation strategies and sustainable development [Nuttall 1998: 175].

Learning from the experiences of indigenous people in the Arctic and from the challenges of environmental protection opens a new dimension in transnational cooperation, between state authorities and inhabitants of the north. In the case of Lapland the situation is much better than the one among aboriginal people in the north of Canada, whose image is that of "pristine survivals from timeless past" (Wolf 1997: 385), "making them candidates for primitivist ethnographic study and not sufficiently post-industrial to be considered as interlocutors in the communication and exchange activities that are addressed in transnational discourse" (Chambon and Dylan 2012: 171). Despite the strong ties of Saami people to their traditions they have mastered the transition to the modern age and network society (see Chapter 2).

In a nature oriented and culturally sensitive milieu like the one in Finnish Lapland, Westerners may find access to the essence of living in the spirit of nature, not just being concerned with it intellectually. If we are willing to learn from the lessons of cultural history we may engage in concerted action against the loss of know-how about the organic embedding of the human cultural space and the living conditions that humans create for themselves in the natural environment. Finnish environmentalism, and in particular experiences from the region of Lapland, may teach us valuable lessons.

The wisdom of such lessons readily accumulates in the essence of maxims that highlight the priority of environmental consciousness (Haarmann 2007: 230ff.):

- *Promoting a comprehensive, culture-based environmental consciousness*
  In our modern understanding, the conceptualization of environmental protection assumes form around the idea that the natural environment has to be protected against human rule. This basis of a protective spirit would have to be expanded so that it would also include a harmonization of the human cultural space with the natural environment. In a wider perspective, respect for nature cannot remain in a defensive opposition against human interests in general, but rather it has to embrace the potential of a respectful interaction. The new consciousness required reconciles the respectful attitudes of humans toward nature that can be found in many cultures with ethical considerations of environmental protection. The high goal is to enhance a deeper understanding of the cooperative interaction of cultural space with the natural environment (Hirsch and O'Hanlon 1995).

- *Activating environmental knowledge as items of local cultural memory*
  In order to safeguard a culture-based respect for nature, those engaged in culture studies are challenged to investigate cultural memory in societies throughout the world. In an ideal sense, such knowledge, rooted in the heritage of many populations, is not only to be studied and documented but also activated. For this purpose, items of environmental knowledge from a wide array of local cultures could be stored in

databanks and made available for environmentalists. In Lapland, the heritage of ancient environmental knowledge, embedded in the traditional Saami shamanism (*noaiddástallan*), is being revived (Helander-Renvall 2006).

• *Reconciling traditional instructions about the respect for nature with modern reasoning about environmental protection*
      The respect for nature is indivisible. It would be presumptuous to unilaterally favor the traditional environmental knowledge rooted in local cultures over the reasoning about environmental protection as a result of enlightened ethics. Both mainstreams of knowledge contribute effectively to a new environmental consciousness, with one (traditional knowledge) having matured as the instructions of ancestors inherited by the present generation, and the other (modern knowledge) exploiting the potential of enlightened reasoning. Yet, traditional indigenous knowledge, encapsulated in cultural memory, provides a favorable basis for reconciling environmental considerations. The Saami concept of *sieidi*—gift giving or gift mutuality—is illustrative of this.

> In gift reciprocity and mutuality, the ultimate goal is to secure the physical, social and spiritual well-being of the individual, community and the entire social order. The responsibility toward the "other" that is embedded in the *sieidi* giving, for example, is mutual and is different from pure self-interest interested only in accumulation. Rather than accumulating wealth, the goal of gift reciprocity is to recognize and sustain the relationships in and with the world. The land itself as well as the spirits and guardians inhabiting and looking after it are considered equals that need to be respected and honored rather than endlessly exploited [Kuokkanen 2006: 265].

• *Safeguarding traditional environmental knowledge as cultural heritage*
      The concept of cultural heritage is perceived by many as referring to the material testimony of a local culture's history—to artifacts, such as Nefertiti's bust in the Egyptian museum in Berlin-Charlottenburg; monuments, such as Angkor Wat in Cambodia; friezes of rock art, such as the site at Astuvansalmi in southeastern Finland; or to entire architectural complexes in the historical centers of many cities, such as Avignon (France), Venice (Italy), Vilnius (Lithuania) or Porvoo (Borgå) in southern Finland. They are all found in the UNESCO listings of world cultural heritage. In addition to the great variety of material manifestations of local heritage, we are also challenged, with respect to the construction of our future worldview, to safeguard the invisible forms of thought that through time have shaped the human mindset. This applies in particular to those ideas and patterns of protective reasoning that relate to environmental knowledge.

## Buildings and the Space Between Them: Modern Finnish Architecture in Contact with Nature

For years, architectural programs throughout the world have focused on making the human living space more humane. This effort favors a symbiosis, in the original sense of the Greek term for "living together," of the cultural habitat and the natural environment (Swan and Swan 1996). Symbiosis as a philosophy for the future is grounded in a reconciliation of cultural ends and economic interests as well as in the respect of humans towards other lifeforms.

> The unavoidable shift toward sustainability, and the consequent interest in phenomena of nature and ecological principles, will certainly help to reroot architecture in its local soil. Instead of eliminating the special demands created by the climate, northern architecture is destined to use these conditions again as inspiration for essential architectural motifs. The recent, somewhat romantic ice architecture—such as ice hotels, bars, and chapels—and international exhibitions of artistic ice structures also indicate an interest in the exotic dimensions of the North. On the other hand, technology and new materials already permit architecture that reacts to the changes of seasons and weather in the ways that all life-forms in nature adapt to the ever-changing conditions of survival [Pallasmaa 2010: 35].

Modern Finnish architecture has been known for the symbiotic dialogue of the living space it creates with the natural environment. There are early manifestations of this orientation. When new neighborhoods were designed in the rapidly growing cities of the postwar period the ecological spirit to reconcile the living space with nature was at work. An illustrative model of this presents itself in the "garden city" of Tapiola which is a part of the city of Espoo near Helsinki. The name is derived from Tapio, which is the divinity of the forest in Finnish mythology. Here, the Latin saying *nomen est omen* holds true.

The beginnings of the garden city Tapiola are in the early 1950s (Tuomi and Paatero 2003). The space was designed for some 30,000 inhabitants and the housing program was realized in five phases, between 1952 and 1965. The architect who designed and built the garden city was Heikki von Hertzen, executive of the Housing Foundation which set things in motion. In his writings, one finds the principles of symbiosis, of the natural space with the living space (Hertzen and Spreiregen 1971):

- closeness to nature, recognition of the aesthetic value of nature, respect for the intactness of natural contours of the landscape which have to be preserved;
- dominance of nature, with architectural forms of secondary significance;
- intentional variation of multistory buildings with low houses, to create variety and spaciousness;
- striving for a working town, not a "dormitory" (people work in the garden city, in close contact with nature);
- striving for an integrated network of job opportunity so that handicraft workers, entrepreneurs and academic people can work and live side-by-side.

Many new houses have been built in Tapiola since the 1960s. Some modern residents in the area say that, in time, the original intention of landscaping—integrating the natural environment and the living space—got lost. Whether this impression holds true remains in the eye of the beholder. Anyway, the idea of a harmonious relationship with nature lives on in people's cultural memory.

This relationship can best be expressed by using the kind of natural material for construction that is available in abundance in Finland and which has been used for the longest time in the history of architecture in the country (for building houses and bridges, landing stages and boats, harbor installations and watch towers, etc.), and this is wood. Wood is used for the interiors of modern structures, such as the Finlandia Hall in Helsinki, and for designer's creations (see Chapter 7). The architect Juha Ilonen has said, "Wood is related to sustainability but, especially for Finns, it's also related to our national identity" (quoted by Chela 2013). Ilonen thinks that wood will be used more frequently in the future.

In some places, one finds ambitious manifestations of the spirit of wood. In Jyväskylä (south-central Finland) the country's highest wooden structure, the Puukuokka Condominium, was erected in 2014. This multistory building in the middle of a wooded surrounding is made entirely of fir. The walls are not painted but left in their natural color. The Puukuokka Building received the 2015 Finlandia Award for Architecture (Laitalainen 2015).

## Breaking the Rules: Talvivaara— The Black Sheep of Environmentalism

The Finns not only talk about respect for nature and environmental protection, they are ready to take action at the highest (governmental) level once there is evidence for an imminent danger to the environment. A spectacular case of confrontation between a mining company and state authorities monitoring the regulations of environmental protection is the decline and fall of the Talvivaara Mining Company. This company is Finnish-based (with location in Sotkamo in eastern Finland) and concentrates on the mining of nickel and zinc. It operates one of the biggest nickel mines in the country.

The mining of nickel has a longer history in Finland. Before World War II there was nickel mining in the region of Petsamo, then part of Finland. Nickel deposits were discovered in 1921 and, in 1935, companies from Canada and France started to operate mines. Petsamo had been frequented by tourists since it bordered the shore of the Barents Sea. Since 1931 when a road from Sodankylä via Ivalo as far as the northern coast had been completed, people from other parts of Finland could drive up to Petsamo by car. Already after the Winter War of 1939–40, the mining area of Petsamo had become a matter of dispute between Finland and the Soviet Union. Toward the end of the Continuation War, in late summer of 1944, the Red Army occupied the territory and, in 1947, the whole region (including the mines) had to be ceded to the Soviet Union.

The deposits that the Talvivaara mining company exploits have been known since 1977 when they were discovered by the Geological Survey of Finland. At that time mining the deposits was not profitable when applying the existing technology. Mining became profitable as late as the beginning of the 21st century. The Talvivaara Mining Company was founded in 2004, and production started in late 2008. Later, in 2010, also uranium (in the form of yellowcake) was mined, as a by-product. From the beginning of its operation the company had problems with properly organizing waste disposal. The pollution effect of the effluent that was discharged into an artificial pond had been underestimated. There was a constant leak of uranium and various other toxic metals that kept polluting the environment. The monitoring authorities demanded improvements in waste management but, despite repeated attempts, the company did not succeed in controlling the leaks of its toxic tailings.

The environmental problems caused by the operations of the mining company raised much negative attention amongst politicians, local media and EU authorities in Brussels. In an editorial column of the daily newspaper *Helsingin Sanomat*, the leaks of the mining companies were called "a large-scale failure, that casts a shadow on the efficiency of the Finnish society as a whole" (Mukka 2012). The Ministry of Employment and Economy declared a stop on mining operations in early 2012, and the Safety Investigation Authority, a governmental agency, started their investigation of the case. In October 2013, a limitation of the waste discharges was ordered by the Vaasa Administrative Court. Eventually the company declared its bankruptcy in November 2014. Members of the former directorial board of Talvivaara were charged with negligence and with breaking the laws of environmental protection. The trial began in July 2015. In May 2016, the members of the former directorial board were sentenced to pay fines amounting to millions of euros. The trial will continue at a court of appeal.

For several months, representatives of the Finnish government and of the mining company have been looking for foreign investors to provide resources for a restart of the enterprise (Talvivaara Mining Company, from Wikipedia; retrieved 5 May 2015). There was vivid interest among foreign enterprises for a takeover of Talvivaara but not enough capital available. In summer 2015, the Finnish government decided to take over—to take care of the measures necessary for environmental protection and to continue mining. Future economic development will show whether mining will become profitable or whether the Finnish state will be left with the burden of cleaning up the mess of the former owners without compensation.

## *The Mystery of the Northern Lights*

Since ancient times, people living in the North have wondered about this impressive natural phenomenon that came to be known as the Northern Lights (Aurora borealis, or "Dawn of the North"). Northern Lights can be observed in areas that extend beyond about 60° northern latitude which include:

- Europe: Finland and the northern part of Scandinavia, northern Scotland and Iceland;
- Greenland;
- America: northwestern Canada and Alaska;
- Asia: northern Siberia

Under certain conditions, Northern Lights can be seen further south, but only on rare occasions.

Lapland is the region where the frequency of Northern Lights is the highest in Finland (about 7 times in 10 nights). Northern Lights may appear throughout the year but they cannot be seen at all times with a naked eye. Since the sky during the summer season is not dark at night the intensity of Northern Lights does not come to bear. The best periods to see Northern Lights are September through October and March until early April; these periods offer the greatest probability (in statistical terms). Everything depends on the weather conditions. If the sky is cloudy then the visibility of Northern Lights is minimal, if not zero.

The light shows (auroral displays) of the Northern Lights offer a great variety of colors. The most common are light green and pink. All the colors of the rainbow can be on display. The light in the sky is streaming and forms extremely diverse patterns: rays, clouds, curtains or patches. The natural phenomenon of the Aurora is displayed at various distances from the surface of the earth, ranging from some 80 kilometers (50 miles) to about 640 (400 miles). There is a rhythm in the auroral activity, and this is a cycle of 11 years. A recent peak in activity was 2013.

Although the phenomenon of the Northern Lights has been studied by scientists for decades it is not (yet) possible to forecast the occurrence of this natural phenomenon with any accuracy. The time for any reliable forecast is limited to two hours maximum.

This means that anyone who wants to watch a light show in the night sky has to be prepared to reach places with good visibility at short notice. Tourists who make plans for a trip to Lapland to see the Northern Lights have to cope with a kind of suspense that will always surround the mystery of this light show. Those who are engaged in the tourist business in Lapland have made provisions for special services to their customers. Some hotels in Lapland (near the Lemmenjoki national park) offer accommodation for visitors in ball-like structures with a glass roof where one can admire the nightly sky while in bed. Forecasts are closely followed by the hotel personnel and a special wakeup service alerts visitors to an upcoming light show.

The factual explanations, given by scientists, for the phenomenon of the Northern Lights stand in stark contrast with the romantic atmosphere as experienced by those who watch them. Already in the 1880s scientists had speculated about a connection between the activity of the flaring sunspots and the reaction of the earth's atmosphere to the "solar wind" that transports gas particles our way. Yet, concrete evidence for this connection came through investigations in the 1950s when the flow of charged particles ejected from the sun's hot spots was proven. The stream of gas particles from the sun collides with the earth's magnetic field that keeps the particles in the polar region (Merrill 2010).

The collision produces different light shades depending on the height above the earth's surface and on the type of particle. For instance, oxygen molecules produce shades of pale yellowish green at a height of some 60 miles while most shades of red are due to the collision of oxygen particles with the earth's atmosphere at high altitudes (up to 200 miles). Nitrogen particles are responsible for purple and shades of blue (http://www.northernlightscentre.ca/northernlights.html; retrieved 9 February 2015).

The Northern Lights have attracted people's imagination since ancient times, and Finnish as well as Saami mythology know tales about how the auroral light influences the life of human beings (Helander-Renvall 2006). In Finnish, Northern Lights are called *revontulet* ("fox fires"). In this name one finds an association with an old tale, with a mythical fox as protagonist. The fox moves across the winterly landscape and sweeps the snow with its tail, causing the snow flakes to spray into the sky (Jokinen 2007).

Among the Saami there was the belief that the Northern Lights, which are called *guopvssahasat* in the Saami language, were the souls of the ancestors whose energy irradiated into the sky. People, and especially children, were expected to show their respect for the celestial fires. In historical times, shamans adorned their drums with pictures of the auroral fire. They believed that one could summon the lights' energy for shamanistic purposes. In the Saami language, there is a special terminology to describe the behavior of children who noisily bustle about, running here and there, often changing direction. The literal translation of this expression in Saami is "to behave like the Northern Lights." This description is based on Saami people's common observation of the movements of the Northern Lights that not only quickly shift shape but also make a bristling noise due to the electric charging of the atmosphere.

There are many other beliefs in the cultures of the northern regions associated with the Northern Lights. For the Vikings the celestial lights were the spirits of dancing maidens. Less joyful are beliefs among the Inuit of eastern Greenland who think that the fires in the sky are the spirits of children that were stillborn. In Canada, some Inuit groups (in the valley of the Yukon river) take the Northern Lights for animal spirits.

## *The Gold of Lapland*

In those regions of the world where gold is found, early discoveries have usually triggered a gold rush, attracting many adventurers in search of their fortunes. Those who come to strike gold, hammering it out from the rock or washing it from rivers, may be lucky and find enough to make a fortune, or they may fail and end up in misery. Stories are told about those who go out in search of the precious metal, and many of these stories are associated with Finnish Lapland where gold was found in the area around Lake Inari.

The history of gold mining in Lapland reaches back into the 19th century. The oldest finds, made along the Ivalo river that flows into Lake Inari, triggered the local gold rush in the 1870s. The "Golden Village" (Finnish Kultala) on the shore of the lake quickly transformed into the center for gold prospecting. The waters of the Ivalo river harbor true treasures, indeed. The largest gold nugget that was ever found in that area (at a place on the Luotto river, in 1935) weighed 393 grams. Nowadays, some of the old trails connecting gold mines and places for washing gold have been integrated in an open-air museum in the wilderness surrounding one of the landmarks of Lapland, the Hammastunturi ("Tooth Mountain").

Another area where gold has been washed for more than a hundred years is the Lemmenjoki river in the municipality of Inari (Inari 2012). The largest gold nugget in that area, weighing 282 grams, was found in 2004. In summer, tourists arrive at a small village, Njurgalahti, and are taken to the places where gold panning is still practiced along the Lemmenjoki river. According to one story, a man with the name Jaakko Isola buried a gold treasure somewhere in the area, and there are always some new adventurers who look out for it.

Not only have some of those who came to Lapland in search of gold made their fortune, the booming tourist business also offers prospects to many an entrepreneur. At Tankavaara (in the vicinity of the Urho Kekkonen National Park and Saariselkä) a gold mining village has been established. Legend has it that in the old days a man named Aslak Peltovuoma, had a vision about the gold of Tankavaara in a dream. He set out to find it, and he did. The atmosphere in the village recalls the spirit that is known from the Klondike area in Alaska. A "Golden Road" (E 4) connects Tankavaara with Vuotso, a Saami village near Sodankylä in southern Lapland. During the past 150 years, more than 2100 kilograms of gold have been washed from the rivers in Lapland.

The impressive amount of more than 2000 kilograms of gold washed from the rivers is dwarfed by the extraction of gold from the rocks by applying mining techniques on an industrial scale. The gold mine that operates in the region of Kittilä, the Kittilä mine (also known as Suurikuusikko mine), is the biggest in Europe. The owner of this mine is a Canadian consortium (Agnico-Eagle Mines). The Kittilä mine started production in 2008. In 2012 alone, it produced some 5500 kg (= 176,000 ounces) of gold (Partanen and Niemelä 2014). Most of the income, however, has to be spent to cover the enormous expenses for the operation of the mine (http://www.mining-technology.com/projects/kittila-gold/; retrieved 29 November 2015):

- the operation of the crusher and the grinding mill to process the ore extracted from the rock;
- further processing of the crushed ore in flotation cells;
- heating the concentrated ore under pressure to separate the gold from sulphide material.

In summer of 2015, leaks in the vast waste water reservoir of the mine were recorded. Experts follow the repair work of the dams of the reservoir closely, hoping that the Kittilä mine does not become, like Talvivaara, another environmental problem.

Gold from Lapland is especially appreciated because of its purity (some 95 percent) and its price on the world market is above average. Gold is worked to produce jewelry, and workshops are found in Tankavaara and Rovaniemi. Besides gold, semiprecious stones (e.g., dark red almandite, garnet, green epidotite, corundum)—cut from rocks or washed out from the waters—are used for making jewelry.

The magic of gold and its history, spiced with narratives crystallizing around the fortunes and misfortunes of gold prospectors—all that is embedded in a wide landscape shrouded in mysteries and imbued with awe-inspiring natural phenomena such as spectacular sunsets and the glamour of northern lights. The stories of prospectors have been told in books and films. The gold of Lapland is always remembered, as in the name of a popular beer, "Lapin kulta" (Lapland's gold), the bottles of which feature a wide landscape against the background of a golden sunset.

Based on recent explorations of the so-called green-stone layers with relatively high concentrations of gold, it has been estimated that the green-stone belt that stretches from the northern to the southern part of Lapland is far more extended than previously thought (Mainio 2016).

## The Gold Museum of Tankavaara Where the Time Stands Still

Tankavaara has another attraction, and this is the Gold Museum which offers exhibits about both past and modern prospecting for gold, not only as related to Lapland but also in a worldwide comparison, with information about the history of gold in more than twenty countries. The museum is a nostalgic place. In fact, it is a museum with its own time, where the clocks have been standing still ever since it was established in 1972. The information about gold history that is presented in museum handouts and booklets is fanciful and hopelessly outdated since it reflects the level of knowledge of about half a century ago. It is claimed that gold was the oldest metal that was worked and that the earliest finds of artifacts made of gold come from ancient Egypt and are dated to the third millennium BCE.

According to the present state of research on the history of metal-working the earliest instances are associated with copper that was first smelted around 5400 BCE in the Balkans (Pernicka and Anthony 2009). There is no information, in the Tankavaara Gold Museum, about the oldest gold treasure of the world, found in Varna (Bulgaria) in 1972. Scientific analysis has shown that the various artifacts made of gold found in a necropolis of the Copper Age date to around 4500 BCE (Slavchev 2009, Haarmann 2012: 96ff.)—that is, they are much older than the oldest Egyptian artifacts.

# 2

# Where Do People Live and What Languages Do They Speak?

*Natives, Newcomers and Social Networking in a Multicultural Society*

Finland has been inhabited for some 10,000 years. The country could not have been settled much earlier. A few thousand years further back in time the land mass that is Finland today was covered by a thick sheet of ice during the last Ice Age. Even after the melting of the ice, a process that began some 12,000 years ago, there was no way to settle the land because most of it was under water. For thousands of years, the land mass of Finland has been steadily rising and it is still rising. During any recent hundred year period the rise amounts to one meter, and such a measure shapes coastlines and whole landscapes. When the first settlers came to Finland many parts were still flooded while others were already habitable (Salo 2013/I: 61).

The first to arrive were not kin to the modern inhabitants of the country, neither the Finns nor the Saami. The first people are called "ancient Laplanders" and their language "ancient Laplandish" (Paleo-Laplandic) in the scholarly literature (Aikio 2012: 64, 80ff.). The ancient Laplanders did not arrive from the south but they came from areas on the northern coast of Scandinavia. These areas had been ice free earlier than other areas in the north and had been used as refuge by some groups at the end of the Ice Age. That ancient population spread to some parts of Lapland and further south (figure 12).

One finds proof of their existence in a number of foreign elements (lexical borrowings) that were adopted, from the language of the first settlers, by the Saami language; e.g., *fieski* "winter pasture of the wild reindeer," *gabba* "completely white reindeer," *skuolfi* "owl," *njárga* "cape, land point." The fact that the Saami terminology for reindeers "has also preserved large numbers of substrate [i.e., Palaeo-Laplandic] words suggests that Palaeo-Laplandic groups had a profound impact on the practices and culture of wild reindeer hunting among the prehistoric Saami" (Aikio 2012: 86).

Other indicators of Palaeo-Laplandic influence are irregularities in the genetic profile of some local populations in Lapland and, in some non-indigenous traits of Saami culture

## Postglacial Colonisation of Northern Europe

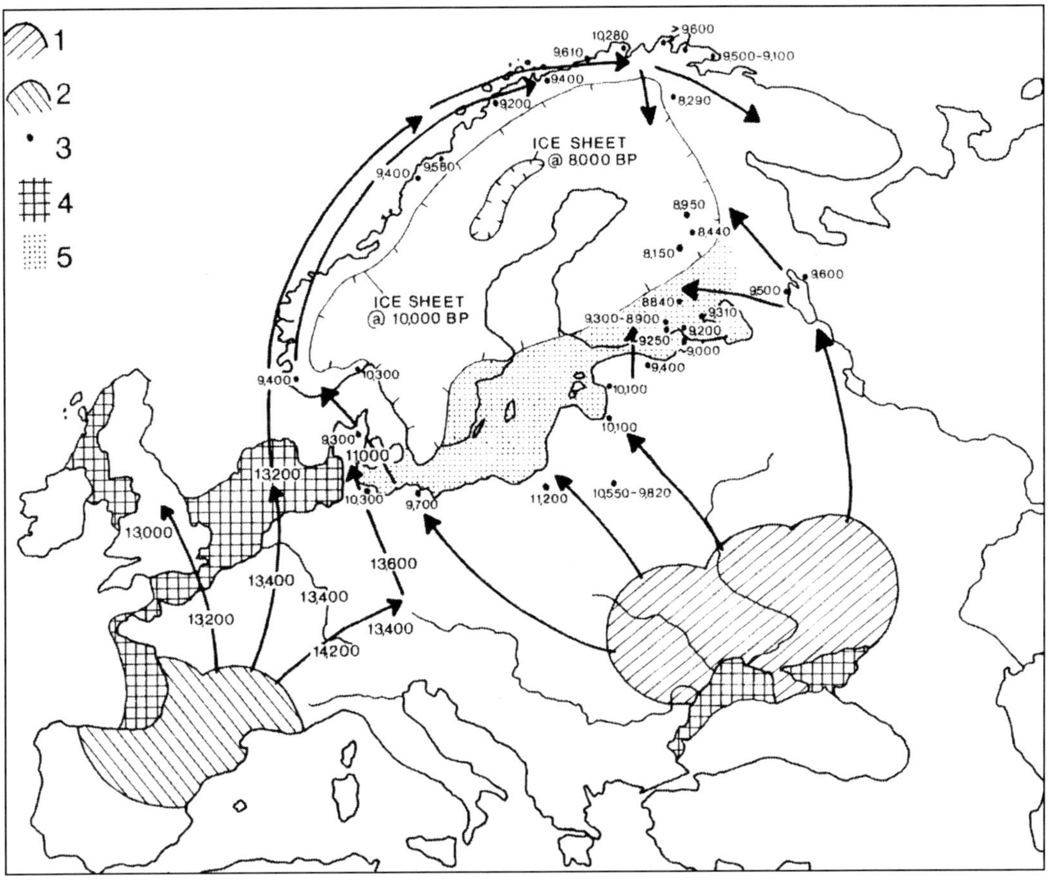

1. Recolonisation from eastern Europe.   2. Recolonisation from southwest Europe.   3. First regional settlement.   4. Late Glacial coastlines.   5. Yoldia Sea.

**Figure 12: The early colonization of Fenno-Scandia (from Marek Zvelebil, "Innovating Hunter-Gatherers: The Mesolithic in the Baltic," in Geoff Bailey and Penny Spikins, eds., *Mesolithic Europe* [Cambridge: Cambridge University Press, 2008], 23).**

that give an impression of great antiquity. The ancient Laplanders eventually assimilated completely to the surrounding Saami population, sometime around the middle of the first millennium CE.

The area of spread of the population that spoke ancient Laplandish extended south of Lapland. Since these people settled the area of the northern lakes they are called Palaeo-Lakelanders. Manifestations of their former presence also come through in Finnish. About one third of the Finnish vocabulary is of unknown origin. This means that words belonging to this category do not belong to the lexical layers which find their parallels in cognate languages, of Finno-Ugrian affiliation. Such expressions were adopted as borrowings. Since those borrowings stem neither from Slavic nor from Baltic or Germanic languages they are assumed to be very old and the source may well be identified as ancient Laplandish. Among those loanwords are geographical terms of frequent use (e.g., *niemi* "peninsula").

## *The Saami—Masters of the Arctic Region*

The Saami range among the native peoples of Europe. Commonly, only a few populations are recognized as truly "native" in Europe, and these are the Saami people in the far north, the Basques in western Europe (in northern Spain and southwestern France) and, on the eastern periphery of Europe, the indigenous peoples of the Caucasus. Why are these called "native" peoples, but other Europeans not? The main criteria for such strict definition of "native" is associated with the extreme age of local settlements of those populations.

The modern Saami are the offspring of the oldest population in northern Europe that can be traced back as a coherent group. Their ancestors arrived in Finland from the south short after the last Ice Age had ended, the big ice-shield had melted, and the terrain was suitable for human settlement.

As a comparison, the Basques are a much older population than are the Saami. The ancestors of the Basques are connected with those people who painted the walls of the Paleolithic caves (Haarmann 1998). Those paintings were made during a long span of time, between ca. 33,000 and ca. 18,000 years BP. There is genetic evidence linking the Basques to Caucasian peoples. The far-distant ancestors of the modern Basques came from the east, some 41,000 years ago and, when they settled in western Europe, they found the previous inhabitants still there, the Neanderthals.

What comes to mind when thinking of the homeland of the Saami, Sápmi ("Lapland"), and of the indigenous people, their culture and customs, is their exoticism.

> Sápmi and the indigenous Sámi who have resided there for thousands of years still continue to fascinate the wider world, their exoticism being retained in the popular imagination despite the arrival of mass travel and modern technological infrastructure in the Sámi homeland many years ago. But today this fascination has gone global [Kent 2014: 259].

The Saami are the only people in Europe that permanently live above the Arctic Circle, that is, above 66° north latitude. They have a long experience with what it means to spend more than half of the year amidst snow, ice and cold weather. And when it comes to the measure of cold, Lapland holds the record in all of Finland. The seasonal changes are marked and sometimes extreme. A year may pass when summer temperatures oscillate around + 25° C for weeks while, in winter, it may be freezing cold, with temperatures between minus 20° C and minus 30° or even colder (-40° C), for weeks and months. People in Finland are accustomed to the cold, and this is especially true for those living in Lapland. There is a saying that every Finn and Saami knows: "Standing the cold is a matter of how you dress."

Indeed, today clothing that wards off the cold is easily available and practical to master extreme conditions. But in the old days when people in Lapland, in winter, moved outdoors to go on a sledge ride, things were different. Then, it was quite a challenge to sit in a sledge, drawn by reindeers, for hours, enduring the biting frost. Some of the early travellers to Lapland described winter clothes of Saami in their accounts (figure 13).

The experiences of Saami people with the weather in winter, handed down from one generation to the next, have crystallized in the Saami language. The ways Saami have learned to deal with winterly weather conditions are reflected in the Saami terminology for natural phenomena.

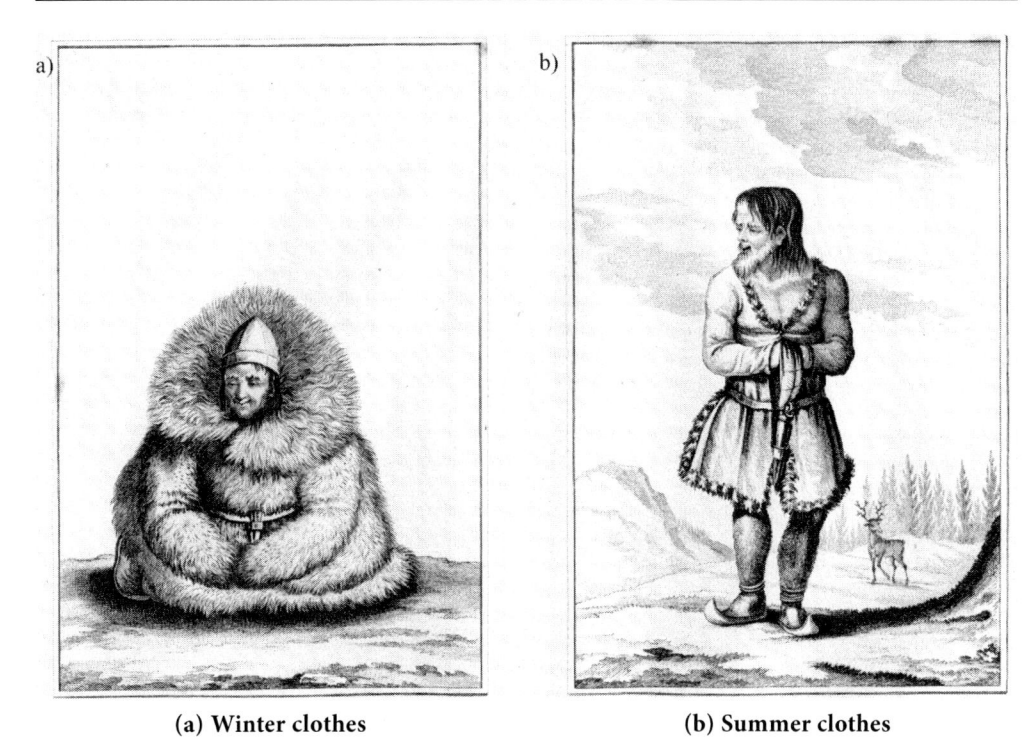

(a) **Winter clothes**        (b) **Summer clothes**

**Figure 13: Saami fashion in the 18th century (from Clarke 1819).**

## Saami Terms for Snow

In Saami, there are more than 20 expressions which specify different conditions of snow and ice. This specialized vocabulary demonstrates the working of the principle of "linguistic relativity," which manifests itself in many languages in manifold ways. While languages usually have but a few general terms for natural phenomena the vocabulary in certain languages shows great variation. An example of linguistic relativity is the concept "rain," which has produced dozens of different expressions in Hawaiian for specifying various types of precipitation (Kent 1993: 377ff.).

In the case of the common concept "snow" linguistic relativity is true for Saami. The Saami terminology for snow is highly complex.

> The physical condition of different layers is essential, but the relation to changes of weather and temperature conditions is often integrated in the meanings. Very basic in the meanings is also the quality and quantity of snow, judged according to the practical needs of people and animals [Magga 2006: 25].

### TERMS FOR SNOW IN SAAMI
(selected from Itkonen 1986–89)

*ääinig*   "new snow, fallen on the bare soil, enabling the tracing of tracks"

*ceeyvi*   "snow that was whipped hard by harsh winds; this snow is so hard that the reindeer cannot break the crust to search for food beneath"

*cuanguj*   "snow crust, hardened snow"

*čaerga*   "thin hard snow (the lower layer that remains when the wind blows away the upper soft layer)"

*čyehi*   "snow fallen in autumn that has hardened over time"
*kamadoh*   "hard snow in spring that breaks easily and with a noise when one steps on it"
*kerni*   "snow with a thin icy surface"
*kolšša*   "hard and slippery snow cover"
*lavkke*   "snow fallen on icy ground which is so slippery that the reindeer cannot stand firmly"
*muovla*   "very soft snow so that someone who comes skiing sinks down to the bottom"
*purga*   "swirling snow in a blizzard"
*rine*   "a thick layer of snow that has accumulated on the branches of trees or in the nooks of branches and the trunk of a tree"
*seeli*   "snow that is soft from the surface down"
*senjes*   "old coarse snow that cracks easily, under a layer of new hard snow"
*skälvi*   "high and hard snow plate that one can find near a river bank or around the edge of a rock"
*syeyngis*   "soft and smooth snow where the reindeer may dig a hole to reach for food"
*šleätta*   "wet and soft snow"
*šohma*   "slush on the ice (of a river or lake)"
*šolkka*   "snow that has been trodden hard by reindeer"
*vasme*   "thin layer of new snow"
*vocca*   "fresh snow that is so light and loose that the wind blows it away"

But why has the Saami language developed so many different terms for snow while the Finnish language has not? There are substantial reasons that may explain this contrast-rich terminology. The experiences with snow produced the variety of terms in Saami because the speakers were in need of such differentiation and this has to do with the way of subsistence in historical times in Lapland, depending on an animal that had long been indigenous to the northern region. The fauna of northern Eurasia is rich in birds (especially water fowl), in many small animal species, and also some larger ones such as bear and elk (moose). There is one animal inhabiting the vast northern plains and which is of special interest for the people who live there, and this is the reindeer, known in North America as the caribou.

The northern plains where the soil is permanently frozen and only the surface melts during the warmer season, is treeless. Shrubs, grass, moss and lichen grow there. This ecosystem with its sparse vegetation is known by a name that has become an item of the international vocabulary: tundra which is of Saami origin (*tundâr* "uplands").

In order to understand the great variation of terms for "snow" it is necessary to highlight reindeer herding under winterly conditions. Reindeer herding is a standard Saami form of subsistence. This has always been so, and still is today. Not everyone can engage in reindeer herding. Those who are allowed to do so have to be permanent residents of Lapland, and they have to prove that they are of Saami descent. The definition of Saami is not exclusively associated with the language as a marker of Saami ethnicity. In the present, the majority of ethnic Saami (about 3,900) no longer speak the language of their ancestors but have assimilated to Finnish as their mother tongue. An ethnic Saami has Saami ancestors, meaning that at least one of the grandparents had to be a Saami.

Reindeer herding is a lucrative business, and every single animal is a valuable asset to any herder. Without the ethnicity-oriented restrictions one could imagine that the herding business in all of Lapland would be controlled by a few monopolists who would dictate the conditions for the meat market and fur trade. In Lapland there are quite a few Saami millionaires who have made their fortune with reindeer herding but the danger of monopolization by a few is not in sight.

For all of its history, the business of reindeer herding has been managed by members of the Saami community. How far back does this tradition reach? There have been all kinds of speculations about the origins of reindeer herding. Estimates previously given for the beginnings of reindeer herding (thought to date back some 2500 years at most) were all too short. New insights allow us to pinpoint a date for the origins that is far more remote. Evidence for the new retrospective comes from rock paintings found beyond the Arctic Circle, at Alta in the Norwegian part of Lapland. There is one scene showing reindeer in a fenced area (figure 14), dated to 4200–3600 BCE. These fences resemble corrals that have been used up to the present by Saami reindeer herders.

**Figure 14: Rock engravings from Alta (Norway) showing a reindeer herding scene (after Helskog 1988).**

In the scene from Alta, a fully-developed herding practice is visualized. This practice of rounding up reindeers in corrals has persisted into our days. Once a year in autumn, reindeers are selected to be distributed (according to ownership) and slaughtered for meat, fur and bones (for making tools or souvenirs) or used for breeding.

The evidence shows that the tradition of reindeer herding in the western part of Eurasia dates to the fifth millennium BCE. However, from the rock pictures it cannot be concluded whether the reindeer driven into the corral were wild or domestic. The former can be assumed for the Alta scene. When looking at prehistoric rock art it is essential to take into consideration that the relationship between human beings and animals might have been perceived, by the creators of the pictures, in a much more intimate way than the modern observer can imagine.

These figures are a part of communication between humans, and between humans and non-humans, within an understanding of what was needed for procuring reindeer that probably was somewhat different from today. Some of the figures associated with the corrals are not connected with driving and killing reindeer from a modern context, but their association indicates connections once existed, if not in driving and killing, then in narratives, myths and rituals [Helskog 2011: 25].

## The Saami Have Many Words for "Reindeer"

Since earliest times, the wild reindeer have been hunted. Still in the 12th century, "the Mountain Sámi ... continued to pursue a nomadic life in which wild reindeer hunting were the primary activities" (Kent 2014: 216).

The Saami vocabulary has a rich and highly diversified terminology relating to reindeer herding and breeding. In this specialized domain, we find manifold expressions for describing various features of the animal. In western languages, English for one, there is one general term for "reindeer" whereas, in Saami, there are dozens. A reindeer is not just a reindeer, it is male or female, young or old, has a thick or scanty fur, is of grey or white color, is quick-tempered or calm, etc. Among the languages of Europe, the Saami reindeer terminology is unique because only Saami engage in the herding of this animal.

### TERMS FOR REINDEER-HERDING IN SAAMI
#### (selected from Seurujärvi-Kari and Ruotsala 2005: 332)

*gabba* "a completely white reindeer"
*jievja* "a white reindeer"
*luosttat* "a reindeer with white flanks"
*čuoivvat* "a grey or white-tipped reindeer"
*muzet* "a black reindeer"
*miessi* "a reindeer calf"
*čearpmat* "a reindeer in its first winter (female and male)"
*vuonjal* "a reindeer in its second winter (female)"
*varit* "a reindeer in its second winter (male)"
*áldu* "a reindeer in its third winter (female)"
*vuobirs* "a reindeer in its third winter (male)"
*barfi* "a reindeer with antlers with many branches"
*biikasággi* "a reindeer with vertical horns"
*čaločoarvi* "a reindeer with skin peeling from its antlers"
*nálat* "a reindeer with its antlers cut off"
*njabbi* "a female reindeer with delicately shaped antlers which slope back a little"
*nulpu* "a reindeer without antlers"
*gisor* "a small, young and worn-out reindeer"
*livat* "an exhausted reindeer"
*rávzi* "a sick, feeble reindeer"
*rotnu* "a cow that did not calve in a particular year"
*heargi* "a castrated, draught reindeer"
*sarvvis* "an uncastrated male reindeer"
*stáinnat* "a female reindeer which never calves"
*spáillit* "an untrained, castrated male reindeer"

Saami specialized reindeer terminology extends to various phenomena and activities relating to animals and herding:

*eallu* "a big reindeer herd (between 200 and 500 animals)"
*bálgat* "the grazing of reindeer on the summer pasture"
*ruovgat* "the grunting sound made by a reindeer"
*dápmat* "the process of taming a reindeer"
*ráidi* "a reindeer herder who in the winter looks after the draught reindeer of residents"
*ráidu* "a reindeer caravan, with the animals harnessed to a sledge one behind the other"
*rátkin* "the separation of the reindeer in a corral"
*sivlá* "a holding corral (the reindeer are first rounded up in a holding corral to settle down before they are separated and earmarked)"
*girdno* "a circular part of the holding corral of reindeer (where a smaller part of the reindeer herd is separated)"
*suohpan* "a long, tarred lasso (used for catching reindeer)"
*spágat* "packsaddles for reindeer"
*vuohtaráipi* "a reindeer's trace"
*siida* "a reindeer village, a mountain camp (consisting of one or, as a rule, several families of reindeer owners with their animals)"

Since the origins of reindeer herding in Lapland date to remote times, it can be conjectured that also the specialized Saami terminology of reindeer herding is of great antiquity. And, most probably, the specialization of terminology for reindeer herding developed contemporaneously with the special vocabulary for natural phenomena. Why and how are these terminologies interconnected?

The weather in winter is of great concern to reindeer herders. If there is too much snow the animals cannot dig up enough food to survive the cold season. If the snow cover is too hard and the animals cannot crush it with their hoofs the chances of survival are poor. Therefore, changing weather conditions put herders on alert, and it is of utmost importance to be knowledgeable about how various conditions of the Arctic winter may affect the herds. It may be necessary to drive a herd to a different pasture where conditions are more favorable. For that purpose the herder has to visit various locations to gather information about the snow quality. The capability to handle changing weather conditions—especially from the standpoint of herding—and the knowledge of how natural phenomena interact with herding probably provided an incentive for the development of the parallel specialized terminologies in these strongly interrelating domains. The conditions of the one domain (winter weather) dictate human actions in the other domain (reindeer herding).

The specialized terminologies were an efficient tool to facilitate and support communication among the herders, and this tool was transferred, in the intergenerational chain, from the older herders to the young. The specialized use of the Saami language served insider communication among the Saami populations of herders. For longer than two thousands years, herders have settled together, forming kin groups and clans.

Individual Sámi families, generally related to one another, tended to settle together in a so-called "*siida*" (a Sámi community or village) in groups of eight or twelve. Aligned with one another, these *siida* were in turn organized into a "*vuobme*" (a regional network of settlements). In the second millennium AD these formed the basis for the establishment of Kemi, Torne, Lule and Pite "*jälldet*" (i.e., Lapp areas), the former two in Finland (under Swedish sovereignty until 1809) and the latter two in Sweden [Kent 2014: 21].

In the old days, herders would travel in a sledge drawn by reindeers to survey the herds and to control the pastures. Those days are long gone. Nowadays, a herder would perform the same activities by driving a snowmobile. The traditional way of transport, the wooden sledge drawn by reindeers, has been revived in the tourist business. People come from all over the world to enjoy reindeer-sledge riding in Lapland during a Christmas holiday.

The specialized terminologies for snow and herding have disappeared from Saami people's daily lives. Most Saami in Finland no longer speak the language of their ancestors. Ethnographers, scholars of Saami folklore and linguists recorded the specialized terminologies in the 19th and 20th centuries, so the bulk of the historical vocabulary has been secured. What reindeer herders of today may still know of this traditional vocabulary are fragments of what their parents and grandparents had at their command. Since there is no equivalent, in Finnish, to the specialized Saami terminology, modern herders must get along with a more general vocabulary, which in turn might require more paraphrasing talk about weather conditions and herding activities.

The reindeer plays a significant role in Saami mythology and themes associating the reindeer with shamanistic magic have been on the agenda of filmmakers. The best known of these artistic manifestations of old Saami beliefs in the supernatural is the film *Valkoinen peura* ("The White Reindeer"), directed by Erik Blomberg in 1952. The plot of the film is tragic: The protagonist is a young beautiful woman named Pirita, played by Mirjami Kuosmanen. Pirita is married to Aslak, a reindeer herder. Her husband often is away for days so Pirita gets lonely. In order to alleviate her loneliness, Pirita consults a shaman who invests Pirita with shapeshifting power. Pirita can transform into a white reindeer that lures men into a fateful relationship with the vampiric creature. In the end, the vampiric reindeer is chased by Aslak who hunts down and kills the alleged animal with a spear. The dying reindeer transforms and, in the snow tainted with blood, lies Pirita, Aslak's loved one.

In 1953, the film won the special award for Best Fairy Tale Film at the Cannes Film Festival. Several years later, in 1957, it won the Golden Globe Award for Best Foreign Film in the United States.

## Modernization in the Arctic Region:
## Mass Tourism and Santa Claus

Well into the 17th century hunting wild reindeer and fishing had been the main forms of subsistence among the Saami population in the north. During the Middle Ages, the Saami had adopted animal husbandry (cattle, sheep, goats) from their Scandinavian neighbors, the Vikings. In the southern regions that were inhabited by Saami they also practiced some agriculture although this has never been of much importance in the Saami lands. The domestication of reindeer led to the establishment of individually owned farms, and reindeer herding became the major activity in the north.

Traditional lifeways of the Saami in Finland were kept up well into the 20th century. Great changes occurred in the settlements of the far North during World War II. According to an agreement between Germany and Finland, some German troops were stationed in Lapland. Between 1941 and 1944 Finns and Germans had cooperated, fighting together, as allies, on the Russian front. When Finns and Russians agreed upon an armistice in autumn 1944, one of the conditions was that the Finns drive out German troops from Finnish territory. For formal reasons, the former Finnish-German allies turned into enemies, and Finnish troops were forced to push the German units to the north, in an attempt to drive them out of Finnish territory into German-held Norway.

The German troops withdrew in an orderly fashion. In early September 1944, Germans and Finns reached an agreement, kept secret from the Russians, that the Germans would inform the Finns about their moves and directions of their withdrawal so that clashes between their troops could be avoided. The Russian observers who monitored the actions, claimed that the pace of withdrawal was too slow and they demanded that Finnish troops be more active. This eventually led to the decisive confrontation of Germans and Finns in the Lapland war that lasted from September 1944 to April 1945. Most of the civilian population in the northern part of Finland had been evacuated earlier, to Sweden or to southern Finland. The withdrawing German troops applied a tactic in Lapland which had been used earlier in Russia: "scorched earth." The town of Rovaniemi and many rural settlements were burned down, altogether almost half of all constructions in Lapland. When the war ended Lapland had been devastated.

Like the mythological Phoenix that rose from the ashes so Lapland rose to modernity. The infrastructure was rebuilt from scratch. The modernization efforts paid off and eventually enhanced the growth of tourism to the region. During the past decades, Finnish Lapland has experienced a dramatic modernization at a rapid pace. The number of those who are engaged in the tourism business has been steadily growing since the late 1990s. There are more employment opportunities in tourism than in any other economic domain.

> The significant economic role of tourism has made it also a socially and politically important issue in regional policy-making. Indeed, tourism and tourism development arguments are used as a medium for many socio-cultural, economic and land-use goals and actions on the regional and local scales in Lapland [Kaján and Saarinen 2014: 191].

Lapland offers a great variety of attractions, natural and touristic. People come from afar to experience the white nights of Lapland when the sun does not set, to admire the spectacle of the northern lights in their changing colors and contours or to enjoy the autumnal scenery of Lapland during the short period of *ruska* (at the beginning of September) when nature changes its colors. Among the preferred touristic activities are hiking, riding in a sledge drawn by reindeers, fishing, kayaking, skiing, snowmobile driving or sitting around an open fire eating grilled fish or sausages. The most modern trend in tourism is trekking without carrying all the gear along. Groups of trekkers move in the open landscape while their gear is transported, on an independent route, from one overnight place to the next in their itinerary (Weaver and Bird 2015).

Among the major attractions are the places associated with Santa Claus. In Scandinavia there are various stories about the homeland of Santa Claus. According to Finnish and Saami folklore, the real home of Santa Claus is in Finnish Lapland in the Korvatunturi fell ("Ear Fell"). Korvatunturi is located in the Urho Kekkonen National Park in eastern Lapland, in the border zone between Finland and Russia (see figure 12 for natural parks in Finland).

Folk tradition has it that, in the Korvatunturi, Santa Claus has his secret workshop where he manufactures toys with his assistants, the elves of Lapland. Around Christmas,

Santa Claus drives into the world in his sledge, drawn by reindeer and loaded with presents for the children. This story was publicized in a popular radio program for children in 1927, the host of which was Markus Rautio. The program's name was *Markus-sedän lastentunti* ("Children's hour with uncle Markus"). The story of Santa Claus in the Korvatunturi has been visualized in the film *Rare Exports: A Christmas Tale* (2010) (http://www.lifeinlapland.com/articles/lapland-travel-tips/real-home-santa-korvatunturi.html; retrieved 2 December 2015).

The home of Santa Claus for tourism is at a different place, in Santa Claus Holiday Village (10 kilometers north of Rovaniemi) in southern Lapland, and there Santa Claus has his office (Joulupukin kammari). This office was opened in 1985. Closely connected with the village is Santa Park. In 2010, Rovaniemi was officially declared the hometown of Santa Claus.

The amusement park of Santa Claus Village is located on the Arctic Circle (as it was positioned in 1865), marked by a white line that is drawn across the park. Visitors who cross the line enter the Arctic region. There is a Santa Claus post office, and mail sent from there gets a special postmark. Santa Claus has his own office where he receives visitors, children and adults alike, to chat with them and to have photos taken (figure 15). Santa Claus' receptions are appreciated as venues attracting media attention, by politicians and VIPs from around the world.

**Figure 15: Representatives of three generations, among them the author, visiting Santa Claus in Lapland (Santa Claus Office, Rovaniemi; www.santaclauslive.com).**

## Cultural Heritage in a Box: The Treasure of the Skolt Saami

We "all know" that the adventures of Indiana Jones, the treasure hunter, are fantasy. But do we really know? Sometimes, real life offers surprises that make us feel as if we were participants in a fairy tale. That is the impression one gets when listening to the story that stands behind the most recent entry in the UNESCO Memory of the World Register. This entry, the Archive of the Skolt Saami of Suonikylä was adopted at the 12th meeting of the International Advisory Committee for the Memory of the World Program, held at Abu Dhabi (UAE) in early October 2015.

The Archive of the Skolt Saami is called *Gramota*, which is Russian and literally means "written document." Finnish *Raamattu* "Bible" and Estonian *raamat* "book" stem from the same source. The document in question is a scroll kept in a box made of fir wood in 1865. From 1942 onward this box was kept in the National Archive (Kansallis-arkisto) in Helsinki. The Skolt Saami had no knowledge of the whereabouts of this box until, in 1996, the *Gramota* was "re-discovered." It is now kept in the Saami Archive (Saamelaisarkisto) in Inari (Lehmusvesi 2015).

The *Gramota* finds itself in prominent company in the World Register. Among the 348 documents that have been registered so far are the Magna Carta, the Gutenberg Bible and Beethoven's Ninth Symphony. This Saami archive is a treasure in its own class. It is a document of world memory associated with a native people, in this case one of the most ancient populations of Europe. The scroll is 9 meters long and contains a collection of official papers, signed by dignitaries and Russian Tsars. The contents of the papers are rights which were granted to the Skolt Saami relating to their fishing grounds and to the areas for their reindeer to graze. The oldest document is from 1601, the newest dates to 1775.

During World War II, the Skolt Saami were evacuated from the region of their original settlement, in the area of Petsamo. That area had been part of Finland from 1920 until 1944, after which it had to be ceded to the Soviet Union. The Skolt Saami were resettled in the northeastern part of Finnish Lapland, in the region of Sevettijärvi. They number some 500 members nowadays. The *Gramota* had been among the belongings which the Saami had taken with them. For unknown reasons the box had remained in the stern of a boat carrying refugees. It was found by an officer of the army unit that organized the evacuation who transferred it to Rovaniemi and from there to the National Archive in Helsinki. The Skolt Saami believed that the *Gramota* had got lost when they were on the trail to the west.

When, in the mid–1990s, the Saami museum Siida gathered materials and artifacts for an exhibition of the culture and the Saami ways of living they also asked the National Archive for potential exhibits. The Siida sent a trusted man, Pekka Fofanoff, who went to Helsinki to fetch objects for the exhibition. To his great surprise he could identify the *Gramota* among them. The scroll was carefully examined and extensive restoration work done. In 2012, the *Gramota* was transferred to the Saami Archive in Inari. The community of the Skolt Saami consider the scroll their national treasure.

## On the Ways Saami Speak Finnish

One of the areas where Finnish has been in contact with several languages for many generations is Lapland (Finnish Lappi). Three Saami languages (Skolt Saami, Inari Saami, northern Saami) are spoken by only about 1,700 people in the Finnish part of Lapland. Nowadays all mother tongue speakers of any Saami variety in Lapland speak Finnish as their second language.

In the processes of language shift, historical and recent, certain phonetic and prosodic traits in the habits of the former Saami speakers have persisted, and their functioning becomes apparent in the way these people speak Finnish. Among the most resilient features of the local variety of Finnish spoken in Lapland is the aspiration of consonants; for example:

| | |
|---|---|
| *Ordinary spoken Finnish* | *Finnish spoken in Lapland* |
| *mettässä* "in the wood" | *met-hässä* |
| (*metsässä* in written Finnish) | |
| *mä oon ollu* "I have been" | *mä oon olhu* |
| (*minä olen ollut* in written Finnish) | |
| *koskaa* "ever" | *koskhaa* |
| (*koskaan* in written Finnish) | |

In all Saami languages, there is a complex system of consonants, also including the opposition of non-aspirated and aspirated sounds. The habitual aspiration of consonants in colloquial Finnish in Lapland, in the speech of Saami speaking Finnish, stems from interference with Saami varieties.

## *Finns: Modern Europeans with an Exotic Language*

The ancestors of the modern Finns were organized in tribal groups of Finnic affiliation. They came to Finland from two directions. One was the connection on land, the Karelian Isthmus, that connects Fenno-Scandia with continental Europe. The other was a western trail, and those who frequented this connection crossed the Gulf of Finland by boat, starting from the northern shore of Estonia and arriving on the southern coast of Finland. For a long time, the development of the western group remained separated from that of the eastern group. These cultural complexes only gradually merged. Still, there are marked differences between western and eastern dialects of Finnish and, in the genetic profile of the Finnish population, the western genome deviates significantly from the genetic pool of the eastern population (Lappalainen et al. 2006).

When the Finnic tribes arrived in Fenno-Scandia they did not find virgin territory but there were the early inhabitants, the ancestors of the modern Saami. They had occupied campsites and settlements far south of their present area of settlement. In southern Finland, one finds place names with the element Lapp- (e.g., Lappeenranta, Lapinjärvi, Lappee). This was the name for the older lexical root in the ethnic name by which the Saami were called by their neighbors; i.e., *lapper* (in Norwegian), *lappar* (in Swedish) and *lappalaiset* (in Finnish).

The contacts between early Saami settlers and Finnic immigrants were not always friendly, which can be inferred from the remnants of prehistoric fortifications at some locations in southern Finland. Hiidenvuori is such a place which most probably had been a dwelling site for Saami who had fortified the slopes of the mountain on the island.

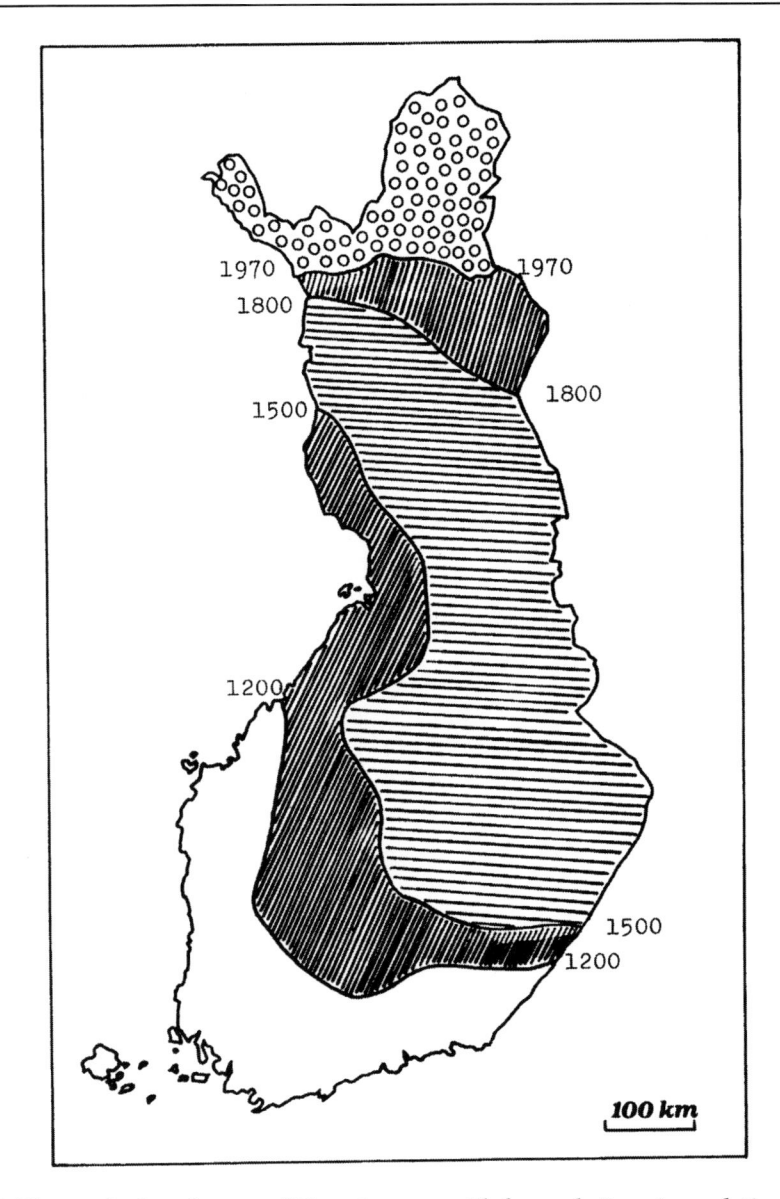

**Figure 16: The gradual settlement of Finns in areas with formerly Saami population (drawing by the author).**

In a prolonged process, the Saami were driven ever further north, up to the borders of the land they currently inhabit (figure 16).

Who were those Finnic tribes that made Finland their homeland? Were they different from the Saami population? Did they have anything in common with the people they encountered in the north? These questions invite us to have a closer look at the majority population of present-day Finland, the Finns and their ancestors.

Are the Finns Europeans? This question seems unnecessary. The Finns are Europeans and this does not have to be explained, it is self-evident. Are the Finns native Europeans? This question requires an answer with some explanation. With respect to peoples, cultures and languages the concept "native" is applied rather randomly. It has been mentioned earlier that the Saami are among the native peoples of Europe whose status is commonly recognized.

The traditional definition of how the concept "native" is understood has been a matter of some debate, and there are those who would extend the meaning of "native" to also include many other national groups of Europe that developed in this continent, though not being of the remote ancestry of the Saami and Basques. In a recently published encyclopedia of the native peoples of the world, more than 70 ethnic groups are specified as "native" to Europe (Danver 2013). The Finns are among them because Finnish ethnicity emerged in Europe.

## The Coming of Finnic Tribes

The Finns did not migrate from somewhere outside this continent to their historical homeland. And yet, the ancestors of the Finns came from somewhere outside Scandinavia. Those were Finno-Ugric tribes, hunters and gatherers who inhabited the region west of the Ural mountains, on both sides of the Middle Volga river. Those hunters pushed north and eventually arrived in Finland on two routes. Some groups crossed the Karelian land bridge between the Gulf of Finland and Lake Ladoga, other groups crossed the Gulf by boat departing from the northern coast of Estonia.

Those who migrated to Finland were not yet Finns in the modern sense, and among the different local groups there was hardly that kind of self-awareness of belonging to the same linguistic-cultural community that is known from historical times. The old tribal division has been preserved in some form, and the people from Karelia are aware that they are different (*eri heimo* "of a different tribe") from the people in Savo or Häme. According to a popular view the name forms by which the Finns call themselves and their home country: *Suomi* ("Finland") and *suomalainen* "Finn; Finnish" are related to the term for swamp, bog: *suo*. This folk-etymological explanation is no longer valid because, in light of recent linguistic research, the alleged association of Suomi with *suo* is untenable (see Chapter 3). Yet, many still believe that he Finns are literally the "swamp people; people living in the land of swamps." Indeed, Finland was covered with swamps in prehistory and for the longest time of its history. Many swamps were dried out, and the turf has been a source of energy for centuries. Nowadays, its use is reduced because of environmental considerations, and swamps are protected as the natural habitat of many species of wildlife. For a long time, the self-awareness of the Finns was characterized by a local-tribal consciousness, which was transformed when the Finns experienced their national awakening in the course of the 19th century, resulting in the emergence of a Finnish national identity.

The Finns are Europeans, they are Scandinavians, and yet, they are different. Foreigners often take Finns to be alike Swedes, which is wrong. There is much convergence between Finnish and Swedish culture, but there is no genealogical relationship between the languages, nor do people in Finland and Sweden have a common genetic ancestry. The gene pool of Finns contrasts with that of Swedes although this does not show when comparing external anthropological features (Cavalli-Sforza et al. 1994: 268ff.). As to their origins, Finnish and Swedish are unrelated because they belong to different ethnic populations and language families. Swedish is affiliated to other languages in Scandinavia such as Norwegian, Danish and Icelandic, which are Germanic languages and of Indo-European affiliation. Finnish forms part of the group of Baltic-Finnic languages, other languages of this group being Karelian, Estonian, Izhorian and Votic. The Baltic-Finnic languages belong to the Finno-Ugric branch of the Uralic family (Abondolo 1998: 2ff.).

## Finnish Communities in Fenno-Scandia

There are some 5 million speakers of Finnish (*suomen kieli* "the Finnish language," short form *suomi* "Finnish") in Europe. These are native speakers. Most of them live in Finland (Suomen Tasavalta "the Republic of Finland," short form Suomi "Finland") where they make up about 90 percent of the population. The political status of Finnish differs in the various regions of its spread. Finnish is but one of Finland's official languages, the other being Swedish.

Finnish minorities live in neighboring states, in Sweden, in Russia (in and around the city of St. Petersburg) and in Estonia. The number of persons of Finnish descent outside Europe is estimated at 1.2 million, most of whom live in North America (see below).

The most numerous group of Finns living outside Finland in a European country is found in neighboring Sweden, with some 700,000 people of Finnish descent (Sweden-Finns, Ruotsinsuomalaiset). These are representatives of the first, second and third generations of migrants from Finland to Sweden. Finnish migration increased in the 1950s and reached a peak around 1970, at a time of high unemployment rates in Finland. Based on interviews made between 2005 and 2007, researchers found out that Finnishness (relating to language, culture and customs) is a firm ingredient of identity among the Finnish residents in Sweden (Björklund 2012).

The Finnish population in the valley of the Tornio river (Tornedalen), along the Swedish-Finnish border, number some 50,000. This group enjoys the status of an acknowledged minority. The status of the Finnish-speaking groups in Estonia and Russia is that of minorities without territorial rights. This means that there are no state-run schools for the Finns to be taught their mother tongue.

There is a small Finnish minority in northern Norway, known by the name Kvener (in Norwegian) and Kveenit (in Finnish) (Saressalo 1996). The area of historical settlement of Kven Finns are Troms and Finnmark in northern Norway to which Finns migrated from Finland in the 18th and 19th centuries. No definite information about the actual number of Kvens is available. In a Parliamentary inquiry on national minorities in Norway, conducted in 2001, the number of Norwegian citizens of Finnish descent was estimated at 10,000 to 15,000. A person is considered a Kven if at least one of the grandparents spoke Finnish. According to a government report of 2005, those who still speak Finnish number between 2,000 and 8,000. When Norway, in 1999, signed the *Convention for the Protection of National Minorities* the Kvens were recognized as an ethnic minority and their language as minority language. Kvens were among the people from Scandinavia who emigrated to America. The mother of U.S.-American actress Renée Zellweger (known from, e.g., *Bridget Jones's Diary*) is a Norwegian of Kven descent.

There are about 300,000 second-language speakers of Finnish. Most of them are Finland-Swedes who mainly live in three areas of historical settlement in Finland: in the southern coastal strip, in the southwestern coastal strip and, in the Åland archipelago (Finnish Ahvenanmaa), including one main island and several smaller ones.

Today, long-resident Finns are found in western Europe (i.e., Germany, France, England, Spain), in the Americas (i.e., the USA, Canada, Brazil), in Australia, and in Japan.

## Who Is Finnish and Who Is Karelian?

Finns and Karelians are closely related. This holds true in a wider perspective although there are marked differences both in their languages and cultures. The culture of the majority of Finns has been strongly influenced by the Protestant tradition while, among the Karelians, the historical development stood under the patronage of the Russian Orthodox church. Finnish has adopted many Swedish loanwords while, in Karelian, the bulk of borrowings is of Russian origin. Finnish and Karelian cultures have unfolded on a continuum, with a Finnish gravitation in the west and a Karelian gravitation in the east.

In order to substantiate the differences between the two groups it is essential to contrast Karelian cultural history and the Karelian language against the Finnish settings. The Karelians live in the North of Russia, in an area bordering Finland. The number of ethnic Karelians (*karjalaized*) has been in a process of steady decline. So has their speech community. In the 1920s, some 240,000 Karelians were counted. That number had dropped by half by the late 1950s and was 93,000 according to the Russian census of 2002. Today, not more than 52,000 Karelians still speak their native language. In all areas with Karelian population there is a marked trend toward assimilation, resulting in language shift to Russian, and Karelian customs fall into oblivion. Most Karelians inhabit the republic of Karelia which, administratively, is an integral part of the Russian Federation. Despite the fact that the Karelians are name-giving to their own republic their portion of the population is less than 10 percent. The great majority of the inhabitants of Karelia are Russians. Karelian settlements are scattered outside Karelia in different areas of northern Russia, in the Tver region and around Novgorod.

The earliest mentions of Karelia stem from Scandinavian sources of the 8th century. From that time onward there has been a continual influx of Russian population in Karelia. In the 12th century, Karelia (in the form Korela) and the Karelians (*koreliane*) are mentioned in a document from Novgorod. The Russian Orthodox Church started its missionary campaign among the Karelians while the region was under the rule of the Russian state of Novgorod which was organized as a feudal republic. Most of the Karelians became Orthodox Christians during the Middle Ages. For centuries, starting in the 13th century, Karelia became an object of dispute in the conflicts between two great powers, Russia and Sweden.

Territorial borders shifted several times, but the most decisive development was the political separation of the territory with Karelian population since the early 14th century, a separation which continues up to the present. Today, the western part of Karelia belongs to Finland, and the eastern part to Russia. A long period of Russian-Swedish warfare came to an end with the conclusion of the peace treaty of Stolbova in 1617. Swedish supremacy was at its height in the 17th century when Karelia, as far as the northern coast of Lake Ladoga, formed part of the Kingdom of Sweden. Swedish authorities initiated a rigid campaign to make the Karelians renounce their Orthodox confession and turn to the Protestant faith. During those years of oppression many Karelians left their homes, moved to the region of Tver and settled in the Valdai Hills. Their number is estimated at 25,000 to 30,000 persons.

In the aftermath of the Bolshevik coup d'état in October 1917 the Karelians favored a union with Finland that became independent after the civil war of 1917–18. However, the newly established Soviet regime opposed the separation of Karelia from Russia. Finland made an initiative to put the Karelian question on the agenda of the League of Nations, the predecessor of the United Nations. A resolution was given in favor of Karelia's independence but this had no effect on the political development. The territory was organized as an autonomous Soviet Socialist Republic (i.e., Karelian A.S.S.R.) within the borders of Soviet Russia. In 1940, the status was upgraded to that of an independent Soviet republic (i.e., Karelo-Finnish S.S.R.) but reduced again to an A.S.S.R., in 1956. Since 1991, Karelia has been a republic, with Petrozavodsk as its capital, in the new Russian federal state.

Karelian folklore is rich in epic songs which have been collected, as part of Finnish literature, in the voluminous work of the *Kalevala* (see Chapter 7). While, in Finland, Kalevala poetry played a crucial role in the movement of national awakening in the 19th century, among the Karelians, it was esteemed as a medium of their folklore, not as a vehicle for any national movement, because something like a national awakening did not happen in Karelia. Epic poetry which was so popular in Karelia, has been preserved there longer than in other communities of Baltic-Finnic peoples in the Baltic region.

As a written language, Karelian has never been widespread and the literary tradition was never continuous. In the early 19th century, some books of religious literature were published, among them a prayer book in 1804 (in the Olonets dialect) and a translation of St. Matthew's Gospel in 1820 (in the Tver dialect). In the 1920s and 1930s, literature was published in various Karelian dialects. The project promoted by the Soviet Finno-Ugric scholar D. Bubrich to create a common written standard for Karelian on the basis of the Cyrillic script was short-lived and ended in 1939.

For decades, Russian has dominated all domains of literacy in the areas with Karelian population. The preservation of Karelian cultural heritage is mostly an agenda of Karelian activists but, among a broader Karelian public, it is fading. Since 1989 Karelian has been written again and is used in elementary schools. Karelian is recognized as a regional language in Karelia but it does not share equal rights with Russian, which functions as the official language of the republic. Finnish, which is mutually intelligible with northern Karelian, is granted official status alongside Russian.

## Finnish: Some Specifics

Finnish is most closely related to Karelian, and to Ingrian (Izhorian), spoken in Ingermanland, in the western part of the Leningrad district (Leningradskaia oblast'). These three languages together with Votic, Veps (both spoken in Russia), Estonian and Livonian (spoken in Latvia) form the Baltic-Finnic (Fennic) group of languages (Abondolo 1998: 97f.).

This group is one among several groupings of Finno-Ugric languages, the others being Finnic-Volgaic (Mordvin: Erzia and Moksha, Mari: Mountain and Meadow Mari), Finnic-Permic (Komi, Komi-Permiak, Udmurt), Ob-Ugric (Khanty, Mansi), Saami, and Hungarian, the latter being most closely related to the Ob-Ugric languages (Austerlitz

1990). Saami actually represents several languages which were formerly collectively referred to as Lappish (Korhonen 1981).

The Finno-Ugric languages are one of two major branches constituting the Uralic phylum of languages. The other branch are the Samoyed languages (Enets, Nenets, Nganasan, Selkup), most of whose speakers live in the Siberian part of Russia. Regarding the geographical distribution of Uralic languages in Eurasia, those of the Finno-Ugric branch have predominantly spread in northern Europe, while those of the Samoyed branch are spoken in northern Siberia.

The distribution of regional varieties of Finnish shows two major groupings: a western and an eastern dialect cluster (Viitso 1998: 97; figure 17). The local variations of Finnish have their origin in the historical movements of Baltic-Finnic tribes on the mainland and around the Gulf of Finland. The profile of the western dialects was shaped in an area where the descendants of two older tribes settled, the Finns Proper (*varsinais-suomalaiset*) and the Tavastians (*hämäläiset*). These Finnic people mainly came from regions south of the Gulf of Finland, from what is nowadays Estonia, between ca. 500 BCE and the beginnings of the CE.

The eastern Finnish dialects have originated from the Finnic population that migrated into Finland through the Karelian Isthmus. These Finns belonged to the third major tribe, the Karelians (*karjalaiset*). There is a continuum of dialectal features connecting the eastern dialects of Finnish with the local varieties of neighboring Karelian and Lydian. That the development of the spoken language of the eastern Karelians diverged from that of the southeastern dialects of Finnish in the course of time is due to the influence of cultural and political boundaries.

Standard written Finnish has eight vowels. In addition to the five vowels of the English sound system (a, e, i, o, u) there are the front vowels ä, ö and y (in Finnish orthography for ü). The length of sounds is phonemic in Finnish, which means that the meanings of Finnish words change, depending on whether a vowel is short or long. All eight vowels may be short or long. This phonemic distinction raises the total number of Finnish vowel phonemes to 16. In addition to the simple vowel phonemes (monophthongs), Finnish knows various combinations of single vowels to form

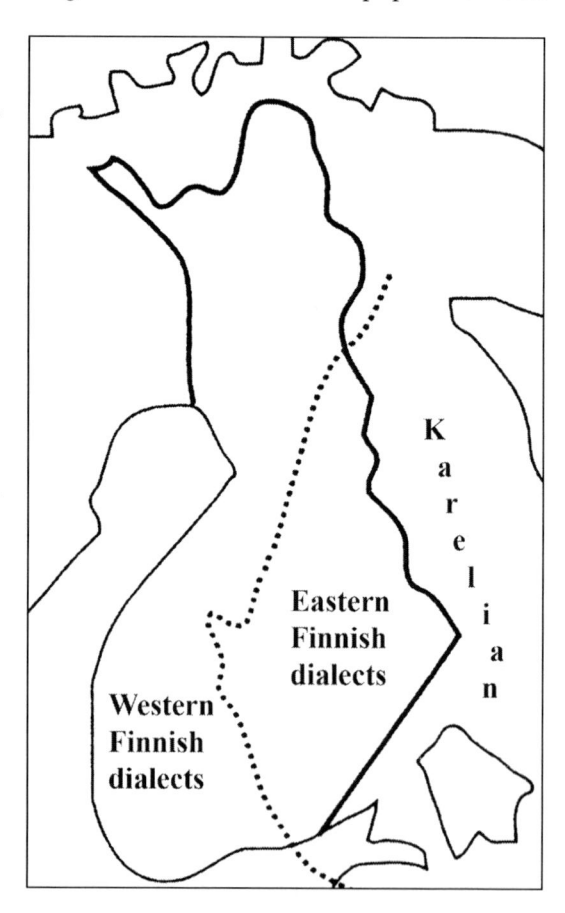

**Figure 17: The division of Finnish dialect areas (drawing by the author).**

diphthongs (two-vowel combinations; e.g., *tauko* "pause") and triphthongs (three-vowel combinations; e.g., *kauan* "long").

In Finnish, there are 15 simple consonants, of which the plosives (e.g., p, t, k), liquids (l, r), nasals (m, n) and s may appear as short or long sounds. Among the peculiarities of the Finnish consonant system is the absence of voiced plosives in initial position (e.g., b-, d-, g-). These sounds only occur in recent loanwords (e.g., *bussi* "bus," *disketti* "disquette," *galluppi* "gallup"). Long consonants occur in word-medial position only. There are no restrictions as to the association of vowels and consonants in syllables. Short vowels may be associated with short or long consonants. The same is true for long vowels (e.g., *satumaa* "fairyland," *sattuma* "accident," *satama* "harbor," *saattama* "accompanied"; *tapan* "I kill" versus *tapaan* "I meet," *hän tappaa* "he kills" versus *hän tapaa* "he meets").

Given the richness of monophthongs and diphthongs which contrasts with the fairly restricted set of consonants, in Finnish speech, vocalic sounds have a higher frequency than consonants. By its specific proportions of vowels and consonants in the phonetic chain, Finnish distinguishes itself from the great majority of languages in Europe. When counting the sounds in the phonetic chain of a variety of languages, the following proportions of consonants (per 100 vowels) can be identified for individual languages (Hakulinen 1979: 15):

> Finnish—96; Italian—108; Ancient Greek—117; Spanish—122; Welsh—122, Latin—127; Turkish—132; Sanskrit—138; Hungarian—141; French—141; Kazan Tatar—141; Biblical Gothic—144; Russian—150; Swedish—161; German—177; Czech—188.

Since the 16th century, Finnish has been written in the Latin script. The orthographic means of rendering the phonemic opposition of short and long sounds in writing devised by the father of the Finnish written language, the Protestant bishop Mikael Agricola, has persisted into the modern period. Shortness is indicated by a single letter, length by doubling the written sign; e.g., *kirja* "book" with a short vowel in each syllable, *saamaan* "for receiving" with a long vowel in each syllable, *reilu* "fair" with a short intervocalic consonant (-l-), *hallitus* "government" with a long intervocalic consonant (-ll-).

In a worldwide comparison of writing systems, Finnish is the only language where the sound structure is almost perfectly rendered in writing. There is only one exception to the functioning of the principle of sound-written sign equivalence in Finnish orthography, this being the -ng- simple sound, as in English *sing* or German *Hang* (e.g., *kuningas* "king" or in *ongelma* "problem").

Among the most prominent properties of Finnish word structure is regular alternation of the word stem, or to be more precise: changes within the stem which occur in conjunction with the addition of specific elements. These alternations (called *astevaihtelu* "gradation" in Finnish) are governed by a multiple set of specific rules which cause phonemic changes in the stem of words. Altogether there are 130 stem classes. Of these, 85 are classes of noun inflection, and 45 are classes of verb inflection. Attempts to reduce the number of classes to a few or only one have so far been unsuccessful (Haarmann 2003: 880ff.).

Of the various techniques to produce systematic alternation (i.e., consonant gradation, consonant assimilation, vowel mutation, vowel loss), consonant gradation is the most widely applied technique. In consonant gradation, two grades are distinguished, a strong grade and a weak grade. These correlate with specific syllable types. The strong grade correlates with an open syllable, the weak grade with a closed syllable. Open syllables are those ending in a vowel, closed syllables end in a consonant. The sound changes which occur when consonant gradation operates may be quantitative (e.g., pp : p, *piippu* "pipe" / nominative case: *piipun* "pipe" / genitive case) and qualitative (e.g., k : ø, *joki* "river" / nominative: *joen* "river" / genitive).

Word formation in Finnish knows the following techniques: derivation by means of a suffix; derivation by means of a prefix; compound words. Given the highly inflectional nature of the Finnish language, Finnish words can be very long. The longest word recorded by the Guinness World Records is comprised of 61 letters (*lentokonesuihkuturbiinimoottoriapumekaanikkoaliupseerioppilas* "A non-commissioned officer apprentice, being an assistant mechanic of an airplane's jet turbine motor"). The term for a certain technical part of a nuclear plant has 66 letters (*atomiydinenergiareaktorigeneraattorilauhduttajaturbiiniratasvaihde* "a nuclear plant reactor's condenser turbine wheel switch") (Karilas 2003: 226).

Finnish grammar possesses a complex case system. Only a few languages in Europe such as Estonian, Hungarian, and Basque have case systems matching the complexity of the Finnish system (figure 18). The Finnish case system includes numerous functions that are expressed in other languages using prepositional phrases.

| Case | Suffix | Singular | Plural | Function |
|---|---|---|---|---|
| Nominative | *-ø; -t* | *nainen* | *naiset* | definite (quantity) |
| | | *vesi* | *vedet* | |
| Accusative | *-n; -t* | *naisen* | *naiset* | definite (quantity) |
| | | *veden* | *vedet* | |
| Genitive | *-n* | *naisen* | *naisten* | pertaining to |
| | | *veden* | *vesien* | |
| General local cases: | | | | |
| Essive | *-nalä* | *naisena* | *naisina* | as |
| | | *vetenä* | *vesinä* | |
| Partitive | *-alä; -tlä* | *naista* | *naisia* | indefinite (quantity) |
| | | *vettä* | *vesiä* | |
| Translative | *-ksi* | *naiseksi* | *naisiksi* | (transformed) into |
| | | *vedeksi* | *vesiksi* | |
| Interior local cases: | | | | |
| Inessive | *-ssalä* | *naisessa* | *naisissa* | in |
| | | *vedessä* | *vesissä* | |
| Elative | *-stalä* | *naisesta* | *naisista* | from (inside) |
| | | *vedestä* | *vesistä* | |
| Illative | *-Vn; -hVn* | *naiseen* | *naisiin* | into |
| | | *veteen* | *vesiin* | |
| Exterior local cases: | | | | |
| Adessive | *-llalä* | *naisella* | *naisilla* | at, with, on |
| | | *vedellä* | *vesillä* | |
| Ablative | *-ltalä* | *naiselta* | *naisilta* | from |
| | | *vedeltä* | *vesiltä* | |
| Allative | *-lle* | *naiselle* | *naisille* | to (local) |
| | | *vedelle* | *vesille* | |
| Instructive | *-in* | *naisin* | *naisin* | in form or role of |
| | | *vesin* | *vesin* | |
| Comitative | *-ineen* | *naisineen* | *naisineen* | accompanied by |
| | *(-ine)* | *vesinee* | *vesineen* | |
| Abessive | *-ttalä* | *naisetta* | *naisitta* | without |
| | | *vedettä* | *vesittä* | |

**Figure 18: The Finnish case system (sample words *nainen* "woman" and *vesi* "water"; from Harald Haarmann, "Finnish," in Thorsten Roelcke, ed., *Variation Typology* [Berlin: Mouton de Gruyter, 2003], pp. 866–904; p. 883, fig. 32.12).**

In Finnish, negation is not expressed by adding a negative pronoun or adverb to a verbal expression, but by using a negative auxiliary, the stem of which is *e-*. The negative auxiliary is inflected like other verbs and distinguishes person: *en* "I ... not," *et* "you ... not," *hän ei* "he/she ... not," *emme* "we ... not," *ette* "you (pl.) ... not," *he eivät* "they ... not." Tense and mood, but not person, are indicated by the main verb which is negated, e.g., *hän ei nuku* "he/she does not sleep," *et mennyt* "you did not go," *en tulisi* "I would not come," compare English I don't like, he doesn't like, I didn't like.

One of the most exotic features of Finnish is the unusual construction for expressing possession. Foreigners take it as natural that, in every language, there is a verb "to have." What may seem natural to outsiders is not natural to the Finns. In Finnish, there is no special verb with the meaning "to have." Certainly, one can express the idea of having something in Finnish, but this is done by using a nominal construction. In order to say "I have a mobile phone" a Finn would paraphrase *minulla on kännykkä* which literally means "a mobile phone is with me." The phrase is made up of the following components: *minä* "I" (*minulla*: stem *minu-* + *-lla* illative case) + *kännykkä* "mobile phone."

## Finnish Americans and American Finnish (Finglish)

Finnish has been spoken in the Americas as early as the 17th century. The first colonists, "many of them Finnish immigrants from Värmland" (Hovdhaugen et al. 2000: 99), who came to settle in the New World founded a colony called New Sweden on the lower Delaware river, as early as 1638. The colony was integrated into the Dutch-held territory in 1655.

Among the people from Finland who went to North America were also Finland-Swedes. One of them is known as an explorer, Pehr Kalm (1716–1779), who is also known as Peter Kalm in English sources. Kalm studied in Finland (at the Academy of Åbo) and in Sweden (at the University of Uppsala). His domains of expertise were botany and agriculture. In 1747, Kalm visited the colony of New Sweden, on a mission assigned to him by the Royal Swedish Academy of Sciences. His task was to find plants and their seeds that could be cultivated in northern Europe.

Kalm was the first European visitor to give a scientific account of Niagara Falls, in a letter to Benjamin Franklin, dated 2 September 1750.

> Benjamin Franklin published Kalm's letter in his Pennsylvania Gazette on 20th September 1750. The same description also appeared as an appendix to Bartram's travel book, published in London in 1751. This was the first article to make Kalm known in London. When he was back home Kalm drew up a new and more complete account of Niagara.... The description was published by Gjörwell in 1782 in "Upfostrings Sälskapets Tidningar" [Kerkkonen 1959: 116].

After returning to Europe, Kalm wrote several books about his travels (Benson 1987, Robbins 2007).

Some of the notable figures of American history are of Finnish descent. One of the early immigrants who settled down in New Sweden was a Finn called Martti Marttinen who arrived in North America in 1654. Since his surname was too difficult to pronounce for foreigners he changed it to Morton. Martti's great-grandson, John Morton (1725–1777), was among the selected group of those who signed the Declaration of Independence in 1776, Morton signing for Pennsylvania.

The industrialization of North America offered an incentive for many Europeans to emigrate from rural areas and make the journey to the New World, with hopes for a prospective future. For many decades, there was a shortage of work force. The immigrants helped narrow the gap. There were also economic factors that drove Europeans away from their home country, for instance the consecutive crop failures in Finland, in the 1860s, that were responsible for an increase in the emigration movement. Most Finns who immigrated to North America in the 19th century settled in the region around the Great Lakes where, today, most Americans of Finnish descent are living (Björklund 2005). Other areas with Finnish settlements are in the northeast, in Florida and along the West Coast. Some 700,000 people with Finnish ancestry are among the citizens of the U.S. (Kostiainen 2014).

The vernacular spoken by the descendants of Finnish settlers in North America has developed specific features in contact with English. While, in the context of language contacts in northern Finland, Finnish as the dominant language has adopted features of the non-dominant language (varieties of Saami), in the Finnish settlements of North America, the contact situation of Finnish is completely different. In all areas of American Finnish settlements, English dominates in almost all domains of language use, and Finnish is non-dominant. The only exception is private language use at home. In its function as a home language, Finnish dominates or is at least co-dominant with English (Virtaranta 1992). American Finnish is called Finglish (Finn + English) or Fingliska (Finn + engelska). As recently as the 1980s, these labels were considered pejorative. Nowadays, however, there has been a renaissance of local consciousness, favoring the acceptance of a name which denotes linguistic identity.

Finglish is not the name of an individual variety with specific structural features. Rather Finglish is to be understood as a blanket term for characterizing a contact situation, that of the non-dominant Finnish under the influence of the dominant English. The inroads of English into the vocabulary of American Finns are selective. When Finns entered the American workforce they found jobs in the lumber industry easily. That domain was familiar to the Finns from their home country and, since there were always other Finns working at the same place they could communicate in Finnish. Different was the situation in the mining industry.

> Finnish miners and mill workers found themselves in new work environments where they were faced with a host of strange concepts and terms. They also found themselves working beside men who often knew little or no Finnish. Loanwords like *maini* ("mine" F *kaivos*), *proospäkätä* ("to prospect" F *etsiä*) and *trillari* ("driller" F *porakoneen-käyttäjä*) reflect the linguistic needs of the situation ... Finnish American milling vocabulary shows a high degree of loaning from English [Virtanen and DuBois 2000: 61].

Also many terms of daily use have been borrowed from English into American Finnish although the associated concepts are familiar to all Finns coming from Europe; e.g., *vamili* (< family F *perhe*), *leiki* (< lake F *järvi*), *hilli* (< hill F *mäki*). And yet, the concepts are not necessarily the same in Finnish and American culture. In the Finnish social context, *perhe* has a much more restricted meaning than the American idea of family. The borrowed term *vamili* reflects this extension of a more traditional concept.

The impact of English on Finnish in America has been massive, even radical. It is possible to speak intelligible (though stylistically poor) Finnish by making extensive use of borrowings and by inflecting these elements according to Finnish morphophonemic rules; e.g., *pussaa* (< push) *se peipipoki* (baby buggy) *kitsistä* (< kitchen) *petiruumaan* (< bedroom) "Push that baby buggy from the kitchen into the bedroom."

The Finnish-English contacts reflect settings where a dialectal variety of Finnish functions under the situational pressure of the dominant English. Finglish, in fact, stands for a dialectal continuum of Finnish varieties which have been transported overseas and which are embedded in conditions of bilingual language use. Of the local varieties of Finglish, more than half are based on dialects of South and North Ostrobothnia as well as on western Savo dialects (subsumed under *pohjalaismurteet* in Finnish terminology). About one quarter of the Finglish local varieties are spoken by people who themselves or their ancestors emigrated from northern Savo and Kainuu. About 15 percent of Finnish immigrants to America came from Häme and the area of transitional Southwest. Dialects from the Southwest and Southeast are poorly represented in the mosaic of Finglish.

## Finland-Swedes: The Nordic Input in Finland and Its History

Finns and Swedes have been neighbors since the Middle Ages. The far-distant ancestors of both Finns and Swedes had also lived in neighboring areas, some 8,000 years ago. The habitat of the Indo-European pastoralists and their herds were the steppes of southern Russia while Uralian hunters and gatherers roamed the woods further north. The forest-steppe zone on the Middle Volga river was a contact area of the two groups (Parpola 2012).

The presence of the Swedish-speaking population in Finland has a history that reaches back more than a thousand years. The Åland Islands, geographically situated in the northern Baltic Sea halfway between Finland and Sweden, formed part of the cultural sphere of the Vikings in the early Middle Ages. Yet, Viking settlements were abandoned in the 11th century. For some time, Finnish groups occupied some places until a systematic resettlement of the islands by Swedes. By the ninth century, the coastal areas of Finland had been explored by settlers from Sweden who came by boat, crossing the Gulf of Bothnia. Ever more settlers arrived with the intention to stay (figure 19).

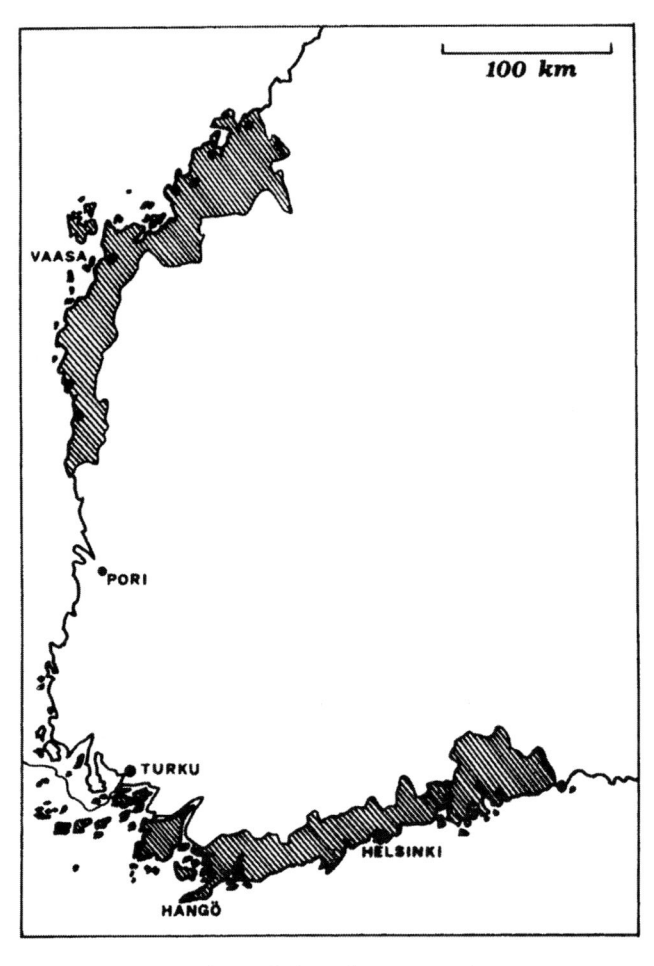

**Figure 19: Areas with Swedish settlements on the west coast and on the south coast of Finland (drawing by the author).**

## The Coming of Christianity

The Swedish newcomers settled on the western and southern coast of Finland. Swedish people's interest in Finland was the exploration of profitable fishing grounds and the occupation of arable land, both of which were available in plenitude along the coast and further inland. Those who came from Sweden brought a cultural good to Finland that would change the very foundations of Finnish society, Christianity (Purhonen 1998). Their enterprise was later backed up by Swedish authorities that organized three crusades (the first around 1150, the second in the 1240s, and the third into Karelia in 1293). The crusades were carried out following various aims; two were to militarily secure occupied land that was annexed to the territory of the Kingdom of Sweden and to spread Christianity among the native population.

There are various accounts, including legend, how Christianity rooted among the Finns. According to some the spread of the new religion was peaceful and did not encounter any significant opposition. According to others, the Finns did not accept the foreign faith without resistance. Despite the successful outcome of the first crusade, missionary work was interrupted by the murder of a Christian dignitary, the bishop Henry. He is known as Henrik (in Swedish) and as Henri or Heikki (in Finnish). Henry, the murdered victim, became a popular figure in Finnish folk tradition. The early history of Christianity and Swedish rule in Finland crystallizes around the figure of bishop Henry who is commemorated both by the Catholic and Protestant churches of Finland. Whether Henry is an historical figure has remained a matter of dispute, but his memory lives on in popular tradition and in Finnish schoolbooks (Heikkilä 2005). As to Henry's life, no reliable proof exists about any of his activities. He is said to have come to Sweden from England and may have been ordained as archbishop of Uppsala. He allegedly joined King Eric on his crusade to Finland where he engaged in missionary work in the region of Turku.

Legend has it that Henry was murdered by a Finnish peasant called Lalli. Lalli pursued Henry while the clergyman was driving a sledge over the ice of Lake Köyliö and slew him with his axe. Henry had been falsely accused by Lalli's wife of having stolen food for himself and provisions for his horses while resting at Lalli's home. In the liturgical calendar, the day of his death is commemorated as January 19, 1156, and January 19 is Henry's name day in Finland and in Sweden.

Henry is remembered as a Christian martyr. Since 1296, he has been referred to as a saint in papal records. His image first appears on the seal of the bishop of Turku in 1299. Henry's grave is unknown although, according to legend, his bones were translated to the church of Nousiainen, at a distance of some 140 km from Köyliö. In the church, there is an (empty) sarcophagus, with pictures of King Eric's crusade. The island of Kirkkokari, in Lake Köyliö, is a place of pilgrimage for the Catholic church in Finland. An "Ecumenical pilgrimage of St. Henry" is organized for the route between Köyliö and Nousiainen.

The Swedish clergy did not give up but continued their effort to conquer souls among the Finns. Christianity proceeded at varying pace, and it took centuries before parishes had been established in all parts of the country. In the 13th century there were only two towns—Turku (founded 1229) in the southwest and Viipuri (founded 1293) in Karelia—where Christian-oriented culture dominated; "elsewhere in the country pagan customs coexisted vigorously among the common people alongside forms of Christian culture" (Nuorteva 1997a: 523).

Such were the conditions during the early centuries of Swedish rule in Finland after the southwestern regions of the country had become part of the Kingdom of Sweden. Those who brought Christianity to Finland in the Middle Ages were Swedes, but those who struggled to eradicate shamanism in Lapland were Finnish priests. And this struggle lasted well into the 18th century (Rydving 1993).

The Swedish campaign to spread Christianity among the Finns was not the only enterprise to make this religion popular in Fenno-Scandia. Another trail originated from the south, and this was the missionary movement of the Orthodox church whose priests made efforts to convert the eastern Finns and Karelians.

> In order to express the new concepts the church had to resort to loan words, taken from Swedish in the west and Russian in the east. The Roman Catholic Church used such words as *synti* (sin, the older word being *pattoinen*, Estonian *patt*), *rippi* (confession), *kirkko* (church), *luostari* (monastery), *munkki* (monk), *messu* (Mass), *paasto* (Lent). The Greek Orthodox Church of Karelia correspondingly took Russian loan words, such as *räähkä* (Russian *grjech*), *tsasouna* or *säässynä* (Russian *tsasovna*), *manaster* (Russian *monastyr*) and *monahko* (Russian *monach*) [Talve 1997: 233].

## Swedish Social Institutions in Finland

During the times of Viking activities, Finns became engaged in the long-distance trade between Scandinavia in the North and Byzantium in the South. Finnish traders established themselves at Novgorod in northwestern Russia. The oldest quarters in the town of Novgorod had inhabitants who distinguished themselves by their ethnic affiliation: Slavs, Balts and Finns.

As a consequence of intensifying contacts, also the Finnish heartland became subject to outside influence. Foreign political patronage over Finnish lands increased from the 12th century on. By the 13th century, Finland had become a part of Sweden which exposed the country and its Finnish settlers, like a buffer zone, to Russian expansionist intentions. Especially destructive were Russian raids on Finnish settlements in the 16th century. The political border between Sweden and Russia shifted many times, and every time it was drawn anew through Finnish territory (http://modersmal.skolverket.se/finska/index.php/opetus/ylaeaste-lukio/suomi-tietoa/880-suomen-rajat-1323-1944; Paavolainen 1958; figure 20).

The only exception was the border that was established with the peace treaty of Stolbova in 1617 when the political power of Sweden was at its height and all coastal areas around the Gulf of Finland were Swedish-held territory. Then, the Swedish-Russian border was fixed at a distance from the Finnish heartland.

Since the Finns were Swedish subjects, the development of their religion and culture followed the trends in other parts of the Kingdom of Sweden. When, in the 16th century, the Lutheran version of Protestantism was adopted by the king of Sweden, Gustav Vasa (reigned 1523–1560), the new religion was transferred to all parts of the Swedish empire and its citizens. Protestantism spread among the Finns and is nowadays professed by some 83 percent of Finland's population.

Since 1634, the governing body in Sweden was the State Council with 25 members. The majority were Swedish aristocrats and only some were Finns. In great contrast to the social conditions in neighboring Russia, the peasants in Finland were free and not

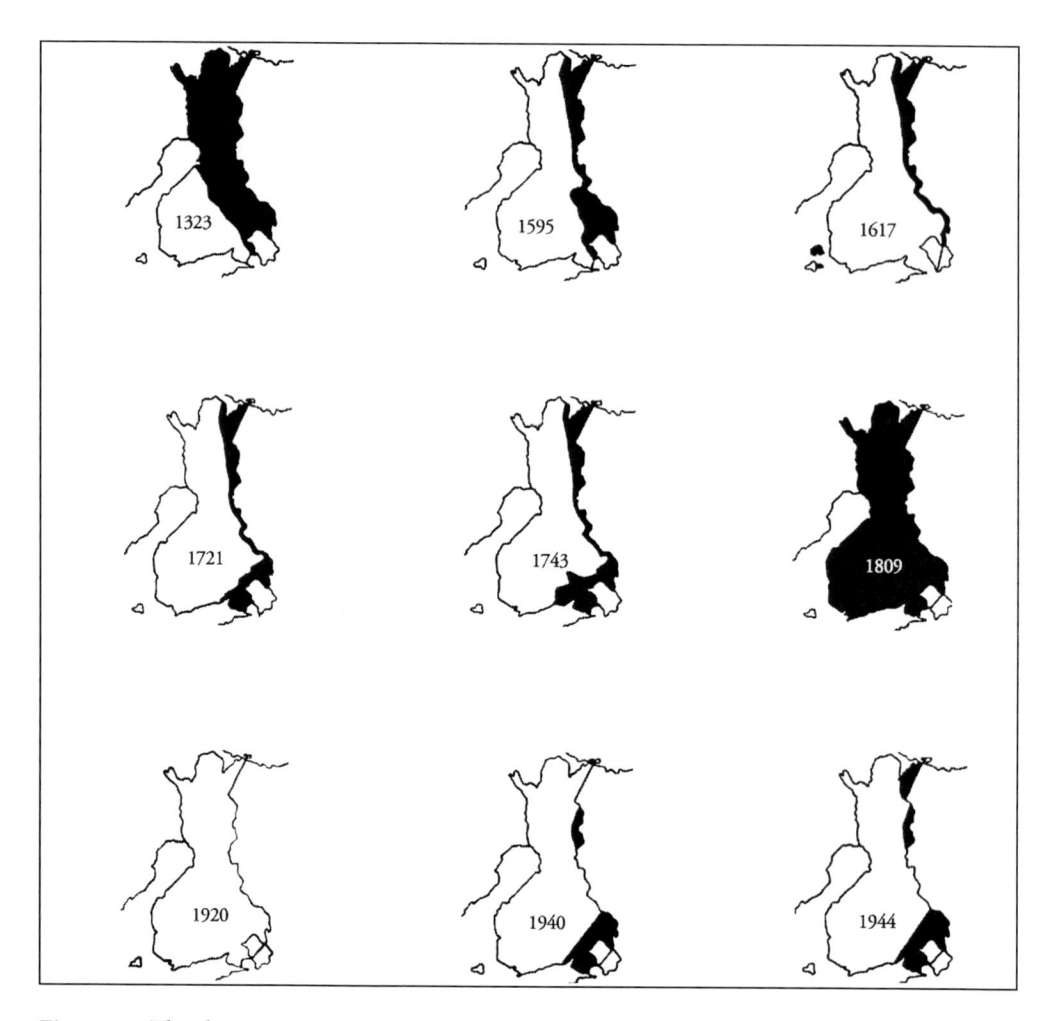

Figure 20: The changing territorial borders of Finland since the Middle Ages (Finnish Authorities; Ministry of Education; http://modersmal.skolverket.se/finska/index.php/opetus/ylaeastelukio/suomi-tietoa/880-suomen-rajat-1323-1944; Paavolainen 1958).
Key:

Areas in white are those regions of Finland under Swedish rule (until 1809) and since the times of Finland's independence (1917/1920). Areas in black are those regions of Finland that were occupied by Russia or ceded to Russia.

1323: Treaty of Nöteborg (Finnish Pähkinäsaari, Russian Oreshek, German Schlüsselburg), dividing Finnish territory between the Kingdom of Sweden and the Novgorod Republic

1595: Treaty of Teusina between Sweden and tsarist Russia

1617: Treaty of Stolbova between Sweden and Russia

1721: Treaty of Nystad between Sweden and Russia

1743: Treaty of Turku between Sweden and Russia

1809: Treaty of Hamina; Sweden acknowledges the annexation of Finland to the Russian Empire; the Diet convenes at Borgå (Porvoo) and tsar Alexander I confirms Finland's constitution (dating to the times of Swedish rule) and religion; Finland becomes part of Russia, as a Grand Duchy

1920: Treaty of Tartu (Dorpat) between independent Finland and Soviet Russia

1940: Treaty of Moscow after the Winter War (1939/40) (see Chapter 4 for the events of this war)

1944: Treaty of Moscow after the Continuation War (1941–44) (see Chapter 4 for the events of this war)

bound by serfdom. Even during the period when Finland formed part of tsarist Russia (between 1809 and 1917) the social order established by Swedish authority, including the freedom of the peasantry, persisted.

## The Impact of Swedish on Finnish

For some 600 years, the Swedish and Finnish languages have been in contact and, for the longest time of this history Swedish functioned as the language of prestige, as the medium of administration, jurisdiction and higher education. Swedish-speaking people in Finland have their own cultural life, have their own theater, schools and two universities, produce their own writers who write in Swedish (e.g., Jörn Donner) and have their own Finland-oriented Swedish literature (Stenwall 2001). Although the written variety of Swedish used in Finland follows the same norms as Swedish in Sweden, the Swedish *spoken* in Finland differs from Swedish in Sweden. What catches everybody's ear who listens to the two varieties, to the language used in Sweden (*rikssvenska*) and to Swedish in Finland (*finlandssvenska*), is that the latter lacks the kind of musical intonation which is typical of the former. In Finland-Swedish, some expressions from older Swedish have been preserved which have come out of use in Sweden.

The prestigious role of Swedish and its importance in Finnish society explain why there are some 4000 Swedish loanwords in Finnish but only a few Finnish borrowings in Swedish. Expressions of Swedish origin are found at all levels of Finnish language use, in the written and spoken language, in the vocabulary of local dialects and in slang. Among the Swedish loanwords are many expressions of daily life with a wide range such as Finnish *juusto* "cheese" (< Swedish *ost*), *sänky* "bed" (< *säng*), *katu* "street" (< *gata*) or *ranta* "beach" (< *strand*) and also elements of more specialized terminology such as *vanki* "prisoner" (< *fånge*), *kivääri* "rifle" (< *gevär*) or *pora* "drill" (< *borr*). The series of terms for the days of the week in Finnish are borrowed from Swedish, either as direct loans or in the form of calques:

> *maanantai* "Monday" (< Old Swedish *manadagher*; Modern Swedish *måndag*)
> *tiistai* "Tuesday" (< Old Swedish *tisdagher*, Modern Swedish *tisdag*)
> *keskiviikko* "Wednesday," literally "middle week" (< calque based on the model
> of Old Norse *midvikudagr*)
> *torstai* "Thursday" (< Old Swedish *thorsdagher*, Modern Swedish *torsdag*)
> *perjantai* "Friday" (< Old Swedish *freadagher* or *friadagher*, Modern Swedish *fredag*)
> *lauantai* (< Scandinavian: Old Norse *laugardagr*, Old Swedish *lögherdagher*,
> literally "bath day")
> *sunnuntai* "Sunday" (< Old Swedish *sunnodagher*, Modern Swedish *söndag*)

A number of Swedish words that were integrated into the vocabulary of Finnish slang are also used in common spoken language; e.g., *satsata* "to invest in; to make provisions for" (< *satsa*), *tienata* "to earn" (< *tjäna*), *likka* "girl" (< *flicka*).

Hundreds of Swedish borrowings have penetrated the vocabulary of western Finnish dialects. Such terms are used by dialect speakers but are unknown in the standard or written language. In the South Ostrobothnian dialect, one finds expressions such as *hantuuki* "hand-towel" (< *handtuk*; for Finnish *käsipyyhe*) or *ranstakka* "fire-iron" (< *randstak*; for Finnish *hiilihanko*). Some modernisms of Swedish origin are widespread in certain Finnish dialects but are not used in the common Finnish language; e.g., *telefooni* "telephone" (< *telefon*; for Finnish *puhelin*) in the southwestern dialect of Turku and in the local speech of people in Ostrobothnia (Grönholm 1988: 21, 163). This expression is an international neologism in Swedish itself which appeared in Swedish language use not earlier than 1870. In Finnish standard language this older expression was replaced, in 1897, by the genuine term *puhelin*, coined by the Finnish purist movement.

## Russian-Speaking People: One Language—Two Ethnic Groups

During Swedish rule when Finland had been a part of the Kingdom of Sweden, relations with neighboring Russia had been mostly bellicose, and Finnish civilians in the eastern part of the country suffered the most in the wars with Russia. The southeastern part of Finland (east of the Kymi river; called "Old Finland" in Finnish, *Vanha Suomi*) was occupied by Russia in the 1740s.

At a time when Russia was an ally of France under the rule of Napoleon and Sweden had joined the anti–Napoleonic alliance, France supported Russia with its intentions to annex Finland, an objective that was achieved after a military campaign against Sweden. The short war with Sweden, in 1808–09, did not produce an overwhelming victory for Russia. It could be expected that Sweden would have renewed military actions. Tsar Alexander I (ruled 1801–1825) made a swift and far-sighted decision.

> Concerned about the international situation and anxious to pacify Finland as quickly as possible, Alexander I may have been persuaded to shift from his initial declared intention of incorporating Finland into Russia as a conquered territory towards a more accommodating approach. Orders were issued by the military governor Friedrich von Buxhoevden in June–July 1808 for the election of a deputation of members of the estates. This deputation presented a memorial to the tsar in St Petersburg, asking for a general meeting of the estates of the land "to obtain the nation's voice in those matters which concern the wellbeing of all and the common good." On 1 February, Alexander issued the order for the estates to convene in the small town of Borgå for a general *Lantdag* (provincial diet) on 22 March 1809 [Kirby 1995: 5].

The Tsar participated in the *Lantdag* personally. In his speech—given in the language of diplomacy of the time, which was French—Alexander raised Finland's citizens to the status of "a respectable nation" (*nation respectable*), promised to take the "sentiments of the nation" (*sentiments de la nation*) into consideration and expressed his hopes for a favorable future development of "this nation, externally serene and internally free" (*cette nation tranquille au dehors, libre dans l'intérieur*) (Protocoll 1809).

In a noble gesture aimed to minimize unrest among the Finnish population, the Tsar granted Finland the status of a Grand Duchy within the Russian Empire. From a formal standpoint, this meant the continuation of Swedish institutions, and also of Swedish as the internal language of administration. The title of a Grand Duke of Finland had originally been among the titles of the King of Sweden, and it was transferred to the Tsar who became Grand Duke of Finland (in Russian *kniaz' velikiy Finlyandii*). "An authoritarian ruler elsewhere, the Czar of Russia became in 1809 the constitutional monarch of Finland with powers limited by the old Swedish constitution" (Pesonen 1985: 12).

Finland's state ties with Russia are in the past but there has been an influx of Russian-speaking people into Finland, which now has a Russian-speaking minority that is not a coherent group of ethnic Russians. There are two ethnic groups with Russian as first language (or native language, respectively): ethnic Russians and Ingrians with Finnish ancestry.

## Russian-Speaking Immigrants

Russian-speaking people came to Finland in four waves. The most recent of these movements has been the most populous:

(1) The early period of Russian-speaking immigrants dates to the 19th and early 20th centuries, during the period when Finland, as a Grand Duchy, formed part of tsarist Russia. Those who came to Finland were soldiers of the tsarist army, civilian workers and merchants. Of the merchants, hundreds settled in the Grand Duchy. One of the merchant families that stayed in Finland are the Sinebrychoffs who founded one of the big breweries in Finland. The descendants of those ethnic Russians no longer speak Russian but have long since become integrated into the Finnish majority.

(2) A strong motivation for emigrating from former Russia emerged after the Bolshevik coup d'état in October 1917—which was no revolution despite persistent Soviet claims—when Russia plunged into civil war. Finland, which had gained independence as the result of a civil war of her own, became the haven for refugees from Russia. The high point of emigration from the newly established Soviet state was in the early 1920s when some 33,000 Russians took refuge in Finland. Some of the descendants of those refugees still know the language of their ancestors but most experienced a shift to Finnish in the intergenerational transition.

(3) During the later decades of the Soviet regime (starting in the 1960s), a new motivation for Russian emigration to Finland arose. Russian women became interested in Finnish living standards and quite a number of them managed to establish social relations with Finnish men while they visited the Soviet Union as tourists. Emigration for Soviet citizens was granted once legal documents of their marriage with foreigners could be presented to Soviet officials. Thousands of Russian women married Finnish men and established families in Finland.

(4) A recent wave of immigration to Finland was initiated by the changes that took place in the process of the disintegration of Soviet rule, which officially came to an end with the dissolution of the former Soviet state and the establishment of modern Russia in 1991. Since the 1990s, there has been immigration of Russian-speaking people into Finland, and they belong to two ethnic groups. One group are ethnic Russians, among them guest workers and, since the 2000s, *nouveaux riches* who have settled in eastern Finland with their families to avoid conditions of social insecurity in their home country. The other group were Ingrians (see below).

Those immigrants who came with the first two waves (up to the 1920s) are called "Old Russians." As of today, there are more than 65,000 Russian-speaking people living in Finland of whom about half are Ingrians. Some 30,000 are citizens of the Russian Federation. Many of those who speak Russian are among the urban residents in the cities of the south, some 12,000 in Helsinki, 4,000 in Vantaa, 3,000 in Espoo.

## Russian-Speaking Ingrians

Some of their ancestors of the Ingrians had moved from Finland across the Gulf of Finland to the coastal area of what became known as Ingermanland (Ingria), west of St. Petersburg. The Ingrians settled in the south in the 17th century, and they set out to explore land for farming, at a time when all the land around the Gulf of Finland was under Swedish rule (Kepsu 2014). When, in the 18th century, Ingermanland was occupied by Russia the long period of Ingrian-Russian contacts began. Yet, the Finnish-speaking population in Ingria kept their language and home culture for a long time. Still in the 1920s, in the early days of the Soviet Union, social cohesion among the Ingrians was strong. "All business and administrative work in this area [Ingria] was conducted in the Finnish language because the majority of the population was Finnish and the level of Russian language knowledge was lower than in other areas" (Zadneprovskaya 1999: 93). During World War II and in the postwar period, many of the Ingrian communities rapidly disintegrated.

The core of the Ingrian population are descendants of the local Fennic population in the eastern Baltic region, and their language (Ingrian-Finnish) has developed distinctive features since the end of the first millennium CE (Laanest 1986: 4). Ingrian has been under prolonged pressure from Russian. The Ingrian vocabulary has been heavily influenced by Russian loanwords, and many terms have even replaced expressions of daily life such as *ostrov* "island" (< Russian *ostrov*, Finnish *saari*), *kulakal* "fist" (< R *kulak*, F *nyrkki*), *traapit* "stairs" (< R *trap*, F *portaat*, colloquial F *raput*).

In the period after World War II, Finnish was stigmatized, in Ingria, as the language of fascists and "enemies of the people." As a consequence, many parents would not teach their children Ingrian-Finnish but Russian and would speak Russian even at home.

> Those people who speak good Finnish or Ingrian-Finnish tend to be as old as 70 years. While many people who are 50 or 60 years of age speak Finnish, they know Russian much better…. Many middle-aged people do not speak (or understand) Finnish, while their (now often deceased) parents were able to do so very well. A young speaker of Ingrian-Finnish is a rarity anywhere in the region [Ilkka and Muusa Savijärvi 1999: 46].

The immigration of Ingrian Finns in the early 1990s has been characterized as "the third wave of Ingrian-Finnish migration to Finland" (Nevalainen 1991: 296). The first wave came as refugees after the establishment of Soviet power in Russia in 1918. The second wave came in 1942–43 during the siege of Leningrad by the German Wehrmacht. In a move of reconciliation, the former president of Finland, Mauno Koivisto (in office from 1982 until 1994), granted Ingrians the right to return to their ancestor's home country. Thousands of Ingrians seized the opportunity and immigrated to Finland (Malinen 1999). As part of their integration into Finnish society Ingrians had to take courses in Finnish to learn the language of their forefathers as a second language.

## Russian Loanwords in Finnish

Contacts between Russian tribes pushing north and Baltic Finns in the area around the Gulf of Finland date to the early Middle Ages. Since then contacts have continuously unfolded, at times interrupted by wars, up to the present. In the course of time, Russian lexical borrowings entered the Finnish vocabulary. Most of these loanwords are found in the eastern dialects of Finnish. Since the modern literary language includes features of eastern dialects, there is also a greater number of Russian borrowings in its vocabulary as compared to the older literary standard, based on the western dialects where one finds only a few Russian elements. The number of Russian borrowings in written and colloquial Finnish amounts to some 350 expressions (Plöger 1973).

There is an older layer of borrowings (e.g., *risti* "cross" < *krest, ikkuna,* western dialect *akkuna* "window" < *okno, riesa* "nuisance" < Old Russian *greza, palsta* "patch of land" < *polosa, raja* "border" < *kraj*) which are less numerous than the more recent ones (e.g., *urakka* "contract; piecework" < *urok, tarina* "tale, story" < *starina, kiisseli* "jelly" < *kisel, piirakka* "pirog" < *pirog, torakka* "cockroach" < *tarakan*). Russian loanwords are most frequent in epic folklore of which the national epic *Kalevala* is composed. The epic tradition has been most vivid in the eastern region of Finland and, thus, language use associated with folklore has retained many words of Russian origin which are unknown in the modern standard language.

Russian expressions have also infiltrated Finnish slang (e.g., *safka* "food stuff" < *zakuska*). A popular expression which is also widely used in colloquial language, is *mesta* (< Russian *mesto* "place") which may refer to a pub, to a disco or to a place where an indoor festival takes place.

## Russian in Finnish Media

In addition to the languages of the indigenous Finnish citizens (Finnish, Swedish, Saami) Russian is also used in the Finnish broadcasting network. News in Russian are broadcast once a day in the afternoon. The largest Russian-language discussion forum, Russian.fi, was introduced to give the Russian-speaking residents of Finland a chance to exchange views. The site is frequently visited by Russian speakers. Yet, a new kind of problem emerged after the Melanesian aircraft MH 17 had been shot down over eastern Ukraine in July 2014. The forum was flooded by messages that obviously were sent from "journalist"-agents stationed in Russia with the intent of discrediting criticism by Finnish political leaders and whitewashing Russian actions. The Finns use the word "trolling" (as *trollata*) to describe this phenomenon practiced by Russian media ever since the crisis in Ukraine started. "Trolling" messages are highly offensive and aggressive in their rhetoric and extremely Russian-nationalistic. This behavior resembles similar activities during the Cold War, but modernized (shifted to digital media). The webmaster of the forum, Veronika Solovian, had to close down the forum several times to dispose of the junk messages (http://yle.fi/uutiset, 18 July 2015).

## *Jews in Finland: Merging with the Majority*

Nowadays, there are some 1,500 Jews living in Finland who form one of the numerous diaspora groups of Jewish population in many parts of the world. They speak Finnish (or Swedish) and share living conditions with the majority population. The ancestors of these Jews came to Finland long ago. The first recorded Jewish resident in a Finnish town was Jacob Weikam who Fennicized his name as Veikkanen and who settled in the town of Hamina (on the southern coast), in 1782. The Jews who came to Finland in the 19th century, during the period of the Grand Duchy (1809–1917), were merchants or craftsmen. Others served in the tsarist army and were allowed to stay in Finland after their retirement. Once Finland had been established as an independent country, Jews received full citizenship.

## Jewish Culture and the Ashkenazim

The transfer of Jewish culture to northern Europe is associated with a long trail of migration across this continent. Although the region of origin of Jewish populations is the Near East there are markers of Jewishness in Europe which are typically European, and these are the languages that are used only in Jewish communities. One is Yiddish, which is the exclusive marker of Ashkenazic Jewry. The Jewish version of Spanish, Judeo-Spanish, marks the identity of Sephardic Jews in Europe. Both of these languages once flourished as media of literacy and high culture. Yiddish still does but mostly outside Europe, in the USA. The number of speakers of Yiddish and Judeo-Spanish drastically declined, as the result of ethnic cleansing since the Middle Ages and, in particular, the Holocaust crimes committed by the Nazis during World War II. The Holocaust (from Greek *holos* "whole" and *kaustos* "burnt") is known as the Shoah in Hebrew.

In 321, Jews are first mentioned as citizens of the town of Cologne on the Middle Rhine. In the early centuries of the present era, the Jews in Europe lived in the Rhine valley and in adjacent areas. In the Talmud, Ashkenaz is identified with the part of the Roman empire called Germania. From the sixth to the 11th century more and more Jews migrated, from Mediterranean countries to the towns along the big rivers (such as the Seine, Rhine, Danube). In the early Middle Ages (eleventh century), Ashkenaz referred to Franco-German communities (Wigoder 1989: 81ff.).

In time, Jews became the target of resentment among non–Jews. The Ashkenazim were envied because of their economic success and they raised suspicion among the surrounding majority because of their religious life in segregation. In successive actions the Jews were persecuted and expelled from western Europe, from England (1290), France (1306, 1394), and Germany (13th and 15th centuries). As a consequence of rising tensions and interethnic frictions, Jews were driven to the East, to Poland, Lithuania, Ukraine and, later, to Russia where their history remained as troubled as before.

In their medieval communities of the Rhineland the Jews had adopted the local language, Middle High German, which they spoke in a typically Jewish way, spiced with Hebrew words and biblical phraseology. This language became known as Yiddish and it was transferred to the East by Ashkenazic migrants. In contact with the languages of eastern Europe (with Polish and Russian in particular), grammatical structures and vocabulary were affected by foreign influence. One of the typical features of Yiddish as a Jewish language is its fusion character, and "fusion processes can be found in literally every nook of the language" (Weinreich 1980: 32f.); e.g., *poyerte* ("peasant woman") with a German root and a Hebrew suffix, *gotenyu* ("Lord") with a German root and a Slavic component, *sedl* ("small park") with a Slavic root and a German ending, *kolboynik* ("rascal") with a Hebrew root and a Slavic suffix.

During World War II, a bizarre situation arose, with democratic Finland fighting against the Red Army in alliance with Nazi Germany. After the outbreak of the Continuation War, in June 1941, Finnish units fought on the front in Karelia in concerted actions with troops of the German Wehrmacht. Among the Finnish soldiers there were some 300 Jews. These Jews had a field synagogue, in the presence of Germans as their "comrades in arms." Jews were not prosecuted in Finland, but a certain number of Soviet refugees of Jewish affiliation were handed over to German authorities, in November 1942. The numbers given in the historical sources vary, mentioning either 39 or 74. Further deportations were suspended, as a consequence of protests by the Archbishop of the Finnish Lutheran Church and by the Social Democratic Party (Rautkallio 1988).

A surreal situation emerged when two officers (Leo Skurnik and Salomon Klass), and a member of the organization of female paramilitary personnel (Dina Poljakoff), all of Jewish affiliation, serving on the Finnish front, were nominated for the German award of the Iron Cross for their bravery, fighting alongside German army units. All three refused to accept the award (STT-IA, Verkkouutiset, 5 December 1997).

The ancestors of the Finnish Jews came from Russia. They were Ashkenazim. Whether those who immigrated to Finland still spoke Yiddish or had already assimilated to Russian is not known. Anyway, they brought with them Hebrew as the sacred language of Judaism. Even before the immigration of Ashkenazim to Scandinavia, Hebrew had been part of the high school curriculum in the 17th century, and Nordic scholars had published studies on the Hebrew language (Hovdhaugen et al. 2000: 37f.).

## Romani–Finland's Gypsies: Between Ethnic Boundary-Marking and Social Integration

Groups of Roma migrated into the Kingdom of Sweden in the 16th century and also came to Finland, then Swedish territory. The Romani people of Finland (or Finnish Kaale, respectively) call themselves *Finitiko romaseele* (*Suomen romanit* in Finnish). Roma is the plural form of *rom* ("man"). This name is nowadays also used by non–Roma because Gypsy is considered a derogatory term.

In the Middle Ages, when knowledge about the origin of this people was scarce and uncertain, they were sometimes confused with the Egyptians (*Aiguptoi/Aiguptianoi* in Greek) which is the source of the name Gypsy. This name form is still in use in English and in Spanish (*gitano*). The Roma are known under various other names in the languages of Europe. Widespread are name forms which are derived from Greek *Tsigganoi*: *Zigeuner* in German, *zingari* in Italian, *tsiganes* in French, *cygane* in Russian, *cigányok* in Hungarian. In some countries the Roma are referred to as "people with black skin" (Finnish *mustalaiset*). The Roma were also known by local names such as Sinti in Germany, Manouches in France or Calé in Spain.

Like the members of other ethnic groups that have lived in Finland for many generations, the Roma possess citizenship and are equal before the law. Roma follow the curricula of Finnish education and they participate in communal affairs. During World War II there were about one thousand Romani soldiers serving in the Finnish army. The Roma in Finland number some 5,000, yet the number of those speaking Romani is only a portion of the total. Finnish and Swedish are the languages most frequently used.

## Roma—Their Long Trail from India to Northern Europe

The Roma's land of origin is India but the formation of regional groups is a European phenomenon. The Roma are of Indo-European stock and their language is one of the Indo-Aryan languages. The presence of Roma in Europe is first documented for the 12th century. In the course of the 15th century Roma appeared in the big cities of western Europe: in Germany (1407 in Hildesheim, 1418 in Frankfurt), in Flanders (1420 in Brussels), in Italy (1422 in Bologna) and in France (1427 in Paris). In the early 16th century the Roma reached Scandinavia and England.

In the minds of Europeans the Roma have a reputation for being talented musicians. In fact, among the Roma one finds many professional musicians and some have gained international recognition in the world of entertainment, such as the Roma guitarists Django Reinhardt and Tchavolo Schmitt. Also the Roma community in Finland has produced musical talents such as the singer Anneli Sari (b. 1947) who has performed since the 1960s, in Finland and France, or the members of the Hortto Kaalo Band (*hortto kaalo* meaning "really dark").

There is a marked influence of Roma musicality in the history of local music in many countries, in Romania, Bulgaria, and elsewhere. Well-known are the traditions of flamenco in Spain and of csárdás in Hungary. Roma music also inspired some of the composers of classical music, Franz Liszt (1811–1886) and Johannes Brahms (1833–1897). Seemingly, the affiliation of the Roma with musical professions has a long record.

When the Roma set out on their migrations they professed Hinduism but during the Middle Ages the Roma adopted Christianity (mostly Catholicism in southern countries, and Protestantism in Scandinavia). Romani, the native language of the Roma, belongs to the Indic branch of Indo-European languages and it split from the central Indic continuum some 800 years ago. In Europe the Romani language has developed four major divisions, and one of these divisions is Romani spoken in northern Russia, Finland and Scandinavia.

Since the Roma have lived in diaspora communities—like the European Jews—their language (Romani) has been influenced—like Yiddish—by a multitude of languages with which it has come in contact (Matras 1995). The oldest layer of lexical borrowings in Romani are loanwords from Greek. The sources of other borrowings are Romanian, Bulgarian, Serbian, Swedish and other languages of northern Europe. The impact of contact languages on Romani can be traced even into domains where one would find indigenous terms in English, numerology for one; e.g., 1—jek (Indic), 4—tschetteri (< Latvian), 7—efta (< Greek).

The first accurate assessment of the Roma, their origin and linguistic affiliation, was given by Johann Christian Christoph Rüdiger in a treatise of 1782 where he argues for the homeland of the Roma in India and for the kinship of Romani and Sanskrit. Rüdiger stands out among his contemporaries in that he is the first to claim human rights for the Roma as a discriminated people.

Despite their far-reaching integration into Finnish society there are significant differences of worldview between the Roma and the Finnish people,

> and the two groups have often been characterized as mirror-images or antitheses of each other. Finnish peasant society valued close, continuous, and diligent relation with the land as an inherent good; sedentary farming was seen as morally superior to itinerant trade. In contrast, Finnish Rom have traditionally viewed farming as suitable only for those whose wits do not equip them for better work. Diligence itself is not viewed as an a priori good; rather, cleverness and skill in one's chosen profession is what carries greatest prestige [Virtanen and Du Bois 2000: 58f.].

Social cohesion in the Finnish Roma community is enhanced by a tendency to favor in-group marriage and to observe marked social hierarchies. The relations between children and their parents are not specifically marked in language use. Children usually do not use terms like "mother" or "father" but call their parents by their first name. The roles of men and women in Roma society are strongly divided. Women usually wear the traditional ethnic dress of "Gypsy" women while men dress like Finnish men. On the occasion of celebrations and feasts men have their meal in a room separated from women and children. Stereotypes about Roma culture are widespread among Finns and partly explain the reservation of the latter in social interaction with the former (Tong 2015: 3ff.).

## *Refugees from Outside Europe: Resettling and Constructing Identity in the New Homeland*

Finland is home to various ethnic groups (of which of course the Finns form the majority). Alongside those national groups that formed part of the population when the country gained independence (in 1917)—Finns, Finland-Swedes and Saami—there is a kaleidoscope of minorities, of older immigrants such as Roma and Russians, and of recent immigrants such as Estonians, Ukrainians, Somali and Syrians. Accordingly, the linguistic mosaic of Finland is diversified, with some 40 languages, most of them spoken by groups of immigrants. Despite this high number of individual languages, Finland's population is, linguistically, considerably homogeneous. The proportions show a great majority (some 90 percent) of people speaking Finnish as their first language. The number of speakers of minority languages counts for less than 1 percent of the population for each linguistic group.

Several languages, now spoken by thousands of people, are newcomers to Finland. This is true for Somali, Arabic, Kurdish, Albanian, Bosnian, Vietnamese and some other immigrant languages that had been unknown in this country before 1990. Among the immigrant languages are some where the number of speakers has increased dramatically during the past ten years (e.g., Russian, Somali, Albanian, Turkish, Italian). In some cases the number has doubled or even tripled (Estonian, Thai, Chinese, Spanish, Polish, Hungarian, Bengali, Tagalog, Portuguese, Ukrainian, Latvian, Lithuanian). The overall number of speakers of the various immigrant languages (except Russian) amounts to some 224,000 (4.2 percent).

The Somali community in Finland has grown dramatically during the past decades. The first Somali to arrive in Finland, not more than 44 in 1990, did not come directly from Somalia but from a Soviet Union that was disintegrating. Those early refugees were university students who had studied in the Soviet Union and left the country on the eve of its dissolution. By 1995, the number of Somali in Finland had risen to over 4,000. By that time the civil war in Somalia had taken its toll and had caused many inhabitants to leave and seek shelter in Europe. In 2012, the Somali community had grown to almost 15,000 individuals, the largest ethnic minority of non–European origin in the country. Somali citizens have difficulties finding suitable jobs, and unemployment rates are higher among the Somali than among native citizens.

The total number of immigrants in Finland—both humanitarian immigrants from outside the EU and EU citizens from other EU countries—is rather small, compared to the situation in other countries where the number is many times higher (e.g., Sweden, Germany, France). Yet, in view of the relatively small population the overall impression of Finland as a multilingual and multicultural country holds true. What is found here is a mosaic society with many facets and, though on a smaller scale, Finland has to cope with all the problems of integration that are well known in other multicultural countries.

The prolonged war in Syria has driven many Syrians out of their country, and they seek refuge especially in EU countries. The problems of the refugees do not start once they have entered the country that offers a safe haven, but much earlier. Many come to Europe on illegal routes, putting their trust into refugee smugglers and loan-sharks to whom they become indebted for many years after they have resettled in their new home-land. Among the Finnish population Syrian refugees meet with less prejudice than the refugees from Somalia who are often suspected of supporting rival clans in their former home country or even terrorist movements financially.

In former years, politicians and sociologists spoke about prospects for integration, for refugees to resettle and become equal members of the majority population. Yet, It has been noticed already in the 1990s that there are many cultural and social impediments for progress with integration, and a smooth merging with the majority is elusive (Valtonen 1998). The success of integration ultimately depends on the resettled person's ability to learn the language of the country's majority—that is, Finnish. It takes longer to get a grasp of Finnish, compared with English. There is nothing in Finnish that would corre-spond to the level of basic English. The complex Finnish grammar puts a strain on lan-guage learning on all refugees and immigrants.

Most job offers require Finnish language skills, and speaking pidgin Finnish will not do. Those refugees who make an effort to become integrated into Finnish society and who manage to climb over the communication barrier, learning proper Finnish, are the ideal image. Yet, many fall below the standards of language skills required for work in Finland. As a consequence, if work is available it is most probably a low-paying job for unskilled workers. Statistically, the percentage of jobless foreigners in Finland (relating to their total number) is increasing more rapidly than the corresponding percentage of jobless Finns. At the same time, the number of foreigners on the Finnish labor market is growing (Härmä 2015).

Integration into Finnish society may be hard to achieve for many refugees. Yet, there are refugees who stand out in the ways they have merged with the majority and, at the same time, have not lost their individual identity as representatives of a foreign culture. Among the prominent cases of successful integration are entrepreneurs, doctors, journalists and activists in political life. An outstanding figure in the political arena is Nasima Razmyar (b. 1984), who was born in Kabul, the daughter of an Afghan diplomat representing the Democratic Republic of Afghanistan in the Soviet Union (Moscow). Her family emigrated to Finland when the Taliban overthrew the Afghan government in 1993. Nasima has grown up in Finland. She became a member of the City Council of Helsinki (in 2012) and, with the elections of April 2015, made it into the Finnish Parliament representing the Social Democratic Party.

In 2010, Nasima was honored by naming her Refugee Woman of the Year. This title is awarded each year since 1998, by the Finnish Refugee Organization, to a refugee woman. Recipients of the award have been women from Iraq, Kenia, Somalia, Kampuchea, Makedonia, Afghanistan, Bosnia, Kosovo, Myanmar and South Sudan.

During the past two decades Finland has developed into a truly multicultural and multilingual society. This is especially felt in the metropolitan area of Helsinki, with the three urban agglomerations of Helsinki proper, Espoo and Vantaa. In this region, some 130 languages are spoken, in addition to Finnish and Swedish, as of the beginning of 2015 (Räty 2015). The languages with the most speakers are Russian (16,600), Estonian (11,700), Somali (8,000), English (5,500), Arabic (4,200) and Chinese (3,000). One finds classes in schools in Helsinki where some ten languages are spoken. Although a common image of Finland in the world today is not that of a multicultural society, the reality though, proves otherwise.

For all those who immigrate, as refugees, to Finland to start a new life here, communication with state officials cannot rely on English only. Even if a refugee masters Finnish swiftly he or she may, occasionally, have to cope with reserve, mistrust or even blunt prejudice on the part of the locals when interacting with them. In Finnish society, a genuine sense of humanitarian solidarity with foreigners who try to adapt to Finnish living conditions is widespread and any rejection of the principle of a multicultural society is restricted to disparate groups of radicals. In a recent opinion poll among university students, a general trend toward humanitarian support for immigrants can be observed. "The experience of living abroad and having contacts with immigrants enhance solidarity with immigrants, but there is a surprisingly weak interest in supporting the integration of immigrant groups more than other groups in need of support" (Sjöblom-Immala 2013: 126).

## *Language Choices in a Multilingual Society: Communicative Networks and How They Function in Finland*

In Finland, a multilingual country, about 90 percent of the total population or 4.87 million (2013), speak Finnish as their first language. Although the absolute number of Finnish-speakers is slightly rising, the percentage has been decreasing. In 1990, it was still 93.5 percent. The Swedish-speaking population in Finland ranks second, with 290,000 speakers, or 5.3 percent. The absolute number of their speakers as well as the percentage have been continually decreasing. In 1990, there were still 297,000 speakers (5.94 percent). Speakers of Russian (66,400 / 1.22 percent) rank third (STV 2014: 112).

In its long history—as part of Sweden, later of Russia and as an independent country—Finland has had various official languages. The first was Swedish during the period when Finland was a part of the Kingdom of Sweden. Swedish remained the official language also in the Grand Duchy albeit under Russian political supremacy. Russian never dominated official language use although the Senate of the Grand Duchy had to communicate in Russian with the tsarist bureaucracy in St. Petersburg.

Finnish was a latecomer in the official domain and it owes its functional breakthrough into the domain of state affairs, as a language of administration, to Tsar Alexander II (ruled 1855–1881). The ruler was inspired by Johan Vilhelm Snellman (1806–1881), the driving force of Finland's modernization in the 19th century, who professed a Finnish-language nationalist ideology. Alexander II took much interest in the modernization of his Grand Duchy and enacted economic and cultural reforms. Among his efforts to raise the standards of civic culture in Finland was the Language Prescript of 1863. "This decree placed the Finnish language on a path to becoming co-official with Swedish" (Lavery 2006: 177). After a twenty years' period of transition, the use of Finnish in administrative affairs was officially acknowledged.

The present-day use of official languages in Finland is the most complex in the country's history and it has contributed greatly to the social balance among the different national groups. In Finland, Finnish and Swedish serve as media of communication in administration, and they are on equal footing. State affairs are handled in these two languages, with Finnish as the most frequently used. Official documents are given in both Finnish and Swedish, and all announcements given by state institutions are bilingual.

The official status of Saami is different. Its administrative functions are limited to the northern province of the country, to Lapland. Here, as in the rest of Finland, Finnish is the major official language, and Saami, in official use, is an additional means of communication. In Lapland, too, official announcements are bilingual, in Finnish and Saami. What puts a strain on administration in Lapland is the fact that there is not only one Saami language but three independent local varieties that are officially used. This means that official documents concerning Lapland (e.g., regulations for fishing or hunting) are given in three local versions of Saami.

The Finnish Constitution stipulates equality of the major languages, Finnish and Swedish, concerning the proportions and territorial distribution of their speakers. The territorial principle as a means of language politics is applied in many multilingual countries of the world. A language is granted official status in local administration if a considerable portion of the resident population speaks it. This principle is applied at the communal level.

## Regulations of Finnish-Swedish Bilingualism

The regulations for administrative language use, referring to the major languages, Finnish and Swedish, came into effect through a language act, given in 1922. The regulations of this act were modernized—and slightly modified—in 2003, as a consequence of the modernization of Finland's Constitution in 2002. In the new version of linguistic legislation, in addition to the older technical regulations, the cultural values of bilingualism and the role of language for an individual's identity are highlighted and safeguarded (Tallroth 2012).

In the western, southwestern and southern parts of Finland where most of the

Swedish-speaking population live, there is a mosaic of municipalities with varying language use, depending on demographics. There are municipalities which are monolingual Finnish, others where administrative language use is bilingual (Finnish-Swedish) and others which are monolingual Swedish ("Ruotsin—ja kaksikieliset kunnat—Taustatietoa 2008–2013"; www.kunnat.net/kielitietoa; retrieved 9 February 2015).

Of the 320 municipalities of Finland, 32 are bilingual, with locally varying majorities of either Finnish or Swedish (STV 2014: 74). The basic criterion for a municipality to be acknowledged as bilingual is that at least 8 percent of the local population speak a different language from the majority or that their number is at least 3,000 (figure 21). If the size of the minority does not fall below 6 percent, the municipality may remain bilingual.

---

I.    Area with Finnish as official language

      (population: 3.683 million)

      Number of municipalities: 271


II.   Bilingual area with Finnish and Swedish as official languages

      (population: 1.722 million)

      Number of municipalities: 30

         A.    Bilingual area with a Finnish-speaking majority

               (population: 1.582 million)

               Number of municipalities: 18

         B.    Bilingual area with a Swedish-speaking majority

               (population: 0.14 million)

               Number of municipalities: 12


III.  Area with Swedish as official language

      (population: 45,284)

      Number of municipalities: 19

---

**Figure 21: Monolingual and bilingual municipalities in Finland (Finnish Authorities; Statistics Finland; STV 2014: 74).**

Public signs, announcements and municipal documents are given, as needed, in one or two languages. In Åland all municipalities are monolingual Swedish and this is the only language of administration. On the mainland, most bilingual municipalities have a Finnish majority (e.g., Helsinki-Helsingfors, Turku-Åbo, Porvoo-Borgå, Hanko-Hangö). Those municipalities with a Swedish majority are fewer in number (and include Inga-Inkoo, Kristinestadt-Kristiinankaupunki, Nykarleby-Uusikaarlepyy, Raseborg-Raasepori). The similarity of name forms of bilingual municipalities is in most cases recognizable despite the phonetic differences between Finnish and Swedish (e.g., Espoo-Esbo). In some cases, though, differences are marked (e.g., Jakobstad-Pietarsaari, Turku-Åbo, Kauniainen-Grankulla).

The conditions of administrative bilingualism are monitored and newly assessed in intervals of ten years. In many municipalities, the proportions of the language groups (of Finnish-speakers vis-à-vis Swedish-speakers) has changed considerably. Still in the second half of the 19th century, the inhabitants of the cities of Finland were overwhelmingly Swedish-speaking. In 1880, the great majority of Finns (94.5 percent) lived in rural areas and only some 5.5 percent were urban (Jutikkala 1953). At the same time (1880), in stark contrast to this, the proportions for the Finland-Swedish population were the reverse, with 65.7 percent urban as against 34.3 percent rural population (Engman 1995: 192).

The cities and bigger towns have experienced especially great changes in the proportions of the language groups. The decrease of Swedish speakers in Helsinki is shown thus—1880: 55.3 percent > 1970: 10.6 percent > 2013: 5.9 percent. In Helsinki, the majorities of Swedish- and Finnish-speakers had already changed toward the end of the 19th century. The proportions of the two language groups showed an equal balance in 1890: 45.6 percent Swedish-speaking vs. 45.5 percent Finnish-speaking. By 1900, the majority had tilted toward the Finnish speakers (50.7 percent), as against 42.5 percent for the Swedish-speaking inhabitants (Schoolfield 1996: 140).

Toward the end of the 19th century, the percentage of Finnish-speaking people gradually increased also in other urban centers. By 1900, the portion of the urban population among Finns had risen to 10 percent, by 1921 to 13.5 percent. Earlier majorities of Finland-Swedish urban citizens continuously shrank and eventually turned into minority status. Turku (Åbo) was the first town in the area of Swedish settlement where the Swedish-speaking inhabitants were in the minority (42 percent) by 1880.

In other cities, the change from majority to minority occurred in later decades; e.g., Porvoo / Borgå (1880: 88.7 percent > 1970—44.6 percent), Vaasa / Vasa (1880—87.2 percent > 1970—29.3 percent) (Klövekorn 1960, Väestölaskenta 1973). In other towns, the decrease of the Swedish-speaking population is steady and continuing up to the present: Hanko (1880: 77 > 2013: 42.8), Kokkola (85 > 13.1), Kristinestad (89 > 55.4), Jakobstad (99 > 55.8), Kaskinen (100 > 28.5). The decrease has been moderate in only one town, Nykarleby (1880: 99 > 2013: 87.3).

In the smaller municipalities, the general tendency is also a decrease of the resident Swedish-speaking population although the dynamics differ among municipalities, with varying patterns of demographic movement and linguistic assimilation. For the most part, those Finland-Swedes who are no longer brought up in the language of their parents make a shift to Finnish.

Most of the monolingual Swedish municipalities are found on the islands of the Åland archipelago with its population of 28,700 (2013); i.e., Brändö, Eckerö, Finström, Föglö, Geta, Hammarland, Jomala, Kökar, Kumlinge, Lemland, Lumparland, Mariehamn, Saltvik, Sottunga, Sund, Vårdö. There is only one municipality on the mainland which is monolingual Swedish, and this is Närpes (Finnish Närpiö) in the coastal area of western Finland (Ostrobothnia). Until 2014, there were two other municipalities with Swedish as the only official language, Korsnäs and Larsmo, but these are now officially bilingual.

## Regulations of Finnish-Saami Bilingualism

In 1991, the official status of Saami in administrative language use on the communal level has been confirmed and, in 2003, an extended language act has been given to safeguard the linguistic rights of the Saami speech community. In Lapland, four municipalities are bilingual, with Finnish and Saami as official languages. These are Enontekiö (name in northern Saami: Eanodat), Inari (name in Inari Saami: Aanaar; in northern Saami: Anár; in Skolt Saami: Aanar), Sodankylä (in Inari Saami: Suádigil; in northern Saami: Soadegilli; in Skolt Saami: Suä´djel), Utsjoki (in northern Saami: Ohcejohka; in Inari Saami: Uccjuuhâ; in Skolt Saami: Uccjokk). In Enontekiö, 10.8 percent of the local population speak Saami, in Inari 6.4 percent, in Sodankylä 1.6 percent and, in Utsjoki 46.6 percent.

The regulations for the Saami language in official function are not just nominal but are of practical and symbolic significance. The use of Saami as an official language is the highest level that a minority language can achieve. Saami is taught at school—by instruction through the medium of Saami and through the teaching of Saami as a subject. In comprehensive and upper secondary schools in Lapland there were more than 600 pupils and students in the mid- and late 1990s. The number has dropped slightly since then (Aikio-Puoskari 2001).

The northern Saami language is the variety with most speakers, and it is used in academic teaching, at the Nordic Institute of Higher Learning (Sámi Allaskuvla) at Kautokeino. The first dissertation in northern Saami was published in the late 1990s (Hirvonen 1998). Northern Saami is used on Finnish radio and on TV, and there is a regular news broadcast in this language.

Despite multiple efforts to keep the regional varieties of Saami alive there is a general trend to switch to Finnish as first language in the intergenerational shift. In a revitalization project where language skills and indigenous knowledge are accumulated, priority is given to continuity in language use, especially among members of the younger generation.

One positive example of how to revive and support the development and transfer of Saami languages, identity and cultures is the project *The Language and Cultural Siidas of the Saami* (2001–2004), by using the traditional knowledge and other resources of elders in a genuine cultural environment and community; the project also aims to enable children to switch into Saami-speaking day care, to study through the medium of Saami at school and in vocational training later, and thus to become fully authorized and harmonious members of the Saami community [Skutnabb-Kangas and Aikio-Puoskari 2005: 17].

# 3

# What Makes a Finn and
# What Makes Finnish Society?
## *Defining Finnishness*

How to define a Finn? What spontaneously comes to mind when thinking of Finns is that they speak Finnish. This holds true for most Finns. And yet, there are people who think of themselves as Finns but who do not speak Finnish. Many of the Ingrian Finns did not speak any Finnish before they immigrated to Finland in the 1990s and they had to learn the mother tongue of their forefathers anew. Thousands of people in the U.S. consider themselves to be Finns although they speak English as their first language. They are Finns through descent and they continue some of the cultural heritage.

Language is one facet in the mosaic of ethnicity but no exclusive marker of it (Haarmann 1986). There are many other facets that make the fabric of an ethnic group. To what extent language may function as a major marker of ethnicity will have to be determined on the basis of an analysis of culture-related and language-oriented constituents.

The insight that language is merely one among many features of ethnicity is not new. Observations regarding the complex fabric of ethnicity were made as early as the Middle Ages. The first attempt to specify the criteria by which national populations distinguish themselves was made by Regino of Prüm who perceived, as early as around the year 900, the following distinctions: *Diversae nationes populorum inter se discrepant genere, moribus, lingua, legibus* ("The various nations differ in descent, customs, language and law") (quoted after Bartlett 1993: 197).

The arbiter of membership in an ethnic group is cohesion. This means that membership is stable as long as the sociocultural relations within the group function without disturbance. "Ethnic cohesion is achieved through interaction between members of intimate networks like close family and friends, effective networks such as kinship or occupation, and the extended networks of neighbourhood or social group" (Henson 2006: 19). What holds individuals together in an ethnic group is a complex network of constituents, which may be categorized as follows:

- constituents of human ecology (the relationship between natural environment and cultural space; etc.);

- sociocultural markers of ethnicity (kinship; socialization of the young generation in the context of specific cultural traditions);
- communication systems (visual communication: gestures, tattooing, hair fashion; emblematic and heraldic systems; language-related visual communication such as writing technology; etc.);
- interaction and social behavior (in-group and out-group interaction; customs of inter-ethnic contacts; language-related behavior such as singing and story-telling; entertainment and festivities; organizing professional life; etc.);
- phenomenological markers of ethnicity (self-identification; categorization of others; religion and worldview; value system; etc.).

The emergence of Finnish ethnicity is related to the prehistoric movements of Baltic-Finnic tribes on the mainland and around the Gulf of Finland. The ancestors of the Finns came from the South and Southeast. In the local variations of the Finnish language the spread of early tribal settlements can be discerned. The profile of the western dialects was shaped in an area where the descendants of two older tribes settled, the Finns Proper (*varsinais-suomalaiset*) and the Tavastians (*hämäläiset*). These Finnic people were mainly immigrants from regions south of the Gulf of Finland, from what is nowadays Estonia, between c. 1200 and 500 BCE. The eastern Finnish dialects have originated from the Finnic population that migrated into Finland through the Karelian isthmus. These Finns belonged to the third and fourth major tribes, the Karelians (*karjalaiset*) and the people in the region of Savo (*savolaiset*). There is a continuum of dialectal features connecting the eastern dialects of Finnish with the local varieties of neighboring Karelian.

The Finns distinguish themselves from other ethnic groups by certain properties in their gene pool. The most striking feature is associated with the so-called haplogroup U5 which, most probably, constitutes one of the oldest mitochondrial complexes in the European context (Malyarchuk et al. 2010). Haplogroups are constituents of the mitochondria, the organelles that can be compared, in their function, to a powerhouse of the individual cell. The frequency of U5 is rather low everywhere in Europe, yet it is markedly higher among the peoples of Uralic stock in Finland (Finns and Saami). In addition to being linguistically and culturally most closely related to the Finns, the Estonians also show a high-grade similarity with the Finns from the standpoint of human genetics. The Finnish genome shows the characteristics of an ancient population in northeastern Europe. This prehistoric genetic component makes up about 80 percent of the Finnish gene pool (Nelis et al. 2009).

Although, anthropologically, the Finns are affiliated to other populations of Uralic stock, in the genomic profile of the Finnish people, only some 20 percent of the original Uralic genes have persisted. About 80 percent of the gene pool is of Europid affiliation. This explains why Finns look like other Europeans although their distant ancestors looked more like present-day Mari or Udmurts, Finno-Ugric peoples that have preserved Uralid anthropological features to a greater extent than Finns, Estonians or Hungarians. The admixture of Europid features in Finnish ethnicity stems from the long duration of contacts with populations of Indo-European stock and, later, with Scandinavians of Germanic affiliation (see Chapter 2).

## What's in a Name? How Finns Call Themselves and How Others Call the Finns

Membership in an ethnic group or nation is identified by using a collective name, an ethnonym. Ethnonyms may be the same for insiders and outsiders (foreigners). Those who identify themselves as "English" are called by the same name also by foreigners. The same is true for the French, Italians or Danes. In other cases, the self-denomination of a nation may differ from the name used by foreigners. The Germans call themselves "Deutsche," while French people call them "Allemands," Italians "tedeschi," Finns "saksalaiset" and Russians "nemtsy."

The names for the Finns belong to the latter type of ethnonym, with the self-given name differing from the name form in use among foreigners. Finns call themselves "suomalaiset," their country "Suomi" and their language "suomen kieli" (literally "the language of Finland"). Name forms on this base are common among other people who are linguistically affiliated with the Finns. Estonians call the Finns "soomlaset," the country "Soome" and the language "some keel." The Swedish neighbors use the names "finskarna" / "Finland" / "finska." The same root appears in the German names "Finnen" / "Finland"/ "Finnisch," and in Russian name forms: Finns are called "finskie," their country "Finlandiia" and the language "finskii yazyk."

Names are a crystallizing focus of identity, and this is true for individual (personal names) as much as for collective names (ethnonyms). "Names of all kinds have associations, flavours; they are evocative, and carry messages that are no less powerful for being ambiguous" (Wilson 1998: xi). The origins of the name "Suomi" lie in mysterious darkness. Linguists hesitate to give a single straightforward explanation of the name since various possible sources can be identified, and none can be ruled out with certainty (Itkonen and Kulonen 2000/3: 215f.).

There have been some popular explanations of the name forms that are today rejected by linguists. In one of these fantastic associations Suomi is related to the Finnish expression *suo* (*suomaa*, respectively), meaning "swamp, swampy terrain." Indeed, there are many swamps in Finland which enhance this idea. However, the structure of the name Suomi does not fit in the molds of Finnish name forms for countries. Another popular, though less common explanation is to relate the name to the expression *suomu* ("fish skin"). This would associate the name to ancient beliefs of totemism, including ideas of certain animals as mythical ancestors or figures of reverence in shamanistic cults. Linguists do not give much credit to this explanation, either.

The most fruitful direction for identification of the word "Suomi" is to look for borrowed expressions. In the Bronze Age when Baltic tribes entertained prolonged contacts with Finnic tribes in the Baltic area, the southwestern part of Finland was called *\*šama* by the Balts, and the borrowed form in Baltic Finnic was *\*šämä*, and *\*some* in Proto-Finnic. From this name form are derived the name by which the Saami call themselves (i.e., *sabme*) and the name for the region Häme (derivation *hämäläinen* "someone from Häme") in south-central Finland. Another possible source of borrowing for Suomi is a term for "country" in Baltic (e.g., as in the Lithuanian dialectal form *žāmė*). A relationship with the inhabitants of Finland is established in the Indo-European term for "tribe," found in Baltic as *\*sto-me* and in German as *Stamm* (Kallio 1998).

The origins of the names formed on the base *Finn-* are as mysterious. The first mentioning of this name in the English-speaking world dates to the Middle Ages. In Old English, the name for the people in the North was Finnas which corresponded to the Old Icelandic Finnr. In the 17th and 18th centuries, the term used for Finnish was Finnic. Since the latter half of the 18th century, Finnish has been used as an adjective (Barnhart 2002: 384).

The earliest references to the Finns are much older and date to around the beginning of the present era. In some antique sources, name forms such as Phinnoi (in Greek), Fenni, Skrithfinni (Latin) and others are used in connection with descriptions of people in northern Europe. Most probably, reference is made to the hunter-gatherers of southern Finland which, at that time, was inhabited by ethnic Saami. The name root *Finn-* may be derived from a Germanic source. In German, one finds expressions which may be related: cf. Old High German *fendo* ("wanderer"), Old Middle German *vende*.

In the medieval Icelandic sagas, in the Eddas and in Norse stories, dating to the eleventh through 14th centuries, one finds references to the Saami and Finns which are inconsistently addressed as *finnr* and *finnas*. In some medieval sources from Sweden (inscriptions on rune stones), reference is made to western Finland: *finlont* (in a rune inscription from Söderby) and *finlandi* (in an inscription from the island of Gotland, in the Baltic Sea).

In the etymological history of name forms is revealed the surprising fact that both the self-given name (*suomalaiset*) and the name by which foreigners refer to the inhabitants of Finland (*Finns*) are borrowed terms. For centuries, the Finns referred to themselves predominantly using tribal names (Karelians, people from Savo, Häme, Pohjanmaa, and others). The name *suomalaiset*, in a context of national self-awareness, is a phenomenon that appeared rather late and can be related to the historical development of nationhood among the Finns in the course of the 19th century (figure 22).

## Salient Features of Finnishness

People speak about themselves and about other people, they create an image about who they are, about their ways of living and about their group affiliations, and they create images about people who speak other languages and behave differently. That is part of crafting one's identity. The Finns carry images about foreigners in their mind, as do foreigners about the Finns. Those images imply a collective body of features, which are generalizing. In the case of the features that make a Finn, their wholeness may puzzle foreigners who may get the impression that Finland is a "cultural lone wolf" (Lewis 2005).

When Finns talk about foreigners they mobilize cultural stereotypes. Finns think that Swedes are talkative while Swedes think that Finns are not very communicative. Such stereotyping is common also when Finns talk about Finns from different parts of the country, referring to different temperaments. People from Karelia and Savo are thought of as vivid and extroverted while Finns from Häme or Bothnia are said to be self-contained and not prone to show their emotions. According to the ethnic stereotype, it takes much longer for someone from Häme to open up than for a Finn from Savo.

In every stereotype there is a bit of truth and we cannot do without generalizing

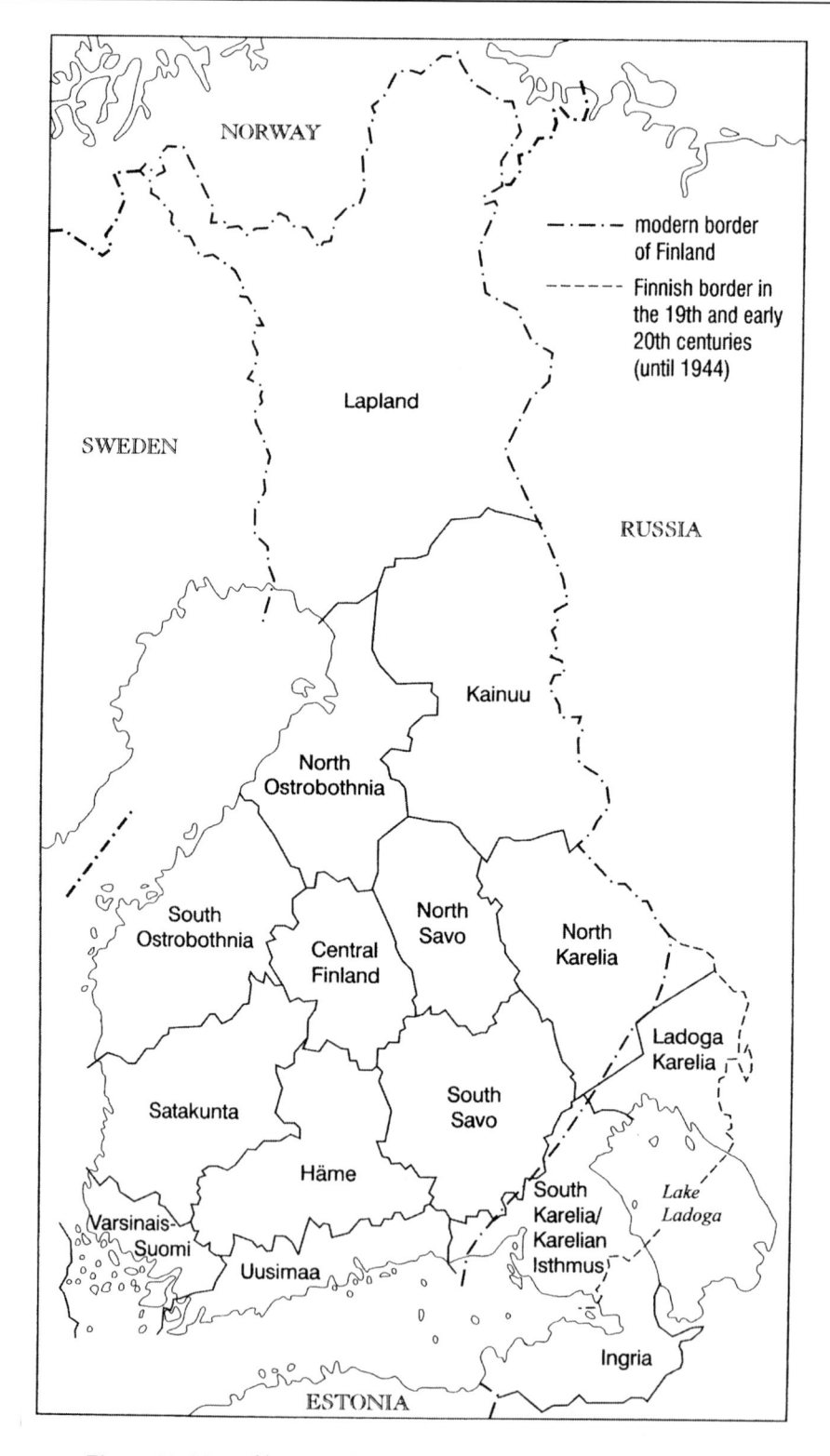

**Figure 22: Map of historical provinces in Finland (Stark 2011: 240).**

statements and evaluations about others. When foreigners are asked what they think about the Finns then they will produce more or less generalizing statements because it is not possible to create images of every individual Finn. Among the typical stereotypes that foreigners carry in their minds is that all Finns love the sauna. There are many Finns who like it and use it regularly. But there are also many other Finns who are not fond of the sauna. The Finns' love for sauna is a stereotype that does not offend anybody. And yet, there are other stereotyping views about the Finns which are disturbing and even offensive. Many foreigners believe that Finns are drunkards. It is true that the consumption of alcohol per capita in Finland is higher than in many other countries but this does not mean that all Finns are heavy drinkers. There are those who drink a lot, but there are others who do not drink any alcohol.

Stereotyping features about cultures and people crystallize in jokes. In one of these, the social behavior of people who like to drink vodka is addressed, highlighting stereotyping features for three different ethnic groups, including a Russian, a Swede and a Finn. The Russian opens the bottle and holds a pathetic speech before drinking. The Swede starts the session with a song. The Finn would open the bottle and just start drinking without further ado.

In this joke there is a core of "truth" that has been observed by many outsiders. Russians and Swedes are perhaps more extroverted and social than Finns. Russians and Swedes prefer to have company when enjoying alcohol while a Finn does not seem to care about company. This does not mean that Finns would be less social than Swedes or Russians. Finns can be as joyful in company and they enjoy celebrations, in a crowd, at birthday parties, weddings or festive events. Yet, a difference in basic attitude shows in the joke, and that is: Finns would not mind drinking alone.

A foreigner may easily get the impression that Finns are more introverted than people from other countries, and this impression keeps repeating in literature and echoing in the media. "The Finns, to foreigners coming from emotive cultures, seem 'closed' and often withdrawn. They are suspicious of melodrama, which confuses them, and secretly believe that people showing this disposition are untrustworthy. They admire coolness and calm judgement" (Swallow 2011: 63).

A survey has been set up, listing the 11 most introverted countries in the world (by Aletheia Luna on LonerWolf), among them Austria, Belgium, Denmark, Finland, Iceland and Japan. In recent years, a number of books have been published analyzing introverted personality patterns and drawing on international comparisons. Special attention has raised the book *Introvert Power* (2008), written by psychologist Laurie Helgoe. According to her findings, the dominant personality pattern among people in Scandinavia and Japan is that of introverts while, in the USA, the number of introverts is considerably smaller. Some 57 percent of the U.S. population identify themselves as introverts although many prefer to avoid the image of being taken for an introvert and try to look like extroverts.

According to Helgoe there is nothing wrong with being an introvert, and there is no reason to feel uncomfortable with the awareness of this trait in oneself or when confronted with other people's negative attitudes toward introverts. Introvert power of Finnish individuals may be the secret of the collective success of Finnish competitiveness in the world and of a small nation like Finland as a player in international economics and politics (see Chapters 5 and 8). Finns do not like to wait for teams to be assembled before setting out to work, and they do not like to talk much about things undone. They would rather just get to it.

Statements about the allegedly introverted nature of Finns may be based on misunderstandings of Finns' attitudes toward problem-solving. Illustrative of such a situation is the evaluation of tango music—so popular among Finns—on the side of foreigners. The kind of melancholy that one finds in the lyrics of Finnish tango "has often, especially abroad, been interpreted as a symbol of Finns' introversion and their feeling of inferiority and communication difficulties, but in reality it represents 'silent information,' a subtle way of handling painful matters" (Jalkanen 2013: 316).

A salient feature of an introverted personality is that such a person is not talkative but rather more the opposite: taciturn. Indeed, when comparing the verbal behavior of Finns with Italians or Greeks, the common impression is that Finns talk much less. And yet, things are changing.

> The taciturn Finn may now be a somewhat outdated stereotype, but it is true that the Finnish attitude to speech and words is an unusual one. In Finland, words have a greater weight than in many other cultures; Finns take words seriously. To interrupt someone is considered impertinent, while loquacity is viewed with suspicion.... Silence and pauses in conversation are not viewed as awkward, but as part of normal communication [Alho 1997: 64].

Covert stereotypes about ethnic groups are always present, even among people who have experience in interethnic contact. When foreigners meet Finns there are often irrational underpinnings involved. Cultural stereotypes may be reinforced in interaction or they may become dissolved. Anyway, practical experience is much more reliable than keeping up one's stereotypes. Life experience tells us that stereotypes emerge easily and it is negative stereotypes in particular that are the most persistent.

## The Environmental Mindset

The Finns share a sense of need for spaciousness. For the longest time in their history they have lived in spacious surroundings, and the custom to leave the city during weekends and holidays for the countryside echoes this history. Finns do not like crowded living areas. There are many jokes portraying this aspect of the Finnish psyche. According to one there is a man who builds himself a home in the middle of nowhere, enjoying the solitude of his natural habitat. One day when he is sitting on the bank of a nearby brook he notices some pieces of chipped wood floating in the water downstream. He gets furious, takes his axe and walks for many miles upstream until he comes across his neighbor whom he threatens with his axe and forces him to leave because he cannot stand the idea of his environment becoming overcrowded.

In cultures where natural resources are not conceptualized as a potential for economic exploitation but are treated as life-supporting factors, an attitude toward preservation of the natural environment prevails.

The ancient idea of keeping a balance between natural and cultural spaces has never been lost among the inhabitants of northern Eurasia, where animistic traditions have created the underpinnings of human consciousness. The Finnish peasants never lived in an environment where everything came in abundance. On the contrary, living in the rhythm of nature and handling one's living space with care shaped the mindset of people decisively.

The Finns are surrounded by nature and forests cover 72 percent of the land. They are forest people at heart. One of their core beliefs is about looking after the environment. Laws, dating back to 1886, promote well-managed, sustainable forestry and these are updated constantly with new and pertinent regulations. This is just one incidence of how long the Finns have been "green" in their outlook. To a large extent, their climate, nature and geography has shaped the Finnish mindset. They perceive themselves at a distance from other cultures, apart and separate—but inextricably mixed with their forests and lakes [Swallow 2011: 63f.].

This model is in stark contrast to the model of unconditional technological progress that produces the mentality of unbridled control of nature. This kind of relationship, denying the human need to comply with nature's conditions, dominates in historical industrialized society as well as in the network society of our information age. The consciousness of the people is directed toward technological advancement and away from the priority of stability. The further advanced the technological development, the more detached its proponents are from the natural life cycle.

The speedy industrialization of Finland in the 19th century and the fast pace of modernization in the postwar period are illustrative that technological advancement and the raising of living standards does not necessarily contradict the principles of a balance between the cultural and the natural space (see Chapter 5).

Symbolic of the sense of people sharing the bonds with nature and enjoying its benefits is the so-called "every man's right" (Finnish *jokamiehen oikeus*), an institution of customary "law" that everybody knows but which is not written down anywhere, neither in the constitution nor in any law book. This right guarantees free movement in the natural environment, wherever an inhabitant of Finland intends to go. "Every man's right which has been valid in Nordic countries since times immemorial is of central significance for the realization of movement outdoors" (Tuomisto 1973: 829). Everybody has the right to move on other people's property (e.g., an area of wooded land, a beach on the shores of a lake) to gather flowers, to pluck wild berries or to take mushrooms, to make a picnic and to walk freely. There is, however, a common understanding that one would not enter the close premises around someone's home without asking permission.

In this every man's right one can sense the very old roots of the Finnish communitarian spirit. Every man's right finds its limits where modern criminal law defines compensation for damage done. If someone cuts trees, illegally, on someone else's property the one who does so will be prosecuted and sentenced to pay for the damage. Nevertheless, every man's right is common knowledge, and there is no use putting up signs which say "no trespassing" or "keep out."

## *Sisu*: The Secret of Finnish Determination and Resilience

Agriculture never was a prosperous domain, given the harsh climatic conditions in the north of Europe. During the 19th century, slash and burn cultivation was still practiced while gradually being replaced by field cultivation. Clearing the woods to gain terrain for plant cultivation in the European north requires much harder labor than in central Europe. All living things have to endure extreme temperature changes, ranging from periods of hard frost in a long winter to sudden heat in a short summer. It may well happen that seeds that are sown in spring do not sprout because of bad weather or seeds cannot be sown at all because of frequent rainfall that keeps the soil too wet.

One may wonder how people manage to live under basically harsh conditions and to cope with the challenges the climate poses. Perhaps it takes people that are carved from a special kind of wood. Indeed, in the image of the national character of the Finns, there is a certain internalized quality, and that is what the Finns call *sisu*.

> *Sisu* can best be described as a strong blend of courage and persistence; a sense of determination that is indifferent to the costs or consequences; a source of mental and spiritual strength that sometimes falls on the side of obstinacy; it is perseverance in action and a stoic and cool display of raw willpower [Chaker 2014: 160].

Finnish *sisu* comes to bear on whatever enterprise Finns engage in. It is hard to say at what level *sisu* works in a person's activities and how strongly it is manifested. Anyway, the power of *sisu* is recalled in some legendary events. One such event was the 10,000 meter race at the Summer Olympics in Munich in 1972 in which the Finnish runner Lasse Virén (b. 1949) participated. In the twelfth lap, Virén got entangled with another runner and fell. For a normal runner, there were two options how to continue. One was to simply let go and leave the track. That would have been unsportsmanlike and would have provoked a bad reaction among the spectators. The other option would have been to rise and move on, keeping one's honor as a participant albeit without any hope of catching up with the other contestants in the race.

As a Finn, Virén chose a third option: the typically Finnish way of *sisu*. He did not abandon the hope to win, he mobilized his will and spurred his physical resources, he rose and caught up with the others in less than 150 meters. He had lost 20 meters and was with the bulk of the pack at that time. There were still 600 meters to go. And that was the crucial moment when Virén switched on the power. In a dramatic drive he rushed to the front and won the race, in 27:38:40 which is still an unbroken record in the Olympics. A legend was born, "an enigma wrapped in glory" (Moore 1977).

Lasse Virén continued the image of the "flying Finn" that had originated with other runners earlier who have become legends. The first Finn to be nicknamed "flying Finn" was Hannes Kolehmainen (1889–1966) who won three gold medals at the 1912 Summer Olympics in Stockholm: "Smiling Hannes" set two new world records. Another legend of a "flying Finn" was Paavo Nurmi (1897–1973), who won nine gold medals, the first at the Olympics in Antwerp in 1920. Later, the saying "flying Finn" was associated with racing sportsmen.

*Sisu* regularly manifests itself during times of crisis. And occasions when *sisu* was called for to endure extreme hardship left their mark on Finnish society and remain present in the ways Finns remember their history. There have been years in Finnish history when crops were ravaged by hailstorms or bad weather. That happened several times on a large scale. The first ecological catastrophe that hit the Finnish population hard were the years of famine from 1695 to 1697. That was the period that has been termed "little Ice Age" because the whole of northern Europe experienced a dramatic climate change to a significantly colder weather.

Toward the end of the 17th century the river Thames in England was frozen during the winter season, as were the canals in Holland. The exceptional experiences of people in those years are documented in the paintings by Dutch artists of people skating or amusing themselves on the ice. The best-known perhaps is the great work *Winter Landscape with Ice Skaters* (ca. 1608) by Hendrick Avercamp. For the Finns there was no time for amusement because a dramatic food shortage caused a famine that lasted several years. It has been estimated that, during those years about one third of the Finnish population was lost to the famine (Lappalainen 2012).

People were desperate and tried to understand why they had to suffer so much. According to the zeitgeist of the 17th century, priests "found" an explanation, claiming that the famine was God's scourge, a punishment for mankind that had been disobedient and lived in disregard of God's will. People did their best to cope with the natural disaster. Those Finns who survived the disaster carried on with a strengthened will.

In the 19th century there came another ecocatastrophe, well-known as the "great hunger years" (Finnish *suuret nälkävuodet*), a period of great famine (1866–68). In May 1867, the temperature was 8° C below the long-time average. Rivers and lakes remained frozen until well into summer. During those years, between 15 and 20 percent of the population in Finland died of starvation. Finns were inventive and ate pine bark, either sliced into thin stripes or—more commonly—ground to produce a kind of flour which was used to bake famine bread, called *pettuleipä* in Finnish. Yet, that foodstuff did not provide even a minimum of the nutrition needed (Häkkinen et al. 1991).

One could have expected a mass exodus of people leaving a country where nature could be cruel and merciless. But those who survived the famine stayed, overcame hardship and continued to cultivate plants, learning from bad experience and focusing on improvements of agricultural techniques. Those people who pressed forward and advanced economic development then professed *sisu*. The typical Finnish mixture of guts and resilience has come during periods of national crisis such as the war efforts to maintain Finland's independence, and this is also true for the process of rapid modernization which the Finns experienced in the postwar era (Oinas 2005: 1232; see Chapter 5).

## Social Cohesion at Work: Trust and Reliability

Factors that determine interaction among members in Finnish society shape the image of the "national" character. These features also contribute to the success of all kinds of economic transactions—they relate to the abstract concepts of trust and reliability. The Finns are known for being trustworthy and reliable: "'a word spoken is a message delivered'—Finns mean what they say and keep their promises" (Alho 1997: 64). In negotiating a contract, once an agreement is reached the partners stick to it and do not try to renegotiate. When a Finn says that he or she will take care of something and makes a promise to do so, one can trust that he or she will do it (except for politicians who may forget about promises they make in election campaigns).

Trust and reliability fit the maxims of a Protestant worldview so these factors go hand in hand for the majority of Finns and Scandinavians alike. These qualities offer enormous benefits for social cohesion among the Finns. Trust is what holds the Finns and their society together (Tamminen 2015). And the Finns' sense of trust extends into all domains.

In the list of those countries which are the least corrupt (World Democracy Audit), Finland ranked first in 2007 and 2012, second in 2011 and third in 2013 and 2014 (Koskinen 2013). In the program of the European Social Survey that has been mapping long-term attitudinal and behavioral changes since 2001, questions about people's well-being are asked, oriented to a set of values (Jowell et al. 2007). Trust is one such value. In the annual survey results, the attitudes among the Finns regarding the measure of trust in other people and in the country's institutions ranks high. The results of the 2014 survey show that, among the Europeans, the Finns rank second with regard to the prime value of trust. There is only one country where this value is hailed even more than in Finland, and this is Denmark.

The fact that the Finnish democratic system functions well and a balance is being successfully kept up between various economic and political interests is due to the measures of trust and reliability. The Finns have trust in the functioning of their political institutions, and this trust is well-founded and can be substantiated. The principle of transparency of proceedings in the juridical system and official administration (including the right to be heard and to receive a reasoned decision) is anchored in section 21 of Finland's Constitution but the idea itself has a much longer history. "One of the people who formulated the principle was the Finn Anders Chydenius [1729–1803] who represented the Ostrobothnian clergy in the Swedish parliament during the 1760s" (Lehtonen 2013: 31).

The perception of lifestyles that function without corruption certainly has a bearing on trust in business relations (Wilhelm 2002). The Finns have a saying about equality in business conduct without the pressures of corruption, *reilu meininki*, or "fair play." A handshake, as confirmation of an agreement among business partners, is worth more than 100 pages of contract.

The Finnish kind of openness and trustfulness makes Finns vulnerable when interacting with people that do not share the same values. Foreigners sometimes claim that it is easy to cheat a Finn. Those who do not care to cheat should be envious of the Finns who get along well in the world of business ethics.

> Equality and social cohesion are traditionally valued in Nordic societies—but they do not feature in the WEF [World Economic Forum] and IMD [Institute for Management Development] competitiveness calculations (Rouvinen & Vartia, 2002, p. 97). A pressing question at present is whether the future business system, innovation system and the society at large will accommodate some of the shared social values of the past [Oinas 2005: 1241].

## *The Finnish Sense for Pragmatism*

Whatever you do outdoors in Finland is dictated by the weather conditions. In the harbors and ports along the coasts of Italy, one may keep boats or yachts in the water throughout the year. This is not possible in Finland, simply because the boats would be crushed by the thick ice in winter. In autumn, people take their boats ashore and turn them upside down for protection against snow and ice. Those who own sailboats have to order a crane to come to the pier and lift the boats onto solid ground where they stay for half a year under a protective cover. In spring, the crane will lift the big boats back into the water.

In Great Britain, in France and in Spain roads can be constructed throughout the year. In Finland, road construction is carried only so long as the soil is not frozen. Construction firms consider themselves lucky if winter comes later than usual and temperatures do not fall too quickly below zero.

Throughout their history, the Finns have learned to adapt to extreme cold weather. The techniques for constructing houses and especially for insulating buildings are far advanced. Among the commodities one finds in Finnish houses is floor-heating, in rooms with ceramic pavement such as bathrooms. In winter, one does not have to wear slippers to keep one's feet warm, one just switches on the floor-heating.

Finns have learned to adapt to push the limits of their activities as far as possible, always keeping in mind that nature has the upper hand. Finns do not lament their fate; on the contrary, nature teaches them to be pragmatic, a quality that shows up in practically all domains of life. To a foreigner it seems that Finns do not easily get emotional and are generally dour.

> Many a newcomer to Finland will think Finns guarded and serious. Indeed, a Finn shies away from any demonstrative behavior. However, I know lots of Finns, and under their very quiet, reserved exterior, they really are quite a bubbly and humorous people. The Finns love to laugh and most of all they tend to laugh at themselves. Their humor is devoid of cynicism and has a startling frankness about it. Their jokes are rarely cutting or bitchy, but more a laugh about their own national characteristics. They have a very natural intelligence concerning their behavior. Rather than getting overconfident and bullish, they tend to self-doubt and use humor to put themselves down—or put themselves back in their place [Swallow 2011: 104].

Pragmatism is a good adviser especially in the political arena. In early June 2015, Finland's president, Sauli Niinistö, announced to the media that he would go to Moscow for talks with Russia's president. Journalists wanted to know what the agenda for his journey was. Niinistö said that he would meet with Vladimir Putin in an atmosphere of consensus with political leaders of other EU countries. When asked whether Finland was expected to function as a mediator between the European Union and Russia and whether Niinistö expects to make progress in talks about the crisis in Ukraine, the president answered that he had no particular expectations. And then he added smiling: "We have a long border with Russia."

Indeed, Finland's border with Russia is long, some 1,340 km (833 miles), which is artificially drawn and not orientated to any landmarks or natural features of the landscape. Near the border, stretching along most parts of the line from south to north, is the most monumental structure the Finns have ever completed, the defense system that was built during 1940, 1941 and 1944. During the first and most extensive phase, work on this defense system (*Salpalinja* or *Salpa-asema* in Finnish) was carried out by some 35,000 men who were provided with supplies by some 2,000 women. These women, called *lotat* (singular *lotta*) in Finnish, participated in war efforts: taking food supplies to the frontline, serving in units on watchtowers to monitor the movements of enemy aircraft, operating switchboards for connecting telephone calls (Hakala et al. 2007). And sometimes, the *lotat* were exposed to enemy fire.

The defense line is comprised of some 350,000 pieces of solid granite rock, each weighing some 3 tons, that were erected and arranged in formations to serve as anti-tank obstacles. Almost 1,000 concrete bunkers and infantry shelters were constructed, of which about 90 percent are concentrated between the Gulf of Finland and Lake Saimaa. This part of the defense line is called the *Luumäen linja* (or *Luumäki-Suomenlahti-linja*, respectively). There are many thousands of entrenchments, ditches and dugouts scattered all along the *Salpalinja*, and many positions for gun batteries. This defensive barrier provided a significant psychological support for the frontline soldiers. The Red Army never advanced as far as the *Salpalinja*; their most massive assault in summer 1944 was stopped in the battle of Tali-Ihantala. Finnish officers had a handbook of regulations. The last page in this handbook concerned the *Salpalinja*. Every officer hoped that they would never have to follow the regulations specified on that page. In fact, they never had to make arrangements for activating the line for combat. The *Salpalinja* was kept in order, secretly, by the Finnish army during the Cold War period (until the 1980s), but it was finally decommissioned in 2003. Since then the remains have been undergoing renovation for preservation as an historical monument. Finland's border with Russia is not only the border of this country with its eastern neighbor, it is, at the same time, the border of the European Union with Russia.

Since it has been the priority of Finnish postwar governments to keep up peaceful relations with Russia, regular contacts between the presidents of both countries and between officials on the ministerial level are observed. As an EU member state, Finland speaks not only in its own voice but often with a mandate from Brussels, as a "bridge-builder," to facilitate negotiations with Russia. Finns are trusted to have experience in dealing with Russian politicians, and this know-how has proven to be advantageous for handling EU-Russian relations.

So when President Sauli Niinistö makes reference to the long eastern border of his country, this statement carries great symbolic weight. It reflects pragmatism of Finland's political leaders along the lines of the so-called Paasikivi-Kekkonen doctrine according to which everything in Finnish politics goes, yet with the warning "Avoid treading on the Big Bear's toes." Two consecutive presidents of Finland, Juho Kusti Paasikivi (in office from 1946 to 1956) and Urho Kaleva Kekkonen (1956 to 1981), constructed relations with the Soviet Union in a way that defined Finland's neutrality (see Chapter 8). The Paasikivi-Kekkonen guideline was extended by president Mauno Koivisto who was in office from 1982 to 1994, and who witnessed the great change when the Soviet Empire crumbled and modern Russia emerged.

## *Cultural Stereotypes in Light of Finnish Realities*

The features that we attach to foreigners are as generalizing and stereotyping as those they attach to us. The more experience we have in interacting with other people the more differentiated the image becomes that we form about ourselves vis-à-vis others. The image we carry in our mind is molded on the basis of cultural stereotypes. With cultural stereotyping, the features with which we categorize populations and their culture may be right or wrong, or somewhat right or only somewhat wrong. Everything depends on how much weight we put on individual stereotypes.

Cultural stereotypes are mobilized easily because they are available in our minds in a kind of stand-by mode. When you ask foreigners what comes to mind when thinking about Finns and Finland, they may answer: sauna and tango. It does not seem far-fetched to consider both as Finnish cultural institutions.

### Finnish Sauna: Myth and Reality

When foreigners think of the Finnish sauna they think of a place to sweat and clean oneself. Basically, it is true that frequenting a sauna is good for your health and enhances your physical condition; you may even use a *vasta* (or *vihta*), a bunch of birch twigs, to beat yourself lightly to stimulate blood circulation. To undergo a sauna is an event, a social gathering for the whole family, a way to think about things, undisturbed, in a comfortable environment. What makes a sauna a venue for social events is not just the common experience inside the sauna but the gathering afterwards. Family members and friends sit together, share a meal and enjoy themselves. This atmosphere has been captured by the Finnish singer Arja Saijonmaa in a book that appeared in 2000.

In historical times, women gave birth to their children in the sauna. That was before the introduction of modern healthcare and maternal facilities in hospitals. In the old days, the sauna was a place for ritual healing and, it was imbued with sacredness. Children were admonished to behave in sauna properly: *Saunassa pitää olla kuin kirkossa* "In sauna you must behave as if you were in church." In the old days there was a direct linkage between sauna—the place to perform a cleaning rite—and the holy Sunday when people would go to church.

> The sacred was embodied most immediately in the Sunday Sabbath, which was referred to as *pyhä* ("sacred"), a term which derives from the pre–Christian word for tabus and restrictions. Sunday began directly after Saturday night sauna. Women cleaned, baked and prepared food for the following day [Virtanen and DuBois 2000: 82].

The traditional spirit of sauna has been eternalized in a famous painting, *Itäsuomalainen sauna* ("Eastern Finnish sauna"), by the artist Pekka Halonen, in 1896.

Sauna is a place for relaxation and for mental reorganization, for problem-solving and for making plans. Finland's long-term president, Urho Kekkonen (1900–1986), once commented on his passion for sauna: "In the sauna I relax physically and invigorate mentally. The calm atmosphere creates harmony. For me, life without a sauna would be completely impossible." The sauna can be the place where important decisions are made, and this holds true for Kekkonen's ways to manage political affairs. He had the habit to invite political guests to a sauna, as a setting to create a memorable atmosphere, tuning one's mind for discussing difficult issues in a relaxed way.

The beginnings of the sauna in Finland are shrouded in mystery, and nobody knows for sure when the culture began. It must be of great age since it is mentioned on many occasions in the national epic *Kalevala*. The habit to heat stones, throw water on them in order to create steam and do some sweating in a closed room is a custom also among the other people of Baltic-Finnic affiliation. Steam baths were in use among the Amerindians in pre-colonial times and this habit is documented for parts of southeastern Europe in pre–Greek times. Finnish sauna became popular at the beginning of the New Era when the older tradition of bath houses in central and northern Europe was abandoned. During the Middle Ages, such houses were a public venue for members of both sexes to meet and to share the same bathtub, naked, accompanied by eating and drinking. The Protestant worldview rejected such sinful habits, and the sauna continued the tradition on a private level.

Sauna is an integral part of Finnish culture (Valtakari 2015) and it is a firm motif in Finland's national image which can be substantiated in statistical terms. There are more than three million saunas in Finland. In relation to the 5.5 million population of the country, there is an average of one sauna per family. Usually, saunas form part of the architectural layout of apartments and houses. Even where there is no private sauna in apartment houses there is one sauna available for all the inhabitants in a bloc. Sauna culture was exported abroad by Finnish immigrants to various parts of the world. In North America one can identify Americans of Finnish descent by their traditional sauna customs.

> The sauna demonstrates both continuities and transformations within Finnish American culture. First and second generation Finnish immigrants living in rural tracts reproduced the sauna and sauna traditions of their homeland unselfconsciously, as a taken-for-granted element of ordinary life. At the turn of the century, many Finnish-American towns also had public saunas as well [Virtanen and DuBois 2000: 61].

Perhaps the most famous sauna in America is the Finnish Baths, built by Alfred Finnilä (1913–2000) in San Francisco. His father, Matti, had emigrated to the U.S. in 1902 and had started a business in Los Angeles. After the earthquake of San Francisco, in 1906, Matti moved to that city and participated, as a mason, in its rebuilding. There he met another Finnish emigrant, Alexandra. The couple married and had two children, one of them being Alfred. Matti opened a Finnish-style sauna, as a place of public healthcare. In the early 1930s, Alfred built another, bigger sauna that became known as Finnilä's Finnish Baths (on Market Street in San Francisco). The sauna facilities were separated for men and women, as were the massage facilities. It has to be emphasized here that the Finnish Baths served as a true sauna, not as a sex establishment.

In 1983—and again in 1984—the Finnish Baths were praised as "the best sauna and massage parlor" in the San Francisco Bay Area (*San Francisco Bay Guardian* No: 37, 1984). In 1986–87, the old structure was demolished and a new building erected, the function of which continues that of the former Baths. The Finnish sauna on Market Street is known as the Market & Noe Center, run by Edna Jeffrey, Alfred's sister.

In Finland, there are many public saunas. In early summer of 2016, a new public sauna (actually a sauna park) was opened in Helsinki, its name is Löyly which means "steam" (and "spirit" in an historical meaning). This showcase of modern Finnish architecture and design, was built by Avanto Architects. The façade of the dome-like building is covered with 4,000 wooden planks, forming a kind of "cloak," all made of natural materials.

## Tango—Finnish Style

Finnish tango is only a few years older than Finland's independence, and yet, tango is as much a part of Finnish culture as is sauna with its long history. The classical song, the mother of tango, is *La Paloma* which was first presented to the public in Cuba, in 1854. *La Paloma* became known in Finland in the 1890s but this did not create a local fashion. The tango took another route over the Atlantic to Finland, this time a detour via Argentina. Before World War I, the Argentinian tango became popular in Paris, and from there, it spread to Finland.

In the summer of 1912, tango music was presented at a famous restaurant (*Kaivo-huone*) in Helsinki. The orchestra that played such melodies had come from St. Petersburg. Those summer performances echoed in Finnish popular culture: the tango was to stay in Finland and bloom. During the following summer season (of 1913), Finland was already "in the grip of tango fever" (Jalkanen 2013: 315). About a year later, a Finn named Emil Kauppi composed the first Finnish tango for a silent film, serving as the accompaniment in a dance scene. Tango music remained popular in the 1920s and 1930s. Most compositions were foreign (e.g., Argentinian, German, Swedish, Lithuanian) and original Finnish ones were few.

The special Finnish touch to tango music emerged during the period of World War II. The lyrics became infused with nostalgia, with themes of epic poetry and with national motifs. There was a marked gravitation toward one's roots, the longing for home, for closeness and solidarity, the melancholic feeling about the uncertainty of the future and one's family. In the lyrics, one finds the motif of a person who listens to the birds or sits under a rowan tree (a sacred tree in Finnish mythology). Tango music became ever more popular, and the soldiers who did service at the front took some comfort from the music to lighten their spirits for the effort to defend their home country. Those who composed tango music were themselves soldiers, like Toivo Kärki (1915–1992)—later called "the supreme god of Finnish popular music"—who served as an artillery officer. In the 1940s, and well into the 1950s, the lyrics for tangos were written predominantly by women, of whom Kerttu Mustonen is perhaps the best known.

Finnish tangos and their lyrics, imbued with "ardent melancholy" (Jukka Ammondt), are the favorite music on Finnish dance-floors, and the melodies resound through the summer nights, at many places in the countryside where Finns spend their weekends and holidays in cottages. Among the most popular melodies are *Täysikuu* ("Full Moon") and *Satumaa* ("Fairy-Tale Land"). Each year, there are singing competitions, and a tango queen and a tango king are crowned. Those singers are the most successful in the entertainment business. Tango is not subject to any fashion trend, it has remained, throughout the decades, a steady component of Finnish entertainment. For the Finns, tango has the value of a popular national anthem.

Tango is not only a genre of song and music, it is also, and very much so, a genre of dance. Since the end of the 19th century, gathering and spending evening pastime in open-air dance pavilions became fashionable among a broader public (Yli-Jokipii 1996). Originally, dancing outdoors was a favorite pastime in the rural areas during the summer season. It then spread into suburban areas. The dancing events in open-air pavilions have remained popular throughout the 20th century and into the twenty-first although there have been setbacks in the 1950s, with the spread of rock music, and in the 1980s, when disco became fashionable (Saarikoski 2014). Yet, open-air dancing is widely practiced nowadays. Among the various dances (waltz, foxtrot, polka) tango is by far the favorite.

## *The Lure of Snow and Ice: Finns and Some of Their Pastime Activities*

If there are people in Europe who have long-term experience with and know how to deal with snow and ice it is the Saami and the Finns in Finland. Climatic conditions determine the pace of life in this country, and people have to cope with restrictions set by snow and ice during several months each year. The climate dictates how you have to build houses in Finland, how cars have to be equipped to function in the Arctic cold and how many icebreakers have to operate to keep the waterways along the coasts open during the winter season. No wonder that icebreaker technology is far advanced in Finland and some of the world's most modern icebreakers have been built in Finnish shipyards.

Snow and ice do not scare the Finns because they have learned how to cope with such weather conditions and, above all, how to profit from them. In winter, the lakes are frozen but that does not prevent the Finns from dipping into them after a sauna. An opening is sawn through the ice and removed, and the space used for a short swim, for cooling down after a hot session in the sauna. This habit is called *avantouinti* ("winter swimming," literally "swimming in the opened water") in Finnish. Winter swimming (or ice swimming) is not for everybody. People with a heart condition should not practice it. When the body that is heated up gets cooled down in a shockwave this puts a strain on the heart although, at the same time, it inspires blood circulation. It has been scientifically proven that winter swimming is of significance for individual health care (Huttunen et al. 2004), and some practice it even without sauna.

As is the case with many other pastimes that turn into competitions, competitive winter swimming is practiced not only in Finland but also in Sweden and Norway, in Estonia, in northern Russia and elsewhere in the world. There is an International Ice Swimming Association. The minimum requirement is that the water temperature in the opening must be below 5° C (41° F). Ice swimming records (relating to the number of participants in a swimming session and to the duration of the swim) are documented in the Guinness Book of Records.

When the winter season is at its height and lakes and inland waterways are frozen, an extended seasonal network of traffic and transportation becomes available. People and machines move on the ice for various reasons. Provided the ice cover is solid enough, sledges, cars and even trucks frequent certain trails to shorten distances between the shore and islands in lakes. During January and February (sometimes extending into March), certain stretches on the southwestern coast are frequented by cars for connections between the shore and islands in the archipelago. Trucks are used in winter to transport construction material over the ice to islands.

Long-term experience with ice conditions has produced certain security standards for various activities. Recommendations have been given relating to the thickness of the ice:

- 6.4–10 cm (2.5–4 inches) for anglers to move on the ice;
- 13–15 cm (5–6 inches) for snowmobiles;
- 18–30 cm (7–12 inches) for light cars;
- 36–41 cm (14–16 inches) for large trucks.

There never is any certainty about the thickness of the ice cover, which is regularly monitored all around the country. There may be places where undercurrents of flowing water prevent a normal growth of ice. Every year it happens that people and machinery break through thin ice at dangerous sites.

Among the popular pastime activities during the winter season is ice fishing (*pilkkiminen* in Finnish), often a social event when anglers meet or compete at contests. Anglers go out on the ice, equipped with drills and angling gear (Gruenwald and Genz 1999). They drill a hole into the ice, sit beside the hole and do angling like in summer. Ice fishing competitions are held at the end of the winter season and their popularity is increasing.

Ice fishing is widely practiced in the colder regions of the northern hemisphere, and there are also contests, like those in Finland, in other countries (including Norway, Latvia, Russia, the U.S., Canada and South Korea).

## Skiing

People who live in countries without snow may wonder how traffic and transportation works when there is regular snowfall and whole regions are covered under thick layers of snow. In historical times when road connections were scarce and waterways were frozen in winter, people drove in sledges from one place to another, and they practiced extensively what the Finns are good at: skiing. Skiing is beyond doubt a typical feature of Finnishness (Turunen 2015). School children in the first grade learn how to ski if they have not already mastered it at preschool age. There are skiing competitions at the end of each term. Learning how to ski is a must for the young ones because many children, in winter, leave their homes on skis to reach their schools.

In Finnish, there are two distinct terms for skiing, one is *hiihtää* which refers to cross-country skiing, the other is *lasketella* in the meaning of Alpine skiing (i.e., down a slope). The former expression is traditional, the latter is a word which has assumed a specialized meaning when referring to Alpine sports as a modern import. Nowadays, Alpine skiing is offered at various winter resorts throughout the country. In Lapland one can do skiing, both ways, starting in November and into May. In the south, the skiing season usually lasts from December until March, sometimes into April.

Cross-country skiing is among the most widely practiced activities for the Finns, and many go skiing regularly during the winter season to keep in good physical condition. Cross-country skiing was originally limited to the winter season but it has become popular also as an outdoor activity in summer. There are two kinds of skiing during the summer season. One is to move on roll skis that are about one meter long and fixed to rubber wheels (called *rullahiihto* in Finnish). The other technique is skate rolling with the help of sticks, like for skiing in winter (called *sauvarullaluistelu*). The latter activity is the more popular.

Alpine skiing has been continuously gaining in popularity although the number of those who practice it is more limited when compared to the cross-country people. Except for the big cities one easily finds a path for skiing near the place where one lives, but to do Alpine skiing one has to drive to a resort. Given the broad backing for skiing skills in the Finnish population, the talents needed for skiing sports are easily acquired. Finns have been performing well in international competitions of both kinds of skiing.

For those who are more engaged in skiing than the average there are opportunities and facilities for ski jumping. This requires yet more special skills. Finland has a legendary figure in this domain, and this is Matti Nykänen (b. 1963) who performed his first ski jump at the age of eight. The Finns call him *mäkikotka* "eagle of the hill" (Theiner 2006). The first event of ski jumping had a decisive effect on Matti's career: he became a passionate participant. Before he was slowed by an excessive use of alcohol in the 1990s he had many records on his list. Matti achieved an exceptional record when he, in Obersdorf (Germany) in 1985, jumped 190+ meters, something nobody had succeeded in doing before him. Competing during the Olympic Winter Games in Calgary in 1988, Matti scored three gold medals in different disciplines—normal hill, large hill, team event. In addition, he won 46 World Cup victories during his career. Matti has remained a legend, the image of the eagle of the hill that people cherish in their memory, despite the vicissitudes that have overshadowed his mature life, linked to uncontrolled behavior when he has drunk too much (e.g., violent fighting, various jail sentences, several divorces). Who knows how persistently the memory of this national legend may last.

## Ice Hockey

In addition to skiing, another type of winter sport comes to mind: ice hockey. This game had a precursor which was "bandy." Originally developed in England as an extension of field hockey, bandy reached Finland toward the end of the 19th century, via Sweden and Russia. In 1927, ice hockey was officially adopted by the Finnish Skating Association, and the first national championship was organized a year later. Bandy, for its part, remained popular in Finland for another twenty years but was abandoned in the 1950s, in favor of ice hockey. Finland's ice hockey team participated in the World Championship in Basel, in 1939, but did not win any game. For another three decades, the Finnish national team (called the "Lions") did not improve its international ranking significantly.

Then came the 1960s, and things changed when the Lions challenged all the "Big Five," the leading national ice hockey teams worldwide. At international championships, the Lions scored victories over the ice hockey teams of the USA (in 1963), Sweden (1965), Czechoslovakia (1967), and Canada (1968). Yet, the Soviet Union remained unbeaten until 1988. The breakthrough to victory over the last of the "Big Five" came at the Olympic Games in Calgary when the Lions beat the Soviet team.

There was still another level to reach for the Finnish ice hockey team: medals at the World Championship. In the 1990s, the Lions advanced to the small circle of those international teams that win medals almost regularly. The games at Prague in 1992 brought the first silver medal, and gold was earned through a victory over Sweden in Stockholm, in 1995. Although Finland was a latecomer regarding the introduction of ice hockey, it was swift in opening the path of this sport for women. As the first country in Europe (and the third in the world after the USA and Canada), Finland organized a team of female hockey players who earned a bronze medal in the first women's Olympic tournament in Nagano (Japan), in 1998.

"In no other European country does ice hockey occupy such a prominent place in the domestic sport scene, and on world level only Canada can compete" (http://jaakiek komuseo.vapriikki.fi/english/history.htm; retrieved 31 October 2015). Ice hockey is a preferred activity for youngsters who dream of becoming a member of the Lions' team one day. TV broadcasts of ice hockey games, both national and international, score among the highest attendance figures of TV programs in the country.

While Finnish youngsters may dream of the national team, those among the Lions who think about an international career dream about joining teams in America, preferably in the USA. Since the 1970s, Finnish hockey players have joined American teams of the National Hockey League (NHL) of the USA. The first hockey player from Finland to join the NHL was Matti Hagman (of Boston Bruins) in 1976. Ice hockey players from Finland who became famous as members of U.S. teams include:

- Sami Vatanen (b. 1991), defenceman for the Anaheim Ducks;
- Valtteri Filppula (b. 1984), forward for the Tampa Bay Lightning;
- Teemu Selänne (b. 1970), called "The Finnish Flash," a former winger for the Winnipeg Jets, Anaheim Ducks, San Jose Sharks and Colorado Avalanche; the Finn with the highest scores in NHL history;
- Jari Kurri (b. 1960), a former right winger and five-time Stanley Cup champion; inducted into the Hockey Hall of Fame in 2001;
- Jarkko Ruutu (b. 1975), a former player for the Michigan Tech, the Vancouver Canucks and the Syracuse Crunch; Jarkko is the brother of Tuomo Ruutu (who plays for the New Jersey Devils) and of Mikko Ruutu (in 2016 a scout for the Ottawa Senators)
- Jussi Jokinen (b. 1983), forward for the Florida Panthers, Tampa Bay Lightning, Carolina Hurricanes and Pittsburgh Penguins.

## Skating

There is another category where Finns have made it to top rankings in championships, and this is skating—figure skating and ice dancing in particular. Figure skating originated in the USA from where it spread to Europe. In 1875, skating performances of the American Jackson Haines at Helsinki and Kokkola brought the breakthrough for this sport in Finland.

The first national figure skating championships in Finland were held in 1908, and the winner of the gold medal was Sakari Ilmanen. As single skaters, women participated sometime later. The first female winner in the history of figure skating was Ludowika Jakobsson in 1917. As pair skaters, women were successful earlier. Ludowika and Walter Jakobsson won gold at the Finnish national championship in 1911. Early on, this team made themselves a name several times at the World Championships: winning silver in 1910, 1912, 1913 and 1922; becoming World Champions in 1911, 1914 and 1923. At the Olympics, Ludowika and Walter won gold, in 1920 and 1924. It took several decades before Finnish figure skaters advanced again to higher rankings, in the 1970s (Kristiina Wegelius, Susan Broman, Pekka Leskinen).

The Finnish skaters who have gained the most recognition in the world are partners in pair—ice dancing, Susanna Rahkamo and Petri Kokko. They made their way up to the top at international championships, in the 1990s: in 1993 winning the bronze medal at the European Championships; in 1994 winning the bronze medal at the World Championship; and in 1995 winning gold at the European Championship and silver at the World Championship.

In international competitions since the 2000s, there have always been Finns with successful ratings, and almost regularly winning medals; but there are some highly contrasting careers. There is the case of the ice dancer Susanna Pöykiö who has had a long career and who won medals at various competitions and through many years: bronze at the Junior World (2001), silver at the European (2005) and bronze at the European (2009). And then there is Kiira Korpi who won bronze at the European in 2007 and 2011 and silver at the European in 2012. In summer 2015, she announced that she would retire because she had been injured in an accident and would not be able to keep up her former skills. Laura Lepistö is the first Finnish woman skater to win gold at the European (2009), and bronze at the World (2010).

In the 2000s, Finland took the lead in the field of synchronized skating, winning medals at the World Synchronized Skating Championships each year since 2000 except 2007 and 2012. There is no other country whose participants in the competitions have been as successful as the Finnish teams (http://www.stll.fi/luistelijalle/lajit/muodostelmaluistelu/ suomalaismenestysta/). As in the case of ice hockey, outstanding members of the Finnish teams for synchronized skating also make it to top positions in the United States. Perhaps the most successful in her field is the choreographer Saga Krantz who became the coach of Team USA 1, the Haydenettes from Lexington, Massachusetts. "Figure skating clubs organize many kinds of activities for kids, teenagers and adults. Those, who aim to become competitive skaters, can choose from a variety of sports: single skating, synchronized skating, pair skating or ice dance" (http://www.stll.fi/in_english/ffsa/history/; retrieved 4 July 2015).

## *Some Unusual Competitions*

Some think the Finns are crazy. One cannot deny that altogether because, in a way, it is true, especially when looking at some rather unusual competitions with which the Finns amuse themselves.

### Wife-Carrying (or Woman-Carrying)

What is sometimes seen as "woman-carrying" in English is called *eukonkanto* (or *akankanto*) in Finnish: "wife-carrying" (*eukko* or *akka* "wife" + *kanto* "carrying"). This is a kind of sport in which a man and a woman engage in a race over an obstacle track. The man takes the role of the runner while the woman is the burden he has to carry. The woman is hanging over the runner's shoulders, with her head hanging down the man's back while her legs are stretched out to the front. Competitions are held each year at Sonkajärvi (in the northern part of Savo in eastern Finland). The race track, some 254 meters long, is in rough terrain and includes two dry obstacles and one water obstacle which is about one meter deep. There is a lower limit to the woman's weight. She must weigh at least 49 kilograms (108 pounds).

It is not known when and where this custom originated but, most probably, it is associated with the historical tradition of bride-stealing. Young men from a village would, during the night, clandestinely approach a neighboring village and steal a young woman as a bride, to become the wife of one of the "thieves." Usually, the man and the stolen bride would not be strangers to one another but, rather, their intention to live together would be ritualized through bride-stealing.

The first wife-carrying competition, with participants from various countries, was held in 1997, and the winning team was from Finland. It is noteworthy that, from 1998 through 2008, the winning team always came from Estonia. Since 2009, again, the world champions have been Finns. From 2009 to 2013, it was the same team (Taisto Miettinen and Kristiina Haapanen) that won the competition each year (Mölsä and Ojala 2015: 63; figure 23).

**Figure 23: The winning couple, Taisto Miettinen and Kristiina Haapanen, during a competition of wife-carrying in 2013 (photograph: Roni Rekomaa; Photo Agency Lehtikuva).**

The Finnish model of woman-carrying championship was copied in other countries, namely in Estonia, Great Britain, the USA, Australia and Hong Kong.

## Mud Soccer (Football)

Mud soccer (or swamp soccer) is an extreme sport that is gaining in popularity in ever more countries of the world. It can be played where marshy grounds or swamps are available, and Finland abounds with such terrain. No wonder why the idea of mud soccer originated in Finland. The Finns are fond of soccer (European "football") but perhaps not as passionately as people in such countries as Germany, Great Britain, Brazil and Argentina. Sports relating to snow and ice are more firmly rooted in this country (see above) but football is not neglected. The extreme version of football, mud soccer, pushes any player to the limits of his or her stamina.

Each year, international competitions of mud soccer sport are organized. In July 2012, the Swamp Soccer Championships were held in Finland (in Hyrynsalmi, northern Finland). Spectators flock around a muddy area that is delimited for the game, and the teams of players do their best to kick the ball across the muddy field to score goals. Apart from being really dirty, mud soccer is very demanding, since it put the utmost strain on the leg muscles when the players sink into the mud and have to try to raise their legs for action on the ball. Footballers say that it is great fun to try mud soccer, but the fun may be even greater for the spectators. And, of course, a mud soccer match attracts many photographers who compete in their own league, trying to take muddy snap shots (http://photoblog.nbcnews.com/_news/2012/07/16/12764939-glorious-mud-photos-from-finlands-swamp-soccer-championships; retrieved 21 June 2015).

## Mobile Phone Throwing

The history of mobile phone throwing started in Savonlinna (eastern Finland), in 2000. That was the time when the Finnish company Nokia was the world's biggest producer of mobile phones (see Chapter 5). Mobile Phone Throwing World Championships have been continuously organized in Finland, on an annual basis. So far, mobile phone championships have been organized in summer, but there are plans to develop this competition into a winter event. The first Mobile Phone Throwing World Championship was scheduled to take place in Savonlinna (at the Castle Olavinlinna), in March 2017.

The idea of mobile phone throwing is no crazy commercial strategy to advertise mobile phone models or producers. On the occasion of the first championship in 2000, the event was sponsored by one of the big insurance companies in Finland. What is intended in connection with this sport is to remind people that mobile phones have to be properly recycled in order to dispose of the toxic material inside the phones in a proper fashion.

> Mobile Phone Throwing is a light and modern Finnish sport that suits for people of all ages. It combines recycling philosophy and fun spirit in active sport. A part of the philosophy is also a spiritual freedom from being available all the time [http://www.mobilephonethrowing.fi/; retrieved 3 October 2015].

The Finnish event served as a model for national championships in other countries, in Norway, Great Britain, Czech Republic, Germany, Liechtenstein, Switzerland, Belgium, Spain (Lund 2008). Those who organize the sport take their work very seriously, and various categories are distinguished:

- the traditional way (throwing the phone over one's shoulders, with the farthest distance winning);
- freestyle (scoring points from the standpoint of aesthetic movements and choreography);
- team throwing (a team may consist of two or three contestants; the scores of their throws are added together);
- junior competition (mobile throwing for youngsters, up to the age of 12).

As for the distances that have been reached, there is a list of world records and of national records. As for the Finnish national records, the distance for men is 101.5 m (Ere Karjalainen, 2012)—as compared to the world record for men at 110.4 m (Dries Feremans, Belgium, 2014), and for women 50.8 m (Eija Laakso, 2006)—as compared to the world record for women at 60.2 m (Tereza Kopicová, Czech Republic, 2012).

## What Holds Finnish Society Together? The Secrets of the Finnish Communitarian Spirit

To look for the roots of the communitarian spirit among the Finns one has to dive deep into the past, as deep as the remote era of prehistory. Prehistory in northern Europe was not dark. Instead, community life then held the key to certain ideals of communal responsibilities vis-à-vis the natural environment and concerning social egalitarianism, something we (re)appreciate today.

The earliest experiences with the sense of belonging to a community are related to the pre–Christian world of shamanism. In the communities of hunters and gatherers, the issue of leadership arose in the context of the relationship between the shaman and the members of the group for whom he acted. This relationship was characterized by the working of a factor that is an essential ingredient of participatory governance: authority. The shaman did not usurp power but was assigned authority to act on the community's behalf and to use this authority in the community's service and for the benefit of its members. Of the two key concepts in a network of sociopolitical conceptualizations, authority and power, the shaman assumed the former, not the latter:

> The essential differences between authority and power lie in the ability to control. Authority rules mainly through persuasion and example, and tradition. Power, while not neglecting these, rules by compulsion. The measure of power is the sanctions it can impose. By sanctions is meant the mechanisms of restrictive and punitive social control that are available to the leaders [Donlan 1997: 40f.].

According to this definitional approach, authority serves chosen leaders in an egalitarian community while the exercise of power is a phenomenon of stratified society. In the world of animated nature, the shaman, with special training for communication between the worlds, acts with the authorization of the community, as a mediator to convey the vital spiritual needs of the community to the forces that guarantee a harmonious balance among the participants in the life cycle (Harvey 2005: 149ff.). Such communication is always carried out under the auspices of "some definite collective goal" (Hoppál 2001: 75). The shaman acts with a mandate from the spiritual powers that inhabit the animated world. But without the responsibility for action vis-à-vis the community the shaman's doing would be futile.

To be effective, the shaman's community would have to share a basic respect for the natural world and common values in association with the group's traditions. The seasonal rituals, dances, feasts, celebrations, offerings—all aspects of traditional life—would reinforce an underlying consciousness of respect and sustainability. Without this context, the shaman would hardly be able to function.

The prevalent shamanistic worldview of the prehistoric era continued to shape the communitarian spirit among the Finns into historical times, and social cohesion could unfold among the local population, without the shackles of feudalism or serfdom so typical of the fate of peasants in Russia. The institution of serfdom determined unconditional social bonds of peasants to a landlord who owned the land and the people who worked it for him. Serfdom in Russia was introduced in the 11th century and abolished as late as 1861. Serfdom was unknown in Sweden, and since Finland formed part of the Swedish Kingdom it was absent there also. The situation did not change when Finland was annexed to Russia in 1809. According to the autonomy status of the Grand Duchy, the older Swedish institutions remained intact which made Finland the only region of Russia without serfdom.

The peasants formed their own estate which was a category based on a mixture of features related to social class and to occupation. In the 18th century, the peasants' estate included the great majority of the rural population. The situation of Finnish peasants was that of crofters (Finnish *torppari* "crofter") who worked on some landowner's estate which was held by them in tenancy (Klinge 1997: 96ff.). Then, the portion of urban citizens in Finland was small compared to their number in Sweden proper (Heckscher 1968: 141).

Early manifestations of communitarianism among the Finns were economic associations that were established by villagers to benefit from common fishing grounds and village owned land and forest areas.

> The economic associations established for the exploitation of various natural resources were based on appropriation under customary law.... The custom applied equally to hunting and fishing in the wilds and to fishing in the islands, where many of the fishing-grounds were controlled by villages or even parishes, in which case they were usually communal.... The voluntary economic associations undoubtedly had roots stretching back to ancient times. Some were loose and disintegrated when a joint venture came to an end (e.g., hunting, fishing and slash-and-burn associations), others were more closely knit (seine, mill, sawmill and lake draining associations) [Talve 1997: 183f.].

## The Long Trail of Women's Participation in Communitarian Decision-Making

Since ancient times the bonds of social relationships among the native populations of Finland have been those of kinship. Within the framework of kinship relations, the roles of men and women are of elementary significance, and this is true in a global comparison of cultures. "It is therefore not possible to understand kinship relations without analyzing the place occupied by men and women, and in a broader perspective the social attributes attaching to each, and which make them different genders" (Godelier 2011: 74).

Equality of the sexes in modern times, in Finland, gives the impression of enlightened reasoning that advocates the participation of both men and women in public life and in state affairs. Common sense informs us that a society can fully profit from its human resources only under the condition that men and women are on equal footing when it comes to sharing responsibilities and participating in decision-making.

Such insights are not new. They were made explicit already in antiquity. There was an ancient Greek philosopher who did not share the conventions of his time and dared oppose traditional clichés of gender roles. This philosopher, the first to address gender issues in society and to advocate the idea that women should be equal before the law and enjoy the same rights as men, was Plato (ca. 424–ca. 348 BCE). In two of his dialogues (in the *Republic* and in the *Laws*) Plato elaborates on social conditions in an ideal society (Haarmann 2016). Plato explicitly stresses the benefits for a state if representatives of both sexes take political assignments, and the philosopher grants women the right to assume responsibility for public affairs in high office, including state leadership. Such ideas were revolutionary for Plato's time when female citizens in the state of Athens did not have the right to vote in democratic elections. It took until the dawn of modernity for Plato's ideas to gradually materialize and for women to actively participate in a country's politics.

In western Europe, the emancipation movement and the rise of modern feminism were a phenomenon anchored in intellectual considerations. The development in Finland differed markedly from western trends. The independent movement of emancipation among Finnish women received intellectual impulses from western Europe at a time when the local drive toward equality of the sexes, nourished by an historical spirit of liberty, had already gained in momentum.

This spirit of liberty, characteristic of Finnish women, has enjoyed a long history.

In Finnish society, the equality of women is no novelty of the modern era, and women in communal service are known from the pre–Christian period. Equality of the sexes is manifested in the division of labor of those who were assigned authority, by the members of their community, to act as leaders, as coordinators of communitarian affairs and as supervisors of ritual life: the shamans. "The shaman served as the religious leader and was considered an expert in mediating the reciprocal interaction between this world and the other realm" (Pentikäinen 1989: 179).

## Female Shamans, Healers and the Christian Witch-Hunt

The tradition of shamanism among the peoples of northern Eurasia includes both male and female shamans. In communities where shamans of both sexes function as mediators between the worlds their roles are distinguished by the different tasks they perform. In connection with the celebration of a funeral, the male shaman would be responsible for the performance of rituals of transcending the world of the living, to gain access to the spirit-world and to escort the soul of the deceased to the netherworld, while the female shaman's responsibility would be to comfort those who suffered a personal loss and to ease the pain of mourning in the community by performing rites of spiritual healing (Haarmann 2000: 10).

A similar role, that of spiritual healing, is traditionally taken by women as the performers of laments among the Finnic peoples (Ingrians, Vots, Karelians) living in the Baltic area (Nenola 2002: 73ff.). "The *itkuvirsi* ("crying song," lament) was seen as an important device for helping conduct the soul of the deceased to the hereafter.… According to tradition, the lament was the only human communication audible to the deceased" (Virtanen and DuBois 2000: 148).

Female shamans among the Saami and the Samoyed peoples of Siberia were held in high esteem (Bäckman and Hultkrantz 1978: 84ff.). Those traditions must be of great antiquity because there is evidence for the presence of women in the Neolithic imagery of northern Europe relating to mythopoetic contexts of shamanism.

Among the finest specimens is an image of a female shaman that features in the largest picture complex of rock art found thus far in Finland, at Astuvansalmi (in the municipality of Ristiina) on the shore of Lake Saimaa (Kivikäs 1995: 64, 261). The female figure whose sex is recognizable from the painted breasts, holds a bow and is the only human being depicted. The figure is centered and surrounded by elks with their heads turned toward her. The site has been identified as a place for the performance of rituals related to hunting magic. In all probability, the female figure represents the performer (or supervisor) of such rituals (figure 24). Near the rock with the painted pictures arrow points were found and, in the surface of the rock, there are small holes, resulting from arrows that were shot at the animal figures in a symbolic hunting performance.

The rock pictures at Astuvansalmi date to the late fourth or third millennium BCE, and they were made by artists from the community of archaic hunter-gatherers in the region.

The responsibility of the female shaman, as a functionary in and for her community, continues in the communities of early agriculturalists, in the era before the emergence of state organization. The significance of female shamanism and its transition from a hunter-gatherer to an agrarian society has been highlighted for southeastern Europe (Haarmann 2013: 157ff.). In northern Europe, and in Scandinavia in particular, the role of the female shaman crystallizes around the central performance of *seidr* ("divination; performance of the seer").

**Figure 24: An image depicting a female figure (shaman) in the rock paintings of Astuvansalmi in Ristiina, southeastern Finland (author's material).**

> Female shamanism appears most strongly in societies which are not primarily based on hunting, or in areas which border such societies. It is often more associated with agrarian societies than is male shamanism, and may be subsumed within a wider spiritual system where the hierarchical religion is more male-dominated. All of these societal characteristics are found in ancient Scandinavia, where *seidr*, the practice most comparable to shamanism, was also dominated by women (in all likelihood this is a reflection of a long-standing preponderance of women as diviners...).... [I]t is, moreover, a broadly shamanic feature..., in that *seidr* would be employed to ensure the welfare and continuance of the "clan" [Tolley 2009: 166].

With the rise of political structures in antiquity, concepts of the prominence of women in community life got lost, with the consequence that men dominated leadership and political decision-making. Most men in Greek and Roman society perceived it as their right and duty to take care of public affairs while women were to be wives, mothers and household managers.

For a long time, the active participation of women in communitary affairs—an integral element of life in pre–Christian communities—was hampered by the Christian worldview. With the advent of Christianity in Finland, the traditional communitarian system was overtaken by patriarchal conceptualizations. Paganism was ideologically stigmatized, and the authority of shamans—called *loihtia* in Saami and *noita* in Finnish—was diminished. Christianity could not accommodate the role of female practitioners of shamanic divination.

> With the aid of determined missionaries, Christianity gradually started to gain more foothold in the Sami territory and eroded the land-based spirituality by banning shamanistic ceremonies, executing the *noaidis,* burning and destroying the Sami drums and outlawing yoiking (*juoigan*), the Sami form of singing, chanting and communicating [see Chapter 7; Kuokkanen 2006: 264].

The treatment of female shamans was more severe than that of male shamans, and women practitioners of pagan customs were prosecuted as witches and accused of sorcery by church authorities, since "all magic rites were interpreted during the period of orthodox Lutheranism as contact with the devil and thus as an offence against the first Commandment. Numerous witch trials were held in Finland, chiefly in Åland and Ostrobothnia, in the mid- and late 17th century in particular" (Talve 1997: 231).

Such prosecutions were carried out over a longer period, well into the 18th century, in Lapland, where shamanism remained vital much longer than in other regions of Finland.

> In both Norway and Sweden the penalty for "sorcery" was death, but the use of capital punishment for the possession of a drum or for sacrifices, was very uncommon.... [T]he death penalty for Saami "sorcery" was abolished in Norway in 1726. The purpose was to get more Saamis to tell about—or "confess," as the term ran—the indigenous practices without fear, and that really seems to have been the result [Rydving 1993: 55f.].

## Farm Households and Self-Confident Farm Mistresses

The agrarian life remained typical of Finnish society into the 20th century, and the farm household, as the basic unit, was the backbone of the Finnish economy and the core of social organization. This unit was comprised of the building for the people, of buildings for the livestock and of the crops, related fields, meadows and forested areas. This unit was kept functioning by the married couple and other persons who worked on the farm. Husband and wife followed the "fitting-together" ideal which was symbolically celebrated by the women in the household by using protective magic.

> According to the representations found in women's magic, women were not only vital components of the complementary, "fitting-together" dyad which was the core of the farm household unit, they were the guardians of the farm household's symbolic boundaries and internal integrity. Women accomplished this "gatekeeping" by using sorcery, protective magic and most significantly, *a dynamistic power believed to be released through their sexual organs*.... It is important to note that in nearly all women's protection rituals, magical force was directed against enemies *outside* the magic user's own household. The only threats from within were perceived to be directed toward breaking up the husband-wife bond, that is, threatening the *structural integrity* of the farm household unit [Stark-Arola 1998: 37].

There was a central factor that attributed to the early awareness among women of their value as farm mistresses in private life and as active citizens in public life. The relationship between husband and wife was determined by a kind of unwritten social contract that stipulated an equal share of work in connection with the division of labor. People were commonly aware "that survival in a culture of scarcity required a gender partnership based on shared toil, and farm production depended equally on the labour contribution of both husband and wife, a situation which resulted in interdependency in daily interaction" (Stark 2011: 22). A major aspect of equality is the sharing of responsibilities. The assumption of responsibilities for women in the public sector may well be anchored in the historical status and attitude of the Finnish farm mistress.

Recently, a certain trend discerned in the history of Finnish women has been highlighted that may be seen as a kind of link between the pre–Christian sense of women's self-assurance in the community and their role in the agrarian society of the Protestant era, and this is the position of the farm maid in the 17th and 18th centuries. Farmsteads were inherited by the eldest son, and unmarried girls without inheritance sought work, as maids, at other farms. This gave them some kind of liberty to make a free choice for work and it gave them opportunities of social contact away from their homes (Miettinen 2015). It was no rare occurrence that a maid married the owner of the farm she had worked for and established a family.

## Women's Rights to Vote in Local and National Elections

One cannot state without some irony that there is only a relatively short time—several decades at most—between the last witch prosecutions and the rise of women's communitarian activism in Finland. It is reasonable to assert that the early revitalization of women's public activities in the 18th century is a product of the sense of liberty among women that had persisted, covertly, throughout the ages, from the prehistoric times of shamanism through the Christian era before it manifested itself again openly and started to bloom.

It is well known that women in Finland were granted the right to vote more than 100 years ago. The Grand Duchy Finland, then part of Russia, was the first country in Europe to introduce women's suffrage. In a worldwide comparison, New Zealand was the first country to grant women the right to vote. That was in 1893, followed by Australia in 1902 and Finland in 1906. Known only to experts of Finnish history is that women already voted in the 18th and 19th centuries, under differing conditions of statehood and citizenship.

The first phase of women's political activities unfolded in the period between 1718 and 1771. That was the period when Finland formed part of the Kingdom of Sweden, which was experiencing a time of evolving civic liberties. The period is known as the Age of Liberty in Swedish history. During that time, female members of guilds who were regular taxpayers had the right to vote in municipal elections (Karlsson Sjögren 2006). That kind of suffrage was renewed under tsarist rule when Finland enjoyed autonomy as a Grand Duchy. Women in the countryside were allowed to vote, in local elections, beginning in 1863 and, since 1872, also in the cities.

One thing that enhanced women's advancement was education. From the introduction of the system of folk-schools (see Chapter 6) it was understood that girls were offered equal chances to become educated. Already in 1788, a school for girls (Töchterschule zu Wiburg) had been opened in Viipuri. Indeed, girls took the opportunity, and the general trend is documented in the archives of Finnish school history (Leino-Kaukiainen 2014: 311ff.). In the latter half of the 19th century, there were more girls than boys attending whatever type of school (SVT IX 43, 44). This is generally true for the level of primary education (Finnish *kansakoulu*) and of comprehensive schools (Finnish *oppikoulu*). The literary level was already high in the late 19th century. Of the inhabitants of the region of Viipuri aged 15 years or older, some 95 percent could read, and of these some 20 percent could also write. By 1910 the percentage of those who could read and write had risen to some 55 percent (SVT VI 9:1, 22, 37, 45:1, 56:2).

The press in Finland had its share in the promotion of reading and writing skills especially among women. Since the mid–19th century, newspapers printed letters written by women, for instance the *Suometar* or the *Tapio*.

> In its first three years (1861–1863), *Tapio* printed at least thirteen letters written by women, and in some cases the editors added their own words of support to shield female writers from potential criticism. A concern with female rural readers and writers seems to have been part of *Tapio*'s official policy from the beginning [Stark 2011: 64].

The Parliament Act of 1906 offered equality of the sexes on the level of national elections, which meant in practice that the Act extended the right to vote that had been exercised by women already on a communal scale. The unicameral parliament of Finland was established, and both men and women could vote and stand as candidates for election. This case of early women's suffrage stands out in that, for the first time in history, women had the right to vote and be elected. The first parliamentary elections were held in 1907 when 19 women were elected as members of the Finnish Parliament. Since then, the participation of women in political decision-making has continued uninterruptedly. The general right to vote provided the basis for women to become assigned to high offices: in 1926—Miina Sillanpää, the first female minister (Minister of Social Affairs) (Salmela-Järvinen 1973); 2000–2006 and 2006–2012—Tarja Halonen, president of Finland; 2003—Anneli Jäätteenmäki, prime minister of Finland.

The proportions of women in parliament and in governments have been increasing. The number of female MPs (members of parliament) in the parliamentary period between 2011 and 2015 rose to 43 percent. Finland's government during the period of 2007–2011 made history since it was the first government in the world with a marked majority of female ministers (12 women vs. 8 men).

There is some resemblance of the history of women's suffrage in Finland to that of the United States although the development was swifter and steadier in the former. The beginnings of women's suffrage in America are associated with the name of Lydia Taft who, in the Massachusetts Colony under British rule was the first woman to vote; in Uxbridge (New England), Lydia voted, on three consecutive occasions, in the town meetings. In New Jersey, between 1776 and 1807, wealthy unmarried women had the right to vote. The historical course of women's suffrage was interrupted for decades, until suffrage is introduced in the Wyoming Territory in 1869. The right to vote was secured for female U.S.-citizens by the 19th Amendment in August 1920.

## Women's Equality in the Welfare State

Gender equality is a major agenda of the Finnish welfare state. Actually, the agenda does not concern women's rights and liberties which are secured by law, but rather the realization of the legally safeguarded opportunities for women. As a rule, the higher the level of professional activity the fewer women are to be found. This is true for the business world as much as for offices in the public sector. Examples of women pioneering in various domains of the private or public sector abound but, statistically, an equal representation of the sexes is not found in every domain. There are many fluctuations and shifting majorities. For instance, in the sector of general health care, the majority of the personnel (doctors, nurses, medical assistants) are women. In the law-oriented professions, the number of female law-students and women lawyers has been constantly rising for many years, and women are in the majority in various sectors.

Among the women who represent different professional domains there are always pioneers, firstcomers who set standards for gender equality. The first Finnish woman to write a dissertation in the field of natural sciences (chemistry) was Lydia Sesemann, in 1874. The first academic dissertation in the humanities by a woman was written by Tekla Johanna Virginia Hultin in 1896. Tekla was a political activist, a member of the Finnish Parliament from 1908 until 1924, and a member of the City Council of Helsinki (1925–1930) (Kanerva 2015). In 1918, Agnes Sjöberg became the first woman of Finland—and in all of Europe—to obtain a doctoral degree as a veterinarian.

The first woman in Finland to write a doctorial dissertation in juridical science was Inkeri Anttila (1946). The first judge from Finland to become a member of the European Court of First Instance (Luxemburg) in 1995, was a woman (Virpi Tiili). The expert who wrote the classical study about intellectual property rights in Finland is a former female member of the Supreme Court, Pirkko-Liisa Haarmann, who is sometimes addressed as the "Grand Old Lady" in her field. And the important office of government arbitrator or state conciliator (Finnish *valtakunnan sovittelija*) has been held by Minna Helle since 2015.

Since 2006, the World Economic Forum (WEF) has monitored the level of gender equality in a Global Gender Gap Index. In the WEF report for 2015, Finland ranks high, together with other Scandinavian countries. In a worldwide comparison of 142 countries the following ranking has been recorded: Iceland—1, Norway—2, Finland—3, Sweden—4. For comparison: the United States is at 28 and Canada 30. In 2006, Finland ranked third in the world and, between 2008 and 2014 the ranking was second.

As for the four indicators of gender equality, with 1 indicating full equality, the position of Finland (viewed from the standpoint of the status of women) is the following (http://reports.weforum.org/global-gender-gap-report-2015/economies/#economy=FIN; retrieved 22 November 2015):

Economic participation and opportunity—0.81 (global ranking: 8)
    Labor force participation—0.95
    Wage equality for similar work—0.81
    Professional and technical workers—1.07
Educational attainment—1 (global ranking: 1)
    Enrolment in tertiary education—1.21
Health and survival—0.98 (global ranking: 1)
    Health life expectancy—1.07
Political empowerment—0.61 (global ranking: 2)
    Women in ministerial positions—1.67

## Giving Profile to the Scandinavian Model of a Welfare State

Although the idea of a welfare state as a model of democratic governance did not originate in Finland, this country was to become a model for its implementation. The history of the welfare system in Finland is congruent with the pace of industrialization: that is, Finland was a latecomer also with respect to the development of standards of health care. Finland had its own history concerning the standards of civil society. The origins of the modern sense of welfare may be sought in the debates about living conditions in the Grand Duchy in the 19th century. The ideas that were articulated then proliferated through the media of the press. The level of literacy was high in Finland, far above reading skills among the other nationalities of the Russian Empire, and literacy, promoted by the efforts of the Protestant clergy, had spread also among the rural population.

> Rural inhabitants' early participation in the press was crucial to the development of a broad-based modern civil society. Only through lengthy discussions in the press on what sort of society was desirable, and how this ideal could be achieved, was it possible to arrive at a loose consensus regarding national goals, standards of truth, and moral ideals such as equality, decency and progress, all of which enabled rapid growth of civil society and its voluntary forms of participation starting in the 1870s [Stark 2011: 239].

The debates that were sparked by the letters of rural writers to newspapers (e.g., *Suometar, Tapio, Sanomia Turusta, Suomen Julkisia Sanomia*) had a double effect. On the one hand they showed the public that the written word was useful for discussing pertinent problems. On the other hand the channel of public opinion—shaping demonstrated that literacy in Finnish was a useful and worthy skill to advance people's interests, providing an incentive to learn to write especially among the rural population (Leino-Kaukiainen 2007: 434f.).

The major breakthrough for the standards of civil society to be raised occurred in the course of the 20th century. The idea of a welfare state had already been entertained in the Scandinavian countries as the "Nordic model" for decades before it gradually materialized after World War II (Christiansen et al. 2006). "As elsewhere in Scandinavia, much of wealth created by the postwar prosperity was funneled into the creation of a universal welfare state…. The welfare state was built on the basis of a broad national consensus" (Lavery 2006: 149).

Sweden took the lead in postwar social development since it was the only country in northern Continental Europe that did not have to cope with war burdens like other Scandinavian countries, either having suffered from occupation (Norway and Denmark) or having been directly involved as a nation at war (Finland). There was a special factor that united the countries of Scandinavia, opened the path for the Nordic model to be established and gave this model an environment in which to become firmly anchored. This factor was a parliamentary consensus which, on the scale achieved in postwar Scandinavia, is a rare phenomenon in Europe's political history. This kind of consensus has been addressed as "consensual democracy" or, with particular reference to Sweden, as a system of "corporatist arrangements" (Held 2015: 182).

> There were two main features of this model: first, the dominance of social democratic parties within a multi-party system, governing either alone or through stable coalitions with other parties of the left or centre. Secondly, the Scandinavian democracies were described as "consensual democracies," where broad consensus-building mechanisms were favoured over majority rule and adversarial politics, and social divisions were neutralized by "over-arching sentiments of solidarity" [Hilson 2008: 38].

The Finnish model of the welfare state is actually an extension and adaptation of the general Nordic model, yet with local developments. Once the social system was set in motion it progressed swiftly and easily caught up with the other Nordic countries. The swift progress may be explained by the pragmatic approach taken by the Finnish government, the orientation of which differed somehow from the political embedding in neighboring Sweden.

> However, while the Swedes, especially the Swedish Social Democrats, declared that they represented the Third Way between Capitalism and Communism, in Finland the dominant strategy was, in turn, to *depoliticize* social policies. Thus, social reforms were discussed as functional needs, pragmatic steps along the road of general progress within the limits of economic resources, or as issues of pragmatic adjustment of conflicting interests in the name of the common national interest [Kettunen 2001: 232].

The Finnish adaptation of the Nordic welfare model stressed the productive perspective of an ideal welfare system that would not become a burden for government spending but, in the long run, stimulate growth. The architect of this idea of "welfare generates growth" in the 1960s was Pekka Kuusi. The Finnish welfare system could build on predecessors which were of local coinage. Welfare started out with a law on industrial injury (1895) and an unemployment insurance law (1917), regulations of pension and disability (1937) and a law on family allowances (1948) (Greve 2014: 72).

The Nordic welfare model is based on the following protective principles:

- the principle of universality or comprehensiveness (the right of all to a basic level of social protection regardless of where they live, their profession or economic position);
- earnings-related benefits for employed persons (including a national pension plan, an employee pension plan, sickness insurance, unemployment insurance, family aid, welfare services, child-care services, services for the disabled, services for substance abusers);
- a strong public sector (health care)

"There is an intensive pre and post natal care service for mother and child, and Finland has the world's lowest infant mortality rate. The state guarantees ten months of fully paid maternity leave for either the mother and/or the father. This maternity leave can be split between them" (Swallow 2011: 86).

- a system based on funding through taxation and contributions;
- equal treatment.

The public sector is the main anchor for these principles. There has been much debate, in recent years, about how to keep up the high standards set by the Finnish welfare system, given the setbacks that the prolonged crisis of world economy has caused. There is wide consensus among all political parties that the principles of welfare are not negotiable. This attitude notwithstanding, there are voices that advocate differing solutions to the problems posed by an explosion of costs in healthcare.

A general program of reshuffling of the healthcare system on the communal level (called *sote-uudistus* in Finnish), making it more efficient and less costly for the citizens who rely on it, is underway. Decision making concerning the implementation of the innovation project led to a crisis of government in November 2015. At the last moment, a compromise was reached so that the renovation could start.

The Finnish system of a welfare state and of efficient education (see Chapter 6) offers, in the domain of healthcare, high professional standards as well as a high-level technological infrastructure of hospitals and clinics. With the backing of such high standards in medicine, globally operating Finnish companies of pharmaceuticals set their own standards of innovation for the export-oriented Finnish economy; e.g., Orion, Biotie Therapies, Herantis Pharma, Forendo Pharma, Oncos Therapeutics. The Finnish Medicines Agency (Fimea) takes responsibility for the testing of some 14 percent of the biological medical products that are subject to the central testing program in the European Union (http://www.goldenbridge.fi/cn/files/2014/10/GB_stronghold_LIFESCIENCE_EN_2014-2015. pdf; retrieved 10 June 2015).

Structural innovation of the whole welfare system is an urgent necessity as leading economists have stated. Without such innovative reshuffling the Finnish welfare system is in danger of "becoming a museum" since the current cost explosion of services may eventually put the system at risk to spiral out of control. On the occasion of a Forum for the Defense of Economy (Taloudenpuolustuskurssi), in August 2015, a leading Finnish economist, Sixten Korkman, brought it to the point when characterizing the Finnish situation in the following way: "Finland has a brilliant past and a bright future but a lousy present" (Liimatainen 2015). It is strange that Finnish economy suffered so long from the world economic crisis that began in 2008. Economic growth was negative for three consecutive years (in 2015: −0.6 percent) while, for other EU economies, 2015 showed moderate growth (+ 0.3 percent for Germany and France, + 0.5 for Lithuania, and + 0.8 for Spain) (Sajari 2015a). Since early 2016 economic growth in Finland has been slightly stronger than the average in the EU.

On the whole, the favorable and supportive measures of the Finnish model of the Nordic welfare state have created an atmosphere for individuals to feel protected and socially secure. In a worldwide Gallup poll monitoring the level of happiness, in July 2010, Finland ranked second after Denmark as the happiest nation in the world. Finland ranks high in the Sustainable Society Index: "Finland is among the top nations under most indicators measuring human and economic wellbeing" (Putkuri et al. 2014: 108).

The Finns are well-tuned to the ways of achieving happiness in life, and of cherishing the striving for it. And the means for people to feel good and to find happiness as a member in a social group may be associated with everyday life, on the grass-roots level. In Finnish, there is a special term for referring to matters of communitarian interest, and this is *talkoot* ("bee"), the meaning of which implies the participation of neighbors in a team. People may engage in *talkootyö* ("team work to carry out communitarian tasks"). In the past, *talkootyö* was a principle of community life that remained unquestioned and functioned without saying. For instance, the roof of a house in a village would need repair which required more than one man. So the neighbors would gather and participate in the repair work, and the wife would provide the workers with food and drinks. After the work had been done people would perhaps sit together and celebrate, but none of the neighbors would expect to be paid for his help.

During times of crisis, the community and, society in a wider sense, profited from the communitarian spirit of *talkoot* that every Finn inherited from previous generations. For instance, during the years of World War II, every Finn who did not serve as soldier at the front and could use an axe had the duty to cut a certain amount of firewood, to facilitate the energy supply in the community. These days, politicians speak of the necessity of *talkootyö*, for members of different parties with different interests to join forces for concerted actions, to meet the challenges of accelerating globalization.

The communitarian spirit creates its own ritual activities, to strengthen social cohesion and stimulate teamwork. The Finns know a tradition of carpet washing at public places. In the past, women would gather at a place where some long boards were placed on some big stones near the lake side or on a beach of the sea. There they would clean the carpets they brought from their homes, using a brush and pine soap, natural soap that is ecologically tolerable and dissolves in water without leaving artificial chemical substances. The time came when washing machines were introduced. The spread of washing machines did not make a difference because carpets are not washed in household machines. The custom of public carpet laundering has remained a stable habit for many during the summer season. Foreigners sometimes wonder what is going on at the laundering jetties that have replaced the simple board levels. Some think that, despite high living-standards in Finland, there might be too few dry cleaners to accommodate the demand for carpet laundering.

What is really going on at the laundering jetties is much more than washing carpets. This gathering would provide the women with the opportunity for chatting and exchanging news about their families and friends. They would not come to the place (by car) only with their carpets and utensils but also with a picnic basket.

> Carpet washing is still one of Finns' favourite outdoor summer activities. A good day for it is a sunny day with a warm breeze. The washers create a strong sense of community together, and reward themselves with treats from their hamper [Ruuskanen-Parrukoski 2013: 344].

The communitarian spirit also shows in the ways language is used. The egalitarian principle of the welfare state is manifested in informal speech and phraseology, avoiding expressions that mark social hierarchy. In the 1970s, the fashion to use informal speech spread from Sweden and soon dominated language among the Finns. Finnish is a language in which the distinction between formal or polite forms and informal or intimate forms is linguistically marked. There are two distinctive address forms, *sinä* (informal or intimate) versus *Te* (formal or polite), and these forms require the use of special forms of verb conjugation: *sinä* combines with the 2nd person singular, *Te* combines with the 2nd person plural. The grammatical association of the polite form with the 2nd person plural, like in Finnish, is also typical of French or Russian. In Italian and Spanish, the polite form associates with the 3rd person singular and, in German, with the 3rd person plural. Using informal address forms is called *sinutella* in Finnish while, using formal address forms, is called *teititellä*.

Informal language use became the ordinary way to use speech in social interaction, and it has been used among people, regardless of sex, age, profession or social status, signaling communication in an open democratic society. The general experience with informal speech in wider use is that it enhances social cohesion and the feel of being members in an egalitarian community. This atmosphere of in-group solidarity in the speech community has dominated social interaction, and it is supportive of other civil liberties, such as the freedom of speech.

For several years already, a shift toward the older system of language use is under way. Formal address forms (*teitittely*) are more often used, and in various contexts where they were not used during the era of linguistic democratization. Waiters in restaurants might nowadays use formal as well as informal speech, switching from formal speech for addressing senior guests to informal speech with younger guests. In a similar way, shopkeepers would switch address forms in contact with their customers. The same trend can be observed in many domains of public services, on the bus, in taxis, airplanes, etc. Does this new inroad of formal speech signal a return to tradition and a drifting away from the familiar behavioral patterns of democratic solidarity? Hardly so, but the intentional distinction of formal and informal speech may bring into focus a nostalgic flair of respectful interaction that had been in danger of being buried under the rubble of plain language use in the media and the internet (http://yle.fi/uutiset/kiehuttaako_sinuttelu_vai_arsyttaako_teitittely/7793900, 10 February 2015).

# 4

# What Do Carl Gustaf Mannerheim and George Washington Have in Common?
## *Impressions from the Drive for Independence*

Every revolution, every struggle for political independence produces its own charismatic personalities. In case such defenders of national interests experience a violent death they are hailed as "martyrs of the cause"; if they stay alive they are celebrated as national heroes and assume the status of icons of national histories written by the victors. Historical icons tend to be persistent. This is the case with George Washington and his role in American history. Finland has its own historical icon, and this is Carl Gustaf Emil Mannerheim (1867–1951).

In the surveys, conducted since 1948, asking the public about the popularity of American presidents, Washington ranks top at the lists, together with Franklin D. Roosevelt and Abraham Lincoln (Skidmore 2004). In Finnish opinion polls, Mannerheim is often named as the "Greatest Finn." Washington and Mannerheim have much in common, not only regarding their popularity in their own country. Both figures had similar military careers, and they both served, as commanders, in foreign armies before they engaged in the decisive struggle for independence. If it were only for those "external" parallelisms, it would hardly be worth writing a whole Chapter on comparing these two military leaders. Yet, there is much more to these personalities than catches the eye of official historiography.

Parallelisms in the lives of Mannerheim and Washington:

- being born into a family where ancestors were of varied cultural backgrounds;
- growing up in a country under foreign rule;
- marrying a rich woman of high social standing;
- making a military career in the service of an Imperial Army;
- distinguishing himself through bravery in battle;
- being at the right place at the right time, and being invested with the right authority for carrying out the historical task;
- assuming an historical role as commander-in-chief of victorious forces in a war of independence;

- lacking aspirations for political leadership;
- freely resigning from military service after victory in the war of independence;
- gaining respect and appreciation as a national figure;
- becoming an integrative symbol of national unity;
- approving of a shift in governance for the newly independent country (from monarchy with a foreign ruler to participatory democracy)
- responding to moral pressure and accepting responsibilities in state affairs (the presidency);
- freely leaving office after serving his country as president, despite the opportunity to continue in high office;
- being engaged in charitable enterprises;
- spending the rest of his life in privacy;
- receiving the honor of a state funeral;
- being remembered as one of the greatest sons of the nation.

Mannerheim certainly was a personality that does not fit into the molds of common clichés. He never gave any interviews and never publicly explained his doings. Understandably, much of the real Mannerheim remained hidden and inspired popular myth-making about his personality, his motivations and activities (Donner 2011). Mannerheim was a patriot and one of a kind.

> The eccentric nature of Mannerheim's patriotism is perhaps nowhere so clearly illustrated as in the matter of language. Born to Swedish-speaking nobility, and quite fluent in Russian and French (which he spoke in the elegant, high-flown manner of the Romanov Court), he could also converse passably in English, Polish, and German [Trotter 1991: 31].

Mannerheim may have picked up some Finnish in his youth but he did not master it and had to learn it as an adult. Still during the civil war, as a commander of the Finnish "Whites," he was in need of an interpreter who passed on orders in Finnish. In his fifties, Mannerheim had achieved a working command of Finnish which he spoke with a strong Swedish accent. While his charismatic personality, as an integrative national figure, may be compared to Washington, Churchill or Charles de Gaulle, Mannerheim was in quite a different position as regards the national language of his country, Finnish, which he had to acquire at an age when people usually no longer learn new languages.

His personal attitudes were exceptional when viewed against the changing currents of world politics and worldview: "he was a cosmopolite in the age of nationalism; an aristocrat in the age of democracy; a conservative in the age of revolution" (Rintala 1969: 36).

## A Glimpse at Family History

The ancestry of the Mannerheim aristocratic family finds its roots in Sweden and ultimately in Germany. The Mannerheim family settled in Finland at the end of the 18th century when Finland was still a part of the Kingdom of Sweden. Members of the Swedish aristocracy residing in Finland served in the Swedish administration of Finland. This custom did not change during the era when Finland was a Grand Duchy within the Russian Empire. Carl Gustav's great-grandfather (given the rank of count in 1825) and grand-father held key posts in the administration of the Grand Duchy.

Finland-Swedes who chose a military career would join the Imperial Russian army. So did Mannerheim who rose to the rank of lieutenant general. In 1891 he was appointed to the tsarina's Chevalier Guard in St. Petersburg. Mannerheim features in the documentary film taken on the occasion of Tsar Nicholas II's coronation (26 May 1896; Vlasov 1994: 90/91).

As an officer of the personal guard Mannerheim became part of the entourage of the Imperial Court at St. Petersburg and he met with the Tsar several times. His social standing enhanced his marriage with a wealthy noblewoman of Russian descent who frequented the Imperial Court. The couple had two daughters. Mannerheim and his wife separated in 1902. They formally divorced in 1919, at a time when society in the newly independent Finland would not tolerate the marital union of a Finnish dignitary with a Russian woman.

When the Russo-Japanese war broke out in 1904, Mannerheim volunteered for duty in the Far East. This was the first opportunity for Mannerheim to show his talents as a military leader and to excel in bravery. He distinguished himself in the Battle of Mukden (1905) and was promoted to colonel. In 1906, Mannerheim was sent on a secret intelligence mission to gather information about the situation in the Russian-Chinese borderland. In a competition known as "The Great Game," Imperial Russia and the British Empire competed for political control over the provinces of Xinjiang and Gansu in western China. Mannerheim, in the disguise of an ethnographer, led an expedition as far as Kashgar in Xinjiang. In July 1908, Mannerheim went to Beijing where he worked on his report for the Russian General Staff.

Mannerheim returned to St. Petersburg in 1909 and was sent to Poland, the greater part of which had been under tsarist rule after the partitions of 1772, 1793 and 1795 (Lukowski 1999). A year later, he was promoted to major general and was stationed in Warsaw. Mannerheim was in command of the Tsar's Life Guard Uhlan Regiment. At the outbreak of World War I he was sent to the southern front where he commanded the Guards Cavalry Brigade. He distinguished himself in combat against the Austro-Hungarian forces and was awarded the Order of St. George in December 1914. This was a turning-point, not only in his career as an officer in the Imperial Russian Army but also for his future orientation in life.

## *The Guidance of Providence*

"Now I can die in peace" is what Mannerheim purportedly said in reaction to his award. The Order of St. George apparently was a highlight in his career as a soldier and he would not have expected any higher honor than this. When there is an exceptional event associated with a figure from world history, the memory of later generations is permeated with a mixture of facts and legends. The combat in which Mannerheim distinguished himself was remembered by his contemporaries in the way that the commander who was charging the enemy in an attack rode in front of his men, surrounded by some of his officers. There was heavy gunfire from the Austro-Hungarian frontline and many men of Mannerheim's cavalry brigade were killed. Bullets showered in and several officers around the commander were shot from their horses. It was like a miracle that Mannerheim was not killed, nor even hit. It was as if providence had a hand in this: Mannerheim's historical task lay in the future.

Here, George Washington and his bravery in the French & Indian war (1754–62) come to mind. In 1755, Washington had joined general Edward Braddock on his mission to confront the French and drive them out from the Ohio valley. The French troops, reinforced by allied Indian fighters, trapped Braddock's men and engaged them in the ill-fated battle near the Monongahela River. Braddock was killed and the British badly beaten. Washington is remembered as having rallied the British soldiers for an orderly retreat. In this Washington succeeded, and he miraculously survived the fighting without a scratch. It is reported that, during the battle, two horses were shot under him and, when taking off his coat afterwards, he noticed four bullet holes shot through it. None of the bullets had hit him. Washington's bravery was duly noticed and he was appointed commander of the entire military force of Virginia. His historical task in the American War of Independence was pending.

Like George Washington who, at the beginning of his military career, professed loyalty to the authority of a king and the British Empire, Gustaf Mannerheim was convinced that loyalty to the ruler of the Russian Empire would accompany him till his death. Washington stood up against an empire, and Mannerheim against a world power. Actually, Mannerheim did not fight against the Russian Imperial Army because this had been dissolved after the Tsar's abdication in early 1917 and his former empire had been taken over by a "bourgeois" government. Mannerheim was promoted to lieutenant general in April 1917 and, in summer of 1917, he was appointed commander of the sixth Cavalry Corps.

The end of Mannerheim's career in the Russian army was undramatic. Mannerheim did not show support for the new rulers in St. Petersburg. The bourgeois élite mistrusted him as a non–Russian and, in September, he was relieved of his duties.

> A stroke of luck removed the Baron from the front during the period immediately before and after the revolution of November 7 [October 7 according to the Russian calendar]. He had fallen from his horse, suffered a sprained ankle, and was recuperating in Odessa; otherwise, loyalist that he was, he would likely have suffered the fate of so many other aristocratic officers [Trotter 1991: 25].

Here, for the second time, at a critical stage in his life, providence saved Mannerheim from being shot by ordinary soldiers rebelling against noblemen commanders. In December 1917, he returned to Finland. There, an unexpected renewal of his military career was awaiting him, with a completely new orientation of loyalties and responsibilities.

## Setting the Stage for Finnish-Russian Confrontation

In the early decades of the 19th century tsarist rule over Finland had little, if any influence on people's daily lives. The Finland-Swedish nobility took care of the administration as had been the case during the Swedish era, with the difference of shifting loyalties oriented to the Russian state. In the 1860s, Tsar Alexander II benevolently supported the modernization of Finland according to the model of society in western Europe. And yet, growing national self-awareness among the Finns caused tensions in later decades.

Although, in 1809, Tsar Alexander I had envisaged a development of the Finnish nation that would be "undisturbed from outside" (*tranquille au dehors*) and "free on the inside" (*libre dans l'intérieur*), by the 1880s, those promises had been forgotten.

Finnish politicians favored Finnish statehood along the lines of the speech of 1809, but Russian authorities rebuffed such an assessment.

> In defence of this constitutional view, in 1886 Senator Leo Mechelin published his famous book about the state rights of Finland, "Précis du Droit Publique du Grand-Duché de Finlande." The Russian historian K.F. Ordin countered this with a 1,000-page work entitled "The Conquest of Finland" (1889), in which he proved by legal means that the Finns' concept of their own country as some kind of "state" was utterly false and without foundation in fact. Finland was a Grand Duchy and a Russian "possession," and that was that! [Smeds 1996: 390].

Finnish-Russian relations experienced a political setback during the "Frost Years" between 1899 and 1917 when the Finns experienced a wave of Russification. In a series of tsarist regulations, the autonomy of the Grand Duchy was systematically curbed. Among the practical measures of Russification was the introduction of Russian as a compulsory subject in Finnish schools and as a vehicle for higher administration in Finland. The tensions fuelled anti–Russian sentiments which found their symbolic expression in a work of art, a painting created by the artist Edvard Isto (d. 1905) (figure 25).

The dramatic scene in the painting shows the Finnish Maiden (Suomi-neito in Finnish) who holds the Constitution of the Grand Duchy, the book of laws of autonomy, trying to protect it from the assault of the two-headed Russian eagle. Isto's painting was done while the artist was in Berlin. His work became an icon of the unified resistance of Finland-Swedes and Finnish nationalists (the "Young Finns"). Copies of Isto's Finnish Maiden found their way into thousands of Finnish homes.

The personification of Finland as a young maiden had become popular in the 19th century and, as a symbol of national unity, it remained in vogue into the era of independence. During Russian rule the Finnish Maiden was valued as a symbol of the strife for political independence. The preferred posture of the figure was one with both arms raised which resembled the contours of the Grand Duchy and the independent Finnish state until World War II (figure 26). In 1944, certain areas had to be ceded to the Soviet Union, and the Finnish Maiden lost one of her "arms" (see figure 20 for the changing territorial borders).

The visual identification of the Finnish Maiden with the contours of the country has become so popular as to shape geographical terminology in everyday language. The northwestern extension of Finnish territory is called *Käsivarsi* ("Arm").

Russification was personified by the governor-general of the Tsar in Finland, the Russian N.I. Bobrikov, who, by 1903, "had what amounted to dictatorial powers; he could dissolve any institution or organization he regarded as 'dangerous,' and he could deprive persons 'likely to cause trouble' of the right to reside in Finland—in other words, he could send his opponents into exile" (Schoolfield 1996: 207). In 1904, Bobrikov was shot by a Finland-Swedish fanatic, Eugen Schauman. Russo-Finnish relations were irreversibly strained by this event.

Things changed dramatically in Russia after the abdication of the last Tsar and the rise to power of a "bourgeois government" in Petrograd (formerly St. Petersburg) in early 1917. After their coup d'état the Bolsheviks overthrew the interim government in October

Figure 25: *Hyökkäys* (*The Attack*) by Edvard Isto, 1899 (courtesy National Museum of Finland).

Figure 26: The Finnish Maiden on a 1906 postcard.

1917. The radicalization of the political scene set in motion a process of segregation which ultimately resulted in the separation of Finland from Russia. Finland's independence was gained at a price, as the outcome of a civil war. The Finnish Senate declared the country's independence in December 1917. However, the Finns were divided as to what concerned the future political order of the country. There were those, later called the "White Finns," who favored a bourgeois governance for their country. And there were pro–Communist groups, the "Red Finns," who also favored independence but in close partnership with the Bolsheviks in Russia. White and Red Finns started to gather the adherents for their cause.

## Mannerheim as Leader of the White Finns in the Civil War

In mid January 1918, the Finnish Senate called upon Mannerheim to take the command of the White Guards that had been set up in various places, functioning as an otherwise nonexistent police force. In practice, there was no Finnish army. The first task of the new commander was to call upon Finnish and Swedish men to join and to organize army units. On January 25, the White Guards were named the Finnish White Army by the Senate.

The paramilitary White Guards were backed up by conservative groups, the Finland-Swedish aristocracy, Finnish industrialists, landowners and middle-class entrepreneurs. They controlled the central and northern parts of Finland. At the outbreak of the civil war the core of the trained forces were the so-called Jägers (Finnish *jääkärit*), a term of German origin meaning "hunters." The Jägers were specialized forces who had been recruited among students and members of the upper middle class in Finland during the years of World War I. Since 1915, more than 1,000 volunteers left Finland clandestinely and gathered in northern Germany, in a camp of the German Imperial Army at Loksted near Hamburg, where they were trained as élite soldiers. The Jägers formed a battalion of their own and, as part of the German Imperial army, they participated in the fights against Russian troops on the northwestern front. By late 1917 the Jägers had been brought to Finland on board German ships that also brought arms supplies. During the civil war, some 2,000 Jägers fought among the Whites.

The arms for the Whites came from two sources. One was the Russian military, with more than 40,000 troops stationed in Finland. Mannerheim, who set up his headquarters in Vaasa on the west coast, managed to disarm large parts of the Russian forces and take over their weapons. Most of the Russian soldiers left Finland and went home, some became activists of the leftist movement and joined the Reds. Another source of supply of arms for the Whites was the Imperial German Army. Everything that could weaken Russia would serve German interests.

The Reds represented the industrial workers whose numbers had increased with the rapid industrialization of Finland in the late 19th and early 20th centuries. The socialist forces were concentrated in the industrial centers of southern Finland (Helsinki, Lahti, Tampere). The Reds received their arms supply from the newly established Russian Soviet Republic.

In March 1918, the Whites gained the upper hand in the civil war with their victories in the battles of Tampere in central Finland and of Viipuri (Vyborg) on the Karelian Isthmus. The White forces were supported by allied troops, an expedition corps of the German Imperial Army. In April 1918, German troops conquered Helsinki and Lahti. The last major fight within the borders of nowadays Finland took place in the region of Luumäki (South Karelia), in May 1918. The rest of the Red forces were either imprisoned or withdrew to Soviet Russia. De facto independence was achieved in May 1918 when a center-right government was formed.

## A Secret Diplomatic Mission and Early International Recognition of Finland's Independence

Germany's support for the Whites was decisive for their victory. At the same time the pro–German policies of the Finnish government were problematic for the image of Finland as a newly independent state. In summer 1918 it became clear that Imperial Germany would not win the war and countries which had established friendly relationships with Germany would be looked upon with suspicion by the Allies. Mannerheim foresaw the political conflict that was arising and distanced himself from the government in Helsinki. In June 1918 he went to Sweden to spend time with his relatives.

Although Mannerheim officially stayed out of touch with Finland's government he unofficially acted in his country's interest when contacting diplomats from the Allied states and explaining to them the need for Finland's independence to be recognized, as a chance for the government to step out of the shadow of a unilateral German-friendly attitude. Mannerheim's effort toward the common good was well received and he was sent as an envoy to Great Britain and France.

The recognition of Finland as a newly independent state turned out to be a highly complex matter. On January 4, 1918, the Bolshevik regime in Petrograd officially recognized Finland's independence. A document was set up and Lenin gave his personal guarantee. Strange as it may seem, Lenin did not command Russian troops to leave Finland, something which the recognition would have automatically stipulated. Nevertheless, Soviet Russia's recognition opened the path for other countries to follow suit. Sweden was the first western state to recognize its neighbor as a sovereign state, and this happened on the same day of Russia's recognition. Within the next few days, also Denmark, Norway, Switzerland and Greece extended the network of international recognition. By the end of the year, 15 states had recognized Finland's independence.

The recognition of states such as Imperial Germany, Turkey and the Austro-Hungarian Empire, seemingly, posed a serious problem for the Allies, who were concerned about the Finnish government's pro–German stance. Finland's independence was recognized by Britain and the United States as late as the spring of 1919. Mannerheim's contacts with British and American diplomats in Stockholm may have had some influence, enhancing political decision-making of those two countries.

In December 1918, Mannerheim returned to Finland where he took over the task of Regent of Finland (Finnish *Valtionhoitaja*; Swedish *Riksföreståndare*). During his term which lasted until the end of July 1919 the political system had to be organized. For some time there had been uncertainty about whether Finland would become a constitutional monarchy or a republic. Before Mannerheim became Regent the Finnish government had asked a German prince (Karl Friedrich von Hessen) to become king of Finland. The prince renounced the offer and Mannerheim saw to it that a republican constitution was introduced. There were monarchist groups in Finland that would have preferred Mannerheim to become king of Finland, but he did not signal any interest to them.

Electing the president was not a matter for the general public but the task of the parliament. Among its members, there was considerable resistance to electing Mannerheim. In the opinion of many, his former role in the Imperial Russian army and his marriage with a Russian noblewoman cast a shadow over the image of the victorious leader of the Whites in the civil war. In addition, Finnish socialists rejected Mannerheim as a "white" general. Mannerheim stood as a presidential candidate but lost the election. The first president of Finland, elected by the parliament, was Kaarle Juho Ståhlberg, in office from 1919 to 1925. For the second time in his career, Mannerheim withdrew from public life and favored private pursuits.

## *Mannerheim as an Integrative National Figure at a Time of Crisis*

Some say that Mannerheim's victorious leadership during the Finnish civil war (January–March 1918) and his achievements for Finland's independence just served to set the stage for his decisive role as a national figure at a time when Finland's independence and democratic system were in a state of siege. The real test for independence came with the worsening of Finno-Russian relations in the late 1930s and with the political tensions that sparked Finland's military confrontation with its neighbor.

In the early decades of Finland's independence, strong echoes of the confrontation of worldviews from the times of the civil war were felt. There were manifestations of political extremism from left and right. The right-wing national movement, the Lapua Movement (*Lapuan Liike*), had aspirations for dictatorship, with Mannerheim as the ruling icon. Yet, Mannerheim did not in any way encourage this idea. He maintained a private life and did not participate in any political activity. Instead, he engaged in humanitarian pursuits. Mannerheim was the head of the Finnish Red Cross (from 1919 till his death in 1951) and he is the founder of the Mannerheim League for Child Welfare (Mannerheimin Lastensuojeluliitto; established in 1920). Mannerheim made extensive travels, to India, Burma (Myanmar) and Nepal, mainly with the purpose of big-game hunting, and he visited various cities in other countries, among them Baghdad, Cairo and Venice.

Through the years, Mannerheim's image integrated itself more firmly with a broader public and the former contrasting evaluations smoothed out. Symbolic of the new zeitgeist was Mannerheim's appointment as chairman of Finland's Defense Council by the third president of Finland, Pehr Evind Svinhufvud (in office from 1931 till 1937). Svinhufvud, as chairman of the Finnish Senate, had appointed Mannerheim commander of the White Guards at the dawn of the civil war, in December 1918. The Defense Council approved of a promise according to which Mannerheim would be appointed commander-in-chief of the Finnish Army should a war occur. Two years later Mannerheim was promoted to the rank of Field Marshal (Finn. *sotamarsalkka*, Swed. *fältmarskalk*). Seemingly, Mannerheim was at the height of his military career. Yet, the true test for his skills as military leader and for the integrity of Finland's independence was still to come.

In the late 1930s, Finland got caught up in the conflicting political interests of Nazi Germany and the Soviet Union. Once an agreement on nonaggression had been signed by the German foreign minister von Ribbentropp and the Soviet foreign minister Molotov, in August 1939, Finland was left to the sphere of Soviet interests. In late summer, the Soviet government made demands to the Finnish government to cede Finnish territory north of Leningrad for reasons of the city's security; this the Finns denied. Bilateral negotiations were held which turned out to be fruitless. In the end, the Soviets issued an ultimatum to which the Finnish side did not respond.

An incident on the Finnish-Soviet border near the village of Mainila, on November 30, sparked the Soviet attack on Finland. This marked the beginning of the Winter War (Sander 2013). The League of Nations, precursor of the postwar United Nations, condemned the Soviet invasion and expelled the Soviet Union from its organization, on 14 December 1939. The world's solidarity lay with the small country that tried to repel the Russian onslaught.

When Mannerheim assumed command of the Finnish Army this was a miniature force when compared to the resources that Finland's enemy mobilized. The Russians outnumbered the Finns 3 : 1, Russian aircraft counted 30 times more than what the Finns had, and the proportions of Russian tank forces, compared with the Finnish, were 100 : 1. Theoretically, the Red Army should have managed to conquer all of Finland within a few weeks. Soviet military leaders did not expect Finnish resistance to be so fierce, and they could not foresee that the Finnish Army would succeed to resist for months (Ries 1988: 79f.).

Yet, there were factors at work that prevented Russian plans for conquest to materialize and ultimately were responsible for the failure of the whole Soviet campaign. At the outbreak of hostilities the people of Finland experienced something they had never experienced before. An exceptional sense of unity dominated all activities in the country. The government did not have to appeal to unity because there was an unstoppable surge of solidarity. Miraculously, conservative aristocratic Finland-Swedes, bourgeois middle-class Finns, social democrats and communists, they all "blew into the same embers" to spur the fire of resistance. The Finnish phrase *puhaltaa samaan hiileen* became a saying that is sometimes called upon for achieving unity in serious matters.

The Finns were all aware of their situation. They stood with their backs to the wall, and they had no choice but to confront the enemy. The Finns mobilized their *sisu* and achieved very high standards of morale. They certainly had no reservations about their commander-in-chief, who became the icon of Finnish resistance. Mannerheim's officers in the general staff complained that their commander-in-chief was never altogether satisfied with any action and he was no easy person to work with. On the other hand, Mannerheim was respected by every member of his staff and by the troops in general.

The Finnish army did not have much anti-tank weaponry. But the Finns knew how to improvise and bolster their defense capabilities by a typically Finnish invention that became known throughout the world: the "Molotov cocktail," a bottle filled with gasoline, with a piece of cloth attached. The cloth was lit on fire and the bottle thrown onto a tank. There were heavy casualties among those soldiers who were courageous and stood up, aimed and threw a bottle. Those brave men immediately became the target for Russian infantry sharpshooters. It was essential for the bottle to hit a certain part of the tank to be effective. That part was a plate above the motor of the standard model of Soviet tanks, the T 34. This plate heated up and turned red-hot when the tank was in action. Every time a bottle exploded and set a Soviet tank ablaze the Finnish soldiers sent their greetings to the Soviet minister Molotov. The Molotov cocktail, together with artillery, proved to be highly effective against Russian tanks. The magnitude of anti-tank warfare can be inferred when looking at the material losses of the Red Army: some 2,300 destroyed tanks and armored vehicles (Tillotson 1993, Appendix 6).

Fighting a war under Arctic conditions was "a frozen hell" (Trotter 1991), but the Finns are used to the harsh climate. Since all Finns had practice in skiing, Finnish army units were accustomed to move on ski through the woods. That gave them a significant advantage over the Russian soldiers who were not trained for winter war. The small Finnish army scored some spectacular victories over attacking Russian forces, destroying huge amounts of Russian weaponry, capturing much needed equipment and taking many prisoners. The Finnish soldiers learned how to cope with being outnumbered on all sectors of the frontline.

Fighting was fierce and relentless. The magnitude of the last battles of the Winter War may be illustrated by the outcome of the battle of Äyräpää (in March 1940), a key stronghold in the hilly terrain of the Karelian Isthmus, held by the Finns and continuously attacked by Soviet troops with heavy weaponry. Soviet artillery was positioned at the foot of the hill and pounded the terrain so that every square meter was turned over. When the battle was over, the Finns counted the casualties. In the hill stronghold, some 1,000 Finns had lost their lives while more than 20,000 dead bodies of Russian soldiers were strewn over the slopes of the hill.

Toward the end of winter Mannerheim and his staff were afraid that, with the melting of the snow, Russian troops would step up their attacks with greater mobility and the risk of their breaking through the Finnish defense lines would increase. The Finnish government agreed to a truce, and hostilities ceased on 13 March 1940. A peace treaty was done in Moscow. Finland was pressured to cede the southern part of Karelia to the Soviet state, and some 400,000 Finns had to leave their homes on the Karelian Isthmus. In June 1941, hostilities flared up again and the Finnish army reoccupied the lost territory. Then, the Finns were allies of Germany, and Finnish and German army units operated together on the Russian front. In summer of 1944, the Red Army launched a series of massive offensives against Finnish troops but they did not succeed beyond the frontlines of the Winter War.

At the time of the great Soviet offensives in summer 1944, the Russian élite units set out to reach Helsinki within a few weeks. In fact, they never reached Finland's capital, and all assaults, for which massive troops were mobilized, were repelled by the Finnish Army and the German allied troops. In the last decisive battle of 1944, at Ihantala, when the Red Army launched a massive offensive to break through the Finnish lines to proceed to Helsinki, the Soviet assault was slowed down and finally came to a halt, thanks to the cooperation of the "comrades in arms," Finns and Germans, with the actions of Finnish infantry supported by heavy German artillery.

Also during the Continuation War (1941–44), the spirit of resistance among the Finns was high. Everybody knew what the consequences would be should Finland be overrun by Russian troops. Mannerheim brought it to the point when he purportedly said: "If Germany loses the war then there is still a Germany that continues; if Finland loses the war, then what will be left is a Russian province." The spirit of resistance remained unbroken till a new truce was negotiated while the Finnish Army suffered heavy losses during the last weeks of the war, with thousands of casualties every day. The Finns, nevertheless, safeguarded their independence, and their country—unlike the fate of Germany in 1945—was not occupied by foreign forces. In late summer 1944, an armistice was concluded. The conditions of the Peace Treaty that followed were severe for the Finns. The borders of 1940 remained in place which meant the final loss of Finland's fertile territory on the Karelian Isthmus.

What was more important than the loss of parts of the territory was that Finland preserved its sovereignty and its political structures. It remained a parliamentary democracy and became integrated into the Scandinavian market economy. Mannerheim, the only figure of prestige, who was respected both by the Finnish people and by the Soviet negotiators of the peace terms, led Finland during the critical phase of transition from war to peace. In early August 1944, he was elected president and he remained in office until March 1946. Mannerheim resigned as president because of his worsening health. In early 1947, he went to Switzerland for an operation and recovery. He spent the rest of his life in the Valmont Sanatorium in Montreux. Mannerheim started to write his memoirs, parts of them himself, but he dictated the text of most parts to his assistants who wrote for him. His memoirs were published after his death in January 1951. Mannerheim received a state funeral and was buried in the Hietaniemi Cemetery in Helsinki.

## *Mannerheim and Washington: The Profile of Humble Public Servants*

Both Mannerheim and Washington were brave soldiers in their early years who fought in battle, fearlessly and tenaciously. Both were brilliant strategists at a mature age, as leaders of their armies. Both entered the realm of civil public life, holding central offices in the parliamentary democracy of their countries. Both were humble and perceived their outstanding positions as reflecting their high responsibilities for the common good of their people. Both could have assumed absolute political power as heads of state but did not. It is the sum of these skills, capacities and, above all, respect for holding high office in the service of democracy that makes both leaders exceptional and exemplary.

Mannerheim was an introvert, and so was Washington. They both were social to the degree demanded by their commands or expected by the responsibilities of their political offices. But neither Mannerheim nor Washington would have regularly sought the company of a crowd, as an audience for presenting themselves and their ideas. They were not selfish, at least not going beyond the attention they could expect, given the nature of their prestigious positions. They made the prestige they enjoyed operational for getting things done, not for any self-glorification.

The officers in the entourage of Mannerheim's general staff who worked with the commander-in-chief on a daily basis in the Finnish Army's headquarters in Mikkeli (eastern Finland) during the Continuation War (1941–44) revealed details of his way of conducting talks. Mannerheim never confronted his staff with ready-made decisions which his subordinates would have to execute. It was customary for Mannerheim to listen to his officers' statements, opinions and advice before he made his decision. Using this strategy as a means to enhance feelings of solidarity among the general staff was hardly intentional. It simply was a typical trait in Mannerheim's personality; he hated to present himself as autocrat.

Similar statements are known about Washington and his way of taking care of his duties. He was not only a skillful general but also an apt administrator. Before making his final decision Washington would listen what his senior staff had to say (Ellis 2004: 197f.). He is described as "systematic, orderly, energetic, solicitous of the opinion of others … but decisive, intent upon general goals and the consistency of particular actions with them" (White 1948: 100).

No matter how outstanding his achievements were as commander of an army, Washington sought privacy whenever he could, not wanting to become involved in politics. In the opinion of some, Washington's decision to resign, in December 1783, as commander of the new republic's army is what makes him a great man. King George III is purported to have said that Washington was "the greatest character of the age" (Brookhiser 1996: 103).

Washington wanted to stay out of politics but accepted the position of president of the Constitutional Convention in Philadelphia. He did little more than supervise the sessions, without much participating in the debates. Similarly, he did not strive to become president of the United States, but he was elected to that office in 1789 nevertheless, and reelected in 1792. He could have run for a third term but he did not, thus setting a precedent observed ever since with the one exception of Franklin D. Roosevelt. He died in December 1799.

Neither Washington nor Mannerheim liked pomp although both men had control over resources that could have provided it for them. The lifestyle of both men was simple without much decoration, favoring orderliness and modesty over an excessive lifestyle. They did not speculate financially, nor with real estate. The land holdings of Washington and Mannerheim were such as simply to establish their homes. Both men rose to such fame that their lives were practically "owned" by their people.

After they had successfully carried out their historical tasks they sought privacy. Yet, fate did not grant them much time, enjoying the privacy of a secluded life, before they died.

# 5

# How Did Finland Modernize?
## The Secrets of Finnish Entrepreneurship, Know-How and Inventiveness

Foreigners sometimes wonder how it is possible that a small country like Finland manages to advance—in terms of technological development, economic competitiveness, educational standards, the level of civic liberties and living-standards—to the range of the top twenty of the world and, in some domains, even achieving top ranking. In 2001, Finland was ranked first, by the World Economic Forum, in a worldwide comparison of competitiveness. This was the first time that a European country had received this top ranking. Ten years later, Finland's ranking had dropped to seventh but, nevertheless, the country finds itself in good company, with Japan ranking sixth, Germany ranking fifth and the United States ranking fourth (World Economic Forum 2010). The situation (as of 2014–15) shows a stabilization of top rankings in competitiveness (http://www.weforum. org/reports/global-competitiveness-report-2014-2015; retrieved 29 November 2015):

- Global Top 10—Finland (4)
- Europe Top 10—Finland (2)
- Innovation Top 10—Finland (1)

In 2010, the level of Finland's human development was characterized by the magazine *Newsweek* as the highest in the world. Finland's system of social security and health care is second to none in a worldwide comparison. The country's capital, Helsinki, features in the top ten list of the best cities in the world, and Helsinki is the only city of northern Europe that has such high ranking. These kinds of ranking, with regard to the country as a whole and to its capital in particular, are likely to contribute to "the creation of a national image" (Oinas 2005: 1238).

The standards of human development in Finland that have been reached today are the result of continuous processes of modernization, not just a single campaign. The Finns themselves may tend to play down the enormous capacity of their society to rapidly adapt to changing conditions. As a matter of fact, this capacity is awe-inspiring.

> Finns gladly cultivate the legend of being a grumpy, unbowing, slow and inflexible people. In reality, ... Finland has morphed from being an imperial (Russian) agrarian economy to a post-modern service- and information-based society in the span of a human lifetime [Schatz 2014: 152].

What stands behind this dynamic modernization? What are the driving forces that have produced such high standards in human development? There is no simple answer to these questions, and one has to look at various factors and their interplay to perceive the magnitude of Finland's modernization. The effects of some of these factors can be traced in the history of industrialization and of the social welfare system. Other factors remain indistinct and are linked to psychological underpinnings that pose a particular challenge to the analyst to single out.

The era when Finland—as a Grand Duchy—was part of Russia, Russian authorities did nothing to safeguard or develop the status of political and sociocultural autonomy. The idea of Finland as an autonomous state-like administrative entity within the Russian Empire was advocated by Finland-Swedes and Finns alike. The second half of the 19th century saw the initiatives of reformers striving for an independent cultural and economic development, always confronted with the reluctance and resistance of Russian authorities.

The benevolent attitude toward Finland of Tsar Alexander II (ruled 1855–1881) furthered the emancipation process of the Finnish language, a major marker of Finland's national identity, being acknowledged, in 1863, as an official language—alongside Swedish—in administration and in the Senate. However, it took several decades before the status of Finnish was secured in all domains of public life. The same reformer who had promoted the acknowledgment of Finnish, Johan Vilhelm Snellman (1806–1881), was influential in the economic sector, too. Thanks to his incentive, Finland obtained the privilege to have its own currency (introduced in 1865) which was the *markka*.

The unique status of the Grand Duchy within tsarist Russia illustrated the political implications of the independent process of industrialization and the achievements of the Finnish economy. During the events of the World Exhibitions that were held between 1851 and 1900 Finland took the opportunity to present itself to the world as a country with an advancing industry and with high standards in various domains of the arts. On the occasion of the world exhibitions in Paris, in 1889 and 1900, the Grand Duchy had its own pavilion (separate from the one for Russia) that attracted much attention from the international media (Smeds 1996: 260ff., 311ff.).

## *Maxims of Entrepreneurship and Finnish Work Ethics*

The swiftness with which Finland became an industrialized country can only be fully understood when one looks at the psychological underpinnings of the Finnish value system relating to work and entrepreneurship.

> The Finns are an extremely conscientious and industrious race. It seems to be part of their national pride that they work hard and study seriously. On the whole, they have a very great respect for education and training and are always working towards long-term good, rather than short-term gain. These people are not lazy or indolent. If there is a job to be done, they just get on and do it with no small talk to interrupt [Swallow 2011: 64].

Industrialization provided the key to technological advance, starting in the early 19th century. The pace of progress of the industrial movement was not even across Europe, and the shift from manual labor to mechanical production unfolded under varying local conditions. In his study *The Protestant Ethic and the Spirit of Capitalism* (German original composed in 1904 and 1905, first English translation in 1930), the German sociologist Max Weber drew attention to the fact that industrialization started much earlier in Protestant communities than among Catholics. One can even state that industrialization, in its early stage, was a phenomenon above all of a Protestant coinage in the countries of northern Europe where this religion dominated community life (Eliaeson and Palonen 2004). Weber's seminal work especially impacted Protestant countries and, in 1998, the International Sociological Association ranked *The Protestant Ethic* fourth in a list of the most influential works of sociology in the 20th century.

In light of Weber's theory about the features that define capitalism, the early rise of entrepreneurship among Protestant communities may be readily related to Protestant mentality and worldview. From a Protestant perspective the pursuit of happiness is a matter of how individuals organize their pursuits. They are responsible for their actions, and success in their endeavors is perceived as divine blessing. While a Catholic might perhaps wait for guidance from above a Protestant might be more likely to go for it and try to please the Lord with his or her doings. This nutshell contrast of worldviews extends to work morale and management of business affairs, but the fundamentally differing traits clearly show. The Protestant religion offered a fertile ground for industrial entrepreneurship, favoring individual initiative.

The Protestant entrepreneurs shared this mindset favoring individual initiative and steady hard work, and this mentality has dominated life in Scandinavia since the 16th century. In the 19th century, the Protestant mindset was made instrumental when the foundations for a nationwide educational system were laid in Finland. The initiator of this endeavor, Uno Cygnaeus, intentionally linked the values of work ethics to the principles of education.

> The concept that work is a "moral responsibility," and it should be perceived as an "honor of man" to accomplish, came from Cygnaeus. Central to his thinking and writings was that education for work should acquaint every child with real work so that every citizen of the future would have a general appreciation and respect for work and not just training for a specific vocation [Dugger 2010: 2].

The cultural heritage of work ethics that had originated in an entrepreneurial milieu early on and had been idealized with the rise of general school education (see Chapter 6 on Finland's educational system) has persisted in the intergenerational chain up to the present. "Work is a respected and almost celebrated value in Finnish society…. A person's work is her bond to the community and plays a major role in forging the social identity of a Finn" (Chaker 2014: 113). It is no exaggeration to speak of the Finnish "cult of work."

When such an atmosphere reigns in professional life, one would expect that this has a bearing on the efficiency of the work that is done. The efficiency of work can be indexed when relating data from the survey of the World Economic Forum on international competitiveness to the data of a 2015 OECD study on the average annual hours an individual worker works (www.stats.oecd.org; retrieved 6 August 2015). There is considerable fluctuation even among the top 10 in the list of competitiveness.

Work efficiency in Finland is high and may be compared with standards in Japan or Canada. These countries have a high ranking not only in terms of international competitiveness but also in terms of being efficiency, which does not show in the rate of average annual working hours. In order to be highly competitive workers in countries like Switzerland, Germany or the Netherlands have to work many hours more because their work is comparatively much less efficient than that done in Finland. According to the surveys, South Korea is the most industrious nation of the world, with an average annual working time of 2256 hours. Yet, in terms of the country's competitiveness it ranks in 22th place. The efficiency of Finland's workforce shows in the relatively low amount of working hours (1704) as compared to the comparatively high competitiveness ranking (7th).

## *Industrializing Finland: A Latecomer but a Fast Developer*

In the pre-industrial era, there were some enterprises that could be seen as forerunners of the later industrial enterprises. Those were mills that operated on the banks of whitewater rapids.

> The first water-driven sawmills were founded in the 16th century (the first record is from Finland Proper [southwestern Finland] and dated 1533). In the 17th century there were crown sawmills in Western Finland, but also single-frame, water-driven sawmills owned by peasant sawmill companies. In the 18th century water-driven sawmills were also founded by the town burghers, mainly along the south and western coasts [Talve 1997: 84].

Among the oldest mills in Finland is the one at Immilä (in the municipality of Nastola, southeastern Finland) that was established in the second half of the 16th century. It is located at the rapids between two lakes, Sylvöjärvi and Ruuhijärvi. Sawmills were established at a later date. At Immilä sawmills have been operating since the 18th century. The mill at Immilä was rebuilt at the beginning of the 20th century, restored in the 1990s and stands nowadays among the historical monuments of Finland's industrialization (Oijala 2007; figure 27).

Figure 27: The old mill at Immilä, now an historical monument (photograph: Kristian Döring).

Small-scale industry began with the establishment of iron works that were founded in the southwest of Finland in the 17th century. Those works processed Swedish iron ore. On the western coast opposite Sweden, traders made their earning with tar burning and furs, and some sawmills operated in the region at an early time. What the people in Finland imported with their earnings were products such as salt, sugar, coffee and precious textiles. Trading was strictly regulated: all shipping with goods from Sweden proper had to be transported via Stockholm.

The population of Finland (under Swedish rule) and that of Sweden proper were united by the Protestant religion, so that trading was a matter among relative equals. Although Finland did not belong to those countries where industrialization began early, such as the United Kingdom and the United States, the development soon gained in momentum once industrial enterprises had been established in various domains. Those who seized the opportunity to establish enterprises in Finland were above all Finland-Swedes, but before long Finns also took part in the industrialization drive.

When Finland became part of Russia in 1809, the country had an agrarian economy and it ranked among the poor regions of Europe. If one takes the gross domestic product per capita as a measure, Finland's figure was less than half that of the leading agrarian states, the UK and the U.S. The country was thinly populated. In 1810, not more than 860,000 people lived in the Grand Duchy (STV 2014: 96). Of these only some 4 percent inhabited cities and small towns. Around 1900, still about 70 percent of Finland's population were engaged, either in forestry or agriculture. These primary industries produced about half of the value of the country's production.

The beginnings of industrialization were modest. In the 1830s, the first cotton factories and some machine shops were established and, in the 1840s, the first steam machines were introduced. During the first half of the 19th century, Finland's biggest natural resource, wood, was exploited on only a small scale, the main reason being a lack of an infrastructure that would have allowed greater quantities of lumber to be transported over greater distances, from inland to the ports on the coast.

In the 1850s, the government of the autonomous Grand Duchy made farsighted decisions and took decisive steps to boost the economic infrastructure of the country. Projects for the construction of railroads and for the modernization of waterways were launched and carried out. In 1862, the first railroad in Finland, connecting Helsinki with Hämeenlinna, was completed. The railroad covers a distance of 95 km (59 miles). The model was the Russian broad track (1,524 mm = roughly 5 feet), which has remained the norm also in independent Finland.

The railroad connecting the Grand Duchy with St. Petersburg, the administrative center of tsarist Russia, was built between 1867 and 1870. The stations along this road, covering a distance of some 442 km (275 miles), were Riihimäki, Lahti, Kouvola, Viipuri and St. Petersburg. This railroad project was carried out during the years of the "Great Famine," offering work to many that would have otherwise perished or emigrated. Workers gave the railroad the nickname "hunger track" (*nälkärata* in Finnish).

Other lines of railroads were completed in the following years:

In 1872, the railroad down to Hangö [Hanko] was finished, joining its more or less ice-free harbor with the capital; in 1874, the line connecting Kervo [Kerava] and Borgå [Porvoo] was laid (enabling people of Runeberg's town to come to Helsingfors by rail, albeit circuitously); in 1876 Åbo [Turku] was joined to

Helsingfors…. The businessmen of Helsingfors regarded the Hangö, Borgå, and Åbo lines with some distaste, since the railroad enabled these harbor towns to compete successfully with the capital, in import as well as in export [Schoolfield 1996: 125f.].

In 1883, the railroad on the western coast to Vaasa (the Ostrobothnian line) was constructed. Various local lines of railroad connections were added in the 1890s.

Once the infrastructure had improved, the products of Finnish sawmills could reach the ports and, through commercial shipping, international customers. In the 1860s, the market of the United Kingdom opened to Finnish lumber products. The booming industrialization process in central and western Europe raised the demand for wood to be used for railroad sleepers and ties, for support pillars in mine shafts, for the production of paper and all kinds of technical construction work. Wood became the driving force for the industrialization of Finland. With the improvement of the inland waterways and railroad connections, Finnish wood could be transported to the coast where harbor facilities were also improved and enlarged. Wood was then transported to central Europe through commercial shipping. Trading contacts with the west intensified and, by 1910, Germany had become the leading trading partner for the Grand Duchy.

Factories were established near the urban centers that were in need of an ever-growing workforce. In the early phase of industrialization, there was only one town where there was a considerable industrial workforce.

Tampere alone had a large industrial population, for Tampere was founded in 1779 as an industrial town after the models of Norrköping and Eskilstuna [in Sweden proper]. In the early 19th century it was the home of Finland's only large-scale undertaking, the cotton mill established by James Finlayson in the 1820s. In 1860 this mill employed a labour force of 1,600 [Talve 1997: 276].

In rural areas, the general population growth was producing a surplus of jobless and landless laborers. With an advancing industrialization, the movement of rural laborers to the urban factories increased, which in turn triggered a major demographic shift. Most of the newly urbanized Finns were industrial workers and service personnel. Finns also went abroad to other cities, above all to imperial St. Petersburg which offered work to many specialized professions. In St. Petersburg, there was a professional group in which Finns even represented the majority: chimney sweepers. Finns not only did handiwork, they also engaged in more specialized labors. For example, among the designers and goldsmiths of the famous Fabergé enterprise were Finns (Tillander-Godenhielm 2011). The biggest urban agglomeration of urban Finns was formed outside Finland. Short before the outbreak of World War I, some 100,000 Finns and their families lived in St. Petersburg.

Social tensions between the middle-class entrepreneurs and the lower-class urban workforce increased, and it was in the urban milieu that the Finnish trade unions originated. Trade unions became legalized in 1883 and, in 1907, the Finnish Trade Union Federation (Suomen Ammattijärjestö, or SAJ) was founded. Workers' interests were represented in the Diet of the Grand Duchy by a political party (founded in 1899) that became the Social Democratic Party of Finland (Suomen Sosialidemokraattinen Puolue) in 1903. From the beginning, cooperation was hampered, between the Social Democrats and the political parties of the middle class that dominated political decision-making in the Diet. This was in part due to the unwillingness of the Social Democrats to abandon their radical image of Marxist ideology, adhering to the dogma of class struggle, favoring the nationalization of farm land against the owners' will and professing overt atheism. Especially the latter aspect of SDP politics caused much alienation even among factory workers, many of whom were religious, professing the Lutheran faith. The representatives of the middle class tended to not take workers' needs into account for decision-making. It took decades, well into Finland's independent history, before a balance of interests would be achieved. One of the first steps in that direction was the land reform of 1918, by which land was secured for small (tenant) farmers and farm workers.

Already during the first years of independence, products of Finnish sawmills such as timber and paper found their way to the markets of western Europe. The export business remained heavily based on wood products, which made up four-fifths of the international trade. Although Finland, during the interwar years, also had developed a metal industry and produced machines, their range was limited to satisfy domestic demands. The dependency of Finland's export economy on sawmill products caused a severe setback with the changing geopolitical situation after World War II, after Finland had to cede wide forest areas and arable land on the Karelian Isthmus to the Soviet Union. The wood export from eastern Finland had to be redirected further west after the loss of the port of Viipuri (Vyborg), in 1944, which had served, as a major trading center. The proportion of postwar wood products (including paper) in the overall volume of export changed significantly, from more than 80 percent in 1950 to some 20 percent in 2005.

## *The Finland-Swedish Impact on Industry and Commerce*

Industrialization in Finland, in the 19th century, would not have made much progress without the initiative of Swedish entrepreneurs (from Finland or Sweden) who provided the capital to get business started and to build factories. Those who determined the pace of industrialization, as entrepreneurs, by enlarging enterprises and opening factories were Finland-Swedes while the majority of the workforce were Finns. For decades, there remained a social division in the process of shift from an agrarian to an industrialized society. Things changed with the rise of the national movement among the Finns, and ever more Finnish entrepreneurs entered the competition with Finland-Swedes (Kuisma 1999: 67ff.). At the beginning of the 20th century, Finns were well-represented in the growing middle class.

Many enterprises founded by Finland-Swedes are still run by Finland-Swedes, such as Wärtsilä, which produces power plants and ship engines. Other enterprises, originally run by Swedes, later merged with Finnish companies to form bigger economic units, such as the Swedish Stora that merged with the Finnish Enso-Gutzeit to become Stora Enso, the world's second largest manufacturer of paper. Another example is Nokia, the former top producer of mobile phones which is now the world's biggest enterprise for communication networks (see Chapter 5). Nokia was founded by Finland-Swedish entrepreneurs and was transformed into a shareholding company, with Finland-Swedish as well as Finnish shareholders.

> Early on, many remote forestry-based industrial communities around the country had emerged as company towns. The basic infrastructure and the gradual diversification of the local economic base grew out of the main employer's activities. The sector was strengthened by domestic rivalry and innovations diffused among competitors across company boundaries [Oinas 2005: 1229].

Finnish-Swedish resources (capital), know-how and management have had a long term impact on Finland's economy. Although ever more Finns have participated, in decision-making and in the leadership of companies, Finland-Swedes have occupied key positions up to the present. An example of the range of Finland-Swedish management in our time is the lifework of Casimir Ehrnrooth (1931–2015), who was born into a wealthy Finland-Swedish family. He inherited substantial holdings from various sectors of Finnish economy, in banking (from the paternal side) and in metal production and forestry (from the maternal side). The founders of big enterprises such as Fiskars (a metal and consumer brands company, founded in the 17th century) and Kaukas (paper factory) were Ehrnrooth's maternal forefathers.

Ehrnrooth's position as president and chief executive officer of the Kaukas company enabled him to arrange the merger with Kymi-Strömberg, in 1985, to form one of Finland's biggest conglomerate corporations, Kymmene. Another merger produced UPM-Kymmene (UPM = United Paper Mills) in 1996, which became the world's third largest producer of paper. Ehrnrooth served in the Nokia Corporation as chairman, from 1992 until 1999. Those were the decisive years when Nokia rose to become the global market leader in mobile phone production.

What makes this figure of Finnish economic life exceptional is that he influenced decision-making during two periods with strongly divergent conditions. One was the period of the 1980s, with Finland's economy booming. The other period, since the early 1990s, was defined by the pressure of innovation to overcome the great recession of 1989–91. Ehrnrooth's contribution to economic innovation and prosperity, through the years of recession into the new era, is widely appreciated (Ahtisaari 2015).

## Finland's Economic Miracle: Standards of Technological Modernization

The postwar decades mark the era of the second stage of modernization of Finland's economy which was much more dramatic than the first (before independence). Economic modernization unfolded hand in hand with the rapid growth of urbanism and international trading contacts. "Over the course of a generation after 1945, Finland transformed itself from an overwhelmingly agrarian to an industrial and urban society" (Lavery 2006: 147). In the early postwar years only some 25 percent of Finland's population lived in an urban environment. In the early 1970s, half of the population was already urban and, at the beginning of the 21st century, the urban population made up more than 80 percent of the total. No other country in Europe has experienced such a rapid transformation of the entire population from predominantly rural to predominantly urban living conditions.

What stands behind this rapid transformation is the symbiotic interplay of factors that define Finnish traditional attitudes and values, and how these factors come to bear.

> Economic systems are embedded in national, deep-rooted social and cultural traditions, which in part explain particular systemic features. It has been argued that, in the Finnish case, such traditions have been instrumental to the nation's capacity to transform itself [Oinas 2005: 1236].

It is true that, in Finland's postwar modernization process, one can observe the working together of vital factors that make up an ensemble which has been termed "cultural capital" by the French sociologist Pierre Bourdieu (1986: 47). This concept has become seminal and has been extensively researched and applied. In the case of Finland's modernization, the Finnish sense for pragmatism, Finnish *sisu* (determination and resilience), the tightly woven bonds in community life, the traditional values of trust and diligence, all that was put to work to achieve what has been termed "the Finnish miracle" by economists and historians.

There was also a certain sociodemographic factor that turned out to become an important player in the process of Finland's modernization, and that was the baby boom of the postwar years. Between 1945 and 1953, birth rates were much higher than the average in Finland's population development. The peak was in autumn of 1945, with almost 12,000 births in August, about 12,600 in September and 10,300 in October. The trend of high birth rates continued until 1953. That populous generation of Finns, born during the early postwar years, continued, since the 1970s, the efforts of their parents who had laid the groundwork for the modern welfare state.

According to a widely popular view—now outdated—of economic development in postwar Finland, the modernization of the country's industries was decisively spurred by Soviet demands for war reparations. Those demands focused on industrial goods, rather than on forestry products. These preferences put Finland's economic capacities to the test and into a forceful drive of industrial expansion. More recent assessments state that Finland had already developed a significant industrial potential during the war, meant to rebuild the economy afterwards. But those resources were immediately absorbed by the efforts to meet the demands of reparations. A further massive expansion of the industrial capacities was required to keep up with the timetable of the reparation plan.

> The hefty war reparations imposed by the Soviet Union placed an incredible strain on the Finnish work regimen. Totally new infrastructures, including new factories, industrial plants producing textiles, pulp and paper, metal products and ships, needed to be built nearly from scratch. During this period Finland, like post-war Japan, operated on a six-day work week. The intensive national work regimen continued until 1966 [Chaker 2014: 114f.].

Finland's reparations activities transformed into Finnish-Soviet trade relations after 1952 when the last transport of reparations goods left Finland. The advancement that Finland's economy made during the early decades of its free trade (freed of the previous burden of reparations) was tremendous, and it can be compared only to the most advanced postwar economies in Europe, Sweden and (West) Germany. Especially significant is the leap between 1950 and 1960, measuring the per capita gross domestic product in U.S. dollars (from Maddison 2003: 50ff.):

> Finland: 1950—4,253. 1960—6,230. 1970—9,577. 1980—12,949. 2000—20,235
> Sweden: 1950—6,739. 1960—8,688. 1970—12,716. 1980—14,937. 2000—20,321
> Germany: 1950—3,881. 1960—7,705. 1970—10,839. 1980—14,114. 2000—18,596

By 2000, Finland had kept up with its neighbor, Sweden, and had even surpassed Germany. When economists speak about recent economic history in the postwar period they mention three exceptional cases which are described in terms of a miracle, and these are "the German miracle" (Henderson 2008a), "the Japanese miracle" (Forsberg

2000) and "the Finnish miracle" (Chaker 2014). Germany was offered support from the Marshall Plan (introduced in 1947), which the country accepted, and Japan received aid from the Dodge Plan (introduced in 1949). Finland was offered aid from the Marshall Plan but the Finnish government rejected the offer in order not to become dependent on foreign financial loans.

Finnish society took the challenge of economic recovery, of payment of war reparations to the Soviet Union and of economic build-up all on its own. That was like going on a marathon under severe conditions. The Finns had no competitors in this, but no supporters either. When comparing the preconditions for economic growth in the three countries, one notices fundamental differences. Without any doubt, the achievements made in Germany and Japan are worthy of great respect. But of all the cases compared here, Finland's rise to high economic and social standards is perhaps the only case deserving of the word "miracle."

The rise of Finland's economy is due to extensive foreign trade relations and these developed in two directions, with the Soviet Union and its allies, the socialist countries of the eastern bloc, on the one hand, and with western Europe and America, on the other. While agriculture and forestry were still dominant before World War II, metal-working, engineering, the timber industry and shipping had gained in importance by the middle of the century. During the past decades, Finland's economy has experienced a booming electronic industry, a boost of its capacities to provide communication networks and an increase in commercial services. In recent years, Finnish know-how, especially in the domains of communication systems, has become the backbone for trade relations with Asian countries.

## The Nokia Story: From Pulpwood and Rubber Boots to Communication Systems

In every country one finds an enterprise that takes the role of flagship for the national economy, setting standards for production, efficient marketing and quality. The exchange of goods in international marketing is accompanied by the crafting and transmission of images about companies and their capacities, and such images may influence the choices and preferences of consumers for certain products. There are always numerous enterprises known among consumers throughout the world for enjoying the image of a national icon, and even if reality changes and the companies experience setbacks the image remains and may be revitalized, once economic success again favors the offered products.

The United States has its iconic car, the Ford, Japan its Toyota, Korea its Hyundai. Everybody knows what a Mercedes is: not just any German car but an iconic brand, and quality and high-level standards are associated with its image. Finland has only one genuinely Finnish car model, and this is Sisu, a truck (foreign cars have been produced under license agreements—Porsche until 2011, and Mercedes starting in 2017, in Uusikaupunki; Perttu 2015).

The flagship of the Finnish national economy is a trail-blazing company for the modernization process—Nokia, in 2016 the internationally leading enterprise for digitalized telecommunication systems. There are some other big companies in Finland which not only hold a share of the international market but also determine the pace of development in their domains. There is Outokumpu, a giant in the timber industry, and Kone, specializing in elevators—a business that has been booming in recent years, particularly spurred by construction activities in China where ever higher buildings are erected.

The productivity of the big firms for Finland's GDP is highly significant. According to the findings of the Doblin analysis of 2005, less than 2 percent of all economic projects produce more than 90 percent of the overall value (Jain 2014). Among the big companies with large-scale projects, Nokia occupies a special position, because of its scale and range. For many years, Nokia's share in Finland's GDP was about one fifth of the annual total.

In many respects, the history of Nokia is unique, yet representative of the overall speedy development of Finnish technological know-how. What is so special about Nokia is its long history that extends from the mid–19th century onward. Nokia has experienced ups and downs, and there were times when the company was challenged by the giants in the arena of international competition.

> At one level, Nokia's transformation is a story of the firm and the struggles related to strategic decision-making. At another, it is a story of the ways in which national institutional environments and corporate strategies mutually shape each other (cf. Morgan, 2005). Without Nokia, Finland would seem different today. But obviously, Nokia would not be what it is had it not emerged in Finland [Oinas 2005: 1232].

By 1995, Nokia had reached a peak: it had become the world's largest producer of mobile phones. International competition put a challenge to the world leader and, after 2010, Samsung's market share increased so that it featured in first rank for several years. Still, in 2013, Nokia ranged second after Samsung among the world's top manufacturers of mobile phones. Only a year later, in 2014, Nokia sold the entire mobile phone production to Microsoft, and the corporation suffered a remarkable setback. Some entertained the vision of "the decline and fall of Nokia" (Cord 2014). But like the Phoenix rose from the ashes so Nokia overcame its setback, rejuvenated and retook its place among the giants of the world. The history of Nokia illustrates how a small company from the north of Europe can conquer the whole world with a product that is needed and wanted by everybody. Its history also illustrates how its business may be ground by the unpredictable mills of the world's markets and what it takes for an enterprise to stay on top.

## Modest Beginnings in the 1860s

The beginnings in the 1860s, a time when Finland's industrialization was gaining strength, were modest. The original enterprise that was later transformed into the Nokia Company was founded by the mining engineer Fredrik Idestam in 1865. The original business of Nokia focused on Finland's renewable natural resources, vast forests which then covered more than 90 percent of the country's surface. Idestam built a wood pulp mill in Tampere (a town in southwestern Finland), on the banks of the rapids called Tammerkoski. A second mill was established, on the banks of the Nokianvirta, near a small village, a center for the Russian fur trade during the times of tsarist rule over Finland. This village, with the name of Nokia, was located about 15 kilometers west of Tampere. In 2014 the town of Nokia counted some 32,000 inhabitants (2014). The name of the village is derived from the Finnish expression *noki* ("soot"). The name *nokia* was given to a black furry mammal, as an euphemism, to avoid calling it by its true name.

The Finns in pre–Christian times were superstitious and feared the wrath of the guardian spirits of animals they hunted.

Idestam's enterprise was changed to Nokia in 1871 and, later, transformed into a shareholding company. The first products of Nokia were mechanical pulpwood and paper. For decades, the company developed within the confines of mechanical manufacturing, while constantly expanding. Idestam's multitalented business partner, Leo Mechelin, was one of the most influential politicians of his time in the Grand Duchy and, as an entrepreneur, he had visions about expanding into the domain of electricity. However, Mechelin's ideas were not shared by Idestam and the vision did not materialize during the time of the partnership. Idestam retired in 1896 and Mechelin took over as chairman of the company in 1898. His position provided the backing for convincing the shareholders of certain profitable prospects and in 1902 Nokia started to generate electricity.

## Engaging in the Production of Electrical Equipment Since the Early 20th Century

Expansion was not only a matter of industrial output but also came to bear in the founding of new businesses, like the Finnish Rubber Works (Suomen Gummitehdas Oy), founded by Eduard Polón in 1898. Finnish Cable Works (Suomen Kaapelitehdas Oy) was founded by Arvid Wickström in 1912. This business opened the path into Nokia's electronic enterprise. The Cable Works produced cables for telephones, telegraphs and electrical appliances. The interests of the three firms were intertwined but as long as Finland formed part of the Russian Empire, the merging of firms was not allowed. The Cable Works went almost bankrupt in the early years of Finland's independence. In 1922, Finnish Rubber Works bought out the Cable Works to ensure electricity supply. The three firms carried out their business activities under a joint ownership of shareholders, until 1967, when they were merged into the Nokia Corporation.

In the decades between World War I and World War II Nokia's activities continued to be diversified. The Finnish Rubber Works developed their production of rubber boots and, later, car tires were added as products. Both rubber boots and tires are being produced to this day. Despite the setback with the electronics business in the early phase of the Finnish Cable Works, this domain would become the cornerstone of Nokia's breakthrough on the international market. The Peace Treaty between Finland and the Soviet Union, concluded in Paris in 1947, set harsh conditions for the Finnish economy, and Finnish Cable Works—like many other companies in Finland—took over the burden of producing considerable amounts of electrical equipment for the Soviet Union as part of the enforced war reparations. In the long run, the Finns profited from the production experience, which served as a springboard for Nokia's product development and design.

Nokia set standards for the broadcasting business and paved the way for communication networking in Finland. The beginnings of the involvement of Nokia in home electronics were not very encouraging. In 1984, Nokia acquired Luxor AB, a Swedish manufacturer of electronic systems (tape recorders, radios, television sets). In 1978, this Nokia-owned company, located in Motala (Östergötland County, Sweden), produced its first model of a home computer (the ABC 80). It turned out that this product was not successful, and the production was discontinued in 1986. There were further cuts in the early 1990s, with the termination of the production of television sets in Motala. Nokia concentrated on the production of receivers for satellite television but, in 1998, decided to sell this part of the business to an American company, Space Craft Inc.

## Digitalization and the Great Endeavor of the Mobile Phone Business

The 1990s were a kind of incubation period for Nokia that was developing an uncharted terrain, the business of mobile phones. Mobile telephony has quite a long history which did not start with hand-held devices. That was many decades after the early experiments with telecommunication from moving vehicles. The first successful mobile telephone service was offered by the German Railroad Company (Deutsche Reichsbahn), starting in 1926, with mobile service offered to first-class passengers in trains on the route between Berlin and Hamburg. The challenges for wireless communication between army units during World War II speeded up the technical development and, in the late 1940s, mobile telephony was established for automobiles, starting with systems devised by Bell Labs in the United States. In 1956, a mobile telephone service (called MTA = Mobiltelefonisystem A), to be used in vehicles, was introduced in Sweden. Ericsson provided the switchboard for this system, and the Swedish Radio Corporation (Svenska Radioaktiebolaget) the equipment for the base station.

The advancement from a mobile transmitter in a moving vehicle to a hand-held device was quite a technical leap although visions of such a use and such a device had been publicized as early as the beginning of the 20th century. In the *Simplicissimus*, a German satirical magazine, a German artist named Karl Arnold published in 1926 a cartoon about the visionary use of mobile phones in the streets of Berlin, and the German writer Erich Kästner, in his children's book *Conrad's Ride to the South Seas* (1931), described a call made by someone walking in the street from a mobile phone that he took from the pocket of his coat. Closer to future realities was the mobile phone in the science fiction novel *Space Cadet* (1948) by Robert Heinlein.

In the 1950s, a Soviet engineer experimented with models of a hand-held mobile phone, but none of those models went into production. Similarly, a model of a cell phone presented by a Bulgarian company in 1965, did not reach any production line. The first hand-held mobile phone was presented to the world by engineers from the Motorola company. Dr. Martin Cooper called his superior, Dr. Joel S. Engel of the Bell Labs, on a device that weighed 1.1 kg, with dimensions far from modern cell phones: 23 cm (9 inches) in length, 13 cm (5.1") in depth and 4.45 cm (1.7") in width. America took the lead in mobile phone development and, in 1983, the first model for commercial use was introduced. Technical development was fast and the early models were soon superseded by more advanced devices. Until the early 1990s, U.S. companies were the leaders in the development, production and marketing of mobile phones.

The marketing strategy for the American mobile phones was to sell the product to people in the business world, to facilitate their commercial negotiations. The image of the mobile phone as a "tool" for handling business affairs dominated marketing into the early 1990s. The association with the world of business was reinforced by the technological innovation of the second generation of mobile phones which was a new variant of communication, text messaging (or SMS = short message service, respectively). The first successful communication via SMS occurred in England, in December 1992. This communication was machine-generated. The following year, as a global inauguration, a person-to-person SMS was sent in Finland.

The innovation of SMS is not the brainchild of a particular person. Teams of engineers in different parts of Europe had experimented with text message technology since the early 1980s (Karlsson and Lugn 2009). There were two main trends to achieve results. In the Scandinavian countries, the technology for SMS was based on the e-mail principle (i.e., the X.400 technique). French and German engineers who formed an international research team (under their first chairman Finn Trosby, a Norwegian) followed the signaling principle for their work. This principle was ultimately adopted. In Finland, Matti Makkonen, a Nokia engineer, was the first to successfully apply the GSM service to the Nokia mobile phone. In autumn 2008, Makkonen received the innovation award given by the British magazine *The Economist* for developing the SMS system. The question whether the GSM service had already been in use to facilitate communication between units of the Finnish army in the late 1980s (the SANLA system) has remained somehow mysterious and may be solved, perhaps as a matter of interest for military historians.

And then, almost out of the blue, a dramatic shift occurred, and this shift is associated with the rise of Nokia to become the world's top manufacturer of mobile phones for more than a decade. The base for a successful mobile phone service is a functioning communication network. Such networks had been operated with an analogical switching system for many years. At a certain stage, growing demands for the development of the mobile phone sector forced engineers to make an elemental choice between two alternatives: developing the analogical switching system further or embarking on the path of digitalization. In the early 1970s, those responsible for technical development in the Nokia company engaged in decisive discussions about technical options. Among those who advocated advancement by focusing on digitalization of PCM (pulse code modulation) networks for telecommunication was the head of implementation services in Nokia Telecommunications Customer Services, Markku Tiili. History proved that his vision led Nokia into the direction of dynamic progress in the 1970s and 1980s, paving the way for its marketing strategy and the achievement of dominant global status (Tiili 2012: 181ff.).

## Selling a New Image of Global Telecommunication: Mobile Phones for Everybody

The reasons for the breath-taking success in international marketing were manifold, but what made the sales strategy appear radically new was the creation of a new image for the purpose of the mobile phone. In this image were two aspects not taken into consideration earlier. Why should the practical use of the mobile phone be limited to the world of business? Why not facilitate communication for all people? And why sell mobile phones only to adults? Young people also need easy means to communicate. And yet, there was a difficulty: young people generally do not have much money, so who would pay for their expensive calls by mobile phone? The SMS technology offered a solution: young people may take advantage and communicate using inexpensive text messaging.

Almost over night a new marketing strategy for selling mobile phones was born (Lindholm et al. 2003). The idea for a new direction in marketing is one thing, its implementation is quite another. The one who was at the right place at the right time and who set his mind to make the new marketing strategy work was Jorma Ollila who had joined the Nokia Corporation in 1985. In 1992, Ollila became the chief executive officer of Nokia, an office he held until 2006. At that time, Nokia offered a broad range of products, ranging from rubber boots to television sets and from toilet paper to mobile phones. Ollila's innovative path of reorganization of technological production and marketing has been termed "unorthodox management."

Nokia's CEO "turned cell phones into a necessity—and took the market" (*Time*, 29 May 2000, pp. 64–65). And the strategy that Nokia's CEO devised by focusing on the production, development and sales of mobile phones proved to be globally successful. Alluding to the magnitude of this success, *The Economist* (14 October 2000, p. 83) called it "a Finnish fable," and Ollila himself speaks of an "impossible success" (Ollila and Saukkomaa 2013). While, in 1994, Nokia ranked second after Motorola in annual sales of mobile phones, in 1995, the company had taken the lead and kept it for more than 15 years: "Nokia rocks its rivals" (Guyon 2002). Between 1996 and 1998 Nokia ranked number one as the world's most electrifying technology company. Those were the days when the future was Finnish.

> Nokia is a giant in Finland. It is by far the country's biggest firm by turnover (29 267 million Euro in 2004; that is 2.4 times bigger than that of the second biggest firm, the Finnish-Swedish forestry company, Stora Enso) and the largest private sector employer (53,511 employees in 2004, of which 43% in Finland) [Oinas 2005: 1233].

In the spring of 1999, Finland was the first country in the world to cross the magical boundary of 60 percent mobile telephone density (i.e., 60 mobile phone subscriptions per 100 inhabitants). Finland still holds a record today, with 172 subscriptions per 100 in 2013. Estonia is close, at 160. As for comparison, the U.S. has a very low density (at 96) (The Finnish Communications Regulatory Authority, Ficora: 28 January 2015; http://www.telecompaper.com/news/finland-leads-the-world-in-mobile-phone-density-in-2013--1061998; retrieved 4 March 2015).

The success of Nokia's international sales of mobile phones remained unrivaled until 2011. The same year, Nokia's board of directors decided to terminate its own Symbian platform and switch to the Windows Phone platform, and this move was staged in connection with a fusion with Microsoft. The aim was to stabilize, for Nokia, an ecosystem that could compete with Google's Android and Apple's iOS. In order to carry out such a monumental change, Nokia elected a new CEO, hired away from Microsoft, Stephen Elop, in autumn 2010. In a "Burning Platform" memo of February 2011, Elop revealed the fundamentals of the new strategy he had devised for Nokia (*BBC Online*. BBC. 9 February 2011; retrieved 19 March 2013). In an interview on Finnish TV, in March 2011, Elop defended Nokia's new direction in its mobile phone business. Elop talked much about failure, offering strategies for its avoidance. In the end, the monumental project failed and cell phone sales dropped worldwide. In the years from 2012 to 2014, Nokia, after many years of leadership, fell to second rank after Samsung.

## Nokia's Decline and Fall and Rise to New Heights

There are those who see Microsoft's intervention, personified and executed by Elop, as an honest attempt to synchronize communication platforms to make Nokia's mobile phones more apt for the U.S. market, that is to abandon the Symbian platform that is isolated in America. And there are others who see, in Elop's activities, a kind of conspiracy, initiated by Microsoft to prepare a takeover of Nokia. According to that view, Elop's role in the Nokia Corporation would have been that of a Trojan horse to facilitate a takeover. In their book *Operaatio Elop* ("Operation Elop," 2014), two journalists of the Finnish magazine *Kauppalehti*, Pekka Nykänen and Merina Salminen, come to the conclusion that Elop's role in the Nokia company was neither that of a promoter of Nokia's mobile phones on the American market nor that of a Trojan horse. According to their assessment, Elop was unsuccessful as CEO because he lacked what would have been required: vision.

In December 2013, the great majority of the shareholders voted in favor of the sale of the complete mobile phone division of Nokia to Microsoft in early 2014. In early summer 2015, it became clear that Microsoft would lay off more than 2000 of its employees will lose their jobs in Finland because the mobile phone section bought from Nokia will be closed.

Since 2014, Nokia has focused on developing and providing communication networks, a division where the know-how of Finnish engineering has flourished for decades. To the surprise of the Finns and the world's public, Nokia announced its intention to acquire the French telecom Alcatel-Lucent, in April 2015. The purchase, worth 15.6 billion euros, was concluded in early spring 2016, and after the integration of this company into Nokia, the enlarged corporation is seen as the world's leading networks operator (Zekaria and Knutson 2015, Sandelin and Partanen 2015).

In August 2015, Nokia announced the sale of its digital navigatory system (HERE) to a consortium of German automobile producers. Nokia's activities are now streamlined and centered on two major domains, electronic development and digital communication networking. Nokia became known worldwide with the slogan "Nokia—connecting people." The essence of this slogan is still valid, only that it shifted from mobile phones to the very basis of telecommunication, the digitalized networks.

## Nokia's Communicative Strategy for International Marketing

The Nokia company's ability to swiftly adjust to changing conditions, as they prevailed during the modernization process and the recent streamlining process, is anchored in its far-sighted communicative strategy for managing international marketing. The working language of Nokia is English, and this is true also for all divisions in Finland. The headquarters of the company is centered in the town of Espoo which, together with Vantaa and Helsinki, forms the southern metropolitan area of Finland. The leadership of Nokia is international although the majority of the company's stockholders are Finns.

The use of English might be a necessity in the inner circle of Nokia's leadership but the decision to use this world language also among the workforce was motivated by the far-sighted vision of internationalization. The major precondition for the requirement to use English is that all personnel in the Nokia company are proficient in that language, regardless of whether it is a worker's native tongue. Every day, when Finns and Finnish-

Swedes go to work they switch to English at the workplace. Proficiency in English is among the high standards of the Finnish educational system that has raised much attention through the PISA studies (see Chapter 6).

## Managing Network Society: A Small Country Mobilizing Know-How and Capacities

Some of the world's biggest ships are built in Germany, and some of the world's biggest ships are built in the USA. Nobody wonders because such production can be expected when all the resources, the accumulated know-how and organizational skills in those big economies are put to work. Some of the world's biggest ships have also been built in Finland. This is quite exceptional.

The biggest cruise ship that ever crossed the Atlantic, the *Oasis of the Seas*, was built in Finland. Its tonnage is 225,282 GRT (gross registered tons), its length is 360 meters (1,187 feet), and it is some 20 storeys high. The keel for this ship was laid in the shipyard in Turku, in November 2007, and the vessel left the shipyard in October 2009. Its home port is Fort Lauderdale in Florida and it is operated by the Royal Caribbean company. The *Oasis of the Seas* is five times bigger than the *Titanic*. The ship is so big that its space is divided into "neighborhoods," into park landscapes, dedicated to differing themes. Finland's shipyards have the capacities to build even bigger ships than the *Oasis of the Seas*.

However, there is a geographical factor that sets limitations. This factor is the bridge that connects the islands of Zealand and Fünen in Denmark. Ships that maneuver through the passage of the Great Belt to reach the North Sea and the Atlantic have to pass under the Great Belt Fixed Link (the Big Belt Bridge) that was completed in 1998. The vertical clearance of the East Bridge for ships is 65 meters (213 feet), and the *Oasis of the Seas* passed through, with its smokestack folded, when the water level of the sea was low. Yet, bigger ships would not pass.

Whether it is cruise ships, ice-breakers, paper mills or astronomical equipment for space projects, Finnish know-how is far advanced but the country has also experienced a swift transition to network society, ranking among the top 15 countries in the world with the highest internet penetration rates. Altogether 91.5 percent of Finland's population were internet users in 2013. High rates are also typical for Iceland, Norway, Denmark and Sweden (http://www.internetworldstats.com/europa.htm; retrieved 21 March 2015). The rates for internet users in big countries such as Great Britain (89.8 percent), Germany (86.2) or the USA (84.2) remain below 90 percent. The average rate for internet penetration in the EU countries is 76.5 percent (as of 2013).

According to the World Payments Report for 2015 (as monitored by Capgemini and the Royal Bank of Scotland), Finland ranks first in the world in payments by credit card (https://www.worldpaymentsreport.com/; retrieved 30 November 2015). Cash as a mode of payment has been decreasing steadily for many years. Many facilities operate with credit card payment only, excluding cash altogether. This is true for certain shops and gas stations. Closely associated with this trend is the increase of online shopping where credit card payment dominates (without postal bill service).

During the 1990s, Finland experienced a transition to a networked society which

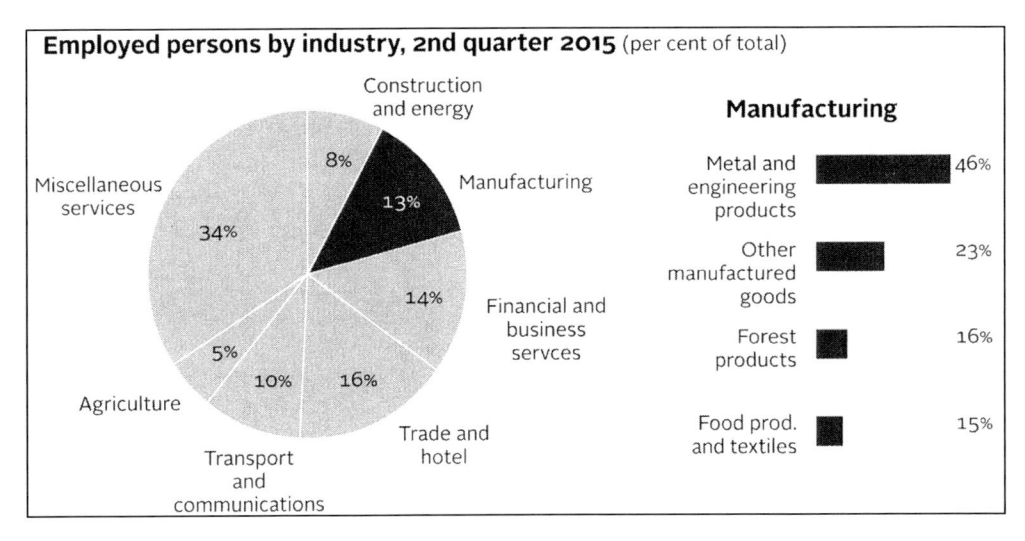

**Figure 28: Finland's economic structure and exports (2014–15) (Finnish Authorities; Statistics Finland).**

has been more rapid and intense than in most other countries of the world. The particular strategies by which Finnish society proceeded toward the developmental stage of the network state have attracted the attention of experts around the world. Around the turn of the century, Finland's stage of digitalization was described by some economists as the "Finnish model" (e.g., Vartanova 1999, Mer 1999, Castells and Himanen 2002). The movement toward integration in western Europe was in concord with this process leading to the institutionalization of a "network state" (Castells 1998: 330ff.), and Finland continues to play the role of a forerunner.

In an interview given to the Finnish newspaper *Helsingin Sanomat* and published on 2 January 2000, the Spanish sociologist Manuel Castells emphasized that Finland holds the edge in this evolution toward a network society (Snellman 2000). According to Castells, technological modernization in Finland is evolving within the framework of high standards in living conditions, whereas in the United States modernization is intensifying, but at the cost of quality of life.

In Finland, the transition to a network society, to the digitalization of industrial production cycles and to the digital processing of information, started out in a sector that, in other countries, was not a major factor of economic development, and this is the traditional sector of Finnish forestry. Well into the 1950s, the export of Finnish products from the forest industries made up about 90 percent of the total income.

> While the Finnish industry and export base has also strongly diversified ever since, especially into metal and machinery, the forest industries have played a significant role in the evolution of Finland's economy and society. Nowhere else has the forest sector similarly been the economic engine of a country; for decades, Finland remained a "forest sector society" [Lilja et al., 1992] [Oinas 2005: 1229].

The forest sector has experienced a dramatic restructuring during the past decades, and its role for Finnish economy is no longer a central one. By 2015, the share of products from forest industry made up about 20 percent of the total exports and those employed in forestry and forest industry make up some 16 percent of the manufacturing domain which employs some 13 percent of the Finnish workforce (figure 28).

# 6

# What Makes Finland's School Education So Efficient and How Important Are the Language Choices for Knowledge-Construction?

The Finns have come a long way with the development of a nationwide education system although the modern system which has earned worldwide attention only emerged as late as the mid–20th century. The beginnings of the concept of national education are associated with the spread of Protestantism in this country. In earlier periods, students from Finland who went abroad to frequent universities in France, Italy or Germany often received financial support from their local dioceses. Things changed in the 16th century, with the shift from Catholicism to Protestantism.

> The confiscation of church property implemented by Gustavus Vasa (King of Sweden in 1523–60) under the auspices of the Reformation broke the economic back of the dioceses. Cathedral chapters were no longer in the position to determine the destinations of student travel or to fund students independently. At the beginning of the Reformation era, studies still served the goals of the church, but now people like the Finnish reformer Mikael Agricola and other scions of the Bishopric of Turku at Wittenberg would turn to Gustavus Vasa for financial support. Study abroad was a part of ecclesiatical policy formulated nationally by the monarch [Nuorteva 1997a: 526f.].

## The Art of Learning Fast: Finnish Education and the Test of Time

The establishment of a national education system aimed to provide every citizen with fundamentals gradually materialized, with modest beginnings in the 19th century. "The old modes of public elementary schooling, the "exchange-schools" (where senior pupils helped beginners) and the "poor schools," had been replaced, in the 1860s, by the new folk-schools, a general and uniform system of basic education" (Schoolfield 1996: 147).

The initiator of the system was Uno Cygnaeus (1810–1888) who gained recognition as the "father of the Finnish folk school." With a grant from the Russian senate, Cygnaeus travelled, in 1858, to study educational systems in central and western Europe.

As a result of his investigations; travels to Sweden, Denmark, Germany, Austria, and Switzerland; and drawing from the best of educational thinking of people like Frobez, Pestalozzi, and Diesterweg, Cygnaeus prepared a report to the Russian senate in 1860.... In this report, he proposed the now famous "Finnish Folk School" as a basic school for all children. The report was the fundamental basis for a law passed in 1866 to establish folk schools throughout Finland for all pupils and to develop universities to prepare teachers to teach in these schools [Dugger 2010: 3].

Cygnaeus was supported by Finland's reformer Johan Vilhelm Snellman who paved the way for the successful law of 1866. Snellman categorically linked the Finnish language to the collective body of the Finnish nation and the process of modernization to Finnish. According to Snellman, "the Finnish nation could survive only through an improvement of Finnish-language education" (Lavery 2006: 177).

Well into the era of Finland's independence, Swedish remained essential for higher education and for social advancement. Alongside the role that Swedish played for the élite, Finnish gained ground and began to challenge the monopoly of the former vehicle of civilized (Swedish-oriented) Finnishness. There were cases of Finland-Swedes changing their language preferences and to favor Finnish. Around the turn of the century

a Finnish-speaking élite emerged, more because of the next generations's schooling; but changing one's language created a Finnish-speaking élite more quickly than schooling alone would have done. Language divided families because some of the family chose Finnish. It also happened that some of the children were sent to a Finnish school and some to a Swedish school. Likewise, it happened that Swedish speakers sent their children to Finnish schools, and, up until the turn of the century often vice versa as well [Engman 1995: 190].

On the older basis, the educational system was extensively reshuffled as part of the Nordic welfare state in the period after World War II. In recent years, the exceptional performance of Finnish students has brought worldwide attention. Regarding the domains of science and literacy the proficiency of Finnish students has been ranked, in the studies of the OECD Programme for International Student Assessment (PISA) for 2000, 2003 and 2006, highest in the countries of the European Union, and worldwide. In 2003, Finland's students ranked second in mathematics. In 2006, Finland ranked first also in this category. The following scores have been recorded for the five best countries in PISA from PISA 2000 through 2006:

| **2000** | **2003** | **2006** |
|---|---|---|
| *MATH* | *MATH* | *MATH* |
| Japan 557 | Hong Kong 550 | Taipei (China) 549 |
| Korea 547 | **Finland 544** | **Finland 548** |
| New Zealand 537 | Korea 542 | Hong Kong & Korea 547 |
| **Finland 536** | Netherlands 538 | Netherlands 531 |
| Australia 533 | Liechtenstein 536 | Switzerland 530 |
| | | |
| *READING* | *READING* | *READING* |
| **Finland 546** | **Finland 543** | Korea 556 |
| Canada 534 | Korea 534 | **Finland 547** |
| New Zealand 529 | Canada 528 | Hong Kong 536 |
| Australia 528 | Australia & Liechtenstein 525 | Canada 527 |
| Ireland 527 | New Zealand 522 | New Zealand 521 |

| **2000** | **2003** | **2006** |
|---|---|---|
| *SCIENCE* | *SCIENCE* | *SCIENCE* |
| Korea 552 | **Finland & Japan 548** | **Finland 563** |
| Japan 550 | Hong Kong 539 | Hong Kong 542 |
| **Finland 538** | Korea 538 | Canada 534 |
| England 532 | Australia, | Taipei 532 |
| | Liechtenstein & Macao 525 | |
| Canada 529 | Netherlands 524 | Estonia & Japan 531 |

By 2012 the scores for Finland had dropped to sixth rank in literacy, fifth in science and twelfth in mathematics, with Shanghai, Hong Kong and Singapore taking the lead, but Finland is still among the best in the world (Välijärvi et al. 2003, 2007, Hautamäki et al. 2008).

The success in the science category is largely due to the efficient implementation of such principles as the practical connection of education with real life that had already been devised by Cygnaeus. He stressed the importance of getting children acquainted with handicrafts (sloyd).

> If Cygnaeus were alive today, he would most likely be a strong supporter of the study of technology by all students from kindergarten through high school. The first priority of a study of technology is to provide technological literacy to all students. This study includes all students who traditionally have not been served by technology programs. Most certainly, Cygnaeus would view the study of technology today as mandatory (not as an elective) [Dugger 2010: 3f.].

This priority of technology education, as formulated by Cygnaeus, experienced a reaffirmation through the teaching of the German educator Ernst Mach (1838–1916), who stressed active participation in the generating of scientific concepts: "A concept cannot be acquired passively, but only by participation, living-through in the domain to which the concept belongs" (Mach 1896: 420). The importance of Mach's teaching is still apparent in Finland's educational system (Siemsen 2010).

On the level of higher education, Finland keeps scoring the highest ranking. According to the report of the World Economic Forum that monitors the efficiency of schooling systems, the following rankings were established for the top 10 countries, for the period 2014–15 (http://www3.weforum.org/docs/img/WEF_GCR2014-15_Education_Image.png; retrieved 29 November 2015):

- HIGHER EDUCATION AND TRAINING—Finland (1), Singapore (2), Netherlands (3), Switzerland (4), Belgium (5), United Arab Emirates (6), United States (7), Norway (8), New Zealand (9), Denmark (10).

The Education Index (as part of the UN's Human Development Index), in 2008, listed Finland—with Denmark, Australia and New Zealand—among the highest in the world. The media speak about "the Finland phenomenon" which is the theme of a documentary film made by Bob Compton and Tony Wagner (from Harvard University): *The Finland phenomenon: Inside the world's most surprising school system* (*Forbes*, 2 May 2011).

Educational experts from many countries have visited Finland to learn more about the fabric of the Finnish school system. Experiments with the Finnish educational model have been under way in Germany, Italy and in other countries. For instance, professional training in the Arab Emirates has been reorganized according to the educational principles of Finland. In 2013, a contract was agreed between Finland and Saudi Arabia for adapting the Finnish-style schooling to that country. In 2014, EduCluster opened a Finnish-style schooling center for professional training in China. When the president of Brazil, Dilma Rousseff, visited Finland in October 2015, she announced plans for the school system in her country to be reshuffled according to the Finnish model.

The global attention which the Finnish school system has gained reflects the elementary value of basic education as established by Cygnaeus. The folk school is not only the cornerstone of the modern educational system in Finland, it is part of a global heritage. "The concept of the Finnish Folk School was cutting-edge and inventive in the total spectrum of education. It laid the foundation for much of what we do (and try to do) worldwide today in the study of technology" (Dugger 2010: 3).

The Finnish Ministry of Education highlights three criteria as responsible for the success of schooling: "the education system (uniform basic education for the whole age group), highly competent teachers, and the autonomy given to schools" ("Background for Finnish PISA success"; http://www.minedu.fi/pisa/taustaa.html?lang=en; retrieved 6 August 2015). One may perhaps add another factor that is likely to enhance social cohesion and the feel of membership in the peer group among schoolchildren, and this is the institution of free school meals.

> In 1943 Finland was the first country in the world to enact a law on free school meals for all pupils, who were obliged to do a reasonable amount of work outside school hours to grow and collect food for the school kitchen. The goal of providing every pupil in compulsory education with a free school meal on every school day within five years was realized in 1948, and the system has endured to this day [Lindroos 2013: 104f.].

For the comprehensive school, of nine grades (decreed in 1998), the principle of equity (education for all) was adopted and implemented. The idea of keeping members of the same age-group together has led to a special situation. While, in Finland, grade repeating is rare, it is quite common in other school systems (e.g., 2 percent of students repeat a grade in Finland as compared to some 40 percent in France). Pupils who fall behind the level of learning are given remedial teaching and additional support to catch up with their classmates.

The level of education in Finland has been continuously rising. In 1980, more than 60 percent of the population had a basic education, 25 percent an upper secondary education, and 13 percent a tertiary education. For the first time, in 2004, the percentage of those with an upper secondary education was higher than for basic education. Difference between the two kinds of education has grown stronger and, in 2012, the proportions had developed as follows: exclusively basic education (31.4 percent); upper secondary education (39.8); tertiary education (28.6) (STV 2014: 368f.).

Various explanations have been given for the success of the Finnish educational system. Whatever singular aspect may have been addressed to explain the success, those musings more or less scratch the surface since what is missing is a view on the organic whole. It turns out that *how* to learn is more important than *what* to learn. The method of how to teach stuff is more decisive for success than paying too much attention to an overcrowded package of data. Moreover, if testing procedures occupy too much time, both of students and teachers, then the prime goal of education becomes blurred.

Pronouncements have been made according to which Finnish students' high level of proficiency may be related to high-grade linguistic homogeneity among school children. The children of the Finland-Swedish community commonly learn Finnish at a preschool age. When these children enter school they already have a good command of Finnish. This means that the quality of teaching and the level of knowledge is equal among Finns proper and Finland-Swedish students.

The number of school children from other ethnic groups in Finnish schools is (still) rather small, given the small portion of minorities in this country. The situation is quite different in Germany where a much greater portion of children are of ethnic origins other than German. While, in Finland, the command of Finnish is at a high level among all school children, the situation in Germany varies greatly among the ethnic groups in the lower grades. Weaker language skills are an impediment to learning while proficiency enhances the construction of knowledge (Ammon 2015: 1072f.). In classes where there is considerable variation in language skills, the overall performance of students is weaker than in homogeneous classes.

Finland's education system started out rather late compared with other countries in Scandinavia and western Europe. Yet, once the project for a comprehensive school system was set in motion modernization quickly gained momentum. A solid infrastructure for the education system was achieved through farsighted planning and smooth implementation and this system developed into a model for other countries. The beginnings of a schooling program in Finland were modest. An elementary education of four years was introduced in 1866 but made compulsory by law much later (in 1921).

> In the course of the modernizing process in Finland, the individual and her / his competence rather than the family or the household became the basis for modern society. The individual was given the responsibility for acquiring the skills, education and wealth needed to improve her / his life circumstances....
> Education, in particular, epitomized the new values linked with individualism. Through it, individuals could be liberated from the shackles of the position into which they were born by gaining access to social mobility... [Koskinen-Koivisto 2014: 95].

Finland experienced a baby boom after World War II (STV 2014: 96), and the demand for schooling put Finnish authorities to the test. Great changes took place, especially new school buildings in cities, towns and rural areas, reflecting an extended program of infrastructure. More decisive was the modernization of teaching methods. The priority lay with activating students' skills (backed up by information), rather than giving emphasis to the mere transfer of data. In this, the Finnish school system deviates from the priorities set for education in countries of western Europe (Kupiainen et al. 2009: 12):

- General western model: Standardization (strict standards for schools, teachers and students to guarantee the quality of outcomes); emphasis on literacy and numeracy (basic skills in reading, writing, mathematics and science as prime targets of education reform); consequential accountability (evaluation by inspection)
- The Finnish system: Flexibility and diversity (school-based curriculum development, steering by information and support); emphasis on broad knowledge (equal value to all aspects of individual growth and learning: personality, morality, creativity, knowledge and skills); trust through professionalism (a culture of trust of teachers' and headmasters' professionalism in judging what is best for students and in the reporting of progress).

The leading principle for school education in Finland is equity. The Finnish educational system functions without tuition fees, and subsidized meals are regularly offered to full-time students. Teaching materials (including school books and technical equipment such as laptops) are subsidized on the level of elementary education although, in the higher grades of secondary education, teaching materials have to be purchased.

Early education does not start with the program implemented in schools, but earlier:

> Early education refers to all-around support for the care, growth, development, and learning of the child. "Daycare" is an administrative term embedded within early childhood education. Daycare is a service for all children below school-start age, ... In Finland the term "preschool" as an administrative and pedagogical term refers to programs serving only 6-year-olds during the year preceding their entry into compulsory education. Preschools can be located in daycare or public school facilities [Niikko 2006: 134].

An essential precondition for teaching methods to bear fruit is the readiness to learn that is promoted in preschool education: respecting each child's individuality, development of social and interactive skills, encouragement for the child to pay attention to other persons' interests.

The preschool facilities are not the places to learn for the sake of instruction. Instead, emphasis is on *how* to learn, and this consequently facilitates integration into school programs. In the ways of inspiring preschool children to learn, the echo of environmental awareness resounds, which forms part of the nature-oriented cultural memory. Preschool children learn about nature, animals and about the elements that define the cycle of life. The overall effect of preschool learning seems to be the stimulation of children's curiosity and this "appetite" to learn more provides an ideal springboard for engaged learning at school.

In Finnish school education, a certain factor is at work which is taken for granted by Finns but which, in a worldwide comparison, is perhaps the exception rather than the rule. This factor is freedom of information, guaranteed by the absence of any ideological orientation, political determination, nationalistic trend or religious dogmatism in the teaching programs that would otherwise cause restrictions to the free access to information or would enhance negative boundary-marking toward foreign cultures. In Finnish schools, lessons are offered, for example, about both the Christian religion and Islam, and history lessons focus on the path of democratic governance, and on that of communist rule for comparison. Pupils are not taught to be happy to be living in Finland. That is an experience everybody can make for themselves.

There is another factor, or better range of factors, where Finnish (and more generally Nordic) school education obviously differs from the educational enterprise in other parts of the world.

> To be sure there are general differences in American and Nordic views about what young children are capable of doing and what they should be allowed to do, as well as differences in the ways in which child-related issues are discussed, debated, and resolved.... Nordic notions about childhood freedom to explore and play were already in place when child care provisions emerged in the Nordic countries. Nordic parents and early childhood teachers seem to readily accept bumps and bruises as inevitable consequences of the *freedom to which children are entitled* as they exercise *their right* to play and explore, unencumbered by oppressive or unnecessarily restrictive adult supervision and intervention. In contrast, ..., American early childhood education typically take a protectionist view, fearful that children will get hurt and that we will then be sued [Wagner 2006: 298].

The core curriculum is comprised of a teaching content that provides valuable attitudes toward society and its members: growth as an individual (development of one's personality), cultural identity and concepts of internationalism (perceiving one's own country as in a web of international relations), media skills and communication, participatory citizenship and entrepreneurship, responsibility for the environment, well-being and a sustainable future, safety and traffic, technology and the individual (figure 29).

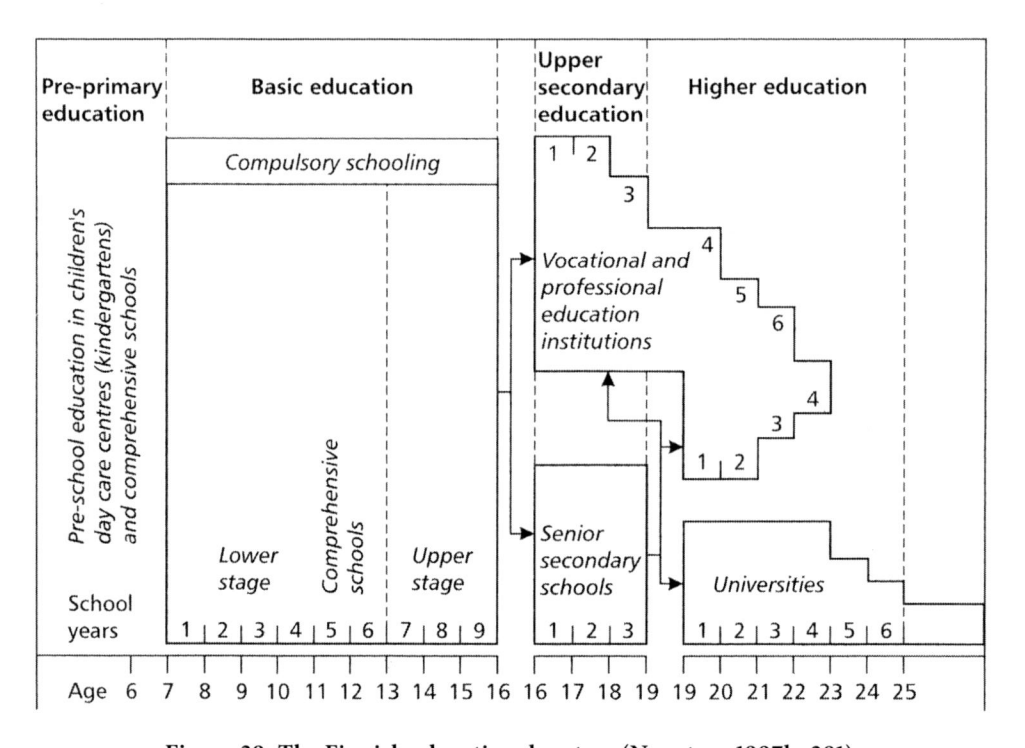

**Figure 29: The Finnish educational system (Nuorteva 1997b: 281).**

In Finland, the profession of the school teacher is commonly respected. There are several reasons for the high standards of teaching skills. In order to have access to programs and courses on the university (tertiary) level the candidate is expected to have good grades and to cope with competition. Salaries for teachers in Finland are well above the OECD average. For many, becoming a teacher is a matter of vocation.

The foundations for the successful school system were laid in the late 1960s and early 1970s, with the Basic School Law of 1968 which was subsequently implemented between 1972 and 1977. Since the 1980s, the education system has been decentralized. The advantage for such a system is that

> the new framework curriculum of 1985 allowed for increased freedom at the municipal and school level while still maintaining high cohesion via the common core curriculum and guidelines for classroom hour distribution. The curricular emphasis on basic skills and knowledge, accentuated in mathematics and science with examples from and a foreseen applicability in real life, can be seen to have further ground the future success of Finnish students in PISA with the very similar goals of its framework [Kupiainen et al. 2009: 12].

The Ministry of Education announced that, starting in 2016, school programs will pay special attention to promoting gifted students. Skeptics say that this shift of focus might favor the emergence of an elitist orientation in education curricula, replacing the older principle of equity. The Ministry's declared intention is to avoid conflict with the principle of equal opportunity but to support talents, as mental capital, at an early stage. In the modern world where demands for global competitiveness in the economic and cultural domains are rising it seems conclusive to offer an educational springboard for the selection and promotion of a creative potential among students.

For several years a shift has been underway in the organizational principles of universities. For long, universities were regarded as institutions that functioned independently and were not involved in the web of competition of the market economy. The traditional kind of competition among universities related to ranking them by the number of students graduating and by the volume of research results published in scientific journals. Competition also focused on aspects of specialization or diversification of subjects and on the structuring of teaching programs. The common ideal of training at the university level in Scandinavian countries was, not long ago, to offer equal quality in every domain to every student.

Since the beginning of the 21st century the management of universities puts more emphasis on entrepreneurial principles. Introducing the element of competition—to the financial and management side but also to the quality of curricula and to the standards of expertise among the staff—has been seen as an asset to enhance flexibility and to activate a sense of realism in touch with the currents of competitiveness in the national economy and in the wider international one. A new type of university has become the subject of a lively debate on the advantages of competitiveness in higher education, as represented by the entrepreneurial university.

> Entrepreneurial universities compete vigorously in the national and international academic markets for excellent staff, for students and for major grants, and they are ruthless at analysing their failures; they will not be satisfied with a modest performance which can be dressed up to look as if it meets the targets set by the State because they will want to succeed in every forum in which they compete [Shattock 2003: 156].

Critics have pointed out that the application of the principle of economic competitiveness to the world of university education might heighten the level of friction and might cause external rivalries that ultimately divert attention from the contents of curricula to the evaluation of their "market value." Long-term experiences with entrepreneurialism in Scandinavian universities are not yet available (Lambert 2009).

The international competitiveness of the Finnish educational system has left its mark, in manifold ways, among former foreign students who have been trained at universities in Finland. One outstanding example may be mentioned here. In 1992, a student from Ethiopia, Hailemariam Desalegn, finished his studies as an engineer (in the domain of water energy) at the Technical University of Tampere. After that he returned to Ethiopia. In 2012, Ethiopia's prime minister, Meles Zenawi, died, and Hailemariam was elected as his successor. Today, Ethiopia has the most booming economy in all of Africa, and this certainly has to do with the prime minister's organizational skills and professional know-how for which the foundations were laid within the frame of the Finnish educational system (Sillanpää and Gröndahl 2015).

## Finnish as a Written Language: From Religious Books to Cybercommunication

Finnish is one of the three non–Indo-European languages of Europe (the others being Estonian and Hungarian) to have achieved the status of a developed language with the functional capability of being used for all spheres of national life, including scientific discourse and university instruction. Finnish has experienced a prolonged process of modernization, starting with the shift in the standards for the written language in the 19th century.

As a written language, Finnish has been regularly used since the 16th century. There are some instances of a rare use of Finnish before that time but the occurrence of texts written in Finnish was random and language use not standardized. The oldest known text in the eastern variety of Finnish, written in the Cyrillic alphabet, is a letter, with words scratched on birch bark. This document, listed as no. 292, was found during the archaeological excavations of the medieval quarters of the town of Novgorod in northwestern Russia, and it dates to the 13th century (Yanin and Zalizniak 1993). During the Middles Ages, people of different ethnic and linguistic affiliation—Russians, Balts and Finns—lived in Novgorod, a major trade center.

Another short text in Finnish is found in a medieval travel book (dated to ca. 1450), apparently written by a German-speaking traveller to Scandinavia who picked up a short phrase in Finnish: *Mynna tachton gernast spuho somen gelen emyna dayda* ... which would look like *Minä tahdon kernaasti puhua suomen kielen, en minä taida* ... "I would like to speak Finnish but I rather don't...." According to the traveller's text—registered in the town library (Stadtbibliothek) in Nürnberg (Germany)—the words in Finnish were spoken to him by the bishop from Turku whom he met (Wulff 1982). Until 1449 this was Maunu Tavast, and from 1450, Olavi Maununpoika.

For long, literature was neither produced in the Finnish language nor in Finland. Books in Swedish were brought to Finland from Sweden. The first book printed specifically for Finland is the so-called *Missale Aboense* (with a text in Latin) which received its name from the town for which it was commissioned, which is Åbo (Turku). The bishop Konrad Bitz had the *Missale* printed in Lübeck in 1488.

The Protestant movement of the 16th century inspired the cultivation of the vernacular language, and the beginnings of Finnish literacy are closely associated with the work of the first Protestant bishop of Finland, Mikael Agricola (c. 1510–1557). Agricola, a disciple of Martin Luther in Wittenberg, is called the father of the Finnish written language. For centuries, Finnish literary production remained in the shadow of Swedish, the prestigious language of the élite.

In the early 19th century, educated people in Finland absorbed the ideas of the Enlightenment and they became fond of their folk culture and ancient heritage. Elias Lönnrot (1802–1884) who worked as a medical doctor in rural communities of Karelia, collected and compiled folk poetry and composed what was to become a national epic, the *Kalevala*. The original version of the epic, the *Old Kalevala*, was published in 1835–36 and a revised and enlarged version, the *New Kalevala*, appeared in 1849.

Lönnrot started his search for the roots of Finnish culture by examining 18th century enterprises to explore Finnish mythology and folk poetry, such as Henrik Gabriel Porthan's *De Poësi Fennica* of 1776–78 and Christfrid Ganander's *Mythologia Fennica* of 1789. He shared the "Romantic view that the runes described an aspect of antiquity and that there existed in them a people's voice" (Pentikäinen 1989: 18). The *Kalevala* became a national icon and furthered national self-awareness among the Finns, as did the paintings in the spirit of the *Kalevala* created by Axel Gallen-Kallela (1865–1931) and the music composed by Jean Sibelius (1865–1957), of which the best know is his *Finlandia* of 1899 (see Chapter 10).

As a written language, Finnish has been in constant use since the 1540s when the first standard language was devised by Mikael Agricola. This old written language was based on the south-western dialect of the region of Turku (Swedish Åbo). The older written language was replaced by a newly elaborated variety. Modern written Finnish is the product of language cultivation in the 19th century. In a long-lasting struggle between 1830 and 1880, when "westerners" and "easterners" among the language cultivators fought for the elaboration of a new written variety (this process is called in Finnish *murteiden taistelu* "struggle of dialects"), the basis of the written language shifted from the former purely south-western dialectal basis—as in Agricola's version of the written language—to incorporate elements from eastern dialects and some artificial creations (Lehikoinen and Kiuru 1991). In its character as an artificial entity, the modern Finnish written language may be compared to modern High German.

Standard literary or written Finnish (*kirjakieli*) has been constantly modernizing. It is used for all domains of literary production, from poetry and literary prose to texts in the mass media (including the internet), in the world of science and in state affairs. Finnish *kirjakieli* is not only used as a written language, but also in formal speech. The vocabulary of the modern written language has adopted many foreign elements, especially from English. Unlike languages in western Europe with their massive layer of English borrowings, the modernization of Finnish through loan-words is comparatively moderate.

Since the 19th century, language cultivators have favored the use of neologisms coined on indigenous elements of the vocabulary. This trend still exerts an influence today. There are numerous expressions of the modern world where Finnish indigenous terminology differs from the internationalisms in other languages; i.e., *tietokone* "computer" (literally "data machine"), *muovi* "plastic" (literally "shaped"), *puhelin* "telephone" (literally "apparatus for chatting").

Functioning as a bridge between formal language and local dialects is colloquial (or conversational) Finnish (*puhekieli*). The selection of structural features in colloquial Finnish depends on the degree of formality of the interaction, on the social and educational background of the speaker, on the nature of the topic which is discussed, and on other factors. Given the diversity of influencing factors, colloquial Finnish may be close to written Finnish or it may encompass dialectal features. There is another widespread variety of Finnish, and this is standard Finnish (*yleiskieli*). This is used in informal speech situations, both in a written form (e.g., letter-writing) and as a spoken variety. Its features draw less on local dialects than colloquial Finnish.

Spoken Finnish may be functionally subdivided further. Among the socially most specialized varieties is slang, which has proliferated in association with various social groups. There is the slang of school children, of criminals and others. The variety of slang which has gained much attention in recent years among scholars is the slang spoken in the capital of Finland, Helsinki.

The origins of this urban slang (*stadin slangi*) go back to the times of an influx of migrant workers from Uusimaa and Häme in the capital, due to the socioeconomic challenges of a rapid industrialization. By the end of the 19th century, the common slang spoken by Finnish and Swedish workers in the capital had assumed features that distinguish it from colloquial Finnish. In the course of time, *stadin slangi* has been continuously transforming to remain a major vehicle of informal speech among the inhabitants of the capital (Heikki and Marjatta Paunonen 2000).

As for the production of belles lettres, the bulk of literature in Finnish is written in a language that is continually modernizing. As in other domains of literacy, also in the realm of belles lettres, lexical and stylistic preferences are apparent in the texts produced by individual writers. This is true for the internationally renowned works written by Aleksis Kivi, Mika Waltari, Väinö Linna or Frans Emil Sillanpää, recipient of the Nobel Prize for Literature in 1939, or by the numerous writers and poets who are less known abroad but have a well-established place in the canon of Finland's literature (Schoolfield 1998).

During the 19th and early 20th century, language cultivators believed that keeping the language as explicit as possible would ensure the "lexical democracy" by which a small child of average intelligence had no difficulty understanding even abstract terms such as *ajankohtainen* "current" (lit. "time + point + ish"), *johdonmukainen* "consistent" (lit. "lead + along + -is"), or *lukemisto* "anthology" (lit. "read + collection"). This resulted in normative attitudes which rejected the use of sounds, words, and constructions regarded as displaying foreign influence. Thus, for example, the older Swedish borrowing *telefooni* "telephone" was marginalized and eventually replaced by the neologism *puhelin* (lit. *puhel(e)-* "to chat" + *-in* denoting an instrument).

In the long run, the nationalistic ideal of lexical democracy had to cope with a serious challenge from the internationalistic ideal of lexical uniformity, with unforeseen possible consequences. Since Finnish has been widely used for scientific discourse both in the past and in the present, there are ready-made chunks available for referring to recurrent concepts, e.g., *satunnais-* "random," *kaksois-* "dual," thus *satunnaispistestereogrammi* "random point stereogram," *kaksoisklikata* "to double-click." Such "bastard words" are no longer regarded as linguistic hybrids to be avoided if at all possible.

Thus, a page of scientific Finnish, filled with words of English-inspired international origin, will contain words that differ radically from other genres of Finnish in phonological structure and inventory while, nevertheless, incorporating many traditional Finnish word-building strategies and ready-made elements.

The vast influx of scientific terminology from international sources coming mainly via a primary stimulus from English but going through a filter that can be understood as the accrued tradition by which Greek and Latin have been pronounced in Finland, provides scientific Finnish with literally thousands of words that violate the traditional phonological constraints of the language (e.g., the preservation of consonant clusters in word-initial position). English has also influenced Finnish syntax and phraseology (Haarmann and Holman 2001: 248ff.).

If "Finglish" is a blanket term characterizing the overall Finnish-English contact and not a specific variety, then this label may be also applied for identifying language use in such fields as computer technology and internet communication in particular. The overall impact of English on written and colloquial Finnish may well be compared, in its intensity, with the processes of fusion in American Finnish (see Chapter 2). Finglish in the European context is as much a product of fusion as in America; for example:

*Kun halutaan seivata* (< save) *tekstejä* (< older loan textum), *kone usein rikleimaa* (< reclaim) *speisiä* (< space) *dokumenteissa* (< older loan documentum) "when one wants to save texts, the machine [the computer] often reclaims space in documents."

English has affected the Finnish lexicon in three ways:

1. It has introduced thousands of new words, and, along with them, the elements of the international Graeco-Latin lexicon needed to construct or adapt a virtually limitless number of international coinages. A text in scientific Finnish will contain words easily recognized by the international community of scholars such as *analyysi* "analysis," *energia* "energy," *ioni* "ion," *materiaali* "material," *mekanismi* "mechanism," *metalli* "metal," and *orgaaninen* "organic."

2. It has provided the already existing and largely native-based lexicon with synonyms, thus allowing for the development of further stylistic differentiation and associative links. The native neologism *muovi* "plastic," from the verb *muovata* "to form," is the generic and normal term for the substance. Nevertheless, the term *plastiikka* is used in the term *plastiikkakururgi* "plastic surgery." The native neologism *tietokone* "computer" (lit. "data; knowledge" + "machine") is the generic and normal term for that concept.

   Modernisms from foreign sources have been integrated into the Finnish lexicon selectively, and the long-range effect of language cultivation is seen in the mixture of borrowings and indigenous creations, some of them synonyms for the borrowings, even in the technical fields; e.g., *disketti* "diskette" versus *levyke* "diskette," *elektroniikka* "electronics" alongside *kännykkä* "mobile phone," *serveri* "server" versus *palvelin* "server."

   Finnish has an extraordinary range of strategies for augmenting its vocabulary by derivational suffixes. Nevertheless scientific Finnish often produces derivatives by ignoring the resources offered by Finnish and loan-translating the structure of the Swedish or English term: *painovalmis* "print-ready," cf. *valmis painettavaksi* "ready to be printed"; *happiköyhä* "oxygen-poor," cf. *vähähappinen* "little-oxygenous"; *käyttäjäystävällinen* "user-friendly," cf. *helppokäyttöinen* "easy-usable." The synonyms given after the words in question represent the same concept using more traditional Finnish word-building strategies.

3. English has provided a motivation for Finnish scientists to invent or redefine already existing Finnish words so that they would more closely parallel their English counterparts with respect to the range of meaning, even if they remain totally different in form. The word *suihku* "shower" has acquired new meanings influenced by English, e.g., *suihkukone* "jet aircraft," *mustesuihku* "ink-jet." As is the case in many other languages, the everyday words *hiiri*

"mouse" and *ikkuna* "window" have acquired special meanings in computer terminology.

Thus, the impact of English on the Finnish lexicon is functionally similar to that of earlier periods of mass borrowing. According to Hakulinen (1979: 364), the influx of Germanic loanwords into Finnish more than two thousand years ago "increased the expressive ability of our language even when they just introduced a synonym to parallel an already existing indigenous term; they have specifically offered opportunities for semantic differentiation and welcome word bases to serve as the basis for new derivatives."

## Which Are the Media of Finnish Know-How? Foreign Languages as Mental Capital

The Finns have cultivated their native language and this has become a flexible medium apt for any function of communication in modern society. Nevertheless, the language is little known outside of Finland, and Finns have always understood the importance of mastering other languages for communication with the world beyond their borders, in addition to which many texts and speeches for occasions, such as toasts, orations, and nowadays, popular songs, advertisements, and restaurant names, have a long tradition of being given in foreign languages in Finland.

The accumulation of know-how in modern Finland, the resources for decision-making in economics and politics and the flow of information through the channels of cultural exchange would not have achieved the standards of today if the Finns had exclusively relied on their national language for knowledge construction. Early on, the Finns have developed a command of foreign languages, to gain access to the currents of international know-how.

Under Swedish rule from the early 12th to the early 19th centuries, and under Russian rule until 1917, Finland was dependent on foreign languages of learning. Within this framework Swedish established for itself a secure if sometimes modest role as a medium for the country's cultured discourse, something that Russian never achieved in Finland. The Finnish tradition of learning did not, as had been the case in France and Germany, produce a distinct set of literati who represented the educated elite of their time and who displayed their skills in belles-lettres and non-literary texts which they served as monuments in the development of the native language. Learning in Finland depended, for most of its history, on individual personalities who accommodated themselves to the internationally recognized educational standards of their times and demonstrated their status as scholars of world rank by publishing their most important works in whichever foreign language happened to be the current lingua franca of the world of learning.

As a rule, those Finns who were able to make a name for themselves in the world of learning before the 19th century were members of the Swedish-speaking population which had settled and evolved in western and southern Finland since the Middle Ages. Before the Academia Aboensis (later Åbo Akademi—Academy of Turku) was founded in 1640, higher education was only available in Sweden (Uppsala) or in western Europe. Modern research reveals that the great majority of those Finland Swedes who went abroad for studying were not aristocrats, but rather members of the urban bourgeoisie or even ordinary people (Nuorteva 1997a: 473ff.).

## Latin and French

In the early years when Finland-Swedes and Finns went abroad in search of knowledge and learning they went to Paris. The first students from Finland were enrolled at the University of Paris in 1313. Later, Finland-Swedes went to Italy while Finns kept frequenting Paris, until a change occurred and attention shifted to German universities.

> The spread of the university system to Germany improved the chances of Finns to study abroad. German universities were located closer and graduation took less time than in Paris. This lowered the expense of study quite considerably. The first German university, founded in Prague, was the most important destination for Finns in the last decades of the fourteenth century. The University of Leipzig inherited its position at the beginning of the fifteenth century, after German masters and students had left Prague, which was torn by national conflict and theological disputes about Jan Hus [Nuorteva 1997a: 524].

During the Middle Ages Paris, Bologna, Marburg, Vienna, Prague and Krakova were among the preferred cultural centers for Finland Swedes to acquire learning. With the rise of Protestantism (adopted as state religion in Sweden in 1523), Wittenberg in Germany became attractive as a center of learning. The most famous representative of Finnish learning in the older tradition, Mikael Agricola (ca. 1510–1557), received his higher education in Wittenberg. Agricola is among the few exceptions in the world of Finnish learning since he was not of Swedish descent, but an ethnic Finn, the son of a farmer in Pernaja. In Wittenberg, Agricola's main tutor was Philipp Melanchthon who wrote a letter of recommendation to the king of Sweden, Gustav Wasa (Nuorteva 1997a: 163).

From the Middle Ages, when Finnish scholars are known to have studied at the universities in Paris, Bologna, Prague, and elsewhere on the continent, until the late 19th century, the preferred language of learned (and scientific) discourse was Latin. Although centuries of Swedish rule had left Finland with a significant and influential Swedish-speaking minority, and Russian rule saw the establishment of a small Russian one, neither Swedish nor Russian, despite serving in various official functions and thus enjoying the status of superimposed languages, ever attained a dominant role in Finland.

## Latin and German

For centuries, the world of learning in northern Europe was dominated by Latin (Hovdhaugen et al. 2000: 32ff.). This was also true after Protestant ideals of favoring the mother tongue as a vehicle of religious education had gained ground. Agricola may have even learned German to a certain degree during his stay in Wittenberg, but Latin was the exclusive means of his academic discourse and writings. The mother tongue—Finnish for Agricola—was meant for practical use. It served as the means for translating biblical texts and for authoring elementary schoolbooks (e.g., Agricola's *Abckiria* of 1543).

The late 19th century began to see the dominant role of Latin yield to German and, to a lesser degree, French, in scientific discourse, in Europe as well as in Finland, although efforts to cultivate a standard which could be the language of an independent nation also saw Finnish begin to be used for specific fields. Finnish independence saw the country fall under the cultural influence of the German-speaking world, thus allowing German to establish itself as the preferred medium for scientific discourse during the 1930s, a position it retained throughout World War II, during which Finland was in a limited alliance with Germany, as well as during the immediate postwar period, when German-educated scholars held key academic posts, despite the fact that Finland, like Germany, came out on the losing side of the war and was under various kinds of political and cultural pressure to loosen its ties with Germany and central Europe.

## Latin and Swedish

Even after the founding of the Academia Aboensis, Latin continued to be used in Finland as a means of academic discourse, as in all parts of the Swedish kingdom. Things changed when, in 1677, O. Rudbeck introduced Swedish at the University of Uppsala. In the 18th century, Swedish competed with Latin, which still retained its dominant status as a language of learning in the context of Finland's society. Throughout the period 1640 to 1827, during which the old university at Åbo (Turku) functioned, Latin was the favored language of natural science and the humanities in Finland.

There are no statistics available as to the distribution of languages of the ca. 20,000 documents printed in Finland between 1488 and 1827. And yet, there is a corpus of thoroughly archived and investigated literature (so-called "Old Fennica") in the State Library of Lower Saxony in Göttingen (Germany) which may serve as a cross-section of older literature produced in Finland (Heininen 1988: 121f.). The 328 titles show the following distribution according to languages: Latin (211), Swedish (84), Finnish (15), German (11), French (3), English (1), Russian (1).

It is noteworthy that, before 1827—the year when the old town of Turku burnt down and the university was devastated by the fire—Finnish ranked third (before German) as a language of academic writing. It is also noteworthy that Swedish experienced its breakthrough as the dominant language of science—at the cost of the rapidly receding Latin—only after the annexation of Finland by tsarist Russia in 1809. By the middle of the 19th century, the three major languages of academic writing in Finland were, in rank order, Swedish, German, Finnish.

## Finnish and German

By the latter half of the 18th century, German had gradually gained in importance in the academic world. Finnish students had been enrolled at the university of Göttingen since 1747, and there had been continuous contacts between German and Finnish scholars. Academic literature produced in Finland was almost regularly reviewed in contemporary German journals (see Kunze 1988 for these activities).

When Finland was separated from the Kingdom of Sweden and granted autonomous status as a Grand Duchy within Imperial Russia, this radical political change had no significant influence on the world of learning. Swedish retained its favored status, and also German continued in its academic function. Academic people in Finland became attracted to a new cultural center where German flourished, and this was St. Petersburg. The Russian Academy of Science had been dominated by German scholars since the times of Catherine the Great (ruled: 1762–1796), and German dominated the scholarly writings of the Academy well into the first half of the 19th century.

Throughout the 19th century, German played a more important role than English, in the Annals of the Academy of Science in St. Petersburg as well as in the production of scholarly texts in Finland. Finnish was the actual winner in the race for dominance in the world of learning. Around 1900 Finnish was competing with Swedish, which was successfully able to retain its recently acquired position as the major language of science in Finland, with German ranking third. After Finland gained independence in 1917, a significant change in the traditional trend of language use in the fields of science occurred: Finnish advanced to first rank, leaving Swedish behind.

In the 1920s and 1930s, German emerged as an international language of science in Finland. Finnish and Finland Swedish scholars wrote entire texts in German, and summaries in German were added to many dissertations. One could have expected that the image of German, as a language of learning in Finland, would have been overshadowed by the consequences of the fateful alliance of Finland and Nazi Germany against the Soviet Union during World War II and that a break with tradition would have occurred in the political atmosphere of the late 1940s, when Finland's politics started out on its cautious course of neutrality, the so-called Paasikivi line (see Chapter 8), and there were no close ties with either German state.

And yet, German continued for some time in its role of first foreign language in school education, and it was used in scholarly writing. The shift to English evolved gradually, detached from politics which was no longer oriented toward central Europe. In the humanities, where German had long been a preferred means of scholarly discourse, it retained this status also in the first decades of the postwar era.

In the field of Uralic studies (i.e., the study of Finno-Ugric and Samoyedic languages and cultures), for example, German was dominant in the pre-war decades, and it ranked second after Finnish well into the 1970s. This is the general picture when placing the material of the *Bibliographia studiorum uralicorum* (Länsimäki 1991) in a chronological order.

## Finnish and English

In the postwar period, English established itself firmly as the dominant academic language in Finland. So far, no comprehensive explanation has arisen for the decline of German as the preferred language of learning. The growing influence of the Anglo-Saxon world—of the United States, in particular—on postwar politics and economy as well as on technological progress may have caused English, as the vehicle of such development, to be favored by scientists and educators (Ammon 2015: 519ff.). Among a wider public, the influence of the American way of life, with Coca-Cola, fast food and American trends in music, may have provided an incentive for English to become popular. In a way, English nourished a cosmopolitan feel in western European societies, and Finland participated in favoring English as the medium of modernity.

The shift toward English, coupled with school reforms of the early 1970s which made English an all but compulsory primary and secondary school subject, have resulted in a Finland in which English is not only widely spoken but also a national resource used both for special effect, as in advertising, as well as for the primary production of texts belonging to an increasing number and variety of genres. As recent as this trend is, it continues the tradition of Finland preferring foreign languages for scientific and other highly valued texts.

There is a practical reason for this trend of favoring English. Those scholars who had participated since the 1980s in scientific discourse no longer learned German as their first foreign language. Instead, it was English and if they learned German at all (as an additional foreign language) their proficiency is likely to have remained at a lower level, compared to their English skills. The members of the younger generation who prefer to write in English may be able to read some German, but language skills do not suffice for using this language actively.

English owes its continually growing influence in Finland to the general importance of the Anglophone countries in the world economy and in the world of learning. Since the 1970s English has ranked third after Finnish and Swedish in scholarly writings. This is true for the humanities. In many other domains English has challenged Swedish, and in some even Finnish. In many domains of the natural sciences, Finnish has been practically excluded from scientific writing.

Among the examples illustrating the latter trend are chemistry, biotechnology and engineering. In the domain of biochemistry, English dominates almost exclusively as the language of doctoral dissertations. Finnish or Swedish are never used. English also dominates in the domain of engineering where doctoral dissertations have been published in that language for decades.

## English as the Icon of Modernity and of Intercommunication

As has been the case elsewhere in western Europe, Finland has experienced a trend toward the increasing influence of English in various domains of public and private life. In addition to the educational impact of English as the first foreign language taught in school and the Anglo-American influence in the world of business and entertainment which has continuously strengthened its grip on Finnish culture since the 1950s, English also enjoys the role of promoter of globalization and the network society, leaving its imprint in lifestyles and verbal behavior.

English also has numerous symbolic functions. Since the 1980s, it has ranked high in the strategies of giving fashionable names to Finnish companies and products. This trend of conveying a feeling of modernity with English names is widespread in the business world of many countries (Haarmann 1989: 249ff.).

In commercial advertising of Finnish companies, English is used for keywords or slogans together with the two official languages of the country. Among the younger generation, there has been a strong tendency toward accepting English as an icon of modernity. This is even apparent in spoken language usage which is spiced with elements of English such as *jees* "yes," *pliis* "please," *okei* "okay," etc.

### Domains of a Practical Use of English in Finland

In recent years, Finnish society has experienced changes which favor the passive "consumption" and the active use of English even more today than a decade ago. These developments are quite consistent with what we know about earlier periods of profound change instigated by intercultural contact. Significant this time are that Finland is an active rather than a passive participant and that this more dynamic role would not have been possible without the knowledge of English the Finnish nation has recently acquired.

(a) Trade relations with the West.—Finland's economy has been strongly export-orientated since the postwar era. Strengthening the role of English as a vehicle of commerce are the long-term relations of Finland with countries in western Europe and the Anglophone world. In the other direction, Finnish-Russian trade had developed at a continuously widening scale. However, in light of the post–Crimea political crisis and the economic sanctions against Russia a marked setback has occurred, minimizing the scale of trade with Finland's eastern neighbor.

(b) Membership in the European Union.—Finland has been a member state of the European Union since the beginning of 1995. Although the staff of Finnish officials who work in the EU bodies (Brussels, Luxembourg) and in the European parliament in Strasbourg are multilingual, the main contact language has been English.

(c) Economic boom.—The Finnish economy saw a sharp upturn in its electronic industry in the 1990s, with the Finnish firm Nokia as the top performer. At the beginning of the 21st century, Nokia had grown to become the biggest electronic company in Europe. Nokia's internal communication is English-based (see Chapter 7). In Nokia's global network, English is the main vehicle of business negotiations and contracts. Since electronic development, in a global comparison, is concentrated within the countries of the OECD, establishing and maintaining contacts with English-speaking countries having high electronic standards are an essential asset of Finland's globalization. English is also the main language for conducting business with the countries of East Asia with their booming electronic industry: China, Korea and Japan.

(d) Growing shares on the financial markets.—When international financial markets expand, Finland also participates. The stock exchange in Helsinki and Finnish bankers are involved in the global flow of financial resources, as are foreign investors with an interest in the Finnish economy. English is by far the most important means of communication in this domain.

(e) Increasing the density of global intercommunication.—In the 1990s, the means of global intercommunication have spread rapidly among the Finns, business people, scholars, private users. In terms of broadband, Finland is at the top, with 60 percent of the inhabitants in recent years using a fixed broadband. Both fixed and mobile broadband is used by about 40 percent of Finnish households (http://www.telecompaper.com/news/finland-leads-the-world-in-mobile-phone-density-in-2013--1061998). Communication via the Internet is a factor that further promotes contacts between Finland and the world. As a consequence, English is becoming more essential.

In a worldwide comparison of the density of information flow through the media (the press, radio, television, telephone, mobile phone, computer network) the traditional ranking of so-called "leading" countries has dramatically changed (Vartanova 1999: 21f.). The United States is the only country which has retained its first rank. Formerly leading countries such as Germany and Japan, which were still high-ranking in the 1980s, have lost their privileged status. Since the late 1990s, Finland's ranking has improved, alongside other Scandinavian countries.

The role played by English in the transitional process toward an international, network-based society, particularly regarding the accumulation of know-how in Finnish companies and the resulting international marketing strategies, has been duly noted at an early stage (Huhta 1997).

(f) Finland's public relations in the field of music.—Finns are known in the world for their high standards in music proficiency, especially in the field of opera singing, orchestra conducting and piano as well as violin playing (see Chapter 7). Many Finns have become famous for their professional skills and for their successful performances outside Finland. In Finland itself, international competitions such as the Sibelius competition for younger musicians and international festivals such as the Savonlinna Opera Festival have gained ever more attention abroad resulting in an ever increasing number of foreign visitors. The language for communication among Finns and foreigners in this field has been English.

(g) Finland's public relations in the field of sports.—Finns are known in the world for their strong representation in international championships and competitions in various fields of sports—car racing, ice hockey, skiing and light athletics in particular. Sporting events draw thousands of Finnish fans abroad, and the need for mobilizing English as a language of everyday contact with foreigners has been growing.

(h) Expanding tourism.—Tourism is developing in two major directions. On the one hand, the number of foreigners visiting Finland has been steadily increasing, partly resulting from the growing attraction of Finland as an EU country. On the other hand, Finns spend ever more money on pastime activities, traveling for one. There has been a steady growth in long distance traveling (to Far Eastern countries, to Southeast Asia, to the Americas). In the context of this mutually growing tourism, English is the dominant language, reflecting a general trend which favors English as the major vehicle of communication in tourism (Ammon 2015: 853ff.).

Resulting from the processes highlighted under (b), (c) and (e) are impulses which promote the use of English in the fields of science. International cooperation on the educational level and in the domain of scientific research has been increasing. The intercommunication among Finnish and foreign experts has especially intensified in various domains of electronic technology.

The participation also has a passive aspect in the sense that Finnish society has been under increasing influence from English, as the cultural vehicle *par excellence* of modernity. English has penetrated many functional "niches" of public and private life in Finland, including entertainment, advertising, marketing, and education. Even wider is the range by which English has increased its already well-established role in the domain of information technology and the scientific sector.

## English as a Vehicle of Symbolic Internationalization

English is not only a practical vehicle of modernity but also an icon of symbolic internationalization. The use of English in Finland and by Finns extends beyond the limits of what is practical into the sphere of imagination and nostalgic cosmopolitanism. For many years it has been fashionable to use English for name-giving in various domains of the business world. English elements may be found in the names of companies, of brands and domestic products, and in the specifications of jobs and trained personnel. Strategies of symbolic internationalization are far advanced in the Finnish context. The amount of English-based names for Finnish products has been increasing continuously since the 1990s.

The global range of Finnish goods, above all industrial and electronic, enhances the use of English names for shops, agencies, and companies in Finland. In Finland, English is by far the most prominent source of symbolic internationalization, and English names outnumber those from other foreign sources such as Italian, French or Spanish (Haarmann 1989: 264ff.). The international element FIN(N) can be found in the names of many Finnish enterprises (figure 30). The basic element FIN(N) shares the function of symbolic internationalization with other foreign components (e.g., FINNISH, FINLANDIA, FENNIA). English elements combine with Finnish components to form hybrid names (e.g., Suomen Plastic, Finn-Lasi, FinnSähkö). In the variety of names, a multifaceted network of naming strategies becomes transparent.

# The Role of English for Higher Education and Professional Specialization

Worldwide, English is by far the most widely used language of science, a truism which has become a stereotype. In a study that broadly covers the global functions of English (Crystal 1997), the role of this language as a means of science is not specified or highlighted. This may be explained by the author's understanding that this role is such a self-evident property of English that it requires no mention.

The dominant role of English has been broadly studied and documented (worldwide by Ammon 2001, 2015: 407ff., for Finland by Haarmann and Holman 2001). The lesson to be learned does not lead to a counterattack against the dominant role of English, but rather insightful monitoring of how local cultures react to the global challenge.

## The Passive Consumption of Academic Texts in English by Students

In all sections of university education there has been a growing need for students to read English texts. The situation of university studies in Finland differs significantly from the situation in larger countries such as Germany, France or Spain in that the pressure on students to read foreign languages is not as strong in the larger countries. German

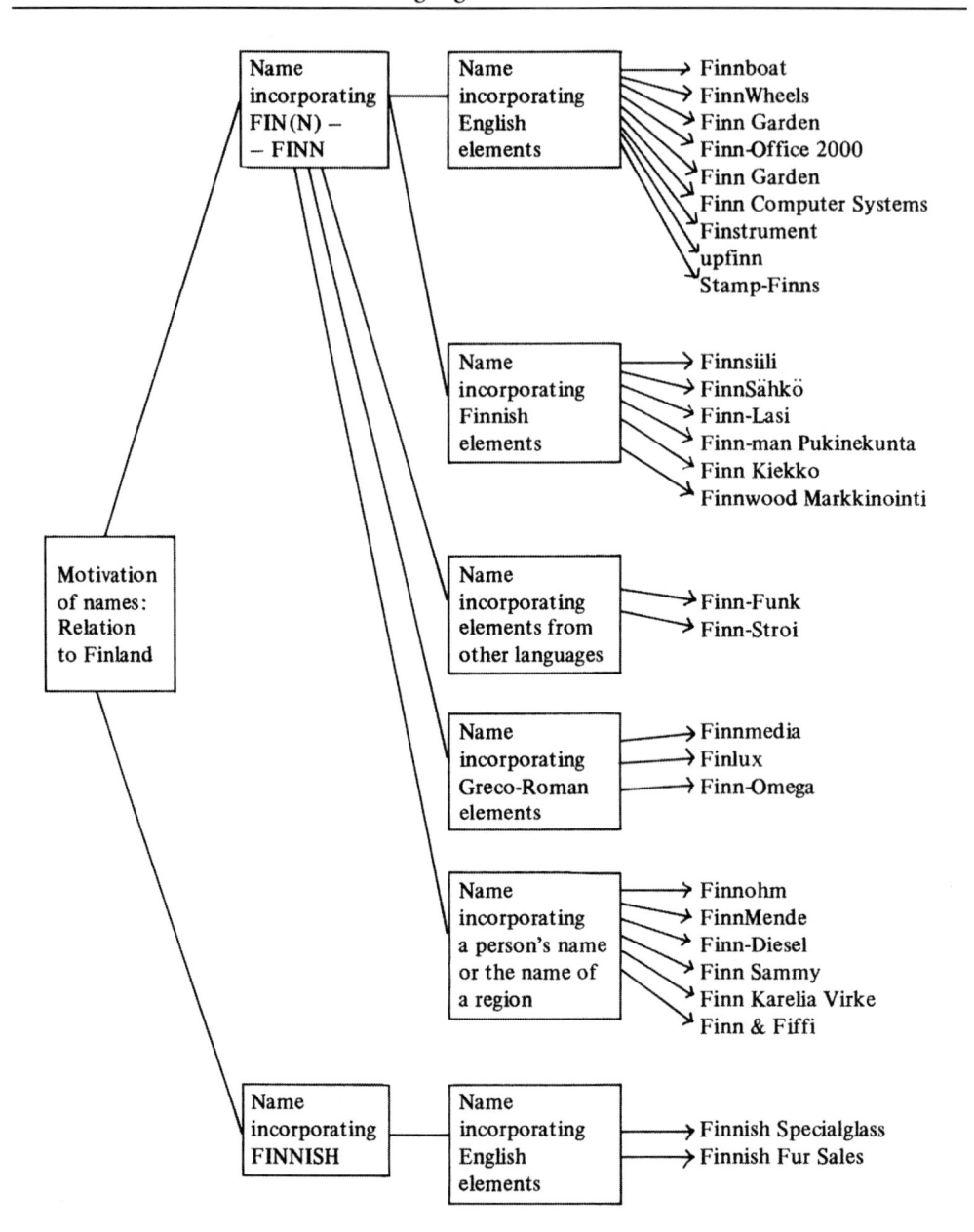

**Figure 30: Name types including the stem FIN(N)—in the Finnish business world (from Harald Haarmann, *Symbolic Values of Foreign Language Use* [Berlin: Mouton de Gruyter, 1989], p. 261, fig. 3).**

or French students would expect to read texts in their mother tongue since many texts essential for studying are available in German or French. In smaller countries such as Finland, translation of scientific texts or textbooks originally written in English into the mother tongue of students is, as a rule, commercially unprofitable, for which reason the same university textbooks are used by Finnish students as are used by their North American and British counterparts.

## The Passive Consumption of Academic
## Texts in English by Scientists

In the context of using literature for teaching or research, the situation of passive consumption of English texts may be the same as with students, however the ends for which the information thus acquired is used differ considerably.

Acquiring information for the purpose of study means accumulating knowledge for two main purposes: passing the exams and becoming trained for professional activities. On the other hand, the reading process for teaching or research purposes produces a higher density of information flow through the medium of English. In addition, the range of literature in English which has to be covered by university teachers and researchers for their purposes is naturally wider than the selected amount of literature required for ordinary study.

The steadily increasing demand for the consumption of English texts by researchers has also produced some negative side-effects. English has become such a strong attractor that, in the scientific writings produced by Finns (judging from the display of bibliographical references), one can notice a phenomenon which has been termed the "Anglo-Saxon bias." This bias is feasible in many sectors of scientific research, in social psychology, genetics, biochemistry, information technology, and others. Research efforts concentrate and become dependent on English literature to such an extent that information in other foreign languages is practically ignored or even voluntarily discarded.

## The Production of Oral English Texts for
## Teaching and Training at the University Level

There has been a growing need for the organization of teaching classes and courses in English at the university level in recent years. In addition to their professional skills teachers have to demonstrate their language proficiency. A high-level proficiency in English is required, a level much higher than the elementary level of everyday usage ("getting along in English"). Raising the level of language skills among teachers and preparing courses in English necessarily results in an even closer connection with the English-speaking world.

## The Production of Written Scientific
## Texts (i.e., Non-Literary Prose) in English

According to the typology of written texts as presented by Kloss (1978: 47), the greatest sociocultural potential of any language is reflected in its scientific literature. English-language scientific texts produced by non-native speakers represent the highest level of their specialized language skills, the highest density of their accumulated knowledge, and the highest grade of readiness for global intercommunication. The choice of English as an active vehicle of science by Finns is an effective means for keeping up with the pace of global scientific development and, in addition, a challenge for actively influencing this development.

Although the university system in Finland is of much more recent origin than in most other countries of Europe, it provides today one of the most comprehensive networks on the continent. For Finland's 5.5 million inhabitants, there are 14 universities and 24 polytechnics. Of the 147,000 students who enrolled in the academic year 1999–2000 more than 3,000 came from abroad to study for a degree. About half of them studied at polytechnics (Vento 1999: 15f.). By 2013, the number of foreign students at institutions in Finland had multiplied markedly, amounting to almost 20,000. According to recent statistics (provided by CIMO, Center for International Mobility), about two-thirds of the foreign students remain in Finland after they have finished their studies (http://www.cimo.fi/services/statistics; retrieved 3 October 2015).

With the exception of students coming from continental Scandinavia who can follow courses in Swedish, foreigners who want to study in Finland usually have no knowledge of either of the indigenous languages of instruction in Finland. Courses in English have been offered for many years at most of the universities and polytechnics.

The range of scientific disciplines in which English courses are organized is fairly wide, covering economics, natural sciences, social sciences and the humanities. The greatest number of offerings, however, is found in fields other than the humanities. Certain fields of study are obviously more attractive for foreign students than others. English courses in economics and business administration as well as in environmental sciences are offered at many institutions at various locations while other fields of study are restricted to one location only (e.g., sports sciences or hypermedia).

In addition to the specialized courses, English is the language of instruction in a number of interdisciplinary courses offered at all universities. The term "course in English" is not yet a clearly defined organizational factor. The prospectus of courses in English at the University of Helsinki says that it "deals not only with courses taught entirely in English, but also with courses that are taught only partly in English or that may be offered in English if demand arises" (Tammivaara-Balaam 1999: 1).

The development of scientific research in the fields of engineering and technology is illustrative of the progress of technical sciences in recent decades and also of the fundamental shift toward English. Of the more than 1,700 doctoral dissertations published since Finland's independence more than half have been produced in recent decades. There is no other field of science where the increase of dissertations is as striking as in technology.

Language choice of dissertations in the technical fields has never been subject-bound. The preferences for indigenous languages of science such as Finnish or Swedish, on the one hand, or for foreign languages such as German, English, etc., on the other hand, have been motivated by trends in scientific orientation. The first dissertation in German was published in 1917, the first in English as late as 1934. French was first used in 1968.

As regards the position of Swedish as compared to all other languages of science, this has always been less used than any of the others. German has been more important than Swedish for writing doctoral dissertations. Until the late 1940s, Finnish and German were equally important as languages of science, and English was still marginal. A shift in the importance of English can be observed in the 1950s and, during the 1960s, the trend becomes marked. From the early 1970s onwards, the immense increase of doctoral dissertations coincides with the growing dominance of English.

There are several specialized fields of technology where the indigenous languages of Finland have been excluded from scientific writing and where English dominates in absolute terms. This is true for analytical chemistry, industrial chemistry, the paper industry, and astronomy. In some other fields, English predominates, with only one or two exceptions of dissertations published in German, Finnish or Swedish. This is the situation in, for example, physics, geology, applied mathematics and construction engineering (Ala-Tuuhonen 1998: 139ff.).

The breakthrough of English in the fields of the natural sciences occurred in the 1970s when the number of dissertations, written in English, tripled compared to the 1960s. The rise continued and, in the 1990s another leap can be observed. The number of dissertations in English almost doubled, compared with the scientific production in the 1980s. The trend toward a steady increase of the corpus of dissertations written in English is continuing while the percentage of Finnish-language dissertations, of the total, has been steadily decreasing (from ca. 15 percent in the 1970s to less than 5 percent in the first decade of the 21st century).

Regarding the publication of scientific literature in the fields of engineering and technology other than doctoral dissertations (Karjalainen et al. 1998), the picture of language choice is more varied. From the end of the 19th century until 1917, Swedish was predominantly used, with Finnish ranking second. The first article to be written in German appeared in 1882, the first book in 1893. French enlarged the range of languages in 1911. In the period between the two world wars there were four major languages used for publications in engineering and technology: Finnish, German, Swedish and English. Since the late 1940s, Finnish and English have been in use. However, the impact of English is not as dramatic as in the case of doctoral dissertations.

The Finnish legal system did not attract much attention among foreign experts before Finland became a member of the European Union. The scholarly discourse about internal legal problems was until 1995 predominantly associated with the Finnish language which is the main working language in all legal institutions of the country. As an example, all laws are written in Finnish first and then are translated into the country's second official language, Swedish.

Regarding the language-subject correlation of juridical publications it can be observed that Finnish is used indiscriminately. As far as inter–Scandinavian aspects of the Finnish legal system are concerned the choice of the language for the scholarly discourse is likely to be Swedish. This shows in the contents of the subjects of juridical dissertations.

The choice of a nonindigenous language for a juridical dissertation has always been subject-bound. If Finns want to contribute to the international academic discussion they choose an internationally acknowledged language of science. The first juridical dissertation in German was published in 1907, the first in French in 1913 and the first in English as late as 1959 (Kangas 1998: 411ff.).

The choice of French for juridical dissertations (and other juridical writings) in Finland reflects a common European tradition. In the 19th century, French was considered the language *par excellence* of international treaties and conventions. This was a function associated with its status as a preferred language in the world of diplomacy. For instance, the original version of the Berne Convention of 1886 on copyright is written in French.

The situation for juridical science has changed dramatically since the mid–1990s.

As a consequence of its official participation in the European integration process, Finland had to accommodate to European standards which, in practice, meant it had to reconcile its corpus of internal laws with EU directives. The construction of the European dimension in the Finnish legal system has made Finland more attractive for foreign experts and, at the same time, has stimulated Finnish lawyers' interest in communicating about Finnish legal matters in light of the EU framework.

Before 1995, the distribution of languages for juridical dissertations in Finland was representative of a rather secluded domain of science. All this has changed, and Finnish juridical science has opened up to international circles. It was soon obvious that, for the writing of doctoral dissertations, and for writings on legal problems in general, English would come to occupy a firm position in foreign language choice. As for the language in which juridical dissertations are written, preference for English has been growing since the beginning of this century, albeit unevenly. During the period between 1999 and 2015, there are only a few dissertations written in foreign languages other than English (two in German, 2004 and 2009, and one in French, 2014) (Language choices for juridical dissertations, Helsinki University: 1999–2015; http://www.helsinki.fi/oikeustiede/tutkimus_ja_julkaisut/vaitoskirja_ja_lisensiaatin_tutkimukset.htm; retrieved 4 July 2015).

# 7

# What Is Known in the
# World About Finnish Culture?
## *Global Manifestations of the Finnish Creative Mind*

Many features of Finnish culture may seem exotic and partly eccentric in the eyes of foreigners although, for the Finns, they form part of everyday life. Certain Finnish institutions are known the world over, like sauna or tango (see Chapter 3), but one might expect that such an exotic culture remains secluded from mainstream developments and unfolds in splendid isolation. The opposite is true. Finnish culture, its peculiar characteristics notwithstanding, has gone global—in various domains at different times—and it has even provided some major impulses for global culture.

The linkage of Finnish national culture with global trends and streams moves in two directions or, in other words, is manifested on two divergent levels. One aspect of how Finnish culture goes global is Finland's access to the international mainstream through its own creative input, thus leaving a typical Finnish imprint on global culture. Another aspect is the organization of international festivals and competitions in Finland. The range of Finland's cultural output worldwide is amazing in its scale and magnitude, which is quite exceptional for a small country. Anyway, such a global input might be expected in light of the accumulation of cultural creativity, professional skills and organizational know-how which Finland offers.

Cultural activities in Finland—and of Finns abroad—cover a wide range. The degree of Finnish global input varies from domain to domain. There are cultural activities in which the Finnish touch is recognized worldwide, for instance architecture or music (see below). There are other domains where international recognition of Finnish creativity is less acute: for example, filmmaking (Lehtonen 2015b). While Finnish filmmaking seems to be predominantly a field of interest for domestic audiences, there are a number of Finnish actresses, actors and filmmakers who have made a career abroad (see below).

Finnish culture has produced an astounding number of representatives who gained worldwide reputation, and this in various domains. The Finns have their own way to live with the images of their celebrities. When foreigners visit Finland they might be puzzled by the lack of T-shirts with pictures of Finnish culture heroes. The explanation is: the Finns do not make the same kind of fuss about famous people that people in other countries do. The comparison of different mentalities on an international scale may produce strange contrasts. For example, in Finland one does not find a T-shirt with the picture of Finland's best known architect, Alvar Aalto. But in the United States, T-shirts featuring him are sold (in the bookstore for architecture in Atlanta, T-shirts are on sale with the pictures of four great architects of the 20th century: Mies van der Rohe, Le Corbusier, Frank Lloyd Wright and, Alvar Aalto; Helsingin Sanomat, 18 July 2015: D 8).

## Architecture

When asked about what comes to mind when talking about modern Finland the answer may well be "architecture" (Nikula 1993, Connah 2005, Pettersson 1989). In its issue of 19 September 2000, the French newspaper Le Monde published an article by its arts critic, Frédéric Edelmann, about Finnish architecture in the 20th century where it says that Finland has produced, in proportion to its population, more great architects of the class of Alvar Aalto than any other country.

Finnish architecture has come a long way from the earliest dwelling, a kind of tent called kota in Finnish and goahti in Saami, which dates to prehistoric times. This elementary structure is a circle of poles, tied together at the top and with an opening to let out the smoke from the fireplace. The sides of the tent are covered with animal hides. When agriculture reached southwestern Finland in the latter half of the third millennium BCE and the hunter-gatherer population gradually became sedentary, a type of rectangular house was introduced and spread to other regions (Talve 1997: 39ff.). The kota was built in Lapland, for accommodation of the reindeer herders in their summer camps, well into the 19th century. Nowadays, kota tents are mostly put up at camping sites, in areas frequented by tourists, to create a nostalgic atmosphere of the lifeways of the ancient Laplanders for foreign visitors.

Architectural forms were not altogether uniform although the basic layout and structure of houses was repeated throughout many generations. Already during the Stone Age one finds some exceptional structures in the north of Finland. In the archaeological area of the town of Oulu, known under the name Kierikki, remainders of a large structure, dating to the fourth millennium BCE, have been found that have been identified as row houses connected by doorways (Pesonen 2002). At Kierikkisaari in the same area, remainders of fenced pits have been unearthed that are thought to have functioned as traps to hunt down elks. It is evident that the Stone Age people of the Scandinavian north had developed advanced schemes for modeling their living-space. Those early settlers engaged in far-distant trade since objects of Baltic amber are among the artifacts retrieved from the settlement.

For the longest time in the history of Finnish architecture the main material for construction has been wood. Since the majority of the Finnish population lived in rural environments until the 20th century, farm houses constructed of logs with corner-timbering dominated the range of building types. Wood has remained a major material, and constructions made entirely of wood or with major parts (interior spaces) elaborated in wood are a specialty of modern Finnish architecture. Among the best known specimens of wooden architecture are wooden churches. The oldest are the church of Vöyri (Ostrobothnia; built 1626 and still in use) and the church of Muhos (on the river Oulunjoki in northern

Finland), dating to 1634. Another old wooden church is found in Lapland, and this is the old church in Sodankylä, dating to 1689. In the Finnish countryside, wooden structures were traditionally painted in red, in the shade of red ochre (called *punamulta* in Finnish). According to modern findings, this color became widespread only in the 16th century.

With the rise of urban architecture in the course of the Middle Ages, another material was favored for constructions, and this material is also amply available in Finland: stone. Well into the modern era, the use of stone in urban areas was restricted to public buildings and wood was widely used for private houses in the towns of Finland. The dense grouping of wooden houses in the town of Turku proved disastrous during a fire that broke out in 1827 and destroyed large parts of the town. Until that date Turku had been the administrative center of the Grand Duchy (i.e., Finland as part of Russia), its capital.

The reaction of tsarist authorities to the devastation of Turku was swift. They decided to choose Helsinki as the new capital. Then, the layout of that city lacked any imperial flair. That changed when Tsar Alexander I appointed Carl Ludvig Engel (1778–1840), of German descent, as the chief architect to design a city center of imperial proportions (Pöykkö 1990). Engel had demonstrated his abilities as an architect with a construction outside Helsinki (a wooden church in Lapua, in 1827) before engaging in the demanding project of the urban design for the new capital.

During the 1830s, until his death in 1840, Engel designed and supervised constructions around the Senate Square in Helsinki, and he accommodated the Palace of the Council of State that had been built earlier (1818–22) with the buildings he designed: the University Building (1832) and the adjacent University Library (1840), and the white Cathedral Church that was completed in 1852. Some say that the Senate Square, with its buildings in the classicist style, is among the most balanced and aesthetic ensembles of wide open urban spaces in the modern history of architecture. The beauty and harmony of the Senate Square came at a price. An older church in the area was destroyed: "the church from 1727, Ulrika's or Ulrika Eleanora's Church, spoiling the grandeur of Senate Square, was torn down and its wood sold at auction just a century after its dedication" (Schoolfield 1996: 16).

The classicist style remained popular and found its manifestation in the major works of architects of the post–Engel era. Landmarks in the urban environment of Helsinki are the Art Museum Ateneum (built in 1887) and the majestic building of the Hotel Kämp (1886) which became the venue for known representatives of Finnish culture. Those buildings were designed by Carl Theodor Höijer (1843–1910).

The specifically Finnish touch was inspired by the movement of national awakening. Here, one architect stands out because of his design inspired by settings of epic poetry in the landscapes of the *Kalevala*, and this is Gottlieb Eliel Saarinen (1873–1950). His specialty was art deco buildings in the 1920s. In his work one can notice a blend of Finnish wooden architecture and European trends such as British Gothic Revival and Jugendstil (Art Nouveau). The latter style is manifested in many buildings in Helsinki (Moorhouse et al. 1987).

Saarinen became known abroad and went to the United States where he designed the Gulf Building in Houston. He held various posts at American universities (from 1924 as a professor at the University of Michigan, and from 1932 as president of the Cranbrook Academy of Art). Eliel Saarinen was awarded the AIA (American Institute of Architects) Gold Medal in 1947. Eliel's son Eero Saarinen (1910–1961) made himself a name among the American architects as a leading figure of the International style. One of Saarinen's students, Edmund N. Bacon, was appointed executive director of the city planning commission in Philadelphia, a post he held from 1949 until 1970.

Saarinen is an early representative of Finnish architecture in the 20th century who gained international recognition (Norri and Wang 2007). Perhaps the best known of the Finnish architects of the 20th century abroad is Alvar Aalto (1898–1976) (Schildt 1984–91). Aalto represents the blend of creativity that springs from the interaction of the two cultural communities in Finland. His father was a Finn, and his mother a Finland-Swede. Aalto was born in Jyväskylä (central Finland). He had made plans to study architecture at Helsinki University but, soon, the course of his life drifted apart. Aalto was drawn into the civil war and he fought as a soldier in the White Army under Mannerheim. He continued his military career until 1923 when he was promoted to reserve second lieutenant.

Still as a student he designed and built a house at Alajärvi, for his parents. In his home city, Aalto started his first business enterprise, an architectural office. Later, the office was moved to Turku (in 1927), and to Helsinki (in 1933). Aalto was multitalented and he worked as an architect, designer, sculptor and painter. In the first two domains he earned world fame, with public buildings in various countries that illustrate his specific modernist style, and with furniture and installations that are both practical and aesthetic (tables, chairs, book shelves, lamps, vases).

The evolution in Aalto's architecture started out from Nordic Classicism, developed into a rational International Style Modernism (by which the architect is also known abroad), to his later Scandinavian Modern Style. Aalto had already designed various buildings in Finland before he was asked to do work abroad. In 1931, he designed the Central University Hospital in Zagreb (Croatia, former Yugoslavia) and several buildings in Estonia and Switzerland. Between 1927 and 1935, the Municipal Library in a "Viipuri" was built ("Vyborg" has formed part of Russia since 1944).

The first building in America that Aalto had designed (together with his wife Aino) was the Finnish Pavilion for the New York World's Fair in 1939. Others were to follow after the war, such as Baker House (Massachusetts Institute of Technology) at Cambridge and the Institute of International Education in New York. Aalto's creations can be found in Denmark (Kunsten Museum of Modern Art at Aalborg), Sweden (the building for Västmanland-Dala nation at Uppsala), France (Maison Louis Carré at Bazoches-sur-Guyonne), Germany (Community Center at Wolfsburg; the Aalto-Hochhaus at Bremen; the Essen Opera House), Iceland (the Nordic House at Reykjavík), Iraq (the post and telegraph office in Baghdad; the Art Museum that Aalto designed was never completed).

The most widely known of the buildings that Aalto designed is the Finlandia Hall in Helsinki that was erected between 1962 and 1971. In the Finlandia Hall, one finds a harmonious combination of materials, both natural (wood) and artificial (concrete). The fabric of the functional parts of the open space of the hall (ceiling, balconies, stage and seating) is Aalto's preferred material for interior structures: wood.

Aalto is also remembered as a designer. Wood has been the preferred material for many of Aalto's creations: various chair, stool and table models, various models of tea trolleys, an umbrella stand, a coat rack, a wall drawer, a bench, a wall shelf. He used metal for various models of ceiling lamps. Aalto's glassware gained an international reputation. In a global perspective, the Savoy vase model (created in 1936), designed for the luxury

Savoy restaurant in Helsinki, was to become the most widely known object of designer glassware in the world (Michl 1991).

Not only architects from Finland gained a reputation in America but also Americans with Finnish ancestry stand out with their work. Among them is Alfred Finnilä (see Chapter 4 for the Finnish Baths he built in San Francisco), who played a decisive role for the construction of the Golden Gate Bridge in San Francisco. Finnilä was engaged with the construction of the bridge from January 1932 until May 1937. Together with the chief architect, Joseph B. Strauss, Finnilä shared responsibility for the raising of the bridge's structures and he oversaw the ironing work during the whole process. Much of the road work, too, was his responsibility. The Bridge Round House at the southeastern end of the bridge was designed by Finnilä and completed in 1938. In 2012, the Bridge Round House was renovated as a specimen of the Art Deco style (https://en.wikipedia.org/wiki/User:Rubert_ABC/Alfred_Finnila; retrieved 7 June 2015).

The preference for natural material in modern Finnish architecture may even be extended to "all-encompassing," as in the case of one of Helsinki's landmarks, the Temppeliaukio (Temple Square) Church or Church of the Rock. This construction, designed by the architects Timo and Tuomo Suomalainen, was virtually carved out of the granite bedrock. The church has a copper dome roof. An Ice Age crevice has been selected as a base for the altar (figure 31).

**Figure 31: The Church of the Rock in Helsinki (photograph: Akseli Niemelä; www.blogfor photos.com).**

Plans for the church were made in the 1930s but they materialized in the 1960s. In September 1969, the Church of the Rock was consecrated. The Finlandia Hall and the Church of the Rock are two of the best known works of Finnish architecture and the most popular attractions for tourists. Among the architectural landmarks of Helsinki is the Kamppi

Chapel or "Chapel of Silence" in the city center. According to Wahlsten and Brookes (2012) "the chapel demonstrates how contemporary architecture at its best can fascinate and inspire." The chapel, which won the Chicago Athenaeum Museum of Architecture and Design award in 2010 is constructed entirely of wood (the exterior of spruce strips, the interior of alder planks).

## Art: Finnish Painting

Before the mid–19th century one could not speak of Finnish "art." There were no institutions such as museums or art schools that would have served as places of inspiration for and professional education of artists. But there were individuals who were looking for opportunities to channel their artistic creativity. They went abroad to study art, preferably to France (Paris) and also to Germany (Düsseldorf). A few returned to Finland, others stayed. The modest beginnings of a domestic (Finnish) tradition of art date to the first half of the 19th century, with the opening of a school for drawing in Turku (1830). In 1846, the Finnish Art Association was founded and opened another drawing school in Helsinki (1848).

In the 1850s, the foundation for Finnish art collections were laid. Tsar Alexander II donated altogether 28 paintings to the Art Association, and this collection was put on public display in 1859. Exhibiting art in Finland was a new cultural experience that attracted the attention of collectors and, through their donations, the collection could be enlarged. In 1864, the Artists' Association of Finland was founded. Yet, it took many decades before Finnish art developed into a mainstream of Finland's culture.

It is difficult to define when the country's art had developed into its mature stage. Art historians speak about the "golden age" of Finnish art when referring to the production of the late 19th century. The spirit of the golden age may be characterized as "the successful synthesis of national aspiration and international movement at the turn of the [20th] century" (Valkonen 1992: 6).

Some of the most influential artists were professionally trained in Paris and got inspired by artistic trends such as realism, naturalism and symbolism. French art left its mark on the works of Akseli Gallen-Kallela (1865–1931), Helene Schjerfbeck (1862–1946), Maria Wiik (1853–1928), Albert Edelfelt (1854–1905), Eero Järnefelt (1863–1937) and Pekka Halonen (1865–1933) (Smith 1985: 45f.). Finnish art developed its own orientation under the growing political tensions produced by the Finnish national movement in resistance to Russification on the side of tsarist authorities. The works of Finnish artists reflect these tensions to various degrees.

> The historical period during which the Golden Age of Finnish art took place was politically sensitive, and this can be seen in some of the pieces from the period in question. Although the extent of the directness of the political commentary varied, the nationalistic sentiment was often present [Ojala 2014].

A national sentiment is most overtly expressed in Edvard Isto's oil painting *Hyökkäys* ("The attack") of 1899, perhaps because it addressed, in a straightforward manner, the contemporary issue of restrictions of Finland's autonomy under tsarist rule (see Chapter 4). The political connotation is more moderate in Albert Edelfelt's watercolor painting *Porilaisten marssi* ("The march of the Pori regiment") of 1900, reviving the memory of the Finnish war of 1808–09, the consequence of which was the annexation of the country by Russia. Aleksi Gallen-Kallela projected his naturalistic style into the thematic pool of the national epic tradition (Kalevala poetry) and created vivid images of the heroic age: *Aino-triptyykki* ("Aino triptych") of 1891, *Sammon taonta* ("Forging of the Sampo") of 1893, *Sammon puolustus* ("Defense of the Sampo") of 1896 and *Lemminkäisen äiti* ("Lemminkäinen's Mother") of 1897.

Abroad, the works of Finnish artists have raised attention in very individual ways. There was no movement of foreign artists that would have favored Finnish art collectively, and international recognition was limited to very few of those who had their own individual styles. For instance, Albert Edelfelt gained recognition by the French public because he had painted a scene in the Luxembourg garden in Paris, under the title *Luxembourgin puistossa* ("In the Park of Luxembourg"). The artist got more attention with the portrait of the famous French scientist Louis Pasteur (1822–1893) which earned him a medal of honor of the National Order of the Legion of Honour.

Helene Schjerfbeck also gained international recognition. In 1889, she was awarded a bronze medal at the Paris World Fair for her painting *Toipilas* ("The Convalescent"). In Finland, too, this particular work has been much praised—it has been hailed as the finest piece in the Ateneum Art Museum in Helsinki (Ateneum 2007: 38). Recently, Helene Schjerfbeck has raised much media attention in connection with a spectacular discovery on the occasion of an exhibition of her works in the Ateneum Art Museum, from June until October 2012, marking the 150th anniversary of the artist's birth. Various private collectors had contributed to the exhibition. When the art works were selected for display the curator, Leena Ahtola-Moorhouse, noticed some exceptional seams with which the canvas was attached to the wooden frame of one of the paintings. This particular painting was examined in the laboratory and the seams were opened. To the surprise of the examining team, another painting—hidden and unknown—was discovered. The theme is a young mother holding her child. In this particular case, the collector who gave one art work for the exhibition, received two back.

In the kaleidoscope of modern Finnish art are found artists with very individual preferences for certain themes. There are three brothers from a Finland-Swedish family, Ferdinand von Wright (1822–1906), Wilhelm Henricsson von Wright (1810–1887) and Magnus Henricsson von Wright (1805–1868) who favored motifs from nature and wildlife. They are all known from their paintings of birds of which the most famous is Ferdinand's *Taistelevat metsot* ("The Fighting Capercaillies") of 1886 (Taiteilijaveljekset von Wright 1986). And there is Hugo Simberg (1873–1917) in whose paintings his special interest in symbolic forms and the supernatural is manifested. His most famous painting is *Haavoittunut enkeli* ("The Wounded Angel") of 1903.

## *Finnish Design and Fashion*

Finnish design forms part of Scandinavian design which emerged in the 1950s, as an expression of the democratic zeitgeist of postwar societies in Scandinavia. Scandinavian design is intended to serve everyone, which means that the products designed are functional and may be used in everyday life (Englund et al. 2007). Finland has become known for its modern design throughout the world, but it is hard to say which designer or which company would be the most prestigious (Finnland 2014: 72f.). The range of modern Finnish design is wide although certain domains are more markedly represented than others.

## Finnish Glassware

Individual designers: Aino Aalto, Kaj Frank, Harri Koskinen, Timo Sarpaneva, Oiva Toikka, Tapio Wirkkala. According to Anu Penttinen, who has a studio in the Nuutajärvi Glass Village and who founded Nounou Design in 2003, "I filter out my visual world from concrete places and human activity, which can end up as abstracts for my glass pieces" (https://www.iittala.com/Designers/Anu-Penttinen/c/Anu%20Penttinen).

Design company: Iittala (since 1881). In the 1920s and 1930s, Iittala products (high-quality crystal) became known abroad. Then, the design was conservative. "Iittala's new designs, based on sculptural art-glass objects, made its first international appearance at the Milan Triennale of 1951" (Aav 1997b: 154f.).

## Finnish Furniture

Individual designers: Alvar Aalto, Simo Heikkilä, Eero Aarnio.

## Finnish Homeware and Ceramics

Individual designers: Kaj Frank, Harri Koskinen, Timo Sarpaneva, Birger Kaipiainen, Heljä Liukko-Sundström.

Design company: Arabia (since 1873) Arabia, a trailblazer in modern Finnish design, was founded as a daughter company to a Swedish enterprise (i.e., Rörstrand) with the specific role of providing Swedish products for the opening Russian market. For decades, the major products were glazed earthenware, and only some porcelain. A change occurred in the early 1930s. "In 1932 Kurt Ekholm (1907–1975), who had been engaged as Arabia's artistic director, developed a range of household goods to respond to the demands of the time and created the factory's famous art division, whose work soon became an important 'shop window' to the world" (Aav 1997a: 18f.).

The designer Inkeri Leivo (d. 2010), who had joined the team of Arabia in 1969, created a series of tableware, called Arctica, which shaped the image of the company decisively. Arctica tableware is all white and its forms are, according to the designer, inspired by nature. Leivo received the Formland-Design Prize in 1988 and is a recipient of the Finland Award for Industrial Design in 1992. Other series inspired by nature or by the Finnish cultural heritage are Lumi ("Snow"; in 2002) and Runo ("Lyrics"; in 2009). In late summer 2015, Arabia announced that the company will transfer its headquarters abroad.

## Finnish Textiles and Fashion

Individual designers: Maija Isola, Mika Piirainen, Aino-Maija Metsola, Maija Louekari, Vuokko Eskolin-Nurmesniemi, Annika Rimala, Jukka Rintala.

Design company: Marimekko (since 1951) (Aav 2003). Marimekko's founder, Armi Ratia, defined her company as "a cultural phenomenon guiding the quality of living" (1962). Marimekko gained global attention and recognition when Jacqueline Kennedy chose seven of Marimekko's dresses for the presidential campaign in 1960, to emphasize her role as a modern, youthful and stylish woman. All seven dresses are exhibited in the Kennedy Museum (Berlin). Since that presidential campaign was a global media event, Jackie and her dresses were in the world's spotlight, and Marimekko has enjoyed prestige abroad ever since (Koivuranta et al. 2015).

For long, Marimekko designs were the only clothing brands from Finland known to the world. Only recently have other fashion designers from Finland earned the attention of customers abroad and international media coverage. In 2012, Siiri Raasakka, Tiia Sirén and Elina Laitinen presented their men's line in Paris, at the Hyères Fashion Festival, and won the first prize. The following year, the prize went to Satu Maaranen (currently working at Marimekko).

The number of Finnish designers working for international fashion firms is increasing: Juha Marttila (at Nina Ricci), Maija Komulainen (at Calvin Klein), and others at Maison Margiela, Balenciaga, Lanvin. In recent years, exhibitions for Finnish fashion design have been organized in New York and in Tokyo. The Pre Helsinki event, with fashion shows and seminars, held each spring, has become a springboard for contacts with the international marketing. "In Finland, we have just started to understand how the fashion world really works. For a long time Finnish fashion was Finlandized and circled around our domestic media, market and demand" (Tuomas Laitinen, lecturer of fashion design at Aalto University, Helsinki, quoted after Pöppönen 2014).

## *Literature*

Finnish literature is multifaceted though not as abundant as other literatures written in European languages. One finds highlights in the tradition of epic poetry and in the movement of national awakening. Some of the historical figures are known abroad, and this is due to translations of their original works, although it is not easy to specify their appreciation and recognition by an international readership. Anyway, there are some objective measures. It is correct to say that Frans Eemil Sillanpää (1888–1964) is an internationally known writer, simply because he was awarded the Nobel Prize for Literature in 1939. It is also true that Mika Waltari (1908–1979) was a writer with an international reputation. In 1945, Waltari published his historical novel *Sinuhe egyptiläinen* (translated into English as "The Egyptian") that has been translated into 40 languages. In 1949, it ranked first in a bestseller list in the United States. Before the appearance of the translation of Umberto Eco's novel *Il nome della rosa* ("The Name of the Rose," 1983) Waltari's Egyptian was the most sold piece of foreign literature in the U.S. for decades.

Aleksis Kivi (1834–1872) wrote the first novel in Finnish, *Seitsemän veljestä* ("Seven brothers"), which was published in 1870. Novel writers such as Aleksis Kivi engaged in the description of the changing conditions of Finnish society in the process of industrialization. So did playwrights, for instance Minna Canth (1844–1897), whose most popular play is *Työmiehen vaimo* ("The Worker's Wife"). Among the post-war writers perhaps

Väinö Linna (1920–1992) is the best known internationally. He participated in the Continuation War (1941–44) and, from his recollection of events and experiences with the unit he led, he started to write after the war had ended. It took three attempts before achieving a breakthrough. The first two novels were not successful but things changed when *Tuntematon sotilas* ("The Unknown Soldier") was published in 1954. It is noteworthy that the reception of the novel in the newspapers was rather critical but the work was received well by the general public. It did not take seven months before some 200,000 copies had been sold. The novel was translated into English and other languages and Penguin Books published a new translation (under the modified title *Unknown Soldiers*) in 2015.

## The National Epic *Kalevala* and Its Legacy

The historical niche in the tradition of literary Finnish is epic prose and poetry which have functioned as an inspiring source for Finnish culture up to the present. Among the masterpieces of literature in Finnish is the *Kalevala*, a collection of epic poetry that was collected and creatively reworked by Elias Lönnrot (1802–1884). Lönnrot was deeply influenced by the epic theory which had emerged during the age of romanticism. The "rediscovery" of the ancient Greek epics, the *Iliad* and the *Odyssey*, and the admiration of epics as the genre highlighting the "genuine roots" of a nation's oral tradition had a decisive impact on Europeans' attitudes toward their own literary tradition (Kuusi et al. 1977: 30f.).

Lönnrot collected specimens from oral poetry in eastern and central Finland, predominantly from the historical landscape of Karelia and, on the basis of the material which he rearranged to form a coherent story, an epic took shape which he called *Kalevala*.

> In fact we are among a people that endows everything with life, and with human and divine attributes. Birds, and beasts, and fishes, and serpents, as well as the Sun, the Moon, the Great Bear, and the stars, are either kind or unkind. Drops of blood find speech; men and maidens transform themselves into other shapes and resume again their native forms at will; ships, and trees, and waters, have magic powers; in short, all nature speaks in human tongues [Crawford 1889 (2014): 25f.].

Traditionally, Lönnrot has been seen as merely having edited the collected poetry which was memorized by trained Finnish dialect speakers. Recent research has shown that the *Kalevala* is not simply a collection of folk poetry but that its contents has been thoroughly organized by Lönnrot who linked the different parts of the epic in a skillful stylistic composition. According to this modern view, Lönnrot is as much a composer of the *Kalevala* as Homer is of the *Iliad*. Both authors based their composition on oral poetry which was transformed into a literary work.

Often, oral epics were presented in the form of songs accompanied by the kantele, a stringed instrument, the Baltic-Finnic equivalent of the Greek lyra. The original spread of the kantele in eastern Finland and Karelia indicates the area from which Lönnrot collected most of his material (see below for music).

Lönnrot was the first to collect epic poetry, and other fieldworkers followed his example. They travelled to many places where the knowledge of the old rune tradition was still alive.

> By the time fieldworkers began collecting Kalevalaic folksong in the nineteenth century, its distribution had become largely confined to a few relic areas. Viena Karelia preserved the epic tradition most extensively, while the Karelian Isthmus showed the greatest flowering and maintenance of the lyric song.... In

Savo, a vibrant incantation tradition preserved the cores of many epic songs [Virtanen and DuBois 2000: 148].

The storytellers had stored in their memory what had been passed on to them from members of the older generation. Thus, in the oral poetry which was written down by Lönnrot, old layers of mythical tradition have been preserved. Some scholars have demonstrated that, in the stories of *Kalevala*, are embedded memories of the world of the Iron Age, going back as far as the second century BCE. As regards the contents and the language in which the collected folk poetry was memorized, the *Kalevala* is considered not only by the Finns to be their national epic, but by the Karelians in neighboring Russia as well (see Chapter 2). "Given the situation of the Finns in the post–1809 world, this folklore nevertheless inevitably gained a Finnish nationalistic interpretation" (Klinge 2012: 79).

A shorter version of the *Kalevala* was published in 1835, an enlarged version in 1849. This work has become the most successful piece of literature in Finnish of all times. The *Kalevala* has prompted a stream of popular literature, including theater plays and operas, and the persistent incentive of classical Finnish epics has created a literary tradition in its own right (Fromm 1980). There also was a profound repercussion of epic themes in the visual arts which concentrated, in the latter half of the 19th and beginnings of the 20th centuries on subjects related to the world of the *Kalevala* (e.g., the paintings of Akseli Gallen-Kallela).

The popularity of the *Kalevala* may also be highlighted when looking at its reception outside Finland. In the span of time between the publication of the short version (1835) and the enlarged version (1849), there was a substantial echo coming from the field of German studies of cultural heritage. Jacob Grimm, in 1845, gave the following evaluation of the *Kalevala*: "Here, if anywhere, there is now a pure epic in simple and thus most moving form, an unprecedented treasure" (quoted after Pentikäinen 1989: 1).

This piece of Finnish literature has been translated into 54 languages, and new languages are added to this list continuously. Among the earliest translations were those into Swedish (1841), French (1845) and Russian (1847); among the more recent are Swahili (1991), Tamil (1994), Vietnamese (1994) and Portuguese (2009). Some translations became themselves the basis for secondary translations into other languages, such as the German version of 1852 by Franz Anton Schiefner. In many languages, one finds successive versions which are based on translations made at different times (in French: 1845, 1867, 1927, 1991; English: 1868, 1888, 1907, 1963, 1988, 1992; Italian: 1909, 1910, 1980, 1988, 2007; German: 1852, 1885, 1967, 2004).

The epic tradition has never lost its attraction for subsequent generations although nowadays the interest focuses more on the living conditions in a natural environment, rather than on the stories told in the *Kalevala*. For the contemporaries of Elias Lönnrot, though, the epic tradition was a living experience for those who visited the eastern region of Finland.

For example, poet Eino Leino, composer Jean Sibelius, painter Akseli Gallen-Kallela, sculptor Emil Wikström and architect Eliel Saarinen went to Karelia in search of the persons and primordial landscapes to use as models in their poetry, music and art. The world of the *Kalevala* was a symbol through which artists strove to convey the deepest experiences of humankind [SKS; http://neba.finlit.fi/kalevala/index. php?m=145&s=273&l=2; retrieved 6 August 2015].

## Sofi Oksanen's *Purge*: An Unconventional Success Story

Foreigners who are familiar with the works of Nobel Prize winner Frans Eemil Sillanpää (1888–1964), represent a small group of Finnish literature enthusiasts. Those who have read the *Kalevala* are a far greater number. The *Kalevala* is a literary institution of Finnishness that has gained in international profile over time. All is different with Sofi Oksanen who has become internationally known in a very individual way.

The success that Sofi Oksanen experienced with her third literary novel *Purge* (2008; original Finnish title *Puhdistus*) is an exception in every respect. It is based on her first theater play *Purge* (first staged in 2007). The novel has an ending which differs from that in the play. Sofi's novel *Purge* received unprecedented attention and recognition. There is no other piece of Finnish literature that would have gained so much regard, in Finland and abroad, as has this single work.

What makes Sofi Oksanen (b. 1977) Finnish is her father, and what makes her Estonian is her mother. Prior to the *Purge* Sofi had published two novels. The *Purge* has by now been translated into almost 40 languages. The protagonists of the novel (as of the theater play with the same title) are two women who look back into their past and are confronted with memories of events during the period of Soviet occupation of Estonia, which lasted until 1991. The reworking of experiences among non–Russian citizens under the Soviet regime, inspired a period of critical remembrance, and the *Purge* can be categorized as the major work in this movement.

The novel received several awards: the Finlandia Prize (in 2008), the Runeberg Prize (in 2009), the Nordic Council Literature Prize (in 2010), the Prix Femina (in 2010), the French FNAC Prize (in 2010). The story of the *Purge* became the theme of a film (2012) and of an opera (2012). In addition, Sofi received the Swedish Academy's Nordic Prize (in 2013) and the Budapest Grand Prize (in 2014) for her entire work so far. She is the recipient of several medals of honor (including the Estonian medal of the Order of the Cross of Terra Mariana in 2010 and the Pro Finlandia Medal in 2012).

The media created for Sofi Oksanen an image of a writer in a class along (e.g., "Sofi Oksanen stands out with *Purge*. This is a family saga like no other"—*Sunday Times* [London] "Best books of 2010"). "Sofi Oksanen has become a literary phenomenon" (*The Times* [London]), and this image is as much Finnish as it is cosmopolitan. Sofi gave the opening speech of the Frankfurt Book Fair in October 2014 which had chosen Finland as its literary theme of the year. No doubt, Sofi Oksanen represents Finnish literary creativity at its best.

## *Finnish Filmmakers and Movie Stars Abroad*

Finland hosts a regular annual film event, the Midnight Sun Film Festival, held in Sodankylä (Lapland) every year in June. Helsinki also offers events for international filmmakers to meet and exchange views with Finns in the film business (Kääpä and Laine 2012). Yet, Finnish films have so far only occasionally been nominated for awards (Kääpä 2012). Finnish filmmakers who are the most widely known abroad are Aki and Mika Kaurismäki (Kääpä 2010). In 2002, Aki Kaurismäki's film *The Man Without a Past* won the Grand Prix at the Cannes Film Festival. A year later, this film was nominated for an

Academy Award. The only other Finish production to range among the Oscar candidates is the film *The Fencer* by director Klaus Härö (nominated in January 2016). The Finnish filmmaker Renny Harlin (b. 1959) who works in Hollywood is known for his action movies. The Finnish-born Nancy Juvonen (b. 1967) has produced films such as *Never Been Kissed* (1999) and *Charlie's Angels* (2000).

Finland cannot compete with neighboring Sweden that brought celebrities such as Greta Garbo and Ingrid Bergman into the world of international cinema, but perhaps both countries are on equal footing when we think of actresses enjoying recognition like the Swedish-born Lena Olin who has become successful in the United States.

The world of international films opened to Finnish actresses and actors in the 1950s, and since then the international public has continuously seen Finnish talents in this field. It is hard to present those personalities in a way that pays people tribute to their individual achievements and to evaluate their position in a world where stars rise and fall and where the chances of success are unpredictable. Some talented individuals of Finnish or Finland-Swedish descent rose above the average and became successful abroad. It is noteworthy that most of them are women and most of them made a career in the United States. The following is a selective list, in alphabetical order:

Irina Björklund (b. 1973); movie and TV actress who won the Jussi Award for Best Leading Actress (1999) and the Shooting Star Prize at the Berlin Film Festival (2004); Irina made her breakthrough with her role as Lotta Kaarina Vainikainen in the film *Rukajärven tie* ("Ambush"; 1999); she had a minor role in the U.S. film *The American* (alongside George Clooney; 2010).

Richard Davalos (b. 1935; father of Finnish descent); winner of the Theatre World Award (performance in Arthur Miller's play *A Memory of Two Mondays*, 1955); Richard played the part of James Dean's brother in *East of Eden* (1955).

Anna Easteden (b. 1976), an award nominated actress; she performed as "Bee Sting" in *Who Wants to Be a Superhero?* (2007).

Samuli Edelmann (b. 1968), an actor who performed in the action movie *Mission Impossible—Ghost Protocol* (2011).

Liisa Evastina (Mannerkoski) (b. 1980), an actress with roles in television shows such as *NCIS* spin off pilot and *NCIS Los Angeles*.

Taina Elg (b. 1930), who started her career as a ballet dancer, performing in Finland, Great Britain and France; as an actress Taina performed in many movies; for her performance in *Diane* (1956) she won a Golden Globe Award for "female foreign newcomer"; in 2004 the actress was honored to become a knight of the Finnish Order of the Lion.

Minna Haapkylä (b. 1973), an actress who has won two Jussi Awards; Minna played the role of Hélène in the French film *Le Serpent* ("Snake," 2006).

Marta Kristen (b. 1945 as Birgit Annalisa Rusanen; her mother is Finnish), an actress who became known as the character Judy Robinson in the popular television series *Lost in Space* (1965).

Christine Lahti (b. 1950; paternal grandparents of Finnish descent), an actress who won the Academy Award for Best Live Action Short Film in 1995; she won two Golden Globe Awards (1989 and 1998) and an Emmy (1998).

Jessica Lange (b. 1949; maternal grandparents of Finnish descent), an actress who won two Academy Awards in the same year, 1982; her career started out with the film *King Kong* (1976); in 1976 she won a Golden Globe Award for New Star of the Year; she won two Primetime Emmy Awards (2009 and 2011); she was the first female recipient of the Kirk Douglas Award at the Santa Barbara International Film Festival (2014); she starred in O'Neill's *Long Day's Journey into Night* on Broadway in 2016.

Maila Nurmi (1922–2008), niece of the legendary runner Paavo Nurmi; Maila gained her reputation through her performance as Vampira, the "Queen of horror," in the 1950s. Her role as vampire protagonist in the film *Plan 9 from Outer Space* (1959) by Ed Wood "remains a cult favorite" (Hinkkanen 2012); Vampira's character continued to be trendsetting over decades.

The number of movie stars with a Finnish background expands when one takes into consideration other cases of Finnish descent: What connects the Canadian-American actress Pamela Anderson (b. 1967) with Finland is her great-grandfather, Juho Hyytiäinen, who emigrated to America in 1908 and changed his name to Anderson, and the American actress and former Miss America (1984) Vanessa Lynn Williams (b. 1963) had a DNA test made and was told that she has 12 percent Finnish ancestry.

## What Makes Finnish Music Attractive for the World? Composers, Conductors, Opera and Jazz

The story of Finland's contribution to the world of music abroad goes back into the 19th century. The country has attracted worldwide attention as the venue for several international musical events with high standards. Nowadays, five such are especially outstanding, one of them being a competition. There is the Kuhmo Chamber Music Festival, founded by Tuulikki Karjalainen and Seppo Kimanen, that has been held annually for more than forty years. An event of competition is the International Jean Sibelius Violin Competition that has been organized, since 1965, by the Sibelius Society of Finland and the Sibelius Academy, in Helsinki (see below). The third major event is the Savonlinna Opera Festival held annually (see below). The other two are Pori Jazz and the pop music Flow Festival.

Of the events in the domain of classical music the Savonlinna Opera Festival attracts the greatest number of visitors. About 70,000 attend annually, and of these some 17,000 people come from abroad. Some of the festivals that present modern music are frequented by more visitors. Of these, the Pori Jazz Festival and the Flow Festival in Helsinki are the most popular. Both were founded and are organized by Finns. The Flow Festival was started in 2004, and in the first year there were 2,000 attendees; in August 2015, some 80,000 people attended and more than a hundred artists performed. Yet, even these numbers are dwarfed by the Pori Jazz Festival, which attracts more than 150,000 people every year (see below).

### Traditional Finnish and Saami Music

Traditional Finnish melodies may be familiar to only a few foreigners although the most typical of the accompanying traditional instruments, the stringed kantele, is more widely known. Vocal music "includes rune-melodies and laments, cattle-calling songs and other signaling melodies" (Asplund 1997: 110). The melodic character of the traditional folk music was restricted, and the composition of the scales was a mere pentachord. Accordingly, the earliest model of the kantele had five strings, made of horsehair. In folk music, rune-singing (or Kalevala singing) dominated—and proliferated into epic, lyric and ritual song genres (the latter performed at weddings). In the old days, many people possessed the skill of rune-singing. These skills were developed further by experts, master singers. When Elias Lönnrot started to collect Kalevala runes he received most of his material from master singers.

The kantele is regarded by Finns as their national instrument although it is not confined to Finland but is more widely spread beyond Fenno-Scandia (Sarmela 1994, map 89) into other Baltic-Finnic groups such as Karelians, Vots and Ingrians. The original five-string kantele was still played in the early 19th century. Later, models with 10, 14 and even 20 or 30 strings were used. In a modern version, the kantele has been used as a concert instrument since the 1920s. Concert music including the kantele has enjoyed increasing popularity since the 1950s. Concert versions may have up to 40 strings. Modern folk music draws on the heritage of Finnish-Karelian traditional tunes. There has been a trend of folk music to search for the roots, and this movement is responsible for folk music to enter the mainstream of popular music.

The most ancient form of music that has survived to this day is singing in the traditional style of the Saami *joik* or *yoik* (*juoiggus* in Saami). The *joik* is a style of chanting resembling that among native Americans. The melodies are pentatonic. The theme of a *joik* song may be spiritual and it is usually dedicated to a person (at the time of birth) or an animal or it may refer to the forms of a landscape. The *joik* singer may be accompanied by a drum. The *joik* tradition reaches back to the times when shamanistic rites were practiced. This musical style has had a renaissance in connection with the roots revival, and there are pop singers who specialize in *joik*, like Jonne Järvelä (member of the band *Shaman* or *Korpiklaani*). The exotic flair of the Saami *joik* attracts foreigners, and Saami-style music may enjoy international media attention. One such occasion was the visit in Lapland of the British actress Joanna Lumley to whom a Saami elder dedicated several *joiks* (*The Times*, 6 September 2008).

## Jean Sibelius and the *Finlandia*

Before Finland's independence, one gifted composer stands out, and this is Johan Julius Christian Sibelius (1865–1957). He is better known as Jean Sibelius, Jean being the French version of the name form Janne (a colloquial variant of Johan) by which he was known as a boy. Jean Sibelius composed music in the spirit of the Finnish national awakening, and he is considered by most Finns to be Finland's greatest composer. He is certainly the one who is internationally best known. The most popular visual impression of Sibelius worldwide are photos that show him smoking a cigar (Sirén 2000).

Of all his works, the most widely known, within Finland and abroad, is *Finlandia*, opus 26, originally composed in 1899, as a symphony. This piece of music, for which words were written in 1941 by Veikko Antero Koskenniemi, became the most popular national song of Finland, ranking with the national anthem, the *Maammelaulu* ("Song of our

Country"). *Finlandia* was composed as a piece for orchestra but, in 1900, Jean Sibelius arranged it for piano. As it grew in popularity, the composer remodeled the original symphonic poem to become a hymn, the *Finlandia Hymn*. What made *Finlandia* popular is the original context for which it was intended and the conditions under which it was performed. The original was intended to express protest against an increasing censorship in cultural affairs during the era when Finland formed part of tsarist Russia. Sibelius "defined the musical life of a nation, and his works—above all his tone-poem *Finlandia*, with its turbulent opening and final hymn-tune—were the soundtrack to Finland's slow struggle towards independence" (Service 2011). It was first performed in July 1900. The message it encapsulated was well received among the Finns, but performances had to choose various neutral titles for the hymn, not to disclose its national impetus.

The melody of *Finlandia* has become so popular that it is chosen, sometimes, for contexts involving turbulence and suspense that do not have anything to do with Finland. Renny Harlin, a Hollywood filmmaker of Finnish descent, chose it as background music in some scenes of his action thriller *Die Hard 2* (1990; with Bruce Willis).

In addition to the *Finlandia,* Jean Sibelius produced a wealth of other musical compositions, among them eight symphonies: No. 1 (Op. 39; 1898–99), No. 2 (Op. 43; 1901–02), No. 3 (Op. 52; 1907), No. 4 (Op. 63; 1910–11), No. 5 (Op. 82; 1915, revised 1916, revised again 1919), No. 6 (Op. 104; 1923), and No. 7 (Op. 105; 1924). Symphony No. 8 (mid–1920s until 1938) was not published by the composer.

A Sibelius monument was unveiled in September 1967, the work of the Finnish artist Eila Hiltunen who gave her sculpture the title *Passio Musicae* (http://oppiminen.yle.fi/juhlapaivat/jean-sibeliuksen-paiva-suomalaisen-musiikin-paiva-812; retrieved 3 February 2015). The monument was erected in the Sibelius Park in Helsinki. On the premises of the UNESCO headquarters in Paris there is a smaller version of Hiltunen's sculpture and a variation of this same grand memorialization of Sibelius can be found in the courtyard of the United Nations building in New York.

Another form of commemoration is the Jean Sibelius Violin Competition. The competition is held every five years and is a truly international event as can be seen from the composition of the jury, with members from many countries. The jury in 2015 had the following members: Pierre Amoyal, Cho-Liang Lin, Serguei Azizian, Sigrún Edvaldsdóttir, Pekka Kauppinen, Sung-Ju Lee, Gerhard Schulz and Krzysztof Wegrzyn. The chairperson of the jury was the Finnish composer Veli-Matti Puumala.

Through the years, participants in this competition have come from many countries around the world, and laureates are from neighboring Russia, from other European countries (Germany, Denmark, Finland, Hungary, Romania, Georgia, Armenia, Iceland, Greece), and from countries outside Europe (Israel, Japan, Canada, the United States, China, South Korea). The winner of the 2015 Violin Competition is the American Christel Lee (b. 1990). So far, only one candidate from Finland has won the competition, and this is Pekka Kuusisto (b. 1976). He began to study music at the Sibelius Academy in 1983 and continued his studies in the U.S. (at the Indiana University School of Music from 1992 to 1997). In 1995, Kuusisto won the Jean Sibelius Violin Competition and has performed in many concerts; he is also interested in folk music (Sirén 2015).

The year 2015 was a jubilee year. In autumn, the 150th anniversary of the birth of Sibelius was celebrated. Events to honor the composer were organized not only in Finland but also abroad. The Finnish Radio Symphony Orchestra went on a tour to Japan where they gave concerts in Tokyo, Shizuoka, Yamaguchi and Osaka. The Japanese themselves honored the Finnish composer in a concert program dedicated to his memory, that began September 2015 in the Tokyo Opera City Concert Hall and continued through the winter until February 2016 with the concluding event in the Aster Plaza Grand Hall in Hiroshima. The jubilee year saw a boom in literature on Sibelius. Five books have appeared in Finnish. Of these, Turtola's work (2015) is perhaps "the most interesting" (Murtomäki 2015).

## Finnish Composers Beyond Sibelius

The history of Finnish composers (and also of orchestras and conductors) can be roughly divided into three periods: the period before Sibelius, the period of Sibelius and, the post–Sibelius period. Robert Kajanus (1856–1933) is the giant of the pre–Sibelius period. As a composer, Kajanus left more than 200 works. He also was a talented conductor (see below).

Composers of classical music in Finland are known from the late 18th century onward, starting with Erik Tulindberg and Bernhard Henrik Crusell. It is noteworthy that the "father of Finnish music," Fredrik (Friedrich) Pacius (1809–1891), was of German descent. He came to Finland as a music teacher in 1834. Pacius composed the music for the poem *Vårt land* ("Our Land"), written by Johan Ludvig Runeberg (see Chapter 1, figure 4 for the text of the poem). This 1848 composition assumed a unique role in the history of Finnish music: it became the national anthem (called *Maamme* "Our Land"). Opera compositions in Finland started out with Pacius who composed *Kung Karls jakt* ("The hunt of King Charles") in 1852.

---

### Finnish Composers of the 19th and 20th Centuries

The works of many composers are dedicated exclusively to one category of music. This is true for the representatives of classical music such as Oskar Merikanto (d. 1924), Armas Järnefelt (d. 1958), Uuno Klami (d. 1961), Helvi Leiviskä (d. 1982), Erik Bergman (d. 2006), Leif Segerstam (b. 1944) or Kaija Saariaho (b. 1952).

Others composed various kinds of music:

- Ernest Pingoud (d. 1942; the first modernist who also produced classical music);
- Aarre Merikanto (d. 1958) and Sampo Haapamäki (b. 1979) who have produced classical and modernist music.

And there are multitalents who—like Sibelius—compose music of various categories:

- Selim Palmgren (d. 1951; classical, impressionist, opera, choir, vocal); Herman Rechberger (b. 1947; modernist, vocal, ethnic, opera);
- Joonas Kokkonen (d. 1996; classical, neoclassical, opera);
- Einojuhani Rautavaara (d. 2016; neo-romantic, opera, mystical);
- Timo Alakotila (b. 1959; classical, jazz, traditional music—*pelimanni*; tango).

---

## The World of Opera and the Savonlinna Opera Festival

The world of opera opened to the cultured Finnish public in the course of the 19th century, especially the latter half. That was a time also when opera was presented to the

European public by Finnish singers. One stands out because of her international recognition: Alma Fohström (1856–1936), who was born into the family of a rich Finland-Swede, a merchant from Helsinki. Alma was the first opera singer from Finland to perform throughout the world (Toivakka 2015).

She achieved an international breakthrough with her performance in the Kroll Theater in Berlin, in April 1878. During her career, Alma performed in some 200 cities in many countries of Europe, Asia, and the Americas. She sang in the presence of kings and emperors, among them Oskar II, King of Sweden, Wilhelm II, Emperor of Germany, Franz Joseph, Emperor of Austria-Hungary, and Dom Pedro, Emperor of Brazil.

In 1887, Alma participated in a concert in the Albert Hall in London, to celebrate the 50th anniversary of the rule of Queen Victoria. In Russia, three emperors heard Alma's singing, Alexander II, Alexander III and Nicholas II. The great occasion for the prima donna was her performance at the coronation of Nicholas II in 1896. Alma went on a concert tour in 1904 to the Far East, as far as Vladivostok. The outbreak of the Russo-Japanese war cast a shadow on her plans. Concerts scheduled for Japan and China were cancelled.

During her first American concert tour, in 1883–84, Alma performed in Buenos Aires, Montevideo, Sao Paolo and Rio de Janeiro. In Rio she performed for the Emperor of Brazil, Dom Pedro.

In 1885–86, Alma went on a concert tour to the United States where she performed in more than ten cities, starting in New York in November 1885 and finishing in Cincinnati in May 1886. Alma was applauded and celebrated, and the echoes in the press were overwhelming. Dozens of articles appeared in newspapers and magazines. Seemingly, the audience was most enthusiastic in Chicago, Philadelphia and San Francisco (Toivakka 2015: 171ff.). The journalists commented on many features of Alma's personality, her singing and her appearance. The quality of her voice attracted special attention:

> "She has a light soprano voice of the peculiar silvery clearness found only among Scandinavian singers" (*St. Paul and Minneapolis Pioneer*, 25 February 1886).

> "It [her voice] is clear, fresh and sweet and has the tone of a silver bell in her higher notes" (*St. Louis Post Dispatch*, 3 March 1886).

> "Her singing last evening leads to the belief that she is probably the best light soprano upon the operatic stage in this country at list. Her voice is not only remarkable for its range and pure vibrant quality, but her execution appears faultless" (*The Daily Interocean* [from Chicago], 12 February 1886).

> "It is marvelous to hear the full and clear volume of sound emitted by this petite donna, whom one compared to an Arctic snowflake, and another to a caged snowbird, she looked so fair and pure" (*The Call*, 24 March 1886).

The impresario who organized the tour in America, James Henry Mapleson, spoke with respect and adoration of Alma. His memoirs mention many memorable performances and he emphasizes how Alma impressed the audience (Mapleson 1888/II): "Fohström acted her part [Zerlina in *Fra Diavolo*, Auber] with much grace and dainty naiveté" (p. 169f.), "The following evening Mdlle. Fohström appeared as "Lucia di Lammermoor," and met with very great success" (p. 179), "San Francisco: The second evening Mdlle. Fohström made a most brilliant success" (p. 182). Alma returned to the U.S. in 1888. She became the first opera singer from Finland to perform at the New York Metropolitan Opera (Toivakka 2015: 266).

Alma was celebrated as the "Finnish nightingale," and "Nightingale" (Russian *Solovei*) was the title of a solo song that had been composed by Aleksandr Aljabjev in 1826 and which Alma sang for the first soundtrack of her voice, which was recorded in St. Petersburg in 1902 (Toivakka 2015: 250). After a long career, more than 25 years as an opera singer, Alma held the post of professor of singing at the Conservatory in St. Petersburg, from 1909 until the Bolshevik coup d'état in October 1917. Afterwards Alma taught music in her home country, Finland, and, from 1920 to 1928, she was a professor at the Stern Conservatory in Berlin. Later, until her death in 1936, Alma taught at the Conservatory in Helsinki (figure 33).

(a) Alma Fohström                   (b) Aino Ackté

**Figure 33: Historical figures in the world of Finnish opera (Museovirasto; Kuvakokoelmat).**

Something that has contributed greatly to the national image of Finland is the organization of the opera festival at Savonlinna in the eastern part of the country. The landmark of Savonlinna is the biggest castle (erected in 1475) ever built in Finland. The castle's name is Olavinlinna (St. Olaf's Castle), and it is located on the shore of Lake Saimaa. The idea to make the castle the place for musical events originated as a sideline, so to speak, of meetings of a circle of nationalist Finns and Finland-Swedes who convened in the castle in the summer of 1907. The agenda of the meeting was the search for Finland's cultural identity amidst a surge of national awakening.

A generation after Alma Fohström, the central figure of Finnish opera music was

Aino Ackté (1876–1944), born into a family of Baltic-German descent (Aghte-Ackte) that had settled in Finland. Aino, a soprano, had already gained international recognition in Paris and New York before the Savonlinna meeting (Pakkanen 1988). Later she was applauded by audiences in Leipzig and London. Aino's major parts were Margareta (in *Faust*), Elsa (in *Lohengrin*), Elisabeth (in *Tannhäuser*), Tosca (the protagonist in *Tosca*) and Salomé (the protagonist in *Salomé*).

The latter role was her favorite. Ackté had followed the presentation of Salomé at the Opera Festival in Cologne in 1906, had studied the role carefully and sang the part for the first time in Leipzig a year later. Her breakthrough in this role came with her appearance in London in 1910. Richard Strauss, the composer of the opera, applauded Ackté as the "the only true Salomé" (http://finnland-institut.de/musikbeziehungen/aino_ackte.html; retrieved 16 April 2015).

It took several years of preparation before Aino Ackté's idea of an opera festival in Olavinlinna Castle materialized. The year 1912 saw the first festival. During the following years four operas were performed, three by Finnish composers. The only non–Finnish opera was *Faust* (by the French composer Charles Gounod). Aino functioned as the director of the festival and she performed the parts of the female protagonists in the operas that were staged in the castle. After the venue of summer 1916, the organization of the opera festival was hampered by the political unrest caused by World War I and by the turmoil of the civil war that followed the Finnish Declaration of Independence in early December 1917 (see Chapter 4).

The memories of the early years never faded and, in the 1960s, another opportunity arose to re-establish the festival. The inaugural performance of the renewed venue at Savonlinna was Beethoven's *Fidelio*, in 1967. Within a few consecutive summers the Savonlinna opera festival developed into a "made in Finland" brand. Each year, there are visitors from many countries. The stage is set in the courtyard of the castle, and a light roof covers the whole of the yard as protection against rain.

The Savonlinna Opera Festival has attracted many opera companies from abroad, among them the Estonia Theatre (Tallinn), the Mariinsky Theatre (St. Petersburg), Covent Garden (London), the Opéra National du Rhin (Strasbourg), the New Israeli Opera, the Los Angeles Opera, the Deutsche Oper am Rhein, the Semperoper (Dresden) and the Volksoper (Vienna). Of the festivals of classical music that take place in Finland during the summer season, the Savonlinna Opera festival certainly is the one best known internationally and the most praised, and it definitely adds to the "national image" of the country.

Since 2010 an Aino Ackté chamber festival (kamarifestivaali) has been organized. This is a venue for lovers of opera and classical music, with events from May through September (http://www.ainoacktenhuvila.fi/kamarifestivaali/yhteystiedot/; retrieved 1 November 2015).

## Finnish Creative Leadership in the Orchestra World

Finland has produced more great architects than most other countries in relation to its small population, and this is the case also for the world of Finnish orchestra conductors (Ropo and Sauer 2007, Sirén 2010). Many attempts have been made to find explanations for the success of the Finnish gatekeepers of classical music that have made their way into the international spotlight. A closer look at their careers reveals the simple truth that musical creativity may find its way onto international forums given two elemental conditions that closely interact.

One is very individual, the other collective and societal. The very motor of promotion of an individual's creativity is the typical asset of the Finnish character: sisu, which provides the key for the endurance of extensive training and nurtures a strong sense of discipline. The other condition defines cultural life in Finland: high standards of musical education. The chain of opportunities for receiving a respectable musical education and training starts with the teaching of music and musical skills at the preschool level, then rising to levels of school education and continuing at music schools.

The most likely reputed institution of higher musical education and professional training is the Sibelius-Akatemia (Sibelius Academy) in Helsinki where most of the successful conductors have studied. This name for an older existing institution was chosen in 1939, with the intention of honoring the Academy's most celebrated former student. The older name had been Helsingfors Musikinstitut (Helsinki Music Institute). The history of the Academy starts out in 1882. The

> ## Notable Gatekeepers of Music from Finland (in alphabetical order)
>
> - Mikko Franck (former conductor of orchestras in Germany, Great Britain, Israel and Belgium, former artistic director and general music director of the Finnish National Opera);
> - Okko Kamu (conductor of the Oslo Philharmonic, City of Birmingham Symphony Orchestra, Copenhagen Philharmonic, Lausanne Chamber Orchestra, Lahti Symphony Orchestra);
> - Hannu Lintu (former conductor of the Helsingborg Symphony Orchestra, conductor of the Finnish Radio Symphony Orchestra);
> - Sasha Mäkilä (assistant conductor of the Cleveland Orchestra);
> - Sakari Oramo (conductor of the BBC Symphony Orchestra);
> - Jorma Panula (teacher at the Sibelius Academy);
> - Esa-Pekka Salonen (former conductor of the Los Angeles Philharmonic, conductor of the Philharmonia Orchestra);
> - Jukka-Pekka Saraste (former conductor of the Toronto Symphony Orchestra);
> - Leif Segerstam (conductor of the Turku Philharmonic Orchestra);
> - Osmo Vänskä (music director of the Minnesota Orchestra).

Sibelius Academy merged with the Theatre Academy and the Academy of Fine Arts in 2013. The new mega-institution is the University of the Arts in Helsinki.

The first permanent orchestra in Finland, the Helsinki Philharmonic Society, was founded by Robert Kajanus in 1882. Later, its name was changed to Helsinki Philharmonic Orchestra. One of the highlights of the orchestra's performance was Beethoven's Symphony No. 9, first heard in Finland in 1888. The memory of Kajanus persists in the orchestration of Finland's national anthem. Kajanus held the post of director of music at Helsinki University from 1897 until 1926. In 1919, Kajanus organized the first Nordic Music Festival. The French honored him with membership in the Légion d'honneur.

There was a smooth transition from the period which bears Sibelius's mark and the years that followed. The central figure during the process of transition was Paavo Berglund (1929–2012), who strongly adhered to the style and works of Sibelius. Sibelius liked the way Berglund conducted the grand master's symphonies. In the 1950s, Berglund started research on Sibelius' major work, the Seventh Symphony, and coordinated various versions with the master's corrections (*A Comparative Study* 1970). This project culminated in the publication of a new edition of the Seventh in 1980. Berglund worked as a conductor abroad. He gave his last concert in Paris, in 2007. The conductor received awards from various countries, including Denmark, France, Great Britain and Sweden.

What certainly strikes the eye of any observer is the dominance of male conductors in the Finnish world of music. Aren't there any female conductors? There are, but they are the exception. According to a false but stereotypical view held even by notable representatives in the world of music, women are not apt for conductor's work. Anyway, there is space, in the world of Finnish music, for female conductors' creativity to unfold.

Susanna Mälkki (b. 1969) is one of the living counter arguments against male chauvinistic views. She started out as a cellist and has devoted herself to conducting since the beginning of this century. Mälkki has conducted many orchestras in various countries, in France (the first female music director of the Ensemble InterContemporain, between 2006 and 2013), Norway (the Stavanger Symphony Orchestra), New Zealand (New Zealand Symphony Orchestra), Great Britain (London Sinfonietta) and the United States (Saint Louis Symphony Orchestra). Mälkki's future work is associated with the Helsinki Philharmonic Orchestra which she will conduct starting in autumn 2016.

Those who look for a colorful personality among Finnish female conductors may find Eva Ollikainen (b. 1982), whose career is full of surprises, also for the conductor herself. Ollikainen's teachers were Jorma Panula and Leif Segerstam. In 2003, she won the Jorma Panula Conductor Competition. It was easy for Ollikainen to get on the list of the Harrison & Parrot agency in London, and she went on many concert tours throughout Europe, organized by the agency. Maybe the workload was too stressful for the conductor in her 20s, maybe her health was affected by the restless life she led, always traveling and performing at different places, always deprived of sufficient sleep. Ollikainen ended up in the hospital with a heart condition and was forced to change her life.

She set out for a voyage to Antarctica where she found snow, ice and absolute silence. "After a long time I felt in harmony with myself. I looked at the starry sky and breathed clean air" (quoted after Pere 2015: B 2). She went to Antarctica once again, this time working on a cruise ship. During that travel she made new friends whom she joined and with whom she started to build a sailboat in Canada. Then, one day, when she was resting, she listened to music and her passion was lit by a spark again. Ollikainen went to live in Copenhagen from where it is easy to go on concert tours in Europe. She had worked in Finland for several years, between 2003 and 2005, as conductor of the Orchestra of the Polytechnics. In November 2015 she conducted the Tampere Philharmonic Orchestra in the Tampere Hall.

And there is another dynamic figure, Dalia Stasevska (b. 1984). Her father is Ukrainian and her mother Finnish. Stasevska has been a student of two Finnish gatekeepers of music, Jorma Panula and Leif Segerstam, and she has worked as an assistant to Esa-Pekka Salonen. Stasevska, who has conducted orchestras in Helsinki, Turku, Oulu, Tampere and Kokkola, directed Mozart's Requiem at the Savonlinna Opera Festival and conducted several opera productions at Kuhmo. Right from the start of her career she has impressed the public and music critics.

From the very beginning it was clear that her approach never sees classical music as a "charming entertainment." Instead she comes across as a fully mature artist whose interpretations have real power and vision. She conducts with immense intensity and control, but at the same time has understanding for small nuances [*Etelä-Suomen Sanomat*, 2015; www.ess.fi].

## Finnish Singers with an International Career

Popular music is so international that almost every country has singers whose songs may be known in other parts of the world. Some Finnish bands and their singers even make it into the charts abroad, for instance HIM, whose album *Dark Light* (released in September 2005) rated 4th in Germany and 18th in the charts both in the U.S. and in Great Britain.

The careers of Alma Fohström and Aino Ackté, highlighted in the foregoing, are illustrative of how different the world of opera music is. In this world, ranking is a matter of prestige, of who works at what important institution and for how long. Most of the Finnish singers who have an international reputation are associated with either the Sibelius Academy or the Savonlinna Opera Festival, or both. The most individual career, deviating from the mainstream education in opera singing, is true for the operatic bass Martti Talvela (1935–1989), who was educated as a primary school teacher in Savonlinna. Talvela started his career as a singer with his debut in Helsinki, in 1960. Since then the man who had a "voice of immense size and wide range" (Loppert 1997) sang in various roles for opera houses in Stockholm, Berlin, Bayreuth, and New York (Hako 2004: 373ff.). From 1972 until 1979 Talvela held the post of artistic leader of the Savonlinna Opera Festival.

Former students of the Sibelius Academy who gained a reputation among an international public may be grouped according to their special training:

- Mezzo-soprano (Monica Groop)
- Soprano (Soile Isokoski, Karita Mattila)
- Baritone (Tommi Hakala, Jorma Hynninen)
- Bass (Matti Salminen)
- Tenor (Peter Lindroos)

Two of the former students did not follow an operatic career but chose the genres of political song, chanson and popular music. These singers are Arja Saijonmaa (b. 1944) and the soprano Tarja Turunen (b. 1977).

Arja started her career as a singer in Sweden, in the 1960s. Her performances became politically motivated once she joined the Greek solo singer Mikis Theodorakis on his world tour in the early 1970s. Theodorakis campaigned against the dictatorship of the military junta in his country Greece that ended in 1974. Arja's career continued in Sweden where her songs have been popular ever since. In 1986, she performed at the funeral of Swedish prime minister Olof Palme who had been assassinated. The song she sang was *Jag vill tacka livet* ("Thanks to life"), composed by Chilean Violeta Parra, and this song became one of Arja's greatest hits. Arja was appointed an UNHCR goodwill ambassador in 1987.

Tarja's talent as a singer was noticed early on, during her years as a schoolgirl at the comprehensive school in Kitee. Her music teacher at the time, Plamen Dimov, was impressed by her skills from the start: "If you gave Tarja just one note, she immediately got it. With the others, you'd have to practice three, four, five times" (quoted in Ollila 2007: 42). As a teenager, Tarja performed as a soloist in various concerts outside school. At the Sibelius Academy she received her decisive training.

In 1996, together with Tuomas Holopainen (one of Tarja's former classmates) and Emppu Vuorinen, Tarja Turunen founded the Finnish symphonic metal band *Nightwish*. The band's first album (*Angels Fall First*), released in 1997, made it right onto the Finnish charts and success continued. In 2004, the album *Once* swept Europe. It topped all other albums in popularity, sold platinum in Finland and Germany. No other album by any other band in any other country of Europe has sold better than *Once*. One reason for the unprecedented popularity of a metal band is the volume of Tarja's voice with a vocal range in three registers (mezzo-soprano, contralto, coloratura soprano). She has a golden throat and she has left an imprint on metal music in a category of her own. Tarja has created a dramatic symphonic style which has been dubbed "opera metal." Her way of singing in the band set standards, inspiring other bands and performers.

Contemporaneous with her success on vocals with *Nightwish*, Tarja performed at the Savonlinna Opera Festival in 1998, with songs from Verdi and Wagner (Ollila 2007: 65). Tarja continued her independent career as a solo singer after the breakup with the band in October 2005. Her separation from *Nightwish* was closely followed by the media, but the true reasons for the breakup have not been made explicit. Obviously, Tarja experienced a kind of renaissance as a soloist, once she was relieved of the restrictions on her vocal range set by singing in a band.

> Now that I can use the whole range of my voice, it feels very nice. I have never sung so low as I did on one of the songs on the new record and there's a song on which I sang my highest notes ever! I really have used a huge range on this album—around three octaves—because the moods are changing in every song and this reflects that [Tarja Turunen, *Kerrang!* interview, September 2007].

Tarja returned to the Savonlinna Opera Festival once again, in 2006. The new powers of her voice shows in her album *My Winter Storm*, released in November 2007. With this album as an independent singer Tarja topped the success of *Nightwish*. It did not take long before *My Winter Storm* was at the top of the Finnish charts, and sales were impressive. The album sold platinum in Finland, gold in Germany and double platinum in Russia (Gold-/Platin-Datenbank. Bundesverband Musikindustrie. http://www.musikindustrie.de/gold_platin_datenbank/#topSearch). Tarja's Storm World Tour, starting in November 2007 and ending in October 2009, was very successful. She performed altogether 95 times, in concert halls of countries in Europe as well as in the Americas.

Undoubtedly, musical education in Finland is the best springboard for Finnish singers to make an international career. Yet there are personalities in the world of Finnish music who have received their training abroad and work in Finland, as is the case with the mezzo-soprano Lilli Paasikivi (b. 1965), who obtained a diploma in singing from the Music University in Stockholm in 1992, and received special opera training at the London Royal College of Music in 1994. She started her professional career as a singer at the Finnish National Opera in 1998. Paasikivi has an international reputation, and she has been invited to perform in many cities worldwide—Berlin, Munich, London, Vienna, Paris, Aix-en-Provence, Oslo, Los Angeles, Cincinnati, Toronto, Sydney and Melbourne. Since 2013, Paasikivi has worked as artistic director of the Finnish National Opera.

## The Pori Jazz Festival

More than 30 jazz festivals are held in Finland every year (at Koli, Kemi, Ylläs, Helsinki, Forssa, Espoo, Kauniainen, Kerava, Tornio, Porvoo, Suovanlahti, Viapori, and other locations). Of these, the Pori Jazz Festival is the most popular. In addition, Pori Jazz is the biggest annual music event in Finland. In 2015, Pori Jazz celebrated its fiftieth anniversary. The event started out modestly, in 1966, with the first jazz festival. The place of venue was the Kirjurinluoto island off the southwestern coast of Finland. The event lasted for two days and was attended by some 1500 visitors. By the 1990s, the number of visitors exceeded 100,000 and, since the beginning of the new century, an international crowd of 150,000 or more gathers for the festival every year. In 1985, the length was extended to nine days. Pori Jazz is among the best known festivals in Europe and is the biggest summer event in Finland.

As for a description of the genres of music that are represented at Pori Jazz the following have been mentioned: jazz, blues, soul, funk, hip hop, Afro-Cuban, Brazilian, world music, pop music. Pori Jazz can count many international celebrities among its performers, such as Tom Jones, Alicia Keys, Benny Goodman, Bob Dylan, Björk, Chaka Khan, Elton John, Fats Domino, Joe Cocker, Kylie Minogue, Paul Anka, Phil Collins, Ray Charles, Carlos Santana, Stevie Wonder, Chuck Berry, Little Richard, Sting and many internationally known bands.

The festival is organized at the Kirjurinluoto Arena, an open-air concert park. Outside the park, there are other places of venues for events in smaller circles. A major attraction for summer visitors is the "Jazz street" in Pori, bordering the banks of the Kokemäenjoki (Kokemäki river) where smaller music events are organized in clubs. The annual festival takes place in the latter half of July.

## *The Moomins and Their Valley*

When Tove Marika Jansson (1914–2001) designed her stories about the Moomins and created illustrations for them she dreamed of a career as an artist. At the time when her stories were still in the planning stage, work as an artist seemed more important to her than writing. The world success of her stories about the Moomin family must have demonstrated to her that she was a multitalent, a skillful writer as well as a creative artist. Tove was born into a Finland-Swedish family. She is sometimes referred to as a Swedish-speaking Finn, which is not the same. Her reputation and her vision of a peaceful world made Tove cross many ethnic boundaries, not only those between Finland-Swedes and Finns, and her overall image in the world makes her an icon of Finnishness in a comprehensive cultural sense (Gieseking 2014: 103ff.).

The adventures of the Moomin family—with the father (Swedish: Mumintroll, Finnish: Muumi, English Moominpappa) and the mother (Muminmamma, Muumi-mamma or Moominmamma) as parents and many other fairy-tale characters—were told to the world, beginning with the publication of the first book, in Swedish, by Schildts in Finland, in 1945. Altogether nine books, five picture books and one comic strip appeared in the following years, until 1993. The first book was *Småtrollen och den stora överswämnin-*

*gen* (translated into English as *The Moomins and the Great Flood*). The ninth book, published in 1970, has the title *Sent i November* (translated into English as *Moominvalley in November*). While eight of the Moomin books were translated into English during the 1960s and 1970s, an English translation of the first book appeared as late as 2005. The reason given for the late transmission of Tove's project into the Anglo-Saxon world is that the first book was not successful, so that its popularity of later years leans on the success of the subsequent titles of the whole series. The picture books were published between 1952 and 1993. The stories of the Moomins have been translated into German, Polish, Japanese and many other languages and the Moomins feature in television series and films.

A special element in the world of the Moomins are their songs. The lyrics are written by Tove and the music composed by Erna Tauro. In their songs, every character is individualized by typical features. The singing Moomins also went on stage, for the first time in Stockholm, in 1959. Even a Moomin opera was composed, by Ilkka Kuusisto in 1974.

The Moomin characters and their adventures have been popular in Finland for decades and they have become a stable component of "national identity" (Meek 2001). Even daily language use among the Finns has produced certain phrases that draw on association with Moomin characters. For instance, when a Finnish mom says good night to her children and wants to make sure that all their toys have been put away, she would ask "Are the Moomins back in the valley?"

The Moomins are well known outside Finland, in the English-speaking world and in Japan. What nobody could foresee was the surge of a "Moomin boom" (*muumibuumi*), an unprecedented wave of popularity which made the Moomins a truly cosmopolitan phenomenon. The Moomin boom started in Japan, where the popularity of the characters went sky-high in the 1990s, with adventures in an animation series of more than 100 parts. The Daiei company adopted the Moomins as mascots in their shopping centers. Finnair had Moomins painted on their planes that frequent the Helsinki–Tokyo route.

A permanent achievement of the Moomin boom is the fun place for children, the Moomin World theme park which was built next to the old town of Naantali (near Turku in southwestern Finland). The Moomin world (Swedish *Muminvärlden*, Finnish *Muumimaailma*) is the village where the Moomins live, with the Moomin House (painted in the color of the blueberry) as its center. The theme park is visited by many families during the summer season (mid–June to mid–August). The control of the whole Moomin business still lies in the hands of the Jansson family which has turned down offers from the Walt Disney Company that was interested in purchasing the theme park.

Maybe, one day, the Moomin world in Naantali will not be the only fun park dedicated to Tove Jansson's heritage. For some time already a Finnish company (FinTech Global) has been engaged in a project to establish a Moomin fun park in Japan. For this purpose the company has acquired land near the city of Hanno. FinTech Global is cooperating with a Japanese firm (Moomin Monogatari) that will carry out the construction work. The intention is to have construction completed by 2017 when the park will be opened to the public. The stakes are high, and about a million visitors are expected annually. Should such expectations materialize the fun park at Hanno would be a Moomin park in its own class. The number of visitors to the Moomin world in Naantali is much more modest, in the range of 200,000 annually (Lehtonen 2015a).

In the Art Museum of Tampere in central Finland, there is a special section, the Moominvalley, with some 2,000 exhibits that are all based on Tove Jansson's books. Here, her skills as artist and illustrator are perhaps best manifested.

The popularity of the Moomins seems limitless, and ever more souvenirs featuring the world of the Moomins enter the market. In view of the increased commercialization of the Moomins enthusiasts of the first day have articulated their concern that the original philosophical message for children—living in peace and cooperating with others—might become banal through the iconization of the characters. As things are, the Moomin movement has developed a growing magnitude.

## Angry Birds *and Other Computer Games*

Computer technology is not only extensively used in Finland, advanced stages of it have also been developed by Finnish experts in the field. Finnish ingenuity went global with the Finnish software engineer Linus Torvalds (b. 1969) who developed the Linux kernel (git). This kernel turned out to become the most popular device in operating systems. For his achievements, Torvalds was awarded the Millennium Technology Prize (awarded by the Technology Academy Finland), in 2012, and the IEEE Computer Society Computer Pioneer Award in 2014. Torvalds lives in the U.S. (Dunthorpe, Oregon) with his family.

The development of video games in Finland started out in the early 1980s, with the introduction of a home computer model, the Commodore 64. From early on, Finnish game companies created new games or devised localizations of imported games. It did not take long before video game making developed into a domain of Finnish industry. In 2003, the Nokia company introduced N-Gage, a sixth generation hand-held gaming device. By 2007, more than two million N-Gage devices had been sold. Such sales, though, were no match for the most successful sixth generation device at that time, the Nintendo Game Boy Advance. The sales had been over 81 million.

Since the beginning of the 21st century, the Finnish video game industry has been booming on the international markets. Still below the record figures of big export companies such as Kone or Neste Oil, the Finnish computer game industry, nevertheless, is thriving and is the only domain of Finnish economy for which an exceptional growth is expected. One of the greatest surprises in computer game industry was the launching of the game *Angry Birds* in December 2009. *Angry Birds* were created by the Finnish company Rovio Entertainment (founded in 2003). Within the next year more than 12 million copies had been sold. The game proliferated on the international markets in various versions and adaptations. By January 2014, *Angry Birds* had been downloaded more than two billion times (Long 2014). This game has been called "the largest mobile app success the world has seen so far" (Eriksen and Abdymomunov 2011).

Since its first appearance, various genres of the game have been developed and made available on the market, among which are puzzles (2009, 2010, 2011, 2012, 2013), racing (2013), role-playing (2014, 2015), side-scrolling shooter (2014), tile-matching (2015). Characters of the *Angry Birds* feature in a cookbook published by Rovio Entertainment and, in 2012, a paperback book was published by National Geographic, under the title *Angry Birds Space: A Furious Flight into the Final Frontier*. Angry Birds Comics have been published by IDW Publishing since June 2014. The Finnish company Olvi offers Angry Birds soft drinks. A computer-animated feature film, *The Angry Birds Movie*, was released in May 2016. This is a cooperation project between Rovio Entertainment and Sony Pictures Image works. An English-language version was shown in the United States, and a Chinese version in China.

Another Finnish success story with worldwide sales is Supercell, founded in Helsinki in June 2010. Its CEO is Ilkka Paananen. In 2013, Supercell has been referred to as "the fastest growing game company ever" (Strauss 2013). By the end of 2014, Supercell had developed into the world's biggest company for computer games (Saarinen 2014). The company has released three successful games: *Clash of Clans*, *Hay Day*, and *Boom Beach*. In October 2013, two Japanese enterprises (GungHo Online and SoftBank) acquired 51 percent of Supercell. Since summer 2015 SoftBank is the sole external shareholder, owning some 73 percent of all shares.

An interesting link has been established between computer games and performance levels in school education. While Finland had ranked high in earlier years of the PISA reports, by 2013 it had dropped considerably, out of the top ten, and this with respect to all domains (math, reading skills, science; see Chapter 6). According to a widely-held popular opinion, computer games are blamed for the decrease in performance. Arguably, young people spend too much time playing video games instead of doing homework or attending to themes favored in school programs. On the other hand, positive explanations relating to computer games for an improvement in certain skills have been given. In statistical terms, the level of boys' skills in English is higher than that of girls. At least one concrete reason for this discrepancy can be given: boys spend more of their leisure time than girls playing English-language video games. So far, scientific analysis has failed to prove any direct negative link between performance at school and the playing of computer games (Desai et al. 2010).

# 8

# Do the Finns Have a
# Recipe for World Peace?
*Minding One's Own Business and That
of Others in a Cooperative Fashion*

Many people throughout the world wonder why there are so many conflicts and local wars and why partisans in conflicts seem to be incapable or unwilling to come to a peaceful agreement. Cynics may comment that human beings are an underdeveloped species that is prone to excessive violence and military confrontation. And there are voices that convey a quite different message; e.g., "Peace is a question of will. All conflicts can be settled" (Martti Ahtisaari, 2008). The one who made this pronouncement is a peace broker with an international reputation from whose services people have profited in many parts of the world (see below).

The Finns fought wars to defend their independence, and they fought wars that were not theirs. They were agents at the command of the powers that ruled Finland without Finnish participation. That was the case with the Thirty Years' War (1618–1648), when Finland formed part of the Kingdom of Sweden. As a Protestant country Sweden sided with other Protestant countries to fight against Catholic supremacy in Europe, and Finnish soldiers participated in the war under Swedish command. The Swedish king, Gustav II Adolf (also known in Anglo-Saxon literature as Gustavus Adolphus) who was killed in a battle in 1632, was an experienced military leader who relied on his special forces, the Finnish cavalry. The Finns became (in)famous with their battle cry *hakkaa päälle!* ("hit [with the sable]; cut in !"). From this war cry derives the name Hakkapeliter by which the Europeans knew the Finnish cavalrists.

In the 19th century when Finland was under Russian rule, Finnish troops—usually under the command of Finland-Swedish officers—had to be loyal to the Tsar. Until Finland's independence, many Finland-Swedes and Finns served as officers in the Russian army. As a consequence of one of the wars of the Russian Empire against its neighbors, the endeavor of Finnish peacekeeping missions in the world took shape.

## Prelude: Finland's Contribution to Securing Bulgaria's Independence

Finland's history of peacekeeping missions in the world extends beyond the modern era, into the 19th century. A Finland-Swede with a special mission is still well remembered in Bulgaria today, and this is Johan Casimir Ehrnrooth (1833–1913) (Ehrnrooth 1967). What associates a Finland-Swede with Bulgaria was the Russian-Turkish war (1877–1878), the outcome of which was the liberation of the former Ottoman colony and the founding of the modern nation-state of Bulgaria. As an officer (commander of a division) in the tsarist army, Ehrnrooth was wounded in this war and promoted to lieutenant general.

After the war, Tsar Alexander II devised plans for the newly independent Bulgaria to become a kind of buffer state between Russia and the Ottoman Empire. The German-born Alexander von Battenberg was selected as Duke of Bulgaria since he was the favorite of Russia's ruler. Ehrnrooth was freed from military service and sent to function as adviser to the new ruler of Bulgaria. In April 1880, Ehrnrooth was appointed defense minister. About a year later, in 1881, there was rioting in Bulgaria and the Duke left the country. In this difficult situation, Ehrnrooth had to take care of state affairs, and he functioned, in addition to being defense minister, also as minister of the interior and of foreign affairs, and eventually he became chairman of the ministerial council, which corresponds to the office of prime minister. Ehrnrooth put an end to the riots and stabilized the political situation. When Alexander returned to Bulgaria, he was made absolute ruler of the country by the National Council.

Ehrnrooth resigned from his political offices and returned to Russia where he was reenlisted into the register of officers of the tsarist army. In his later years, Ehrnrooth worked for the Finnish Ministry which was represented in St. Petersburg. In April 1891, Ehrnrooth retired and he was also granted leave from the army. Ehrnrooth spent the rest of his life in Helsinki. The task that Ehrnrooth carried out and brought to a successful conclusion would be nowadays called "crisis management." A hundred years later, in the 1980s, another political representative of Finland engaged in international crisis management. That mediator for peace is Martti Ahtisaari (see below).

## Finnish Peacekeeping Missions in the World Since the 1950s

Postwar politics of the Finnish governments have been devoted to the principle of neutrality, including good-neighbor relations with the Soviet Union and, nowadays, with the modern Russian state. Finland's neutrality was appreciated by both western and eastern countries during the era of the Cold War and it provided favorable conditions for Finnish peacekeeping missions with UN mandates in many parts of the world.

In 1955, Finland was admitted to membership in the United Nations. Only one year later, the first Finnish detachment of 250 infantry soldiers participated, as members of the UN Emergency Force (UNEF), based in Egypt, in peacekeeping in the Sinai and the Gaza Strip. Since then Finland has contributed continuously to UN-authorized peacekeeping missions throughout the world. For more than half a century, Finnish soldiers have participated in various UN peacekeeping missions, involving more than 40,000 ser-

**Figure 34: A female soldier of the Finnish peacekeeping force in Afghanistan being greeted by an Afghan girl, Mazar-i-Sharif, 31 January 2013 (photograph: Jussi Nukari; Photo Agency Lehtikuva).**

vicemen. In light of this input, Finland is rightly referred to as a "great power in peacekeeping," and this has become a notion of national pride (figure 34).

Yet, the high standards of humanitarian considerations involved are somehow overshadowed by the reality of organizing peacekeeping missions. The reality is that such missions are expensive (for Finland) and they bear the risk of tragic outcome, with Finnish soldiers losing their lives and becoming victims, in ambushes, suicide bombings or open combat. In political rhetoric, the peacekeepers' motivation to apply for participation in a UN mission are described as stabilizing living conditions and helping people in crisis areas, but for the average applicant (at an age of 27), more mundane reasons come to bear. In 2010, a survey was conducted, with the following results as regards the applicants' motivation: gaining professional experience (36.5 percent), salary (20.8), desire for variation (10.4), the challenge of the task (9.4). Only 4.2 percent of applicants gave the humanitarian input (helping people) priority (Kotilainen 2011).

Whatever the reasons for Finnish volunteers to participate in UN peacekeeping activities, their input and their efforts have been significant. The list of UN missions with Finnish participation is impressive (see a survey of missions until the early 1990s in Tillotson 1993: 291ff.). There were in 2016 four UN-led operations in which Finland is participating:

- UN Interim Force in Lebanon (UNIFIL)
- UN Truce Supervision Organization in the Middle East (UNTSO)
- UN Military Observer Group in India and Pakistan (UNMOGIP)
- UN Mission in Liberia (UNMIL)

In addition, Finland has participated in NATO-led operations: Kosovo Force (KFOR), authorized by the UN Security Council Resolution 1244 (issued in 1999), and Afghanistan (ISAF), authorized by UN Security Council Resolutions 1386, 1413 and 1444.

By the early 1990s it had already become clear that Finland, with its efforts in international peacekeeping, was in its own class, and this image has not changed.

---

UN (United Nations) missions
OSCE (Organization for Security and Co-operation in Europe) missions
EU (European Union) missions
EUNAVFOR (European Union Naval Force Operation) missions
EUTM (European Union Training Mission) missions
EUCAP (European Council Action Plan) missions
NATO (North Atlantic Treaty Organization) missions

**Europe**
OSCE missions (Kosovo, Ukraine, Makedonia)
EU missions (Kosovo, Bosnia-Hercegovina, Georgia, Ukraine, Moldova)
NATO mission (Kosovo)

**Africa**
UN missions (Liberia, Somalia, Mali, South Sudan)
EU missions:
EUNAVFOR ATALANTA mission (Somalian coast)
EUNAVFOR MED SOPHIA (Libyan coast)
EUTM missions (Somalia, Mali)
EUCAP missions:
EUCAP SAHEL (Mali, Niger)
EUCAP NESTOR (Djibouti)

**Near East**
UN mission (Libanon)
EU mission (Palestinian area)

**Middle East**
OIR (Operation Inherent Resolve) Iraq

**Asia**
UN mission (border area between India and Pakistan)
NATO mission (Afghanistan)
EU mission (Afghanistan)
OSCE mission (Tadzhikistan)

---

**Figure 35: Finland's participation in international crisis management (Finnish Authorities; Ministry of Foreign Affairs; http://formin.finland.fi/public/download.aspx?ID=38854&GUID ={93480D5E-EE22-4E3D-BEE5-FF15B0C38C4E}).**

The moral and manpower contribution of Finland towards UN peace-keeping is far beyond the proportion that might reasonably be expected from a nation of less than five million people. This is a record and
standard of which every Finn is justifiably proud. As the international reputation won in the Winter War
fades a little with each new generation, an esteem of a different kind is gradually taking its place. Now
Finland is thought of as the nation to which the United Nations Secretary-General turns without hesita-
tion when the core of a new peace-keeping mission is needed [Tillotson 1993: 305].

## Getting Along with World Powers

Finland is not a member of any military alliance. The option for Finland has been
NATO, and discussion of the conditions of membership flares up, every now and
then. Opinion polls show that Finns do not feel a need to join NATO although the percentage of those who favor an alliance has recently increased. This is due to the political
instability in eastern Europe, caused by the Russian annexation of Crimea and the way
Russia fuels conflict in eastern Ukraine. Finland has remained outside NATO—despite
cooperation with NATO troops in crisis management—and the country did not change
its course of neutrality after the political changes in eastern Europe, that is after 1989–
90, when several of the former socialist states applied for membership in the NATO
alliance.

### Finland's Flexibility to Cope with Foreign Rule: Per Brahe and Alexander II in Focus

Every nation carries memories of its past. Those memories may be light and joyful
when remembering periods of economic progress and social advancement. On the other
hand, memories of the past may be stressful and gloomy when thinking of times of war
and disaster. When the Finns look back into their history they find both. Unfortunately,
there is an abundance of heavy memories relating to the many wars and to the suffering
of the population that nobody can erase. Fortunately, as a counterweight, there are memories of how Finland and its society modernized and how the Finns have mastered the
challenges of globalization.

The Finns have learned to live with those memories in their characteristic way, by
professing a pragmatic attitude. They do not blind themselves with exaggerated pride,
nor do they pity themselves. They do not lament or blame others for things that went
wrong. They take their stand and balance their memories to profit from lessons learned.
This pragmatic mindset readily crystallizes in collective manifestations of national memory. The Finns have their own ways to remember innovative developments during the
periods when they were governed by foreign rulers, and innovative developments can
be judged by their imprints on Finnish society as a whole.

Finland is a rare example of a modern independent state where one finds the statues
of foreign rulers on public display. One was erected in Turku, the other in Helsinki. The
one in Turku features a former governor, representative of the King of Sweden in Finland,
Count Per Brahe the Younger (1602–1680). The one in Helsinki depicts a Russian Tsar:
Alexander II (1818–1881; reigned 1855–1881). After Finland had gained independence, in
1917–18, those statues were not demolished or removed. There are good reasons why they

stand in their place as before, and this has to do with the benevolent attitude they took vis-à-vis Finland and how their vision of prosperity came to bear.

## Per Brahe

Before coming to Finland, Per Brahe gained fame as a military leader, in the Polish War (1626–29) and in the Thirty Years War (1618–1648). Brahe served the Swedish Crown during two terms, from 1637 until 1640 and from 1648 until 1654, as Governor General in Finland. In Finnish history books, the Count is remembered as one of the great innovators of the country. During the few years of his government, Brahe carried out an extensive program of reforms, with the following range:

- measures to reform Finland's administration;
- introduction of a postal service;
- the founding of ten new towns;
- improvement of commerce;
- development of agricultural techniques;
- the promotion of education.

Per Brahe is credited with the founding of the Royal Academy of Turku which he inaugurated in 1640 and of which he became the first chancellor. The statue of Brahe, erected in the Brahenpuisto and revealed in 1888, is made of bronze and was designed by the same sculptor who did the statue of the female seer at the Runeberg monument in Helsinki, Walter Runeberg. At the base of the Brahe statue one finds the following inscription: "I was well pleased with the land and the land with me." The second part of this statement still holds true. Brahe's achievements for Finland are gratefully remembered in history books.

## Alexander II

The relationship of Finland with the Tsars of Russia depended very much on their attitude toward the Grand Duchy and, ultimately, on their political skills as rulers. There was the "bad Tsar," Nicholas II, who imposed restrictions on the liberties that the Finns had gained and practiced a policy of suppression. And there was the "good Tsar," Alexander II who set manifold reforms in motion.

The reign of Alexander I had brought some external innovations, such as the architectural reshaping of the center of Helsinki (see Chapter 7). On the political level, there was practically no activity in the Grand Duchy. The Diet of Finland that had been reassured, in 1809, by Alexander I to be an institution in support of the autonomy of the Grand Duchy, remained dormant and did not convene. Things changed when Alexander II, the liberal ruler, in the 1860s, took special interest in Finland and in the reform of the country's infrastructure, political, economic and cultural (Klinge 1997: 201ff.). Alexander's benevolent support for the modernization of Finland was not motivated simply by the emperor's goodwill. There were pragmatic political considerations that stood behind the Tsar's reform program.

The modernization of Finland was embedded in a wider political scheme. The benefits of the reform program would strengthen the status of the Grand Duchy within Russia and, in the process, the achievements of modernization would serve to distance Finland from its former sovereign, neighboring Sweden. When Alexander II, in 1863, re-convened the Diet of Finland, this meant the practical re-activation of the status of autonomy that Alexander I had granted earlier. The introduction of a separate currency for Finland, the *markka*, in 1860 can be interpreted as symbolic of the process of distancing the country from Sweden.

Within the Grand Duchy itself, Russian politics followed the old wisdom of imperial ruling *divide et impera* ("divide and rule"). Russian interests were oriented toward a weakening of Finland-Swedish prevalence in economic and cultural life. Substantial support of Finnish national culture would strengthen the feeling of sameness among the Finns and such a movement would eventually produce a counterweight against dominance by Finland-Swedes (Schoolfield 1996: 115ff.). At the time of Alexander's reforms, nobody could yet foresee how vigorous the Finnish national movement would become and that it would, eventually, challenge Russian imperial supremacy.

The reforms of the "good Tsar" would not have been fully implemented, were it not for the efforts of the right experts who were given the authority to act at the right time, above all Snellman (see Chapters 2 and 6). The reforms in the economic sector (industrial development, commerce, a railroad network under a separate Finnish administration) and in the cultural domain (the upgrading of Finnish to become an official language alongside Swedish, the introduction of the folk-school) owe their smooth implementation to the organizational talents of Snellman as Finland's major innovator.

The Finns kept positive memories of the "good Tsar" who was assassinated in 1881 and they erected a monument to honor him, posthumously. The sculptor Walter Runeberg crafted the monument to Alexander II that was erected in the center of the Senate Square in Helsinki, in 1894. This monument was neither damaged nor demolished in later periods, even during the times of hardship when Finland was at war with Russia. In their long-lasting memory, the Finns cherish the benefits of the reforms carried out during the rule of Alexander II and from which they still profit today. This monument to the "good Tsar" and its intactness are illustrative of the Finns' sense of pragmatism. The Finns have learned to control their national sentiments, not to blind their common sense with anti–Russian resentment, regardless of how strained Finnish-Russian political relations may be at times.

## The Odds of "Finlandization"

During the era of the "Cold War" (until the dissolution of the Soviet state) many foreigners misunderstood the essence of Finland's neutrality and thought of Finnish politics as following a course of submission to Soviet interests. Western politicians crafted a special term which carries condescending connotations: Finlandisierung (in German), Finlandization (in English). "During the Cold War, scholars and politicians outside Finland defined Finlandization as a small power's servile policy toward its larger neighbor. Finland served for many in the West as a warning example to other democracies facing Soviet power" (Lavery 2006: 139).

The attitude of negative stereotyping of Finland's position in western Europe was unsubstantiated and reflected ignorance; it was mostly ideologically motivated, fuelled by conservative and right-wing circles in western Europe whose representatives tended to downplay the fact that Finland never was a member of the socialist bloc of Soviet satellite states and that the western foundations of Finnish society were reconfirmed in the postwar period. Muddying the discussion about Finlandization in the west was the association of this concept with the ideological background of Soviet superpower politics. Many in the west misunderstood the Finnish course of neutrality as a reflection of Soviet power plays and Communist ideology.

Finlandization was translated into Finnish as *suomettuminen*, which, however, transposed stereotyping attitudes of western politics and does not reflect Finnish political pragmatism. The Finnish way of neutrality is to avoid becoming the target of a powerful neighbor's expansionism. In order to hold a balance for their country, Finnish politicians do their best to remain below their neighbor's political radar.

One of the reasons for misunderstandings about the Finnish position in the west was perhaps a lack of regular contact and experience, on the side of western politicians, with their Russian counterparts. For Finland, establishing relations in an atmosphere of mutual trust with the former superpower, the Soviet Union, meant activation of the sense of pragmatism that has guided Finnish foreign politics for more than half a century.

On the level of global politics Finland's neutrality gained recognition and appreciation. This can be concluded from the constellation of neutral states vis-à-vis the western and the eastern bloc. From the 1950s to the decline of Soviet rule there were only three states which functioned like oases between the ideological currents: Switzerland, Austria and Finland. And there were only three cities where political representatives of the East and the West would meet: Geneva, Vienna and Helsinki. Geneva and Vienna became the venues for negotiations about the reduction of nuclear arms.

## The Conference on Security and Cooperation in Europe (1975)

Helsinki's role as a venue for international politics may have been valued even higher than that of the other havens of neutrality because it was only in Helsinki, not in Geneva or Vienna, that the leaders of the superpowers and the heads of state of many other countries from the east and west once met. That was on the occasion of the Conference on Security and Cooperation in Europe that had been ongoing for some three years before it was concluded in Helsinki in the summer of 1975. The grand finale was the meeting of the delegations, including the heads of state, from 35 countries, hosted by Finland's president Urho Kekkonen.

At the conference, almost all European states were represented, with the exception of Albania and Andorra. From outside Europe, the United States and Canada took part in the conference. As the outcome of their negotiations, the delegations chiseled out accords that were included in the *Declaration on Principles Guiding Relations between Participating States*. This declaration, consecutively signed by the heads of state on 1 August 1975, is also known as *The Decalogue* because it is comprised of ten points:

I. Sovereign equality, respect for the rights inherent in sovereignty

II. Refraining from the threat or use of force

III. Inviolability of frontiers

IV. Territorial integrity of States

V. Peaceful settlement of disputes

VI. Non-intervention in internal affairs

VII. Respect for human rights and fundamental freedoms, including the freedom of thought, conscience, religion or belief

VIII. Equal rights and self-determination of peoples

IX. Co-operation among States

X. Fulfillment in good faith of obligations under international law

The Helsinki Accords (http://www.britannica.com/EBchecked/topic/260615/Helsinki-Accords; retrieved 16 November 2014) did not have the status of a treaty and, thus, they were not binding. So their observation and implementation were totally dependent on the goodwill of leaders and politicians in the signatory states. As history teaches us, none of these accords has prevailed up to the present. But the symbolic value for history books remains (Bange and Niedhart 2008). The Helsinki Accords were the first, and the only, attempt to agree on the basics of international politics during an era of continuing tension. The Helsinki Conference set in motion a process that has been termed "Cold Peace" (Tarkka 2015: 75ff.), this being a more constructive alternative to the permanent "Cold War."

Although many idealists have claimed that the era of the Cold War ended with the fall of the Berlin wall in 1989, the disintegration of the socialist bloc of states in eastern Europe in 1990 and the demise of the Soviet Union in 1991, pragmatists tend to view the period without overt ideological confrontation that began after 1990 as an intermezzo that ended with the occupation of Crimea by Russia in early 2014, and the crisis in eastern Ukraine, fuelled by Russia. Thus, ideological barriers between Russian expansionism and western political doctrines of democratic cooperation have been renewed. It is not far-fetched to view the current state of political affairs as a reactivation of the kind of overt tension that the Europeans experienced before. Can it be expected that Helsinki might become the venue for yet another conference on security in Europe? Finnish political know-how for mediating between parties with differing interests is certainly available.

## The Art of Negotiating: Martti Ahtisaari and His Imprints on World Peace

Finland's international engagement in peacekeeping received worldwide recognition when Martti Ahtisaari, the country's tenth president (in office from 1994 till 2000), was awarded the Nobel Peace Prize in 2008, "for his efforts on several continents and over more than three decades, to resolve international conflicts" (http://www.nobelprize.org/nobel_prizes/peace/laureates/2008/; retrieved 1 May 2015).

The city where Martti Ahtisaari was born, Viipuri (Russian Vyborg), is now Russian territory. When Martti was still a little boy, his family had to evacuate their home in Viipuri since this was ceded, after the Winter War, to the Soviets in spring 1940. The experience of being a refugee at an early age might have decisively impacted Ahtisaari's intentionality to engage in developing aid projects and in crisis management. As a young man, Ahtisaari spent several years in Pakistan, where he led the YMCA's physical education training establishment in Karachi. Starting in 1965, Ahtisaari became active in Finland's political institutions, first in the Ministry of Foreign Affairs and its Bureau for International Development Aid. Since the late 1970s Ahtisaari worked as a UN Commissioner for Namibia (Merikallio and Ruokanen 2011).

## Achieving Independence for Namibia

It is no exaggeration to state that Ahtisaari's mission to achieve independence for Namibia was a truly adventurous one, with many ups and downs and even occasional threats to his safety. The transition for Namibia, from a territorial part of South Africa to an independent state, turned out to become a prolonged and difficult process. Ahtisaari's first experience with Namibia dates to the period from 1977 to 1981 when he, as a UN Commissioner for Namibia, engaged in negotiations with the governments of the states that, at that time, were involved in Namibian affairs.

The 1975 detachment of Angola, former colony of Portugal, from the motherland had resulted in civil war, with ideological polarizations typical of the era of Cold War. There were the leftists and these were supported by Cuban troops that had been sent by Fidel Castro to support the socialist movement. The government of South Africa supported Angola's right-wing fighters (organized as the UNITA) and had deployed troops in southern Angola, to prevent Angolan leftists from instigating insurgency in Namibia and the Angolan government from stabilizing its communist regime.

Ahtisaari's initial efforts to negotiate an agreement on political issues were cut short by a move of the Americans who had a major influence on the UN mission for Namibia. A new political doctrine, a linkage policy, had been devised by Chester Crocker, who had been appointed assistant secretary of state for African affairs and functioned in the administration of the newly elected U.S. president Ronald Reagan (in office 1981–1989). As a basis for negotiations with representatives of Angola, Cuba and South Africa, Crocker advocated a linkage between Cuban troop withdrawal (according to the 1978 UN Security Council Resolution 435), South African troop withdrawal from southern Angola and the transition of the South African held Namibian territory to UN control. For a few years, the Cubans were reluctant to negotiate. Eventually, Crocker's proposals were accepted by Cuban leader Fidel Castro in September 1986, and the South African government followed suit.

Yet, no agreement was reached involving all parties. Diplomats made a detour, with representatives from Angola and the United States engaging in bilateral talks in June 1987. Meanwhile, the civil war in Angola and the clashes of Cuban troops with South African units in southern Angola took their toll. The military situation had ended up in deadlock and, eventually, increasing losses on both sides brought all parties to the negotiating table. Despite various setbacks, an agreement was finally reached. The document, known as the Tripartite Accord or the New York Accord, was signed by representatives of the governments of Cuba, Angola and South Africa, on 22 December 1988.

The political situation changed dramatically when the UN Commissioner for Namibia, Bernt Carlsson, who had been engaged in the negotiations since 1981, was killed in a plane crash on the eve of the signing of the Tripartite Accord. Several months later, in April 1989, Ahtisaari was re-commissioned to lead, as the UN Special Representative, the UN Transition Assistance Group (UNTAG), monitoring troop withdrawal and the withdrawal of South African authorities from Namibia. UNTAG had no resources for military supervision of the implementation of the accord, and their mission was in danger to be jeopardized by repeated incursions of rebels from Angola. These were insurgents in the military wing of the movement for Namibia's independence (SWAPO) whose intention was to drive out the South Africans from Namibia by force.

Ahtisaari was urged, by the South African appointed administrator-general in Namibia, to allow South African troops to rebuff SWAPO's incursions, and Ahtisaari agreed. South African troops and SWAPO guerrillas engaged in fierce fighting in the northern part of Namibia. UNTAG became the target of political populism and found itself in the crossfire of public criticism when various groups manipulated the reignited conflict for their ideological interests. Ahtisaari himself got caught in the crossfire of opposing outside interests. He was openly criticized by representatives of the British Council of Churches who had visited Namibia and blamed Ahtisaari for making too many concessions to the South Africans, by allowing troops from South Africa to be deployed in Namibia to fight rebels. "There is a widespread feeling that too many concessions were made to South African personnel and preferences and that Martti Ahtisaari was not forceful enough in his dealings with the South Africans" (Kinnock 1990: 19). Contrasting with this assessment was the position of the South African Civil Cooperation Bureau (CCB) that launched a campaign to scapegoat Ahtisaari for not being cooperative enough regarding South African interests in Namibia. As was revealed in a hearing of the Truth and Reconciliation Commission in September 2000 (http://www.doj.gov.za./trc/amntrans/2000/200928ct.htm; retrieved 21 September 2015), the CCB had been given the task to assault Ahtisaari in a coup that was planned in July 1989. Ahtisaari did not attend the arranged meeting and, thus, was saved.

South Africa withdrew its troops from Angola by August 1988, and Cuban troops were repatriated between January 1989 and May 1991. In November 1989, UN monitored elections were held in Namibia, and the country became officially independent in March 1990. South Africa still kept a stronghold (the port of Walvis Bay) in Namibia after that date, as an insurance for the new Namibian government to come to terms with the newly established democratic institutions. The South African presence in Namibia ended in late 1992. Ahtisaari was honored, both by the new Namibian government and by South Africa. He was granted honorary citizenship in the new African state and, from the government of South Africa, Ahtisaari received the O R Tambo award for "his outstanding achievement as a diplomat and commitment to the cause of freedom in Africa and peace in the world."

## Negotiating Peace for Kosovo

Kosovo, independent since 2008, is the last part of the former Yugoslav state that gained independence after the dissolution of Yugoslavia, beginning in 1991. There had been continuous ethnic frictions between the Serbian central government in Belgrade and the southern province of Kosovo with its majority population of Albanians (Kosovars). Under the government lead by Slobodan Milosević (president of Serbia, as part of the former Yugoslav state, from 1989 to 1997; president of the new Yugoslavia from 1997 to 2000) there was a surge of Serbian nationalism and, as a consequence, Serbian-Albanian relations in Kosovo became ever more conflict-stricken. The Serbian army started a campaign of ethnic cleansing, either forcing Albanians to leave their homes and emigrate or killing local residents. Many hundreds of thousands of Kosovars fled their home country and were accepted, as fugitives, by various states in western Europe.

The situation became untenable, and hostilities escalated to a full-scale military conflict. Confronted with the terror campaigns of Serbian army units, local Albanians formed rebel groups, later called the Kosovo Liberation Army (KLA), that were armed with weapons smuggled into Kosovo from Albania. Weapons were also obtained from local Serbian police stations and army posts that became the target of sabotage acts and were raided. The nature of armed hostilities between the Serbian army and guerrilla groups changed to a full-scale war. The beginning of the Kosovo War is dated to February 1998. Diplomatic attempts to solve the conflict failed and, in March 1999, NATO forces carried out air strikes against industrial installations in Serbia and Serbian military facilities in Kosovo in a campaign that was labeled "humanitarian war" ("Endgame in Kosovo," *New York Times*, 9 December 2007).

Starting in spring 1999, the heads of western states urged Milosević to step down as president, and Great Britain's Tony Blair made plans to send British ground troops into Kosovo. Martti Ahtisaari led a Finnish-Russian delegation to Belgrade for crucial talks to end the war. It must have been Ahtisaari's personal initiative and Milosević's insight that the Russians would not intervene on behalf of the Serbs that caused the Serbian president to accept the terms proposed by the delegation, on 3 June 1999. After a tumultuous debate over the agreement in the Serbian parliament the proposal was adopted, followed by ratification by the North Atlantic Council. The air strikes were suspended. As a consequence of the UN Security Council Resolution 1244, adopted in June 1999, the Serbian army withdrew its troops from Kosovo, and NATO-led peacekeeping units (KFOR = Kosovo Force) entered Kosovo. The resolution 1244 envisaged transitional UN administration for Kosovo.

Ahtisaari, the architect of the agreement to end the war, assumed a central role in devising a plan to bring political stability to the war torn region. A diplomatic initiative to start negotiations about the future status of Kosovo was made by the Norwegian diplomat Kai Eide who, in October 2005, submitted a UN-commissioned report endorsed by the Security Council. Multilateral talks, involving the political leadership of Serbia and Kosovo and diplomatic representatives of the EU, the United States and Russia, started in February 2006, led by UN special envoy Martti Ahtisaari.

A year later, Ahtisaari had elaborated a draft proposal concerning the status of Kosovo as one of "supervised independence" and had submitted his proposal to the political leaders in Serbia and Kosovo. By July 2007, the draft text had been communicated to the United States and the EU members of the Security Council, and it was subsequently revised several times to respond to Russian concerns about territorial sovereignty. Serbia was willing to grant Kosovo far-reaching autonomy status, yet, independence was out of the question. The term "independence" was not explicitly mentioned in the text of the proposal although politicians in Kosovo and in the western states perceived the context as implying statehood for Kosovo. It became obvious, though, that the positions of western states vis-à-vis those of Serbia and Russia were too far apart, so that the Security Council discarded Ahtisaari's draft proposal.

In January 2008, the Parliamentary Assembly of the Council of Europe called for continuation of the negotiations with all parties about the status of Kosovo. In light of the stalemate of diplomacy at that stage, the Assembly of Kosovo, in February 2008, unilaterally declared Kosovo independent. This step, in practice, meant an unofficial adoption of the contents of Ahtisaari's draft resolution. In May 2008, Russia, China and India called for the talks to be resumed according to the resolution of the Council of Europe. Yet, their call represented a minority position in the Kosovo agenda. Many states spontaneously recognized Kosovo's independence. As of July 2016, their number has risen to 113. In July 2010, the International Court of Justice ruled that Kosovo's option for political independence is legal and does not violate international law.

## Negotiating Autonomy for the Aceh Region in Indonesia

Aceh is a region in the northern part of the island of Sumatra which forms part of the territory of Indonesia. The population in this part of Indonesia suffered great losses when the tsunami hit the coastal villages in December 2004. For decades, between 1976 and 2005, a local separatist movement (the Free Aceh Movement or GAM) fought a guerrilla war against Indonesian government forces in the so-called Aceh insurgency. It had become clear by the 1990s that the Aceh guerrillas would not achieve independence by fighting the government and that military supremacy of the Indonesian army over the region was impossible to reach.

The given stalemate called for diplomatic mediation to end the prolonged conflict. Several attempts were made to achieve a ceasefire and to arrange for subsequent negotiations between the two parties, the GAM and the Indonesian government, but they failed because the positions of the participants in the conflict were too far apart. The Indonesian government would not accept political independence of the region, and GAM would not accept any form whatever of defined autonomy or self-government.

In 2005, Martti Ahtisaari launched a new initiative of mediation.

Using the formula that "nothing is agreed until everything is agreed," he required the two parties to agree on the broad outlines of a political formula before a ceasefire and related security arrangements would be put into effect. This placed great pressure on them to modify their positions [Aspinall 2005: viii].

Both parties made concessions and, after five rounds of intensive negotiations held between January and July, agreed on terms as laid down in a Memorandum of Understanding that was signed, in August 2005, by representatives of the Indonesian government and of the GAM. Aceh was granted far-reaching self-government, though within the confines of the Indonesian state and law.

Many villages and cities in the Aceh region had been devastated by the tsunami. Only after GAM agreed to demilitarize could reconstruction progress. Since peace has been given an opportunity to materialize, the people in Aceh have regained their faith in the future and have engaged in rebuilding their communities. So far, peace holds and, hopefully, the younger generation may grow up without the threat of military confrontation in their home country.

While the autonomy status was negotiated for the Aceh region in Indonesia a nongovernmental organization, specialized in crisis management, gained international media attention. This is the Crisis Management Initiative (CMI) founded by Martti Ahtisaari in 2000. The headquarters of CMI is Helsinki, with another office in Brussels. The organization, in its role as peace broker, has actively contributed to mediating between parties in conflict and to providing stabilizing measures in Liberia and Ethiopia, in the Middle East and in the Black Sea region. Crisis management aims to raise awareness on conflict resolution and is oriented to the following specific goals (https://en.wikipedia.org/wiki/Crisis_Man agement_Initiative; 10 June 2015):

- CMI contributes to conflict resolution through mediation, dialogue and confidence building processes
- CMI seeks to consolidate and sustain peace processes through supporting state capacity and participatory planning and prioritization

As of November 2015, a light counterweight exists to the serious matter of world peace as processed through the mediation of CMI. This is the Christmas calendar publicized by the Finnish Ministry of Foreign Affairs, the first calendar of its kind in the world. In each of its 24 windows, one finds a specific symbol signifying Finnishness. The symbols are designed as Finland-emojis based on the Japanese model of stereotyping signs which are commonly used in digital communication as elements in e-mail messages and in SMS messages on mobile phones.

Among the emojis designed for promoting the Finnish country brand are an elk, a bear, Santa Claus, trees, people in the sauna, a Finnish flag and a very exclusive motif: a stylized picture of Martti Ahtisaari, raising his hand and making the V-sign with his fingers, calling for "world peace" (http://formin.finland.fi/public/default.aspx?cont entid=336964&nodeid=15145&contentlan=2&culture=en-US; retrieved 4 December 2015) (figure 36).

**Figure 36: An emoji symbol featuring Martti Ahtisaari calling for world peace (Finnish Authorities; Ministry of Foreign Affairs; public relations campaign).**

# Epilogue
## *How to Cope with Accelerating Globalization*

Toward the end of the 20th century Finland was regarded by many as a forerunner of the network society, and the digitalization of communication systems in this country made fast progress. That was the time when the Nokia company was the world's top producer of mobile phones. Now, more than fifteen years later, the network society model has proliferated into many regions of the world and Finland is one among many countries where digitalization dominates the public as much as the private sectors and everybody's daily life. Living according to the standards set by network society is an aspect of globalization.

The kind of globalization that world societies have been experiencing since the beginning of this century is but an extension of the modernization process Finland went through in the postwar period. The country's economy, depending heavily on exports, is accustomed to dealing with multilateral trading transactions worldwide. The Finnish economy is highly sensitive to global economic fluctuations. For Finns, globalization is no magic word that evokes fanciful images about steady progress in all domains of life. The Finnish pragmatic sense perceives this phenomenon as it really is, a modern trend which offers opportunities but also produces negative side effects that should not be underestimated. Any economic crisis of great proportions unavoidably produces repercussions in Finland's export business. Finland was drawn into the global recession of 2007/08 and its economy is still under a remarkable strain.

What worsened the situation was the political crisis in Europe, caused by the annexation of Crimea (part of Ukraine) by Russia and by Russian interventions in eastern Ukraine. The shock waves of this disturbance of the political balance in eastern Europe not only damaged the Russian economy (including a dramatic loss of value of its currency) but also hit Finland and its strong trade relations with Russia. The Finnish position in global trade—within the European Union and with overseas countries—also weakened as demand for Finnish industrial and electronic products decreased. Finnish competitiveness is coping with the pressure of innovating market strategies, which are different in nature from the traditional challenges of securing market share. What is called for is a "digital footprint" (Isokangas and Vassinen 2011), an image—created on the net—of a brand that attracts customers.

Recent history has shown ambiguous results of the impact of globalization on national economies and policy-making. Finland, like other countries, has its share of opportunities of free movement of goods and ideas and of great mobility of its workforce within the European Union and overseas. Via cyberspace, Finland is connected with the world as is the world with Finland. Knowledge-construction is no longer possible on a mere national level. On the other hand, Finland is facing an ever increasing stream of refugees from war-torn areas of the world who have to be resettled in Finnish society. Favoring multiculturalism is no longer a national choice but it has become a necessity of crisis management. It can be foreseen that Finland will have to step up its efforts for international peacekeeping since the future scenario of international relationships suggests more, not fewer crises than today.

A major aspect of globalization is energy supply. Finland is linked to an international network of electricity distribution. This is an inter–Scandinavian network but also includes Estonia and Russia. Recent history has taught that the Russian government is willing to use its political power for price manipulation of oil and gas or for cutting supplies temporarily, strategies that were applied in the conflict with Ukraine. Until early 2014, Finland aimed at increasing trade with Russia in the energy sector because of favorable prices for Russian electricity. Such plans were by 2016 on ice and Finnish companies are well aware of the vulnerability of energy import from neighboring Russia. Moreover, since the price for Russian electricity is rising it is ever less profitable and energy imports from Russia have been decreasing significantly. Since Finland has no natural resources of gas or oil, nor significant water power, the country's energy supply relies largely on nuclear energy. Finland is among the few countries in Europe where new nuclear plants are being built. When the nuclear plant under construction, Olkiluoto 3, is operational in 2018, it is likely to provide about one third of Finland's energy demands. After the Japanese Fukushima disaster in early 2011 the German government announced that all nuclear plants in Germany would be closed after a period of transition. The transition period has been extended since it has become clear that not enough alternative energy will be available in the near future. Germany has returned to "dirty" energy resources such as coal while Finland is making efforts to get rid of coal entirely (Kettunen 2015). In the meantime Japan has opened one of its nuclear plants again.

The use of coal has been increasing worldwide. India has announced a doubling of its coal production by 2020. By 2015, some 500 new coal fired power stations had been built in India and 1000 more coal plants are planned in India and Southeast Asia. Japan will construct 40 new power plants operated with coal within the next twenty years. The use of coal is increasing in China where the construction of more than 1,100 new coal plants (with some 2,400 already operating) is envisaged for the near future (Adams 2015). This trend to favor coal runs parallel with a decrease in subsidies for renewable energy. For instance, the conservative government of Great Britain decided in early summer 2015 to cut subsidies for wind energy. The costs for constructing hundreds—or thousands—of windmills are simply too high and the supply will not suffice anyway to meet the growing demands for energy in that country. In August 2015, the British government announced its support for the exploitation of shale gas reserves in the U.K.

The technologies for renewable energy (chiefly wind and solar power) are advanced but the facilities that could be provided would not suffice to compensate for fossil fuels or nuclear energy. Finland offers high-tech to profit from renewable energy and yet, it is somehow ironic: Finland has become a forerunner for the global prospects of renewable energy but the country itself is far from any important use of such resources (STV 2014: 220f.). Things are just the opposite with respect to environmental protection. In this sector, too, Finland offers advanced technology that makes it a leader in a worldwide comparison. Finland can afford to end the use of coal. In the northern part, wind energy may soon suffice to cover the demands of the scarce population in Lapland. In other parts of Finland complete energy supply will be assured to a great extent by two recent nuclear plants under construction.

Finland, nationwide, is a showcase of how efficient environmental protection works, backed up by the mentality of its citizenry who cherish the value of an intact environment. The Finnish respect for nature of course has deep roots, reaching back far into the pre–Christian era.

What then are the other values that have stood the test of time and can be offered, by the Finns of today, to future generations? Values of traditional fabric are Finnish *sisu*, social cohesion and a vivid communitarian spirit, a functioning democratic system without the scourge of corruption, a high-grade equality of the sexes, high standards of living and social security, peaceful relationships with neighboring states and an environment with recreational potential. Trust in the functioning of Finnish society and in the doings of state authorities is another of the properties that has proven its validity. The Finns have trust in their political system because they are confident that it works on their behalf, and they have trust in their educational system because they are aware that no other system can guarantee the kind of equity it provides.

Trust in the working of this network of values creates a consciousness that being born into Scandinavian society is like winning the lottery. This extends to those lucky foreigners who live in Finland and have accommodated to the Finnish way of living. This metaphor of winning the lottery has its own tradition. It goes back to the early 1960s and is attributed to the Norwegian Dag Hammarskjöld who was then Secretary General of the United Nations. In the late 1970s, Urho Kekkonen—then president of Finland—repeated the statement. They both highly valued the achievements of the Nordic model of a welfare state.

Every now and then opinion polls are taken and there has been no significant change in the Finns' evaluation of their lives. In June 2015, some 60 percent of inhabitants in the Helsinki metropolitan area shared the view of the "winning the lottery" idea—but the percentage among people in rural areas is much higher, 73 percent (Koskinen 2015).

And what about the situation of foreigners coming to live in Finland? There were times when foreigners from eastern Europe who had a chance to resettle in Finland definitely profited from Finnish living conditions. Living in Finland gives newcomers a taste of quality, in all domains, from housing standards to education and communal infrastructure, from social security to environmental protection. And, among the great majority of Finns and foreigners alike, there is this special currency of trust in the system, trust that Finnish society flexibly copes with changes and that the right know-how is applied for managing problems once they emerge.

Perhaps it is an advantage for the Finns that their country has its own particular language-barrier that is higher than in many other cultures. The Finnish language is the motor of identity and it fuels a sense of intimacy, of being members of a highly efficient small-size society (but whose productive output is large-scale). One may readily "conclude that [Finnish] success in the future will be about personality and uniqueness. It is therefore critical for individuals, companies and nations to promote personality and harvest uniqueness, encouraging all of us to develop offerings that are powerfully unique" (Chaker 2014: 209).

In recent years, the turbulence of the world economy have forced Finnish entrepreneurs and companies to rethink their marketing strategies, and many enterprises are under pressure to reassess their potential of competitiveness. This is perhaps also the time to remember that there is a sector of economy, with a long tradition, where Finnish know-how is second to none in the world, this being forestry. Throughout recent years of economic stagnation, production and export in the forestry sector have remained rather stable and there are signs of increased productivity. Although only about a quarter of the total GDP, the forestry sector has been constantly innovating (Rantanen 2015).

Does the secret of future success lie with economic fairs such as the one known as Slush, initiated by Finns? Within only a few years, Slush has grown to unexpected proportions. The event that is held annually in Helsinki, in November, started out with some 300 participants in 2008. In November 2015, the event brought together some 15,000 attendees from almost 100 countries, over 1700 startup entrepreneurs and firms and some 800 investors. Slush offers opportunities for startups and tech talents to present themselves, to exchange ideas and to engage in business contacts with investors (http://www.slush.org/; retrieved 29 November 2015). There is reason to assume that some of the companies that will, in the future, hold the keys to progress in the world economy, will grow from startups at the Slush fair.

In the long run, Finnish competitiveness will keep its high standards, provided those who are involved in marketing management and political decision-making will not abandon the time-tested Finnish values. "If something is certain, it is that we will prevail." These are the closing words of the speech, given by the country's prime minister, Juha Sipilä, to the nation on 16 September 2015.

# Appendix I
## *Finland in figures*
(STV 2014; findicator.fi)

## *Area*

- 0.391 million sq. km (94 percent is land; 6 percent is fresh water such as rivers, brooks and lakes);
- number of lakes: 188,000;
- 68 percent of the land is covered by forests (dominant species are pine, spruce and birch); 6 percent is cultivated land.

## *Population*

- 5.5 million;
- Ethnic groups (Finns, Finland-Swedes, Saami; ethnic minorities);
- Languages (Finnish: 89 percent; Swedish: 5.3; Russian: 1.3; plus immigrant languages of EU citizens and of refugees from outside Europe);
- Religions (Protestant-Lutheran: 74 percent; Orthodox: 1 percent; 24 percent are registered in the civil register; religions of the minorities include Islam, Buddhism, Bahai);
- Live expectancy at birth (Women: 83.9 years; men: 78.2);
- Education (81 percent of those aged 25 to 64 have completed upper secondary or tertiary education; 37 percent have university education).

## *Form of State and Government*

- sovereign state since 1917;
- form of government: parliamentary republic;
- parliament: 200 members, elected for four-year terms;
- head of state: president, elected every six years (Sauli Niinistö has been in office since March 2012);

- official languages: Finnish and Swedish;
- political membership: member state of the European Union (EU) since 1995;
- no military alliance.

## *Economy*

- market economy;
- currency: Euro;
- gross domestic product per capita (GDP) in euros: 37,600 (2014); higher than that of Germany, Great Britain or France;
- gross public debt (percent of GDP): 62.5 (in 2015);
- inflation rate: −0.2 percent (mid–2015).

# Appendix II
## *Administrative Regions of Finland*

(STV 2014: 51)

1 *Southern Finland AVI*

2 *Southwestern Finland AVI*

3 *Eastern Finland AVI*

4 *Western and Inland Finland AVI*

5 *Northern Finland AVI*

6 *Lapland AVI*

7 *State Department of Åland*

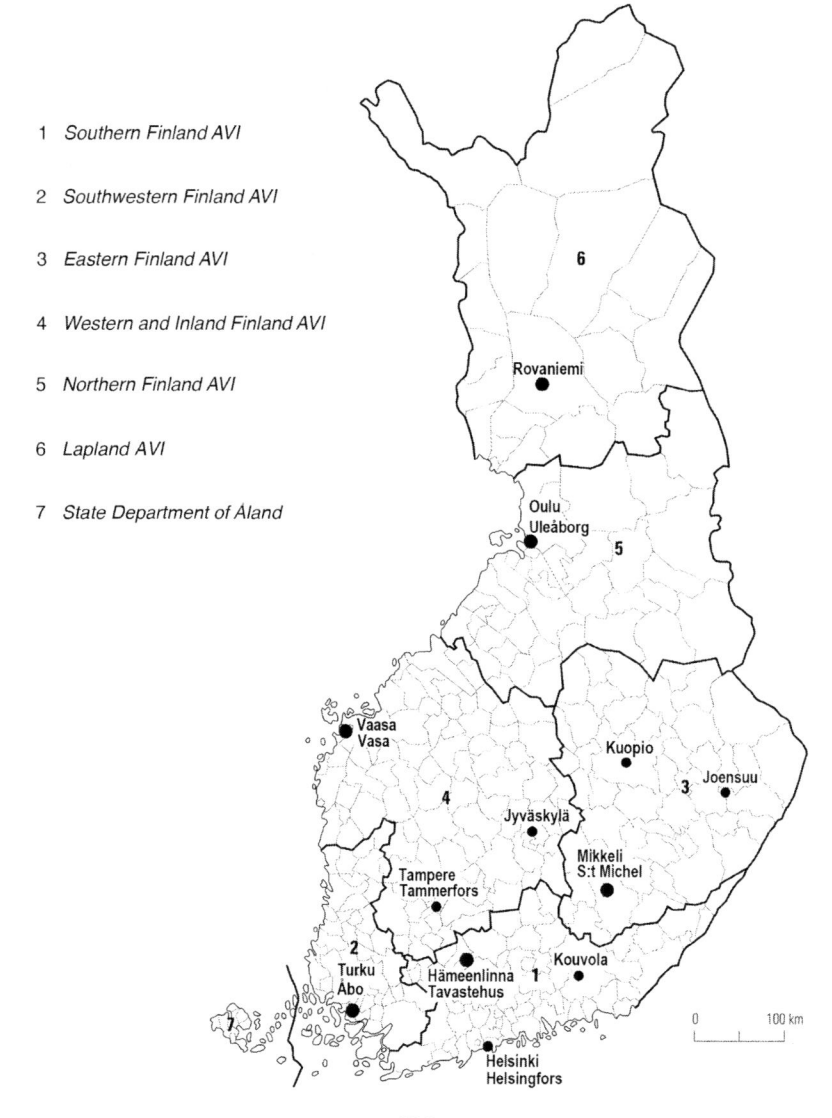

# Bibliography

Aav, Marianne. (1997a). "Arabia." In Alho et al. 1997: 18–19.

_____. (1997b). "Iittala." In Alho et al. 1997: 154–155.

_____. (2003). *Marimekko: Fabrics, Fashion, Architecture*. New Haven, CT: Yale University Press.

Abondolo, Daniel (ed.). (1998). *The Uralic Languages*. London: Routledge.

Adams, Patricia (2015). *The Truth About China: Why Beijing Will Resist Demands for Abatement*. London: Global Warming Policy Foundation.

Ahtisaari, Martti. (2015). "Ehrnroothin Työstä Laman Keskellä Voi Oppia." *Helsingin Sanomat*, 26 July, B8.

Aikio, Ante. (2012). "An Essay on Saami Ethnolinguistic Prehistory." In Grünthal and Kallio 2012: 63–117.

Aikio-Puoskari, Ulla. (2001). *Saamen Kielen ja Saamenkielinen Opetus Pohjoismaissa: Tutkimus Saamelaisten Kielellisistä Ihmisoikeuksista Pohjoismaiden Kouluissa*. Rovaniemi: University of Lapland.

Ajkhenvald, A., E. Helimski and V. Perukhin. (1989). "On Earliest Finno-Ugrian Mythologic Beliefs: Comparative and Historical Considerations for Reconstruction." In Hoppál and Pentikäinen 1989: 155–159.

Ala-Tuuhonen, Leena, Linnea Lindman-Sharma, Eeva Mörttinen and Irma Pasanen-Tuomainen (eds.). (1998). *Teknillisen Korkeakoulun Väitöskirjat 1911–1997: Terpenikemiasta Nanoteknologiaan*. Espoo: Teknillinen Korkeakoulu.

Alho, Olli. (1997). "Customs." In Alho et al. 1997: 63–64.

Alho, Olli, Hildi Hawkins and Päivi Vallisaari (eds.). (1997). *Finland: A Cultural Encyclopedia*. Helsinki: Finnish Literature Society.

Ammon, Ulrich (ed.). (2001). *The Dominance of English as a Language of Science: Effects on Other Languages and Language Communities*. Berlin: Mouton de Gruyter.

_____. (2015). *Die Stellung der Deutschen Sprache in der Welt*. Berlin: Walter de Gruyter.

Anderson, David E., Andrew S. Goudie and Adrian G. Parker. (2007). *Global Environments Through the Quaternary: Exploring Environmental Change*. Oxford: Oxford University Press.

Anthony, David W. (ed.). (2009). *The Lost World of Old Europe: The Danube Valley, 5000–3500 BC*. New York: The Institute for the Study of the Ancient World; Princeton, NJ: Princeton University Press.

Apo, Satu, Aili Nenola and Laura Stark-Arola (eds.). (1998). *Gender and Folklore: Perspectives on Finnish and Karelian Culture*. Helsinki: Finnish Literature Society.

Aspinall, Edward. (2005). *The Helsinki Agreement: A More Promising Basis for Peace in Aceh?* Washington, D.C.: East-West Center Washington.

Asplund, Anneli. (1997). "Folk Music." In Alho et al. 1997: 110–112.

Ateneum Art Museum (ed.). (2007). *Ateneum-Opas*. Helsinki: Ateneum Art Museum.

Austerlitz, Robert. (1990). "Uralic Languages." In Comrie 1990, 175–184.

Autio, Eero. (2000). "Reindeer and Reindeer Antlers Inside the Sun-Symbol of Saami Shaman Drums; Snake, Zigzag Motifs and Horned Antropomorphic Figurines in Finnish Rock Paintings." In Kare 2000b: 174–201.

Bäckman, Louise, and Åke Hultkrantz. (1978). *Studies in Lapp Shamanism*. Stockholm: Almqvist & Wiksell.

_____, and _____ (eds.). (1985). *Saami Pre-Christian Religion*. Stockholm: Almqvist & Wiksell.

Bailey, Geoff, and Penny Spikins (eds.). (2008). *Mesolithic Europe*. Cambridge: Cambridge University Press.

Bange, Oliver, and Gottfried Niedhart (eds.). (2008). *Helsinki 1975 and the Transformation of Europe*. Oxford: Berghahn Books.

Barnhart, Robert K. (ed.). (2002). *Chambers Dictionary of Etymology*. Edinburgh: Chambers (reprint of the 1988 edition).

Bartlett, Robert. (1993). *The Making of Europe: Con-*

quest, Colonization and Cultural Change, 950–1350. London: Allen Lane—The Penguin Press.

Benson, Adolph B. (1987). *Peter Kalm's Travels in North America: The English Version of 1770*, 2 vols. Dover Publishing.

Björklund, Krister. (2005). *Finns Over the Atlantic: An Overview of the Emigration from Finland to North America*. Turku: Siirtolaisuusinstituutti

_____. (2012). *Suomalainen, Ruotsalainen vai Ruotsinsuomalainen? Ruotsissa Asuvat Suomalaiset 2000-Luvulla*. Turku: Siirtolaisuusinstituutti.

Botz-Bornstein, Thorsten, and Jürgen Hengelbrock (eds.). (2006). *Re-Ethnicizing the Minds? Cultural Revival in Contemporary Thought*. Amsterdam: Rodopi B.V.

Branch, Michael. (1985). "Introduction." In *Kalevala* 1985: xi–xxxv.

_____. (1998). "Finnish Oral Poetry, Kalevala and Kanteletar." In Schoolfield 1998: 3–33.

Brookhiser, Richard. (1996). *Founding Father: Rediscovering George Washington*. New York: Free Press.

Castells, Manuel. (1998). *The Information Age: Economy, Society and Culture, Vol. III: End of Millennium*. Malden, MA: Blackwell.

Castells, Manuel, and Pekka Himanen. (2002). *The Information Society and the Welfare State: The Finnish Model*. New York: Oxford University Press.

Cavalli-Sforza, L. Luca, Paolo Menozzi and Alberto Piazza. (1994). *The History and Geography of Human Genes*. Princeton, NJ: Princeton University Press.

Chaker, André Noël. (2014). *The Finnish Miracle: An Inspiring Model and a Few Cool Stories from a Self-Made Nation*. Helsinki: Talentum.

Chambon, Adrienne, and Arielle Dylan. (2012). "The Missing Presence of Aboriginal Peoples from the Transnational Debate." In Chambon et al. 2012: 167–186.

Chambon, Adrienne, Wolfgang Schröer and Cornelia Schweppe (eds.). (2012). *Transnational Social Support*. New York: Routledge.

Chela, Carina. (2013). "The New Edge of Finnish Architecture: Pioneering Projects in Finnish Architecture Are Earning Global Attention and Setting New Trends." Retrieved from http://finland.fi/arts-culture/the-new-edge-of-finnish-architecture/.

Chippindale, Christopher and George Nash (eds.). (2004). *The Figured Landscapes of Rock-Art: Looking at Pictures in Place*. Cambridge: Cambridge University Press.

Christiansen, Niels et al. (eds.). (2006). *The Nordic Model of Welfare: A Historical Reappraisal*. Copenhagen: Museum Tusculanum Press.

Christopher, M. and P. Tatham (eds.). (2014). *Humanitarian Logistics: Meeting the Challenge for and Responding to Disasters* (2nd ed.). London: Kogan.

Clarke, Edward Daniel. (1819). *Travels in Various Countries of Europe, Asia and Africa*, 11 vols. London: Cadell and Davies.

_____. (1997). *Matka Lapin Perukoille 1799* (translated into Finnish, with an introduction and explanations by Jorma Ojala). Pieksämäki: IdeaNova.

*A Comparative Study of the Printed Score and the Manuscript of the Seventh Symphony of Sibelius*. Acta Musica V. Studies Published by the Sibelius Museum. Institute of Musicology, Åbo Akademi University, Turku, Finland, 1970. Retrieved from http://www.abo.fi/institution/musikvetenskap.

Comrie, Bernard (ed.). (1990). *The Major Languages of Eastern Europe*. London: Routledge (2nd printing).

Connah, Roger. (2005). *Finland: Modern Architectures in History*. London: Reaktion Books.

Cord, David J. (2014). *The Decline and Fall of Nokia*. Helsinki: Schildts & Söderströms.

Covey, Stephen M.R. (2008). *The Speed of Trust*. New York: Free Press.

Crawford, John Martin. (1889). "Preface." *The Kalevala*, vol. I, pp. 1–30. Chesterville, ME: Kellscraft Studio, 2014.

Crystal, David. (1997). *English as a Global Language*. Cambridge: Cambridge University Press.

Danver, Steven L. (ed.). (2011). *Popular Controversies in World History: Investigating History's Intriguing Questions*, 4 vols. Santa Barbara, CA: Sharpe Reference.

Daun, Åke. (1989). *Svensk Mentalitet: Ett Jämförande Perspektiv*. Stockholm: Rabén & Sjögren.

Decker, Julie (ed.). (2010). *Modern North: Architecture on the Frozen Edge*. New York: Princeton Architectural Press.

Desai, R.A., S. Krishnan-Sarin, D. Cavallo and M.D. Potenzo. (2010). "Video-Gaming Among High School Students: Health Correlates, Gender Differences, and Problematic Gaming." *Pediatrics* 126: 1414–1424.

Doblin analysis. (2005). *On Innovation Effectiveness* (March). Retrieved from http://www.avsusergroups.org/pag_pdfs/PA2013_11Frigstad.pdf.

Donlan, Walter. (1997). "The Relations of Power in the Pre-State and Early State Polities." In Mitchell and Rhodes 1997: 39–48.

Donner, Jörn. (2011). *Anteckningar Om Mannerheim*. Stockholm: Atlantis Förlag.

Dugger, William E. (2010). "Uno Cygnaeus: The Finnish Visionary Who Changed Education Forever." Retrieved from http://www.iteea.org/Resources/PressRoom/CygnaeusFinlandPaper.pdf.

Edwards, P., and T. Elger (eds.). (1999). *The Global*

*Economy, National States and the Regulation of Labour*. London: Routledge.

Einarsdottir, Johanna, and Judith T. Wagner (eds.). (2006). *Nordic Childhoods and Early Education: Philosophy, Research, Policy and Practice in Denmark, Finland, Iceland, Norway, and Sweden*. Charlotte, NC: Information Age Publishing.

Eliaeson, Sven, and Kari Palonen (eds.). (2004). *Max Weber's Relevance as Political Theorist*. Special issue of *Max Weber Studies*, 4:2.

Ellis, Joseph J. (2004). *His Excellency: George Washington*. New York: Alfred A. Knopf.

Ehrnrooth, Magnus. (1967). *Casimir Ehrnrooth: Kolmen Aleksanterin—Kahden Tsaarin ja Yhden Ruhtinaan—Uskollinen Palvelija*. Helsinki: Otava.

Englund, Magnus, Chrystina Schmidt and Andrew Wood. (2007). *Scandinavian Modern*. London: Ryland Peters & Small.

Engman, Max. (1995). "Finns and Swedes in Finland." In Tägil 1995: 179–216.

Eriksen, Erik Holthe, and Azamat Abdymomunov. (2011). Translated from article in *Dagens Næringsliv* (18 February 2011). "Angry Birds Will Be Bigger than Mickey Mouse and Mario. Is There a Success Formula for Apps?" *MIT Entrepreneurship Review*. Retrieved from http://miter.mit.edu/articleangry-birds-will-be-bigger-mickey-mouse-and-mario-there-success-formula-apps/.

Etu-Sihvola, Heli. (2010). *Lahden Muinaisrannat*. Lahti: Lahden kaupunginmuseo. Retrieved from http://www.lahti.fi/www/images.nsf/files/C3E34E4E96D748D1C225770E001FD41F/$file/Lahden%20muinaisrannat_web.pdf.

*Finnland* (7th ed.). Ostfildern, Germany: Karl Baedeker.

Forsberg, Aaron. (2000). *America and the Japanese Miracle*. Chapel Hill: University of North Carolina Press.

Fromm, Hans. (1980). "Zur Rezeptionsgeschichte des Kalevala." In *Congressus Quintus Internationalis Fenno-Ugristarum*, Turku 20–27. VIII, pars I. Turku 1980: 25–55.

Fukuyama, Francis. (1995). *Trust: The Social Virtues and the Creation of Prosperity*. New York: Free Press.

Funk, Dmitriy A., and Lennard Sillanpää (eds.). (1999). *The Small Indigenous Nations of Northern Russia. a Guide for Researchers*. Vaasa: Åbo Akademi University.

Garlake, Peter. (1995). *The Hunter's Vision: The Prehistoric Art of Zimbabwe*. London: British Museum Press.

*Gelehrte Kontakte Zwischen Finnland und Göttingen zur Zeit der Aufklärung* (Katalog zur Ausstellung aus Anlass des 500jährigen Jubiläums des Finnischen Buches), 1988. Göttingen: Vandenhoeck & Ruprecht.

Gieseking, Bernd. (2014). *Das Kuriose Finnland Buch*. Frankfurt: Fischer.

Godelier, Maurice. (2011). *The Metamorphoses of Kinship*. London: Verso.

Greve, Bent. (2014). *Historical Dictionary of the Welfare State*. Lanham, MD: Rowman & Littlefield.

Griffin-Pierce, Trudy. (1992). *Earth Is My Mother, Sky Is My Father: Space, Time, and Astronomy in Navajo Sandpainting*. Albuquerque: University of New Mexico Press.

Grönholm, Maija. (1988). *Ruotsalaiset Lainasanat Turun Murteessa*. Turku: Åbo Academy Press.

Grünthal, Riho, and Petri Kallio (eds.). (2012). *A Linguistic Map of Prehistoric Northern Europe*. Helsinki: Société Finno-Ougrienne.

Gruenwald, Tom, and Dave Genz. (1999). *Modern Methods of Ice Fishing*. Minnetonka, MN: Creative Publishing International.

Guyon, Janet. (2002). "Nokia Rocks Its Rivals: Flawless Execution Put Nokia on Top. Will Customer Love Keep Growing?" *Fortune Magazine*, 4 March 2002.

Haarmann, Harald. (1986). *Language in Ethnicity: A View of Basic Ecological Relations*. Berlin: Mouton de Gruyter.

_____. (1989). *Symbolic Values of Foreign Language Use: From the Japanese Case to a General Sociolinguistic Perspective*. Berlin: Mouton de Gruyter.

_____. (1990). *Language in Its Cultural Embedding: Explorations in the Relativity of Signs and Sign Systems*. Berlin: Mouton de Gruyter.

_____. (1996). "On the Sub-Naturalistic Style of Rock Carving in Northern Europe: The Finnish Setting in a Comparative View." *Bollettino Del Centro Camuno Di Studi Preistorici* 29: 65–75.

_____. (1998). "Basque Ethnogenesis, Acculturation, and the Role of Language Contacts." *Fontes Lingvae Vasconvm—Stvdia et Docvmenta* 77 (1998): 25–42.

_____. (2000). "The Soul of Mother Russia: Russian Symbols and Pre–Russian Cultural Identity." *Re-Vision* 23: 6–16.

_____. (2003). "Finnish." In Roelcke 2003: 866–904.

_____. (2007). *Foundations of Culture: Knowledge-Construction, Belief Systems and Worldview in Their Dynamic Interplay*. Frankfurt: Peter Lang.

_____. (2012). *Indo-Europeanization—Day One: Elite Recruitment and the Beginnings of Language Politics*. Wiesbaden: Harrassowitz.

_____. (2013). *Ancient Knowledge, Ancient Know-How, Ancient Reasoning: Cultural Memory in Transition, from Prehistory to Classical Antiquity and Beyond*. Amherst, NY: Cambria.

_____. (2016). *Plato on Women: His Revolutionary Proposals for Gender Equality in Areas of His Ideal Society*. Amherst, NY: Cambria.

Haarmann, Harald, and Eugene Holman. (2001). "The Impact of English as a Language of Science in Finland and Its Role for the Transition to Network Society." In Ammon 2001: 229–260.

Haarmann, Harald, and Joan Marler. (2008). *Introducing the Mythological Crescent: Ancient Beliefs and Imagery Connecting Eurasia with Anatolia*. Wiesbaden: Harrassowitz.

Häikiö, Martti. (2002). *Nokia: The Inside Story*. Upper Saddle River, NJ: Prentice Hall.

Hakala, Ilmari, Hely Alhainen, Maria Andersin, Annukka Kiviranta-Koivisto and Missu Saloheimo. (2007). *Lotta Svärd*. Vammala: Vammalan Kirjapaino.

Häkkinen, Antti, Vappu Ikonen, Kari Pitkänen and Hannu Soikkanen. (1991). *Kun Halla Nälän Tuskan Toi: Miten Suomalaiset Kokivat 1860-Luvun Nälkävuodet*. Porvoo: Werner Söderström Osakeyhtiö.

Hako, Pekka. (2004). *Unohtumaton Martti Talvela: Elämäkerta*. Helsinki: Ajatus Kirjat.

Hakulinen, Lauri. (1979). *Suomen Kielen Rakenne ja Kehitys* (fourth corrected and supplemented edition). Helsinki: Otava.

Halmari, Helena. (1997). *Government and Code-switching: Explaining American Finnish*. Amsterdam: John Benjamins.

Härmä, Iisakki. (2015). "Huono Suomi Pudottaa Osaajia Hanttihommiin." *Helsingin Sanomat*, 7 August 2015, A 6.

Harvey, Graham. (2005). *Animism: Respecting the Living World*. London: Hurst.

Haught, John. (2013). "Is Nature Enough?" In Seachris 2013: 173–182.

Hautamäki, J., et al. (2008). *PISA 06 Finland: Analyses, Reflections and Explanations*. Helsinki: Ministry of Education Publications 2008: 44. Retrieved from http://www.pisa2006.helsinki.fi/files/PISA 06_Analyses_Reflections_and_Explanations. pdf.

Heckscher, Eli F. (1968). *An Economic History of Sweden* (3rd ed.). London: Oxford University Press.

Heikkilä, Tuomas. (2005). *Pyhän Henrikin Legenda*. Helsinki: Suomalaisen Kirjallisuuden Seura.

Heikkinen, Sakari. (1997). *Labour and the Market: Workers, Wages and Living Standards in Finland, 1850–1913*. Helsinki: Finnish Society of Sciences and Letters.

Heikkinen, Sakari, and Jan Luiten van Zanden (eds.). (2004). *Explorations in Economic Growth*. Amsterdam: Aksant.

Heininen, Simo. (1988). "Finnische Gelehrte in Göttingen Während des 18. Jahrhunderts." In *Gelehrte Kontakte ... 1988*: 47–77.

Helander-Renvall, Elina. (2006). *Silde: Sami Mythic Texts and Stories*. Rovaniemi: Sevenprint.

Held, David. (2015). *Models of Democracy* (3rd ed.). Cambridge, UK: Polity Press.

Helgoe, Laurie. (2008). *Introvert Power: Why Your Inner Life Is Your Hidden Strength*. Naperville, IL: Sourcebooks.

Hellingrath, B., D. Link and A. Widera (eds.). (2013). *Managing Humanitarian Supply Chains: Strategies, Practices and Research*. Bremen: BVL Group.

Helskog, Knut. (1988). *Helleristningene i Alta: Spor Etter Ritualer og Dagligliv i Finnmarks Forhistorie*. Alta: Alta Museum.

———. (2004). "Landscapes in Rock-Art: Rock-Carving and Ritual in the Old European North." In Chippindale and Nash 2004: 265–288.

———. (2011). "Reindeer Corrals 4700–4200 BC: Myth or Reality?" *Quaternary International* 238: 25–34.

Henderson, David R. (2008a). "German Economic Miracle." In: Henderson 2008b. Retrieved from http://www.econlib.org/library/Enc/German EconomicMiracle.html.

——— (ed.). (2008b). *The Concise Encyclopedia of Economics*. Indianapolis: Liberty Fund.

Henson, Donald. (2006). *The Origins of the Anglo-Saxons*. Hockwold-cum-Wilton, Norfolk: Anglo-Saxon Books.

Hertzen, Heikki von, and P.D. Spreiregen. (1971). *Building a New Town: Finland's New Garden City: Tapiola*. Cambridge, MA: MIT Press.

Hilson, Mary. (2008). *The Nordic Model: Scandinavia Since 1945*. London: Reaktion Books.

Hinkkanen, Tomi (2012). "Finnish Celebrities in Hollywood, Part 1." *Finn Times*, 5 May 2012. Retrieved from http://finntimes.com/?p=2748.

Hirsch, Eric, and Michael O'Hanlon (eds.). (1995). *The Anthropology of Landscape: Perspectives on Place and Space*. Oxford: Clarendon Press.

Hirvonen, Vuokko. (1998). *Sámeeatnama Jienat: Sápmelaš? Nissona Bálggis Girječállin*. Utsjoki: DAT.

———. (1999). *Saamenmaan Ääniä: Saamelaisen Naisen Tie Kirjailijaksi*. Helsinki: Suomalaisen Kirjallisuuden Seura.

Hjerppe, Riitta. (1989). *The Finnish Economy, 1860–1985: Growth and Structure Change*. Helsinki: Bank of Finland Publications.

———. (2008). "An Economic History of Finland." *EH.Net Encyclopedia*, edited by Robert Whaples. 10 February 2008. Retrieved from http://eh.net/encyclopedia/an-economic-history-of-finland/.

Honko, Lauri, Senni Timonen, Michael Branch and Keith Bosley. (1993). *The Great Bear: A Thematic Anthology of Oral Poetry in the Finno-Ugrian Languages*. Pieksämäki: Raamattutalo Press.

Hoppál, Mihály. (2001). "Cosmic Symbolism of Siberian Shamanhood." In Pentikäinen 2001: 75–87.

Hoppál, Mihály, and Juha Pentikäinen (eds.). (1989). *Uralic Mythology and Folklore*. Budapest: Ethnographic Institute of the Hungarian Academy of Sciences; Helsinki: Finnish Literature Society.

Hovdhaugen, Even, Fred Karlsson, Carol Henriksen and Bengt Sigurd. (2000). *The History of Linguistics in the Nordic Countries*. Helsinki: Societas Scientiarum Fennica.

Huhta, Marjatta. (1997). *The Dynamics of Language Training: From an Element of Cost to an Investment in Communication*. Helsinki: Opetushallitus.

Hultkrantz, Åke. (1985). "Reindeer Nomadism and the Religion of the Saamis." In Bäckman and Hultkrantz 1985: 11–28.

———. (2001). "Shamanism: Some Recent Findings from a Comparative Perspective." In Pentikäinen 2001: 1–9.

Hunt, Harry T. (1995). *On the Nature of Consciousness: Cognitive, Phenomenological, and Transpersonal Perspectives*. New Haven, CT: Yale University Press.

Huttunen, Pirkko, Leena Kokko and Virpi Ylijukuri. (2004). "Winter Swimming Improves General Well-Being." *International Journal of Circumpolar Health* 63: 140–144.

Hyvärinen, Heikki et al. (2004). *Hyle: Saimaan Oma Norppa*. Helsinki: Tammi.

*Inari: Mighty by Nature* (2012). Retrieved from http://www.inari.fi/media/tiedostot-2012/muut/matkailuesite-2011/matkailuesite-english.pdf.

Isokangas, Antti, and Riku Vassinen. (2011). *Digitaalinen Jalanjälki*. Helsinki: Talentum (2nd ed.).

Itkonen, Erkki. (1986–89). *Inarilappisches Wörterbuch*, 3 vols. Helsinki: Suomalais-Ugrilainen Seura.

Itkonen, Erkki, and Ulla-Maija Kulonen (eds.). (2000). *Suomen Sanojen Alkuperä: Etymologinen Sanakirja*, 3 vols. Helsinki: Suomalaisen Kirjallisuuden Seura (2nd ed.).

Jaakkola, Jutta. (2000). "The Finnish Tango: Its History and Characteristics." Finnish Musical Information Service (trans. Susan Sinisalo). Retrieved from http://composers.musicfinland.fi/musicfinland/fimic.nsf/0/b07de6da87c46640c2257506005199fe!opendocument&click=.

Jain, Ravindra. (2014). "Innovation Promotion Strategies: A Conceptual Framework." *South Asian Journal of Management* 21: 44–70.

Jalkanen, Pekka. (2013). "Finnish Tango." In Taipale 2013: 315–318.

Jokinen, Anniina. (2007). "Aurora Borealis, the Northern Lights, in Mythology and Folklore." *Luminarium*. Retrieved from http://www.luminarium.org/mythology/revontulet.htm.

Jowell, Roger, Roberts, Caroline, Rory Fitzgerald and Eva Gillian (eds.). (2007). *Measuring Attitudes Cross-Nationally: Lessons from the European Social Survey*. New York: Sage Publications.

Julku, Kyösti (ed.). (1997). *Itämerensuomi—Euroopalainen Maa*. Oulu: Atena.

Jussila, Osmo (2004). *Suomen Suuriruhtinaskunta, 1809–1917*. Helsinki: Werner Söderström Osakeyhtiö.

Jussila, Osmo et al. (1999). *From Grand Duchy to Modern State: A Political History of Finland Since 1809*. New York: Hurst.

Jutikkala, Eino. (1953). "Internal Migration and Industrialization in Finland, 1878–1939." *Scandinavian Economic History Review* 1: 247–251.

Kääpä, Pietari (ed.). (2010). *The National and Beyond: The Globalization of Finnish Cinema in the Films of Aki and Mika Kaurismäki*. Oxford: Peter Lang.

———. (2012). *Directory of World Cinema: Finland*. Bristol: Intellect.

Kääpä, Pietari, and Silja Laine (eds.). (2012). *World Film Locations: Helsinki*. Bristol: Intellect.

Kaján, Eva, and Jarkko Saarinen. (2014). "Transforming Visions and Pathways in Destination Development: Local Perceptions and Adaptation Strategies to Changing Environment in Finnish Lapland." In Viken and Granås 2014: 189–208.

*Kalevala: The Land of the Heroes* (1985). Translated by W.F. Kirby, introduced by M.A. Branch. London: Athlone Press.

Kallio, Petri. (1998). "Suomi(ttavia Etymologioita)." *Virittäjä* 4: 613–620.

Kalmari, Heidi, and Kati Kelola. (2009). *Vastuullisen Matkailijan Käsikirja*. Keuruu: Otava.

Kanerva, Arla (2015). "Tekla Hultin—Itsenäisyyden Nainen." *Helsingin Sanomat*, 5 December, C2–3.

Kangas, Urpo (ed.). (1998). *Oikeustiede Suomessa, 1900–2000*. Helsinki: Werner Söderström Lakitieto.

Kare, Antero. (2000a). "Rock Paintings in Finland." In Kare 2000b: 98–127.

——— (ed.). (2000b). *Myanndash: Rock Art in the Ancient Arctic*. Rovaniemi: Arctic Centre Foundation.

Karilas, Yrjö (ed.). (2003). *Antero Vipunen: Arvoitusten ja Ongelmien, Leikkien ja Pelien Sekä Eri Harrastelualojen Pikkujättiläinen* (20th ed.). Porvoo: Werner Söderström Osakeyhtiö.

Karjalainen, Kristiina, Linnea Lindman-Sharma, Taija Tuoresjärvi and Helena Turkka (eds.). (1998). *Teknillinen Korkeakoulu Kirjoissa ja Kansissa: 150-Vuotisbibliografia*. Espoo: Teknillinen Korkeakoulu.

Karlsson, Svenolof, and Anders Lugn. (2009). *Att Förändra Världen: En Berättelse om Lars Magnus Ericsson och Hans Efterföljare*. Stockholm: Sellin & partner.

Karlsson Sjögren, Åsa. (2006). *Männen, Kvinnorna och Rösträtten: Medborgarskap och Representation 1723–1866*. Stockholm: Carlsson.

Karlsson-Sutisna, Sanna. (2009). *Elämänpuu Kukkii—Livets Träd Bloomer—The Tree of Life Blooms*. Helsinki: Wings Production.

Karonen, Petri. (1999). *Pohjoinen Suurvalta: Ruotsi ja Suomi 1521–1809*. Helsinki: Werner Söderström Osakeyhtiö.

Kaukiainen, Yrjö, Risto Marjomaa and Jouko Nurmiainen (eds.). (2014). *Autonomisen Suomen Rajamaa: Viipurin Läänin Historia*, vol. V. Joensuu: Karjalaisen Kulttuurin Edistämissäätiö.

Kent, Harold Winfield. (1993). *Treasury of Hawaiian Words in One Hundred and One Categories*. Honolulu: Masonic Public Library of Hawaii.

Kent, Neil. (2014). *The Sámi Peoples of the North: A Social and Cultural History*. London: Hurst.

Kepsu, Kasper. (2014). *Den Besvärliga Provinsen: Reduktion, Skattearrendering och Bondeoroligheter i det Svenska Ingermanland Under Slutet Av 1600-Talet*. Helsingfors: Societas Scientiarum Fennica.

Kerkkonen, Martti. (1959). *Peter Kalm's North American Journey: Its Ideological Background and Results*. Helsinki: Finnish Historical Society.

Kettunen, Niko. (2015). "Eroon Kirotusta Kivihiilestä." *Helsingin Sanomat*, 25 November 2015: A 42–43.

Kettunen, Pauli. (1999). "The Nordic Model and the Making of the Competitive 'Us.'" In Edwards and Elger 1999: 128–136.

———. (2001). "The Nordic Welfare State in Finland." *Scandinavian Journal of History* 26: 225–247.

Kinnock, Glenys. (1990). *Namibia: Birth of a Nation*. London: Quartet Books.

Kirby, David G. (1991–95). *Northern Europe in the Early Modern Period*, 2 vols. Vol. 1: *The Baltic World 1492–1772*; vol. 2: *The Baltic World 1772–1993*. London: Routledge.

Kivikäs, Pekka. (1995). *Kalliomaalaukset: Muinainen Kuva-Arkisto—Paintings on Rock: An Ancient Picture Archive*. Jyväskylä: Atena.

Klinge, Matti. (1997). *Keisarin Suomi*. Helsinki: Schildts.

———. (2012). *A History Both Finnish and European: History and the Culture of Historical Writing in Finland During the Imperial Period*. Sastamala: Societas Scientiarum Fennica.

Kloss, Heinz. (1978). *Die Entwicklung Neuer Germanischer Kultursprachen Seit 1800* (2nd ed.). Düsseldorf: Institut für deutsche Sprache.

Klövekorn, Martin. (1960). *Die Sprachliche Struktur Finnlands 1880–1950: Veränderungen im Sprachlichen Charakter der Finnlandschwedischen Gebiete und deren Bevölkerungs-, Wirtschafts- und Sozialgeographische Ursachen*. Copenhagen:

Munksgaard & Helsinki: Societas Scientiarum Fennica.

Koivuranta, Esa, Kati Pehkonen, Tuija Sorjanen and Annina Vainio. (2015). *Marimekko: Suuria Kuvioita*. Helsinki: Into.

Kokko, Hanna, E. Helle, J. Lindström, E. Ranta, T. Sipilä and F. Courchamp. (1999). "Backcasting Population Sizes of Ringed and Grey Seals in the Baltic and Lake Saimaa During the 20th Century." *Annales Zoologici Fennici* 36: 65–73.

Kolbe, Laura (ed.). (2002–04). *Suomen Kulttuurihistoria*, 5 vols. Helsinki: Tammi.

Korhonen, Mikko. (1981). *Johdatus Lapin Kielen Historiaan*. Helsinki: Suomalaisen Kirjallisuuden Seura.

Koskinen, Johannes. (2013). "No Corruption." In Taipale 2013: 50–52.

Koskinen, Matti. (2015). "Suomi On Yhä Lottovoittajien Maa." *Helsingin Sanomat*, 16 August, A10.

Koskinen-Koivisto, Eerika. (2014). *Her Own Worth: Negotiations of Subjectivity in the Life Narrative of a Female Labourer*. Helsinki: Finnish Literature Society.

Kosonen, Pekka. (1993a). "The Finnish Model and the Welfare State in Crisis." In Kosonen 1993b: 45–66.

——— (ed.). (1993b). *The Nordic Welfare State as Myth and as Reality*. Helsinki: University Printing House.

Kostiainen, Auvo (ed.). (2014). *Finns in the United States: A History of Settlement, Dissent, and Integration*. East Lansing: Michigan State University Press.

Kotilainen, Noora. (2011). "Humane Crisis Management—Or Lifestyle War?" *Helsinki Times*, 10 March.

Kuisma, Markku. (1999). "Europe's Wood Basket Transformed: Finnish Economic History in a Long Perspective." In Lehtonen 1999: 50–85.

Kulonen, Ulla-Maija, Irja Seurujärvi-Kari and Risto Pulkkinen (eds.). (2005). *The Saami: A Cultural Encyclopaedia*. Helsinki: Suomalaisen Kirjallisuuden Seura.

Kunze, Erich. (1988). "Zur Geschichte der Wissenschaftlichen Beziehungen Zwischen der Georgia Augusta und der Academia Aboensis." In *Gelehrte Kontakte ... 1988*: 79–120.

Kuokkanen, Rauna. (2006). "The Logic of the Gift: Reclaiming Indigenous Peoples' Philosophies." In Botz-Bornstein and Hengelbrock 2006: 251–274.

Kupiainen, Sirkku, Jarkko Hautamäki and Tommi Karjalainen. (2009). *The Finnish Education System and PISA*. Helsinki: Ministry of Education Publications (opm46(1).pdf).

Kuusi, Matti, Keith Bosley and Michael Branch

(eds.). (1977). *Finnish Folk Poetry: Epic: An Anthology in Finnish and English*. Helsinki: Finnish Literature Society.

Laanest, Arvo. (1986). *Isuri Keele Ajalooline Foneetika ja Morfoloogia*. Tallinn: Valgus.

Lahelma, Antti. (2008). *A Touch of Red: Archaeological and Ethnographic Approaches to Interpreting Finnish Rock Paintings*. ISKOS 15, Helsinki: Finnish Antiquarian Society. Retrieved from https://helda.helsinki.fi/bitstream/handle/10138/19406/atoucho.pdf.

Laitalainen, Juha. (2015). "Puukuokalla Voittoon." *Kamppi-Eira* Nro 24: 15.

Lambert, Bruce Henry. (2009). "Impediments, Inhibitions, and Barriers to University Entrepreneurialism." In Shattock 2009: 142–182.

Länsimäki, Maija (ed.). (1991). *Bibliographia Studiorum Uralicorum 1917–1987: Uralistiikan Tutkimuksen Bibliografia. Bibliography on Uralic Studies, III: Kielitiede/Linguistics*. Helsinki: Suomalaisen Kirjallisuuden Seura.

Lappalainen, Mirkka. (2012). *Jumalan Vihan Ruoska: Suuri Nälänhätä Suomessa 1695–1697*. Helsinki: Siltala.

Lappalainen, T., S. Koivumäki, E. Salmela, K. Huoponen, P. Sistonen, M. L. Savontaus and P. Lahermo. (2006). "Regional Differences Among the Finns: A Y-Chromosomal Perspective." *Gene* 376: 207–215.

Lavery, Jason Edward. (2006). *The History of Finland*. Santa Barbara, CA: Greenwood Publishing Group.

Lehikoinen, Laila, and Silva Kiuru. (1991). *Kirjasuomen Kehitys*. Helsinki: Helsingin Yliopiston Suomen Kielen Laitos.

Lehmusvesi, Jussi. (2015). "Koltta-Aarre Kätkee Salaisuuden." *Helsingin Sanomat*, 15 October, B1–2.

Lehtinen, Tapani. (2007). *Kielen Vuosituhannet: Suomen Kielen Kehitys Kantauralista Varhaissuomeen*. Helsinki: Suomalaisen Kirjallisuuden Seura.

Lehtola, Jorma. (2000). *Lailasta Lailaan: Tarinoita Elokuvien Sitkeistä Lappalaisista*. Helsinki: Kustannus-Puntsi.

Lehtonen, Lasse. (2013). "The Principle of Transparency." In Taipale 2013: 31–35.

Lehtonen, T.M.S. (ed.). (1999). *Europe's Northern Frontier: Perspectives on Finland's Western Identity*. Porvoo: PS-Kustannus/Werner Söderström Osakeyhtiö.

Lehtonen, Veli-Pekka. (2015a). "Japanin Muumipuisto Tavoittelee Miljoonaa Kävijää." *Helsingin Sanomat*, 1 July, B3.

_____. (2015b). "Suomalainen Elokuva Vuonna 0." *Helsingin Sanomat*, Teema 6/15: 82–84.

Leino-Kaukiainen, Pirkko. (2007). "Suomalaisten Kirjalliset Taidot Autonomian Kaudella." *Historiallinen Aikakauskirja* 4: 420–438.

_____. (2014). "Kohti Koulutusyhteiskuntaa." In Kaukiainen 2014: 300–336.

Lemola, T. (2004). "Finnish Science and Technology Policy." In Schienstock 2004: 268–284.

Lewis, Richard D. (2005). *Finland: The Cultural Lone Wolf*. London: Intercultural Press.

Liimatainen, Karoliina. (2015). "Essayah: Suomesta on Tulossa Museo." *Helsingin Sanomat*, 30 August, A10.

Lilja, Kari, Keijo Räsänen and Risto Tainio. (1992). "A Dominant Business Recipe: The Forest Sector in Finland." In Whitley 1992: 137–154.

Lindholm, Christian, Turkka Keinonen and Harri Kiljander. (2003). *Mobile Usability: How Nokia Changed the Face of the Mobile Phone*. New York: McGraw-Hill.

Lindroos, Kirsi. (2013). "Free School Meals." In Taipale 2013: 104–106.

Lommel, Andreas. (1965). *Die Welt der Frühen Jäger, Medizinmänner, Schamanen, Künstler*. München: Callwey.

Long, Neil. (2014). "Two Billion Downloads? We're Just Getting Started, Says Angry Birds Creator Rovio." *Edge*. Future plc. Retrieved from http://www.edge-online.com/features/two-billion-downloads-were-just-getting-started-says-angry-birds-creator-rovio/.

Loppert, Max. (1997). "Martti Talvela." In *The New Grove Dictionary of Opera*. London & New York: Macmillan.

Lukowski, Jerzy. (1999). *The Partitions of Poland: 1772, 1793, 1795*. London: Longman.

Lund, Christine. (2008). "History of the Mobile Phone Throwing World Championships." Savonlinna Festivals. Retrieved from http://www.mobilephonethrowing.fi.

Mach, Ernst. (1896). *Die Principien der Wärmelehre*. Frankfurt: Minerva.

Maddison, Angus. (2003). *The World Economy: Historical Statistics*. Paris: Organization for Economic Cooperation and Development.

Magga, Ole Henrik. (2006). "Diversity in Saami Terminology for Reindeer, Snow, and Ice." *International Social Science Journal* 58: 25–34, doi: 10.1111/j. 1468–2451.2006.00594.x.

Mainio, Tapio. (2016). "Suomi on Kultamaa." *Helsingin Sanomat* 5 January 2016, B8–9.

Malinen, Pirkko. (1999). "The Ingrian-Finnish Remigrants: Factors Preventing and Promoting Integration." In Teinonen and Virtanen 1999: 195–210.

Malyarchuk, Boris, Miroslava Derenko, Tomasz Grzybowski, Maria Perkova, Urszula Rogalla, Tomas Vanecek and Iosif Tsybovsky. (2010). "The Peopling of Europe from the Mitochondrial Haplogroup U5 Perspective." *PloS One* 5: e10285, doi: 10.1371/journal.pone.0010285.

Mapleson, James Henry. (1888). *The Mapleson Memoirs 1848-1888*, 2 vols. London: Remington Publishers.

Martynov, Anatoly I. (1991). *The Ancient Art of Northern Asia*. Urbana: University of Illinois Press.

Matras, Yaron (ed.). (1995). *Romani in Contact: The History, Structure and Sociology of a Language*. Amsterdam: J. Benjamins.

McRae, Kenneth D. (1997). *Conflict and Compromise in Multilingual Societies*, vol. 3: *Finland*. Waterloo, Ontario: Wilfrid Laurier University Press.

Meek, Margaret. (2001). *Children's Literature and National Identity*. Stoke on Trent: Trentham Books.

Meinander, Henrik. (2010). *Suomen Historia: Linjat, Rakenteet ja Käännekohdat*. Helsinki: Werner Söderström Osakeyhtiö.

Melander, Toini. (1951). *Personskrifter Hänförande sig till Finland 1562-1713*. Helsingfors: Valtioneuvoston Kirjapaino.

Mer, Jacques. (1999). *La Finlande*. Paris: La Documentation Française.

Meri, Veijo. (1990). *Suomen Marsalkka: C.G. Mannerheim*. Helsinki: Werner Söderström Osakeyhtiö.

Merikallio, Katri, and Tapani Ruokanen. (2011). *Matkalla: Martti Ahtisaaren Tarina*. Helsinki: Otava.

Merriden, Trevor. (2001). *Business the Nokia Way: Secrets of the World's Fastest Moving Company*. Chicago: Capstone.

Merrill, Ronald T. (2010). *Our Magnetic Earth: The Science of Geomagnetism*. Chicago: University of Chicago Press.

Michl, Jan. (1991). "Alvar Aalto: Savoy Vase, 1936." In Naylor 1991: 716-717.

Miettinen, Tiina. (2015). *Piikojen Valtakunta*. Jyväskylä: Atena.

Mitchell, Lynette G., and P. J. Rhodes (eds.). (1997). *The Development of the Polis in Archaic Greece*. London: Routledge.

Mölsä, Ari and Markku Ojala. (2015). "Intohimona Eukonkanto." *LakimiesUutiset* 7: 62-63.

Moore, Kenny. (1977). "An Enigma Wrapped in Glory." *Sports Illustrated*, 27 June.

Moorhouse, Jonathan, Michael Carapetian and Leena Ahtola-Moorhouse. (1987). *Helsingin Jugendarkkitehtuuri 1895-1915*. Helsinki: Otava.

Morgan, Glenn. (2005). "Introduction: Changing Capitalisms? Internationalization, Institutional Change, and Systems of Economic Organization." In Morgan et al. 2005: 1-18.

Morgan, Glenn, Richard Whitley and Eli Moen (eds.). (2005). *Changing Capitalisms?* Oxford: Oxford University Press.

Mukka, Antero (2012). "Talvivaara on Suuren Lu- okan Epäonnistuminen." *Helsingin Sanomat*, 8 November, kolumni.

Murtomäki, Veijo. (2015). "Kahnauksia, Erotiikkaa ja Sensuroitu Koululaulu." *Helsingin Sanomat*, 9 August, C16-17.

Naylor, Collin (ed.). (1991). *Contemporary Masterworks*. Chicago: St. James Press.

Nelis, M., et al. (2009). "Genetic Structure of Europeans: A View from the North-East." Retrieved from http://journals.plos.org/plosone/article?id=10.1371/journal.pone.0005472.

Nenola, Aili. (2002). *Inkerin Itkuvirret—Ingrian Laments*. Helsinki: Finnish Literature Society.

Nevalainen, Pekka. (1991). "Inkerinmaan ja Inkeriläisten Vaiheet 1900-Luvulla." In Nevalainen and Sihvo 1991: 234-299.

Nevalainen, Pekka, and Hannes Sihvo (eds.). (1991). *Inkeri: Historia, Kansa, Kulttuuri*. Helsinki: Suomalaisen Kirjallisuuden Seura.

Niikko, Anneli. (2006). "Finnish Daycare: Caring, Education and Instruction." In Einarsdottir and Wagner 2006: 133-158.

Nikula, Riita. (1993). *Architecture and Landscape: The Building of Finland*. Helsinki: Otava.

_____. (2014). *Suomalainen Rivitalo: Työväen Asunnosta Keskiluokan Unelmaksi*. Helsinki: Suomalaisen Kirjallisuuden Seura.

Norri, Marja-Riitta, and Wilfried Wang (eds.). (2007). *20th Century Architecture: Finland*. Berlin: Prestel.

Nuorteva, Jussi. (1997a). *Suomalaisten Ulkomainen Opinkäynti ennen Turun Akatemian Perustamista 1640*. Helsinki: Suomen Kirkkohistoriallisen Seuran toimituksia 177.

_____. (1997b). "Schools." In Alho 1997: 280-281.

Nuttall, Mark. (1998). *Protecting the Arctic: Indigenous Peoples and Cultural Survival*. Amsterdam: Harwood Academic Publishers.

Nykänen, Pekka and Merina Salminen. (2014). *Operaatio Elop: Nokian Matkapuhelinten Viimeiset Vuodet*. Helsinki: Teos.

Ó Corráin, A. and S. Mac Mathúna (eds.). (1998). *Minority Languages in Scandinavia, Britain and Ireland*. Uppsala: Uppsala University Press.

OECD (2004). "Learning for Tomorrow's World: First Results from Pisa 2003." Retrieved from www.oecd.org/dataoecd/1/60/34002216.pdf.

OECD (2006a). "Assessing Scientific, Reading and Mathematical Literacy: A Framework for Pisa 2006." Retrieved from www.pisa.oecd.org/xxx.

OECD (2006b). "Document: Releasedpisaitems_Maths.Doc."

OECD (2007a). "Assessing Scientific, Reading and Mathematical Literacy: A Framework for Pisa 2006." Retrieved from www.pisa.oecd.org/document/33/0,3343,en_32252351_32236191_374623 69_1_1_1_1,00.html.

OECD (2007b). "Pisa 2006 Science Competencies for Tomorrows World: Volume I—Analysis." Retrieved from www.pisa.oecd.org/dataoecd/30/17/39703267.pdf.

Oijala, Matti. (2007). *Immilän Myllymäki: Immilän ja Arrajoen Asutushistoriaa* (2nd ed.). Nastola: Immilän Mylly ja Saha.

Oinas, Päivi. (2005). "Finland: A Success Story?" *European Planning Studies* 13: 1227–1244.

Ojala, Elina. (2014). *The Golden Age of Finnish Art.* ENGA14 Finnish Institutions Research Paper. Retrieved from http://people.uta.fi/~eo93098/Golden_Age.html.

Ojala, Jari, Jari Eloranta and Jukka Jalava (eds.). (2006). *The Road to Prosperity: An Economic History of Finland.* Helsinki: Finnish Literature Society.

Ollila, Jorma, and Harri Saukkomaa. (2013). *Mahdoton Menestys: Kasvun Paikkana Nokia.* Helsinki: Otava.

Ollila, Mape. (2007). *Once Upon a Nightwish: The Official Biography, 1996–2006.* Porvoo: Deggael Communications.

Ozorio, Anne. (2007). "Appreciating Sibelius' Luonnotar Op. 70." Retrieved from http://www.musicweb-international.com/classrev/2007/mar07/Luonnotar.htm.

Paavolainen, Erkki. (1958). *Sellainen oli Karjala.* Helsinki: Otava.

Pakkanen, Outi. (1988). *Aino Ackté: Pariisin Primadonna.* Porvoo: Werner Söderström Osakeyhtiö.

Pallasmaa, Juhani. (2010). "The Northern Dimension: Between Universality and Locality." In Decker 2010: 27–35.

Parpola, Asko. (2012). "Formation of the Indo-European and Uralic (Finno-Ugric) Language Families in the Light of Archaeology: Revised and Integrated 'Total' Correlations." In Grünthal and Kallio 2012: 119–184.

Partanen, Seppo J., and Raimo Niemelä. (2014). *Kullankaivajan Opas.* Helsinki: Alfamer (2nd ed.).

Paunonen, Heikki, and Marjatta Paunonen. (2000). *Tsennaaks Stadii, Bonjaaks Slangii: Stadin Slangin Suursanakirja.* Helsinki: Werner Söderström Osakeyhtiö.

Pekkarinen, Jukka, and Juhana Vartiainen. (2001). *Finlands Ekonomiska Politik: Den Långa Linjen 1918–2000.* Stockholm: Stiftelsen Fackföreningsrörelsens Institut för Ekonomisk Forskning FIEF.

Pentikäinen, Juha. (1989). *Kalevala Mythology.* Bloomington: Indiana University Press.

———. (1995). *Saamelaiset: Pohjoisen Kansan Mytologia.* Helsinki: Suomalaisen Kirjallisuuden Seura.

———. (1997). "Forest." In Alho et al. 1997: 120–122.

———. (2007). *Golden King of the Forest: The Lore of the Northern Bear.* Helsinki: Etnika.

——— (ed.). (2001). *Shamanhood: Symbolism and Epic.* Budapest: Akadémiai Kiadó.

Pere, Eeva-Liisa. (2015). "Komeetan Lailla Noussut Kapellimestari Eva Ollikainen Jätti Musiikin Uuvuttuaan: Onneksi Into Palasi." *Helsingin Sanomat* 20 November 2015, B 1–2.

Pernicka, Ernst, and David W. Anthony. (2009). "The Invention of Copper Metallurgy and the Copper Age of Old Europe." In Anthony 2009: 162–177.

Perttu, Jukka (2015). "Onnenpotku Autotehtaalle." *Helsingin Sanomat,* 27 November 2015, A 37.

Pesonen, Pertti. (1985). "Finland: The Country, the People, and the Political System." In Uotila 1985: 11–25.

Pesonen, Petri. (2002). "Semisubterranean Houses in Finland: A Review." In: *Huts and Houses: Stone Age and Early Metal Age Buildings in Finland.* Helsinki: Museovirasto.

Pettersson, Lars. (1989). *Finnish Wooden Churches.* Helsinki: Museum of Finnish Architecture.

Plöger, Angela. (1973). *Die Russischen Lehnwörter der Finnischen Schriftsprache.* Wiesbaden: Harrassowitz.

Poikalainen, Väinö. (2000). "The Prehistoric Sanctuary at Lake Onega." In Kare 2000b: 242–287.

Pöppönen, Hannu. (2014). "It's Time for Finnish Fashion to Take a Big Leap." *Helsinki Design Weekly* (2 December 2014).

Pöykkö, Kalevi. (1990). *Carl Ludvig Engel 1778–1840: Pääkaupungin Arkkitehti.* Helsinki: Helsingin Kaupunginmuseo.

*Promoting Gender Equality in Finland.* The Finnish Ministry of Social Affairs and Health, 2013. Retrieved from http://urn.fi/URN:ISBN:978-952-00-3409-2.

*Protocoll, Hållit i det Högvördiga Präste Ståndet vid Landtdagen i Borgå Stad år 1809.* Helsinki: Osakeyhtiö Kauppakirjapaino, 1899.

Przybylak, Rajmund. (2003). *The Climate of the Arctic.* Dordrecht: Kluwer Academic Publishers.

Purhonen, Paula. (1998). *Kristinuskon Saapumisesta Suomeen.* Vammala: Vammalan Kirjapaino.

Putkuri, Eija, Matti Lindholm and Aino Peltonen. (2014). *The State of the Environment in Finland 2013.* SYKE—Finnish Environment Institute. Publication 1. Retrieved from http://hdl.handle.net/10138/42691.

Rantanen, Lasse (2015). "Vanhat Vahvuudet Elättävät Suomea." *Helsingin Sanomat,* 28 November, A4.

Räty, Reetta. (2015). "Anteeksi, Mutta Mitä Kieltä Te Puhutte?" *Helsingin Sanomat,* Kuukausiliite No 521 (August): 34–43.

Raukas, Anto. (1995). "Evolution of the Yoldia Sea in the Eastern Baltic." *Quaternary International* 27: 99–102.

Rautkallio, Hannu. (1988). *Finland and the Holocaust:*

*The Rescue of Finland's Jews*. New York: Holocaust Publications.

Richardson, J.G. (ed.). (1986). *Handbook for Theory and Research for the Sociology of Education*. Westport, CT: Greenwood Press.

Ries, Tomas. (1988). *Cold Will: The Defense of Finland*. London: Brassey's Defence Publishers.

Rintala, Marvin. (1969). *Four Finns: Political Profiles*. Berkeley: University of California Press.

Robbins, Paula Ivaska. (2007). *The Travels of Peter Kalm: Finnish-Swedish Naturalist Through Colonial North America, 1748–1751*. Fleischmanns, NY: Purple Mountain Press.

Roelcke, Thorsten (ed.). (2003). *Variation Typology: A Typological Handbook of European Languages Past and Present*. Berlin: Mouton de Gruyter.

Ropo, Arja, and Erika Sauer. (2007). "The Success of Finnish Conductors: Grand Narratives and Small Stories About Global Leadership." *International Journal of Arts Management* 9, No. 3: 4–15.

Rüdiger, Johann Christian Christoph. (1782). *Von der Sprache und Herkunft der Zigeuner aus Indien*. Leipzig 1782; reprint with a preface by Harald Haarmann, Hamburg: Buske, 1990.

Ruuskanen-Parrukoski, Pirkko. (2013). "Public Laundering Jetties." In Taipale 2013: 342–344.

Rydving, Håkan. (1993). *The End of Drum-Time: Religious Change Among the Lule Saami, 1670s–1740s*. Stockholm: Almqvist & Wiksell.

———. (2010). "The 'Bear Ceremonial' and the Bear Ritual Among the Khanty and the Sami." In *Temenos: Nordic Journal for Comparative Religion* 46: 31–52.

Saarikoski, Helena. (2014). *Silloin Tanssittiin Tangoa: Tanssikansan Kertomaa 1900-Luvulta*. Helsinki: Kulttuuriosuuskunta Partuuna.

Saarinen, Juhani. (2014). "Supercell Kasvoi Maailman Ykköseksi." *Helsingin Sanomat*, 13 December, B8–9.

Saijonmaa, Arja. (2000). *Sauna*. Malmö: Richters Förlag.

Sajari, Petri. (2015a). "Suhdanne Horjahti taas Huonommaksi." *Helsingin Sanomat*, 14 November, B8–9.

———. (2015b). "Nokian Uudistuminen Pian Päätökseen." *Helsingin Sanomat*, 5 December, B9.

Salmela-Järvinen, Martta. (1973). *Miina Sillanpää, Legenda jo Eläessään*. Porvoo: Werner Söderström Osakeyhtiö.

Salo, Unto. (2013). *Kalevalaiset Myytit ja Uskomukset*, vol. I: *Olevaisuus ja sen Valtius: Muinaissuomalaisten Maailmanymmärrys*; vol. II: *Luonto ja Kulttuuri: Muinaissuomalaisten Elämänymmärrys*; vol. III: *Tuoni, Pohjola, Taivas: Arkeologian ja Kalevalaisten Runojen Tuonelat*. Somero: Amanita.

Sammallahti, Pekka. (1998). *The Saami Languages: An Introduction*. Karasjok: Davvi Girji.

Sandelin, Martin, and Juha Partanen. (2015). *Nokian jalokivi. Tarina suomalaisesta DX 200 puhelinkeskuksesta*. Espoo: Mediakasvo JPA.

Sander, Gordon F. (2013). *The Hundred Day Winter War: Finland's Gallant Stand Against the Soviet Army*. Lawrence: University Press of Kansas.

Saressalo, L. (1996). *Kveenit: Tutkimus Erään Pohjoisnorjalaisen Vähemmistön Identiteetistä*. Helsinki: Suomalaisen Kirjallisuuden Seura.

Sarmela, Matti. (1994). *Suomen Perinneatlas. Suomen Kansankulttuurin Kartasto 2*. Helsinki: Suomalaisen Kirjallisuuden Seura.

Savijärvi, Ilkka, and Muusa Savijärvi. (1999). "Language Contacts in Ingrian-Finnish." In Teinonen and Virtanen 1999: 23–47.

Sawwatejew, J.A. (1984). *Karelische Felsbilder*. Leipzig: E.A. Seemann.

Schatz, Roman. (2014). *Finland: What a Country!* Helsinki: Johnny Kniga.

Schienstock, Gerd (ed.). (2004). *Embracing the Knowledge Economy: The Dynamic Transformation of the Finnish Innovation System*. Cheltenham: Edward Elgar.

Schildt, Göran. (1984–91). *Alvar Aalto*, 3 vols. New York: Rizzoli.

Schmidt, Éva. (1989). "Bear Cult and Mythology of the Northern Ob-Ugrians." In Hoppál and Pentikäinen 1989: 187–232.

Schoolfield, George C. (1996). *Helsinki of the Czars*. Columbia, SC: Camden House.

———. (ed.). (1998). *A History of Finland´s Literature*. Lincoln: University of Nebraska Press.

Scott, Joan Wallach. (1996). *Only Paradoxes to Offer: French Feminists and the Rights of Men*. Cambridge, MA: Harvard University Press.

Screen, J.E.O. (2001). *Mannerheim: The Finnish Years*. London: Hurst.

Seachris, Joshua W. (ed.). (2013). *Exploring the Meaning of Life: An Anthology and Guide*. Malden, MA: Wiley-Blackwell.

Service, Tom. (2011). "Rediscovering the Spirit of Sibelius." *The Guardian*, 12 December. Retrieved from http://www.theguardian.com/music/2011/dec/12/spirit-of-sibelius.

Seurujärvi-Kari, Irja (ed.). (2000). *Beaivvi Mánát: Saamelaisten Juuret ja Nykyaika*. Helsinki: Suomalaisen Kirjallisuuden Seura.

Seurujärvi-Kari, Irja, and Helena Ruotsala. (2005). "Reindeer Terminology." In Kulonen et al. 2005: 331–333.

Shattock, Michael. (2003). *Managing Successful Universities*. Maidenhead: Open University Press.

——— (ed.). (2009). *Entrepreneurialism in Universities and the Knowledge Economy: Diversification and Organizational Change in European Higher Education*. Maidenhead: Open University Press.

Siemsen, Hayo. (2010). "Ernst Mach and the Epistemological Ideas Specific for Finnish Science Education." *Science & Education*, doi 10.1007/s11191-010-9303-6.

Siikala, Anna-Leena. (1994). *Suomalainen Samanismi* (2nd ed.). Helsinki: Suomalaisen Kirjallisuuden Seura.

Sillanpää, Sami, and Jukka Gröndahl. (2015). "Kovimman Kehityksen Maa." *Helsingin Sanomat*, 30 August, B1–3.

Simmons, Ian G. (1993). *Environmental History: A Concise Introduction*. Cambridge, MA: Blackwell.

Simola, Hannu. (2005). "The Finnish Miracle of Pisa: Historical and Sociological Remarks on Teaching and Teacher Education." *Comparative Education* 41: 455–470.

Sirén, Vesa. (2000). *Aina Poltti Sikaria: Jean Sibelius Aikalaisten Silmin*. Helsinki: Otava.

———. (2010). *Suomalaiset Kapellimestarit: Sibeliuksesta Saloseen, Kajanuksesta Franckiin*. Helsinki: Otava.

———. (2015). "Ihme Äijä." *Helsingin Sanomat*, Kuukausiliite no. 524 (November): 30–37.

Sjöblom-Immala, Heli. (2013). *Tervetuloa Suomeen? Korkeakouluopiskelijoiden Asenteita Mittaava ETNOBAROMETRI 2013*. Turku: Siirtolaisuusinstituutti.

Skidmore, Max J. (2004). *Presidential Performance: A Comprehensive Review*. Jefferson, NC: McFarland.

Skutnabb-Kangas, Tove, and Ulla Aikio-Puoskari. (2005). "Exclusion or Inclusion: Linguistic Human Rights for a Linguistic Minority, the Deaf Sign Language Users, and an Indigenous People, the Saami." Retrieved from http://www.deafzone.ch/file/file_pool/action/download/file_id/1380/.

Slavchev, Vladimir. (2009). "The Varna Eneolithic Cemetery in the Context of the Late Copper Age in the East Balkans." In Anthony 2009: 192–210.

Smeds, Kerstin. (1996). *Helsingfors—Paris: Finlands Utveckling till Nation på Världsutställningarna 1851–1900*. Vammala: Vammalan Kirjapaino.

Smith, John Boulton. (1985). *The Golden Age of Finnish Art: Art Nouveau and the National Spirit* (2nd ed.). Keuruu: Otava.

Snellman, Saska. (2000). "Castells Tietää mistä Tässä Kaikessa on Kysymys." *Helsingin Sanomat*, 2 January.

Söderhjelm, Torsten. (1900). *Le Pavillon Finlandais à l'Exposition Universelle*. Catalogue. Paris: Lemercier.

Stark, Laura. (2011). *The Limits of Patriarchy: How Female Networks of Pilfering and Gossip Sparked the First Debates on Rural Gender Rights in the 19th-Century Finnish-Language Press*. Helsinki: Finnish Literature Society.

Stark-Arola, Laura. (1998). "Gender, Magic and Social Order: Pairing, Boundaries, and the Female Body in Finnish-Karelian Folklore." In Apo et al. 1998: 31–62.

Steele, Pamela, and Gyöngyi Kovacs. (2013). "Gender and Humanitarian Logistics: A Situational Update." In Hellingrath et al. 2013: 298–313.

Stenwall, Åsa. (2001). *Portföljen i Skogen: Kvinnor och Modernitet i det Sena 1900-Talets Finlandssvenska Litteratur*. Helsinki: Schildts.

Strauss, Karsten. (2013). "Is This the Fastest-Growing Game Company Ever?" *Forbes*, 6 May.

Suhonen, Seppo (ed.). (1995). *Itämerensuomalainen Kulttuurialue—The Fenno-Baltic Cultural Area*. Helsinki: Vammalan Kirjapaino.

(STV). 2014. *Suomen Tilastollinen Vuosikirja—Statistisk Årsbok för Finland—Statistical Yearbook of Finland 2014*. Helsinki: Tilastokeskus.

(SVT). 1870–1923. *Suomen Virallinen Tilasto*. VI (1870–1923); and IX (1906–1922). Helsinki: Tilastollinen Toimisto.

Swallow, Deborah. (2011). *Culture Shock! A Survival Guide to Customs and Etiquette: Finland*. Tarrytown, NY: Marshall Cavendish.

Swan, James, and Roberta Swan (eds.). (1996). *Dialogues with the Living Earth: New Ideas on the Spirit of Place from Designers, Architects, & Innovators*. Wheaton, IL: Quest Books.

Tägil, Sven (ed.). (1995). *Ethnicity and Nation Building in the Nordic World*. London: Hurst.

Taipale, Ilkka (ed.). (2013). *100 Social Innovations from Finland*. Helsinki: Finnish Literature Society.

*Taiteilijaveljekset von Wright: Suomen Kauneimmat Lintumaalaukset* (1986). Helsinki: Otava.

Takala, Hannu. (2004). *The Ristola Site in Lahti and the Earliest Postglacial Settlement of South Finland*. Jyväskylä: Gummerus.

Tallroth, Paulina. (2012). *Strategy for the National Languages of Finland*. Government resolution. Helsinki: Prime Minister's Office Publications.

Talve, Ilmar. (1997). *Finnish Folk Culture*. Helsinki: Finnish Literature Society.

Tamminen, Tuomo. (2015). "Luottamus Kantaa Suomalaisia." *Helsingin Sanomat*, 9 November, B8–9.

Tammivaara-Balaam, Irmeli (ed.). (1999). *University of Helsinki: Courses in English 1999–2000*. Helsinki: Helsinki University Press.

Tarkka, Jukka. (2015). *Venäjän Vieressä: Suomen Turvallisuusilmasto 1990–2012*. Helsinki: Otava.

Tarkka, Lotte. (1998). "Sense of the Forest: Nature and Gender in Karelian Oral Poetry." In Apo et al. 1998: 92–142.

Taylor, Paul W. (2011). *Respect for Nature: A Theory of Environmental Ethics* (25th anniversary edition, with a new foreword by Dale Jamieson). Princeton, NJ: Princeton University Press.

Teinonen, Markku, and Timo J. Virtanen (eds.).

(1999). *Ingrians and Neighbours: Focus on the Eastern Baltic Sea Region.* Helsinki: Finnish Literature Society.

Theiner, Egon. (2006). *Matti: The Biography of Matti Nykänen.* Egoth: Egon-Theiner.

Thomas, Keith. (1983). *Man and the Natural World: A History of the Modern Sensibility.* New York: Pantheon Books.

Tiili, Markku. (2012). *Kansainvälistymisen Tiellä: Nokialaisen Muistelmia 1965-1975.* Helsinki: Neirol-Kustannus.

Tillander-Godenhielm, Ulla. (2011). *Fabergén Suomalaiset Mestarit.* Helsinki: Tammi.

Tillotson, H.M. (1993). *Finland at Peace and War 1918-1993.* Wilby, Norwich: Michael Russell.

Timonen, Virpi. (2003). *Restructuring the Welfare State: Globalization and Social Policy Reform in Finland and Sweden.* Cheltenham: Edward Elgar Publishing.

Toivakka, Svetlana. (2015). *Alma Fohström: Kansainvälinen Primadonna.* Helsinki: Suomen Musiikkitieteellinen Seura.

Tolley, Clive. (2009). *Shamanism in Norse Myth and Magic,* vol. 1. Helsinki: Academia Scientiarum Fennica.

Tong, Diane (ed.). (2015). *Gypsies: An Interdisciplinary Reader.* London & New York: Routledge.

Trotter, William R. (1991). *A Frozen Hell: The Russo-Finnish Winter War of 1939-1940.* Chapel Hill, NC: Algonquin Books.

———. (2002). *The Winter War: The Russo-Finnish War of 1939-1940.* New York: Workman Publishing; London: Aurum Press (5th ed. of Trotter 1991).

Tuomi, Timo, and Kristiina Paatero. (2003). *Tapiola: Life and Architecture.* Espoo: Housing Foundation.

Tuomisto, Antero. (1973). "Jokamiehen Oikeus." In *Kodin Lakikirja: Käytännön Laintietoa,* vol. II. Helsinki: Otava, pp. 829-832.

Turtola, Martti. (2015). *Rakastan Sibeliusta: Ja Muita Musiikillisia Tunnustuksia.* Helsinki: Tammi.

Turunen, Markku. (2015). *Pitkä Latu: Legenda Suksesta.* Helsinki: Maahenki.

Uotila, Jaakko (ed.). (1985). *The Finnish Legal System.* Helsinki: Finnish Lawyers Publishing.

*Väestölaskenta—Folkräkningen—Population Census,* vol. 1: *1970.* Helsinki: Suomen virallinen tilasto—Official statistics of Finland, 1973.

Vahtola, Jouko. (2003). *Suomen Historia: Jääkaudesta Euroopan Unioniin.* Helsinki: Otava.

Välijärvi, Jouni, Pekka Kupari, Pirjo Linnakylä, Pasi Reinikainen, Sari Sulkunen, Jukka Törnroos and Inga Arffman. (2003). *The Finnish Success in PISA—And Some Reasons Behind It: PISA 2000.* Jyväskylä: Institute for Educational Research.

———. (2007). *The Finnish Success in PISA—And Some Reasons Behind It, 2.* Jyväskylä: Institute for Educational Research.

Valkonen, Markku. (1992). *The Golden Age: Finnish Art, 1850 to 1907.* Helsinki: Werner Söderström Osakeyhtiö (2nd ed.).

Valtakari, Pirkko. (2015). "Finnish Sauna Culture—Not Just a Cliché." Retrieved from http:// www.sauna.fi/in-english/sauna-information/articles-about-sauna/finnish-sauna-culture/.

Valtonen, Kathleen. (1998). "Resettlement of Middle Eastern Refugees in Finland: The Elusiveness of Integration." *Journal of Refugee Studies* 11: 38-60.

Vaneeckhout, Samuel. (2008). "Sedentism on the Finnish Northwest Coast: Shoreline Reduction and Reduced Mobility." *Fennoscandia Archaeologica* XXV: 61-72.

Vargic, Martin. (2015). *Vargic's Miscellany of Curious Maps: The Atlas of Everything You Never Knew You Needed to Know.* London: Penguin Books.

Vartanova, Elena. (1999). *Finskaja Model' na Rubezhe Stoletij: Informatsionnoe Obshchestvo i CMI Finljandii v Evropejskoj Perspektive.* Moskva: Izdatel'stvo Moskovskogo Universiteta.

Vento, Pauli (ed.). (1999). *Study in Finland: International Programmes in Finnish Higher Education 1999-2000.* Helsinki: Centre For International Mobility.

Viitso, Tiit-Rein. (1998). "Fennic." In Abondolo 1998: 96-114.

Viken, Arvid and Brynhild Granås (eds.). (2014). *Tourism Destination Development: Turns and Tactics.* Farnham, Surrey: Ashgate Publishing.

Virtanen, Leea, and Thomas DuBois. (2000). *Finnish Folklore.* Helsinki: Finnish Literature Society; Seattle: University of Washington Press.

Virtaranta, Pertti. (1992). *Amerikansuomen Sanakirja: A Dictionary of American Finnish.* Turku: Institute of Migration.

Vlasov, Leonid. (1994). *Mannerheim Pietarissa 1887-1904.* Jyväskylä & Helsinki: Gummerus.

Vuorela, Katri, and Lars Borin. (1998). "Finnish Romani." In Ó Corráin and Mac Mathúna 1998: 51-76.

Vuoristo, Kai-Veikko, and Nina Vesterinen. (2009). *Lumen ja Suven Maa: Suomen Matkailumaantiede.* Helsinki: Werner Söderström Osakeyhtiö.

Wagner, Judith T. (2006). "An Outsider's Perspective: Childhoods and Early Education in the Nordic Countries." In Einarsdottir and Wagner 2006: 289-306.

Wahlsten, Marianna and Hannah Brookes (December 14, 2012). "Helsinki: World Design Capital 2012." CNN (retrieved 23 July 2016).

Weaver, Fran, and Tim Bird. (2015). "Destination Lapland: Trekking the Light Fantastic." *Blue Wings* (Finnair), September: 30-36.

Weber, Max. (1971). *The Protestant Ethic and the Spirit of Capitalism.* London: Allen and Unwin.

_____. (1978). *Economy and Society*, 2 vols. Berkeley: University of California Press.

Weinreich, Max. (1980). *History of the Yiddish Language*. Chicago: University of Chicago Press.

Wheeler, Stephen M. (2004). *Planning for Sustainability: Creating Livable, Equitable and Ecological Communities*. New York: Routledge.

White, Leonard D. (1948). *The Federalists: A Study in Administrative History*. New York: Macmillan.

Whitley, Richard (ed.). (1992). *European Business Systems. Firms and Markets in Their National Contexts*. London: Sage.

Wigoder, Geoffrey (ed.). (1989). *The Encyclopedia of Judaism*. Jerusalem: Jerusalem Publishing House.

Wilhelm, Paul G. (2002). "International Validation of the Corruption Perceptions Index: Implications for Business Ethics and Entrepreneurship Education." *Journal of Business Ethics* (Springer Netherlands) 35(3): 177–189.

Wilson, Stephen. (1998). *The Means of Naming: A Social and Cultural History of Personal Naming in Western Europe*. London: UCL Press.

Wolf, Eric. (1997). *Europe and the People Without History*. Berkeley: University of California Press (2nd printing).

Wolf, Susan. (2013). "The Meanings of Lives." In Seachris 2013: 304–318.

Wulff, Christine. (1982). "Zwei Finnische Sätze aus dem 15. Jahrhundert." *Ural- Altaische Jahrbücher*, Neue Folge 2: 90–98.

Yanin, V.L. and A.A. Zalizniak. (1993). *Novgorodskie Gramoty na Bereste iz Raskopok 1984–1989 Godov*. Moscow: Rossiiskaia Akademiia Nauk.

Yli-Jokipii, Pentti. (1996). *Changes in Local Communities: The Cultural Geography of Finnish Open-Air Dance Pavillions*. Helsinki: Suomen Maantieteellinen Seura.

Zadneprovskaya, Alexandra. (1999). "The Destiny of Ingrian-Finns and Their Traditional Culture in Their Native Land." In Teinonen and Virtanen 1999: 85–97.

Zekaria, Simon, and Ryan Knutson. (2015). "Merger of Nokia with Alcatel-Lucent Could Put Pressure on Prices." *The Wall Street Journal*. 14 April. Retrieved from http://www.wsj.com/articles/merger-of-nokia-with-alcatel-lucent-could-put-pressure-on-prices-1429016471.

Zvelebil, Marek. (2008). "Innovating Hunter-Gatherers: The Mesolithic in the Baltic." In Bailey and Spikins 2008: 18–59.

# Index